Socioeconomic Evaluation of Megaprojects

The governance and evaluation of 'megaprojects' – that is, large-scale, complex, high-stakes infrastructure projects usually commissioned by governments and delivered through partnerships between public and private organisations – is receiving increased attention. However, megaproject evaluation has hitherto largely adopted a linear-rationalist perspective to explain the frequent failure of such projects to meet the 'iron triangle' of performance criteria: delivering on time, within budget, and according to specifications. This approach recommends greater control and accountability to remedy megaproject 'pathologies'.

Drawing on empirical examples mainly from the transport sector and radioactive waste disposal, this book offers new perspectives to megaproject evaluation. Comprising contributions from leading experts in project evaluation and appraisal, this collection opens up new avenues by suggesting two ways of improving megaproject evaluation: 1) approaches that go beyond the dominant linear-rationalist notion of policy processes, and emphasise instead the objective of opening up appraisal processes in order to enhance learning and reflexivity; and 2) approaches that extend evaluative criteria beyond the 'iron triangle', to cover the various socioeconomic impacts and preconditions for project success.

This volume will be of great relevance to scholars and practitioners with an interest in megaprojects, energy and climate policy, radioactive waste management, urban design, and project planning and management.

Markku Lehtonen is Associate Researcher at Centre CONNECT, ESSEC Business School and at GSPR, École des Hautes Études en Sciences Sociales, France.

Pierre-Benoît Joly, economist and sociologist, is Research Director at the National Institute of Agronomic Research (INRA) and Director of the Laboratory of Interdisciplinary Studies of Science, Innovation and Society (LISIS) at Université Paris-Est, France.

Luis Aparicio is in charge of Social Sciences and Humanities at the R&D Division of the French Radioactive Waste Management Agency (Andra), France.

Routledge Explorations in Environmental Studies

Socioeconomic Evaluation of Megaprojects

Dealing with uncertainties

Edited by Markku Lehtonen,
Pierre-Benoît Joly and Luis Aparicio

LONDON AND NEW YORK

from Routledge

First published 2017 by Routledge

2 Park Square, Milton Park, Abingdon, Oxfordshire OX14 4RN
711 Third Avenue, New York, NY 10017

Routledge is an imprint of the Taylor & Francis Group, an informa business

First issued in paperback 2018

British Library Cataloguing-in-Publication Data
A catalogue record for this book is available from the British Library

Library of Congress Cataloging-in-Publication Data
A catalog record for this book has been requested

ISBN: 978-1-138-65611-6 (hbk)
ISBN: 978-0-367-02688-2 (pbk)

Typeset in Goudy Old Style
by Saxon Graphics Ltd, Derby

Contents

Figures

Tables

Acronyms

Andra	Agence nationale pour la gestion des déchets radioactifs (French Radioactive Waste Management Agency)
AFCN-FANC	Agence Fédérale de Contrôle Nucléaire – Federaal Agentschap voor Nucleaire Controle – Belgian Federal Authority for Nuclear Safety
CAD	Canadian dollars
cAt project	proposed storage solution for LILW or category A waste in Dessel
CBA	cost–benefit analysis
CIG	Commission Intergouvernementale franco-italienne (intergovernmental commission Lyon-Turin)
CIGEO	Centre industriel de stockage géologique (deep disposal centre for French radioactive waste)
CLA	construction licence application
CNDP	Commission Nationale de Débat Public (French National Commission of Public Debate)
CNRS	Centre National de la recherche Scientifique (French National Center for Scientific Research)
CoE	Council of Europe
COGEMA	Compagnie générale des matières nucélaires (since 2006, Areva NP)
COST	European Cooperation in Science and Technology framework
CREM	Centre de Recherche en Economie et Management (Center for Research in Economics and Management)
CSR	corporate social responsibility
CTRL	Channel Tunnel Rail Link
DBFM	Design–Build–Finance–Maintain contract
DiP	Decision-in-Principle in accordance with the Finnish Nuclear Energy Act

DOE	US Department of Energy
DRI/McGraw	an economic forecasting company (US)
EIA	Environmental Impact Assessment
EIB	European Investment Bank
EMCA	Eclectic Multi-Criteria Analysis
EPR	European Pressurised Reactor
EU	European Union
EUR	euro
FNAUT	Fédération Nationale des Associations d'Usagers de Transport (France)
FPH	Fortum Power and Heat Ltd.
FPIC	free, prior and informed consent
Frapna	Fédération Rhône-Alpes de protection de la nature
GDP	Gross Domestic Product
GTK	Geological Survey of Finland
HEATCO	Developing Harmonised European Approaches for Transport Costing and Project Assessment (EU FP6 research project)
IAEA	International Atomic Energy Agency
IAIA	International Association for Impact Assessment
IBA	Impacts and Benefits Agreement
IFC	International Finance Corporation
INEA	The Innovation and Networks Executive Agency (of the European Commission)
InSOTEC	International Socio-technical Challenges for implementing geological disposal – research project funded by the Euratom Framework Programme (FP7)
ISBET	Indicateurs Sociétaux de Bien-Etre Territorialisés (Societal Indicators of Territorial Wellbeing)
IVO	Imatran Voima Ltd., Finnish 100 per cent state-owned power company established in 1932. Known as Fortum Power and Heat since 1998
KBS-3	KärnBränsleSäkerhet-3: a final disposal concept for spent nuclear fuel, developed in Sweden
LAURE	Loi sur l'Air et l'Utilisation Rationnelle de l'Energie (French law on air quality and the rational use of energy)
LILW	short-lived, low- and intermediate-level radioactive waste
LOTI	Loi d'Orientation des Transports Intérieurs (French domestic transport framework act)
LTF	Lyon Turin Ferroviaire company (ch. 4)
LTF	Long Term Fund (ch. 6)
MAMCA	multi-actor multi-criteria analysis

MCA	multi-criteria analysis
MEE	Finnish Ministry of Employment and the Economy
MONA	Mols Overleg Nucleair Afval – Mol Consultation Nuclear Waste
MTF	Medium Term Fund
MTI	Finnish Ministry of Trade and Industry, from January 2008 Ministry of Employment and the Economy
MTP	mega transport project
NATA	New Approach to Appraisal (UK)
NETLIPSE	Network for the dissemination of knowledge on the management and organisation of large infrastructure projects in Europe
NGO	non-governmental organisation
NPP	nuclear power plant
NPV	net present value
NWM	Nuclear Waste Management
OECD	Organisation for Economic Co-operation and Development
OLAF	European Anti-Fraud Office (Office de Lutte Anti-Fraude)
OMB	US Office of Management and Budget
ONDRAF-NIRAS	Organisme National des Déchets Radioactifs et des matières Fissiles enrichies – Nationale Instelling voor Radioactief Afval en verrijkte Splijtstoffen – Belgian Agency for Radioactive Waste and Enriched Fissile Materials
ONKALO	The spent nuclear fuel repository under construction in Finland
PLMCA	policy-led multi-criteria analysis
Posiva	the nuclear waste management organization owned by Teollisuuden Voima and Fortum Power and Heat
PPP	public–private partnership
ProRail	the national railway network manager in the Netherlands
PVB	present value of benefits
QCA	Qualitative Comparative Analysis
R&D	research and development
RFF	Réseau Ferré Français – French national rail network company
RTD	Research, Development and Technical Design
RWS	Rijkswaterstaat, the executive branch of the Dutch Ministry of Infrastructure and the Environment, responsible for the national highway network
SCK-CEN	Studiecentrum voor Kernenergie – Centre d'étude de l'Energie Nucléaire – Belgian Nuclear Research Centre

SEA	Strategic environmental assessment
SEIA	Socioeconomic Impact Assessment
SIA	Social impact assessment
SIMP	Social Impact Management Plan
SKB	Svensk Kärnbränslehantering AB (Swedish Nuclear Fuel and Waste Management Company)
SNF	spent nuclear fuel
SPIRAL	Societal Progress Indicators for the Responsibility of All
STORA	Studie- en Overlegplatform Radioactief Afval Dessel – Study and Consultation Radioactive Waste Dessel
STUK	Säteilyturvakeskus, the Finnish Radiation and Nuclear Safety Authority
TELT	Tunnel Euralpin Lyon Turin company
TEN-T	Trans-European Transport Network
tU	tonnes of uranium
TVO	Teollisuuden Voima Oyj, a Finnish nuclear utility operating the nuclear power plant at Olkiluoto, Finland
UCL	University College London
USD	US dollars
VREF	Volvo Research and Education Foundations
VTT	Technical Research Centre of Finland
YJT	Ydinjätetoimikunta, the Nuclear Waste Commission of Finnish Power Companies
YVL	Regulatory Guides on nuclear safety – Finland

Contributors

Luis Aparicio holds a PhD in science, technology and society from Strasbourg University. He is currently in charge of social sciences and humanities research at Andra, the French Radioactive Waste Management Agency, and an associate member of LISIS (Laboratoire Interdisciplinaire Sciences Innovations Sociétés). He edited the book 'Making nuclear waste governable: Deep underground disposal and the challenge of reversibility' (Springer, 2010).

Anne Bergmans is lecturer and senior researcher in the University of Antwerp's Faculties of Law and of Social Sciences. She holds a PhD in sociology from the University of Antwerp (May 2005). Her research interests are in the fields of science and technology governance, environmental sociology and the sociology of safety and risk, with an empirical focus on questions related to the long-term governance of radioactive waste.

Harry T. Dimitriou is the Bartlett Professor of Planning Studies and Director of the OMEGA Centre at UCL, which undertakes international consultancy and research in decision-making for mega infrastructure projects. He has published several books and many articles. In the past he has held several senior appointments at the universities of Sheffield, Hong Kong and Aalborg, as well as advisory/consultancy posts with UN-Habitat, UNDP, the World Bank, the European Investment Bank, the governments of Hong Kong and Indonesia, the UK Treasury and the World Economic Forum.

Pierre-Benoît Joly is Director of Research at the National Institute of Agronomic Research (INRA) in France. He was the Director of IFRIS (French Institute for Studies of Research and Innovation in Society) and of Labex (Laboratory of Excellence) SITES from 2011 to 2014, and is now the director of the interdisciplinary research laboratory LISIS (Laboratoire Interdisciplinaire Sciences Innovations Sociétés) at the Université Paris-Est. He holds a degree in agricultural engineering (ESAP, Toulouse 1982), a PhD in economics (Université de Toulouse, 1987) and the Habilitation à Diriger des Recherches (Université de Grenoble, 1995).

Mika Kari (M.Soc.Sci.) is research scientist at VTT Technical Research Centre of Finland in the area of foresight, organisational dynamics and systemic change, and a doctoral candidate at the University of Jyväskylä, Department of Social Sciences and Philosophy. He is currently preparing his dissertation concerning 'nuclear communities' and the social acceptance of spent nuclear fuel disposal projects.

Matti Kojo is postdoctoral researcher at the University of Tampere, School of Management. His doctoral thesis 'The public engagement turn in nuclear waste policy' examined Finland's nuclear waste policy from the perspective of political style, with special reference to the process of site selection for a final disposal facility for spent nuclear fuel.

Moktar Lamari (PhD) is in the top one hundred of the world's most quoted scientists in the area of knowledge transfer and knowledge management. He is currently a full professor at the School of Public Administration of the École Nationale d'Administration Publique, Quebec University, Canada. His ongoing research projects examine the impact of web 2.0 and digital tools on knowledge transfer and knowledge absorptive capacity. He won the Louis Brownlow Award in 2003 for the best article published by Public Administration Review; the Elsevier Award in 2002 for the best article published by the journal *Technological Forecasting and Social Change*; and the 2014 award for Outstanding World Research Leader, delivered by the International Multidisciplinary Research and the University of the Philippines. He has published more than one hundred articles and reports, four books and dozens of book chapters.

Markku Lehtonen is researcher at the Centre CONNECT, ESSEC Business School (Cergy-Pontoise, France) and at the Groupe de Sociologie Pragmatique et Réflexive (GSPR), l'École des Hautes Études en Sciences Sociales (EHESS) in Paris. He worked as a research fellow at the SPRU (Science Policy Research Unit) of the University of Sussex from 2005 to 2015, and at the IFRIS (Université Paris-Est) from 2012 to 2014. Markku holds a PhD in environmental economics (Université de Versailles Saint-Quentin-en-Yvelines, 2005) and an MSc in environmental studies (University of Helsinki, 1994). His research focuses on the role of expertise (especially indicators and evaluations) in energy and environmental policy, the evaluation of megaprojects, deliberative democracy, and public controversies over questions of energy and the environment (with a special attention to biofuels and nuclear power).

Başak Saraç-Lesavre recently completed her PhD degree at the Centre de Sociologie de l'Innovation, École Nationale Supérieure des Mines de Paris. She has studied evaluation and valuation processes that are associated with the formulation of very long-term public policies, focusing in her empirical work on the US nuclear waste programme.

Tapio Litmanen is Professor of Sociology at the University of Jyväskylä, Department of Social Sciences and Philosophy. His research interests are in environmental sociology, science and technology studies, and civil society research. He has conducted several research projects on risk and technology issues. His publications deal with, among other topics, nuclear power policy and nuclear waste management.

Line Poulin-Larivière holds a Masters degree in public administration, a postgraduate programme in public management and a Bachelor's degree in international studies. She has experience in policy analysis and programme evaluation. In 2015 she co-authored four chapters in a publication on climate change adaptation in coastal zones, and has presented research results and recommendations to policymakers at international conferences on climate change and policy evaluation.

Jean-René Prévost obtained a Master's degree in Programme Evaluation from the École nationale d'administration publique (ENAP) in 2013, and an Integrated Bachelor's degree in Public Business and International Relations from the Université Laval in 2011. He has participated in several evaluation projects as a researcher at the Center for Research and Expertise in Evaluation (CREXE). Since 2015 he has worked on public programme reviews for the government of Quebec, as an analyst in the Bureau de révision permanente des programmes of the Secrétariat du Conseil du Trésor. His particular interests include the performance of governmental programmes and the organisational challenges associated with programme evaluation in Quebec and in Canada.

Michel Renault is Associate Professor of Economics at the University of Rennes and a research fellow at CREM (Centre de Recherche en Economie et Management – Research Centre in Economics and Management). His main research areas are the history of economic thought and epistemology, social indicators and participatory public policies. He received the award for the best contribution to the third OECD World Forum, "Statistics, Knowledge and Policy: Charting progress, building visions, improving life" in Busan (Korea) from October 27 to 30, 2009.

Thomas Reverdy holds a PhD in sociology, and teaches economic sociology, sociology of work and sociology of organisations at the Grenoble Institute of Technology. His research (at PACTE – social science research laboratory) is focused on the management of projects. His research concerns new projects in high-risk and infrastructure industries, with an ambition to understand the interplay between the practice of forecasting, planning and contracting on one hand, and the need for adaptation and resilience on the other.

Frank Vanclay is Professor of Cultural Geography in the Faculty of Spatial Sciences, University of Groningen, the Netherlands. Frank is an applied social researcher who is primarily interested in social impact assessment and related issues such as project-induced displacement and resettlement; social licence to operate; free, prior and informed consent; and the management of social issues throughout the project cycle.

Marlies Verhaegen is junior researcher in the Society and Environment research group in the Department of Sociology at the University of Antwerp. She holds a Master's degree in Sociology and her current interests are the sociology of risk and uncertainty and modes of participation. These topics relate to her action research on the Belgian project to build a repository for the disposal of short-lived low- and intermediate-level radioactive waste.

Stefan Verweij is postdoctoral researcher in the Department of Planning (Faculty of Spatial Sciences) at the University of Groningen. He specialises in complexity, governance networks, infrastructure planning and implementation, project evaluation, project management and organisation, public–private partnerships, and qualitative comparative analysis. More information can be found at www.stefanverweij.eu.

Jurgita Vesalainen obtained her MA in organisational communication and public relations from the University of Jyväskylä, Finland. Her Master's thesis analysed risk communication concerning nuclear power from an organisational point of view. While working as a research assistant she examined the process of nuclear waste management in Finland, with a special emphasis on the issue of copper corrosion.

E. John Ward (PhD) is a civil engineer specialising in infrastructure planning and appraisal and project risk analysis. He has worked for local government and the private sector as a transport and GIS consultant in the UK. He is a research fellow at the OMEGA Centre, UCL, and a lecturer in Infrastructure Planning and Appraisal at the Bartlett School of Planning, UCL. His research and consultancy interests lie in the fields of infrastructure development using both quantitative and qualitative tools and techniques. As an OMEGA Centre consultant, he has also acted as an advisor to EIB, HM Treasury, and the UK Institution of Civil Engineers and Actuary Profession.

Philip G. Wright is a specialist in strategic planning, urban regeneration/renewal and project appraisal of large-scale infrastructure developments. He has extensive international practice experience in both Europe and Asia. Spending much of his career in Hong Kong, he later provided advice to developers and Network Rail on major railway developments. More recently he was both research fellow at the OMEGA Centre, UCL engaged in applied research into decision-making in the planning, appraisal and delivery of mega transport projects, and an OMEGA Centre consultant on project appraisal for the urban division of EIB.

1 Introduction

Markku Lehtonen, Pierre-Benoît Joly and Luis Aparicio

Broadening the scope of megaproject evaluation[1]

Increasing attention has recently been paid to the governance and evaluation of what have become known as 'megaprojects' (e.g. Flyvbjerg et al., 2003; Flyvbjerg, 2007; 2011), i.e. 'large-scale, complex infrastructure projects usually commissioned by governments and delivered through partnerships between public and private organisations, with multiple partners, high uncertainties, and considerable political stakes' (van Marrewijk et al., 2008: 591).[2] Typical examples include infrastructure construction projects such as motorways, tunnels, bridges, railways or ports, which frequently "respond to global competition among cities for investments, knowledge workers, tourists and prestige" (Bornstein, 2007), and are expected to deliver multiple socioeconomic benefits to the society. A number of characteristics specific to megaprojects render their governance and evaluation particularly challenging. These include in particular: the exceptionally large budgets, and hence considerable economic and political interests involved; considerable temporal and spatial scales; continuous evolution and dynamism – also concerning project governance and the institutional framework; and sharp normative disagreements among parties involved, at different levels of governance. Further challenges arise from the lack of precedents, i.e. similar earlier projects, which would help provide a basis for evaluation; the complex causal relationships between governance measures and policy outcomes; and the high degree of scientific, political and institutional uncertainties involved (e.g. Altshuler and Luberoff, 2003; Flyvbjerg, 2007; 2011; Flyvbjerg et al., 2003; Flyvbjerg and Priemus, 2007; OMEGA, 2012).

The two dimensions of 'the socioeconomic'

Literature and practice in the area of megaproject governance and evaluation have hitherto largely focused on a rather narrow set of approaches and evaluative criteria, neglecting a range of aspects that could conveniently be subsumed under the term 'socioeconomic'. To put it simply, the emphasis has been on evaluating the performance of megaprojects in the light of the 'iron triangle' of success criteria (Dimitriou et al., in this volume) – that is, in terms of their capacity to deliver on time, within budget, and within predetermined project specifications (OMEGA, 2012; see also Giezen, 2012: 781; Shenhar et al., 2001). Current literature in the area often interprets megaproject "pathologies" (Priemus, 2010), i.e. their chronic difficulties in complying with these criteria, as an outcome of strategic and malevolent behaviour by the involved actors. As a result, solutions suggested have largely focused on the needs to increase control, transparency, and accountability, notably through more rigorous and independent *ex ante* evaluations. The contributions in this book explore avenues for extending megaproject evaluation from such narrow framings towards approaches that would truly integrate 'the socioeconomic' concerns.

Our concern for bringing to the fore 'the socioeconomic', and therefore calling for a more complex evaluative perspective, draws on two dimensions composing the term. The first refers to the socioeconomic aspects as performance criteria in project evaluation, including both socioeconomic impacts and the socioeconomic preconditions for successful project implementation. Arguably, the 'iron triangle' considerations constitute only a part of the multiple criteria against which the performance of megaprojects should be evaluated. In particular, the exclusive focus on the 'iron triangle' neglects the implementation processes. In these processes, project goals are constantly redefined through interaction and dialogue among the involved actors and stakeholders – which may or may not include public bodies or individuals beyond the project planners, managers and directly concerned parties. The second dimension relates to the evaluation approaches – the theories, methodologies and paradigms underpinning project governance and evaluation. In this perspective, the key weakness of the narrow framing of megaproject evaluation would lie in its exclusive reliance on a linear-rationalist notion of policy processes (e.g. Albaek, 1995; Adelle et al., 2012) as the interpretative frame. Seen from this angle, greater attention to 'the socioeconomic' would mean embracing the multiplicity of interpretations of policy processes and rationalities motivating human behaviour – an approach that would highlight and take seriously the various uncertainties. In a way, one could even say that this approach feeds uncertainty, by placing uncertainties at the heart of governance instead of seeking to suppress them.[3]

'Opening up' of megaproject evaluation

In practice, the neglect of 'the socioeconomic' has resulted in evaluation approaches that see evaluation as a means of fostering accountability – in a narrow meaning of the term – in order to help 'close down' policy options and perspectives (Stirling, 2008). However, alternative accounts exist in megaproject literature, and are making their way into governance practice. These approaches acknowledge the multiple dimensions and types of rationality, and stress learning, flexibility, reflexivity, and the potentially constructive nature of uncertainties.

A key starting point for the preparation of this book, and a reason why we decided to devote four chapters to nuclear waste disposal projects, was the observation that these projects drive certain megaproject characteristics to their extreme, while representing rather atypical megaprojects in other respects. The extreme length of the timescales involved represents an example of the former – most megaprojects entail long time frames, but seldom raise the kind of true intergenerational justice issues that are typical for nuclear waste disposal. The challenges for socioeconomic evaluation and intergenerational justice are similar to those associated with, for instance, climate change and biodiversity protection. Similarly, in particular because of the dominance of safety as the overriding concern, the state plays possibly an even greater role in nuclear waste disposal than in other megaprojects. Where nuclear waste disposal projects clearly differ from 'conventional' megaprojects – and do not just represent extreme examples of such projects – is in their ultimate *raison d'être*: nuclear waste disposal projects respond to the imperative of solving 'a societal problem', rather than simply seeking to bring added benefits to society in the form of economic development, job creation, etc. Delivering on time and within budget remains important, but secondary to safety as the dominant performance criterion. Partly in reaction to the need to manage the long term and the society, nuclear waste management has seen its own 'participatory turn' (e.g. Sundqvist and Elam, 2010) – an attempt to manage uncertainty by involving the public and the stakeholders. Efforts to 'open up' the socioeconomic evaluation of nuclear waste management face largely similar challenges as the participatory turn.

This introductory chapter first elaborates on the major themes and rationales underpinning the subsequent chapters of the book. The discussion is structured according to the distinction mentioned above: 'the socioeconomic' as an evaluation approach and as a set of evaluative criteria. We then conclude by introducing the remaining chapters of the book.

The socioeconomic as an evaluation approach

Megaproject pathologies and the 'iron triangle' of project performance criteria: strategic misrepresentation and optimism bias

A dominant, 'rationalistic' strand in megaproject governance and evaluation literature focuses on the 'iron triangle' of project performance criteria (OMEGA, 2012: 2). It explains the chronic failure of megaprojects to reach their objectives as a result of project selection dynamics, which would favour the "survival of the unfittest", i.e. the selection and financing of the least viable projects (Flyvbjerg, 2009; 2011). Two main reasons are evoked. First, humans have a systematic tendency to estimate things more positively than objective analysis of empirical evidence would warrant ('optimism bias' or 'planning fallacy') (e.g. Flyvbjerg, 2011). Second, the hypothesis of 'strategic misrepresentation' (Flyvbjerg, 2009; 2011), or 'malevolent design' (van Marrewijk et al., 2008: 599), in line with the rational actor model of human behaviour, postulates that project approval decisions are guided by strategic, rent-seeking behaviour by planners and other key actors. Planners and project advocates would hence have an interest in lying and representing costs and benefits in a manner that would maximise the project's chances of winning public funding (Wachs, 1989; Bruzelius et al., 2002: 145; Flyvbjerg, 2009; 2011: 329; Flyvbjerg et al., 2002; Cantarelli et al., 2010). Strategic misrepresentation would explain failures in most megaproject contexts – i.e. when political pressures are strong – whereas the optimism bias might prevail in less politically contentious situations. The very long time frames would further accentuate the problems, because of the lack of proper accountability structures: project advocates – including politicians – may often no longer be in office when the project reaches a stage in which its actual viability could be assessed reliably (Sanderson, 2012: 437).

A logical consequence of this interpretation has been a repeated call for greater accountability, *ex ante* control, and more effective *ex post* monitoring and enforcement designed to minimise strategic, self-interested behaviour (e.g. Sanderson, 2012). To increase transparency and both public and private sector accountability, greater external scrutiny (e.g. benchmarking, peer review, media scrutiny, financial rewards and sanctions) would be needed. According to this line of argument, deliberative and participatory approaches would be inherently ineffective because of the overwhelmingly powerful economic and political interests at stake (Flyvbjerg et al., 2003: 7).

Alternative readings of megaproject governance and evaluation – which have received less attention in public debate and policy practice – interpret megaproject governance in the light of the multiple alternative rationalities governing the behaviour of policy actors. These interpretations emphasise that since project objectives constantly evolve, even a project that does not fulfil its original criteria may in fact constitute a success in the light of the new criteria. A 'failed' project may therefore over time be reclassified as a success (Dimitriou et al., in this volume). The alternative approaches to megaproject governance and evaluation share a number of common characteristics: they reject the idea that malevolence is the dominant explanation for megaproject 'pathologies'; they emphasise the diverse rationalities underlying actor behaviour instead of adhering to the rational actor model; they stress learning, reflexivity, and the complexity and dynamism of megaprojects; and they advocate an 'opening up' of appraisal and decision-making to a broad variety of perspectives and stakeholders. Some of these approaches see the sources of risk, turbulence and uncertainties in megaproject governance as emanating from outside the project management organisation, while others stress internal factors, such as conflicts and confrontation between mutually conflicting rationalities and project cultures (Sanderson, 2012: 437). Regardless of these variations, the alternative accounts lead to very different suggestions for evaluating megaprojects than the rational-actor based model.

Network governance and 'positive uncertainties'

From the point of view of a 'rationalistic' reading of megaproject pathologies, the multiple uncertainties and complexity in megaproject governance appear as exclusively problematic, insofar as they render the control of projects difficult and accentuate the risks of chronic budget overruns, failure to keep to timetables, and overestimation of the benefits of the project (e.g. Flyvbjerg, 2007: 12–13). Yet

Sanderson (2012) argues that it would be unrealistic to expect that the complexity and irreducible uncertainties inherent in megaprojects could be simply controlled through careful *ex ante* planning of appropriate governance measures.[4] Instead of strategic planning, megaproject governance should therefore focus more on the day-to-day practice of 'real-life' megaproject "governing", the spontaneous processes of emergent work practices, "organising rather than organisation", and project governing "here-and-now" (Sanderson, 2012: 441).

Furthermore, the notion that megaprojects would actually represent clearly definable projects has been called into question. Instead, megaprojects could more usefully be characterised as "programmes of projects" (OMEGA, 2012: 36) or *"networks of people and organizations that work more or less coherently and purposefully to address complex public problems"* (Benjamin and Greene, 2009: 297; see also e.g. Hertting and Vedung, 2012). Given their nature as 'open systems', these 'projects' would exhibit boundaries that are vague, fluid, and subject to constant change (Benjamin and Greene, 2009; OMEGA, 2012). In such a situation, the 'evaluand' – the entity to be evaluated – cannot be clearly defined, i.e. it is not *"programmatically organised or institutionally situated"*, as the conventional approach to policy and programme evaluation assumes (Benjamin and Greene, 2009: 297).

Megaproject governance can therefore be interpreted in terms of a broad range of alternative notions that could conveniently be classified under the umbrella of 'network governance'. Such an approach is generally considered appropriate for solving complex, unstructured problems that require cooperation between a variety of actors from different institutional backgrounds (Benjamin and Greene, 2009; Regeer et al., 2009: 516, 518). From this perspective, uncertainties would appear not merely as problems, but also and above all as opportunities (Hertting and Vedung, 2012). The mutual interdependencies would encourage voluntary, horizontal governance and coordination (*ibid.*, 31), and the conflicts involved in megaproject governance could help to harness the inevitable uncertainties to the benefit of reflexivity, adaptability and exploration of alternative pathways (e.g. Gelatt, 1989). Network governance strategies would emphasise more complex types of "double-loop" or even "triple-loop" learning (e.g. Argyris and Schön, 1978; Reed et al., 2010),[5] adaptation, iteration, and flexible experimentation (Regeer et al., 2009: 518). Given the multiple interdependencies, vertical and horizontal accountability relationships and organisational heterogeneity, decision-making would entail not only rational choice among a set of known options, but also redefinition of the range of available options (Stark, 2000; 2001). Constant technological change and shifting societal preferences and power relations would highlight the challenges of dealing with irreversibility: no single option would be self-evidently the best, since commitment to a given line of action means foregoing other options, whose value cannot be readily estimated (*ibid.*). Ultimately, such considerations echo the dilemma identified by Collingridge (1980): a technology first needs to be implemented if one wants to obtain information about its consequences, yet when implemented, the technology also gains its own inertia and escapes the control of policy actors.

Managing irreversibilities would hence require constant balancing between two objectives: keeping options open to retain the capacity of adapting to evolving situations, and maintaining sufficient control over the system through the reduction of complexity, closing down decisions, and establishing clear lines of accountability. Reflexivity, adaptability, reversibility, and 'opening up' (Stirling, 2008) appear as variants of the 'corrigibility' strategy advocated by Collingridge (1980) as a partial solution to the problem of irreversibility. As for radioactive waste management, a number of countries have sought to build on 'stepwise' and reversible implementation strategies in tune with Collingridge's (1980) plea for incrementalism and for keeping "an exit strategy".[6] Yet technical approaches to evaluation and management of radioactive waste management still dominate, with socioeconomic aspects remaining either underemphasised or being treated predominantly through engineering-oriented approaches.

Accountability versus learning

Accountability is clearly the dominant agenda in public sector evaluation in general, spurred by the rise of neoliberalism, New Public Management and evidence-based policy discourses. Some characteristics specific to megaprojects have further strengthened the position of accountability as a dominant concern in megaproject evaluation. These include the substantial economic resources involved, the increasing implication of the private sector, and the dominance of disciplines such as engineering, accounting and economics in the governance of the often highly technical megaprojects. The conceptualisation of uncertainty and complexity in exclusively negative terms makes greater control and accountability appear as 'natural' recipes in megaproject management. An excessive emphasis on accountability goes hand in hand with an exaggerated trust in the possibility of controlling the projects through careful *ex ante* planning. It has likewise reinforced the dominance of large-N research approaches that focus on statistical regularities between megaprojects across various contexts (e.g. Sanderson, 2012; Verweij and Gerrits, 2013).

Although learning generally constitutes the *raison d'être* of network governance and a key function of its evaluation (Hertting and Vedung, 2012), accountability nevertheless remains crucial. Evaluation should help the public and policymakers to hold project managers accountable for spending and goal achievement. Accountability as such is not to blame – the problem is rather its overly dominant position and the narrow way in which accountability is defined as part of the rationalistic notions of megaproject governance and evaluation. From a rational-actor perspective, accountability would represent a solution to the principal–agent problem – as a means of minimising the risk that the agent would engage in malevolent, strategic behaviour in conflict with the interests of the principal. By contrast, insofar as megaprojects are conceptualised as networks, the multiple overlapping horizontal and vertical accountability relationships should be seen also from a perspective that stresses ethics, shared responsibility and obligation. Principal–agent problems would from this point of view arise not from opportunism, but also from "honest incompetence, miscommunication, organisational routines" and the like (Benjamin, 2008: 326). Accountability would then foster dialogue and greater understanding between the principal and the agent concerning the problem at hand (*ibid.*). Redefining accountability in this way would help reconcile learning and accountability as the two major objectives of evaluation. Defining the boundaries and characteristics of the network and exploring the multiple accountability structures would constitute key tasks of evaluation, in an attempt to foster learning and reflexivity (e.g. Benjamin and Greene, 2009; Hertting and Vedung, 2012).

A perspective recognising the multiple forms and relations of accountability would translate into greater emphasis on the megaproject context (e.g. OMEGA, 2012) and spontaneous, 'real-world' project 'governing' (Sanderson, 2012). Evaluation would from this perspective appear both as an element of top-down project governance, and as an emergent property of spontaneous project 'governing'. Taking these propositions seriously would also speak in favour of the adoption of adaptive evaluation arrangements, arguably needed when evaluation covers particularly long time periods (Hildén, 2009). Evaluation would hence constitute "probing", allowing new, emerging issues to be taken into consideration as information accumulates throughout the successive evaluations repeated during the policy cycle (Hildén, 2009, 10).

Integrating the socioeconomic criteria into megaproject evaluation

Interpreting megaprojects as evolving networks, as open systems whose goals are constantly evolving, also profoundly affects the criteria used for judging project success. Extending the range of evaluation criteria beyond the traditional 'iron triangle' would call attention to 'the socioeconomic', and to *ex post* evaluation and *ex nunc* monitoring (which occurs throughout the evolution of the project) as complements to *ex ante* assessment. The dynamic and emerging nature of the project goals would hence be taken as a starting point for evaluation. While megaproject literature indeed generally recognises such dynamism, different strands of this scholarship contrast starkly in terms of the practical implications they suggest for project management and evaluation. A key dividing line again distinguishes the approaches seeking to 'close down', by reducing uncertainty and strengthening control, from those that focus on 'opening up' (Stirling, 2008), via the exploration of various perspectives, and collective probing of evaluative criteria through stakeholder-oriented evaluation approaches (Benjamin and Greene, 2009; Hertting and Vedung, 2012: 40).

Integrating socioeconomic criteria in project evaluation faces numerous challenges of paradigmatic, theoretical, methodological, and institutional natures. The current dominance of 'rationalistic' notions of policy processes compromises attempts to open up perspectives towards the 'subjective' aspects of the social dimension. The 'subjective' denotes here the symbolic representations and meanings attributed to phenomena by social actors, and the changes in society as experienced and perceived by the actors involved, whereas the 'objective' aspects can be measured through indicators such as employment rate, demographic trends or literacy rate (e.g. Fortin and Gagnon, 2006: 726). 'Objective' information is therefore independent of the observer, while 'the subjective' depends on individual judgement.

Most approaches that seek to evaluate the social dimension have tended to focus on the objective, the measurable, employing methods such as 'social impact monitoring', often reduced to a 'checklist approach'.[7] This type of approach is weak at fostering learning, tending to disempower and objectify people while reinforcing the existing power asymmetries and failing to involve local communities (Rossouw and Malan, 2007). Furthermore, when the social dimension is addressed under the notion 'socioeconomic', the emphasis is typically on 'the economic' (e.g. Vanclay, 2004). The often neglected 'subjective' aspects include: culture; ethics; subjective well being; personal and property rights; people's fears, aspirations and identities (e.g. Vanclay, 2004: 280); and the relationships between society and nature (Littig and Grießler, 2005).

While most megaprojects are specifically designed to foster national, regional and local development by enhancing economic activity, improving infrastructure, etc., radioactive waste disposal represents, instead, an example of a megaproject that entails a local solution to a national – in fact, even global – problem.[8] These projects hence raise issues of justice, such as the respective roles and duties of, on the one hand, the state as the guardian of the general interest and, on the other, the sub-national actors that are often torn between their responsibilities towards the state and those towards their local constituencies. Two central questions stand out in particular. First, to what extent can local communities be held responsible for solving a national problem? Second, what right does the state have to impose upon a community a solution deemed to be in the interest of the nation, even in the interest of humankind? The promise of the various local socioeconomic benefits from the projects – and the economic support measures and 'community benefit packages' – complicates matters further, not least when the project is planned and implemented in an economically less developed area. 'Benefit packages' often generate contrasting reactions at the local level, some actors welcoming them as an indispensable source of development, and others condemning this kind of support as an act of bribery (Cass et al., 2010).

The chapters in Part II of this volume present a sample of the currently available context-sensitive methods and approaches that seek to integrate the subjective and objective sides of 'the social'. The 'political' variant of social impact assessment – SIA (Vanclay, 2004) – presented in Chapter 9, is probably the most widely applied approach in practical policymaking and project assessment, while participatory development of well-being indicators (Chapter 10), and Qualitative Comparative Analysis (Chapter 11) represent more recent attempts to bridge this gap between the subjective and the objective. Chapter 7 makes the case for mixing methods and approaches, including the 'rationalistic' methods such as cost–benefit analysis.

Dealing with the unpredictable impacts and consequences of evaluation

Sanderson's (2012) plea for greater attention to 'governing' instead of 'governance' is grounded in the perception that the rationalistic approach to megaproject evaluation has failed to fully appreciate the diverse roles that evaluation plays in project management and policymaking. Interpreting evaluation exclusively in terms of the rational actor model overemphasises the conception of evaluation as a tool for 'speaking truth to power'. Not only does this perspective presume an evaluator capable of setting herself apart from the evaluation object, but it also tends to underestimate the uncontrollable and unpredictable roles of evaluation in policy processes.

A more nuanced perspective would entail in particular recognising the multiple dimensions of power, including its discursive, ideological, cultural and knowledge-related expressions. Megaproject governance certainly entails strong economic and political interests, but power manifests itself in these contexts also and above all through knowledge. As a rule, the greater the degree of technicality and complexity of the project, the greater the significance of power associated with the use and production of knowledge. Often the key knowledge and expertise tend to be concentrated in the hands of the few, which raises questions such as 'who controls the production and use of knowledge?', and 'is the evaluator perceived as credible and independent?'. When crucial knowledge is held by a limited number of 'canonised' experts, an evaluator without direct access to this privileged group may find it difficult to appear as credible. Conversely, actors outside of such an 'inner circle' frequently contest the legitimacy and independence of an evaluator, or they perceive this as too dependent on the established experts. Literature on network evaluation, in turn, has suggested that in such governance contexts traditional notions of the independence of the evaluator would be unhelpful, because the evaluator would unavoidably depend on the broad range of actors involved at various levels of project governance. The credibility and legitimacy of the evaluator would hence be better anchored in multiple dependencies – the evaluator would be credible precisely because of, and not in spite of, being dependent on a range of actors in the network (Benjamin and Greene, 2009). Chapters in Part I of this volume provide insights on the exercise of power through expertise in megaproject evaluation.

The question of control is crucial also for the role and influence that evaluation can have in policy processes. Many strands of policy and programme evaluation, as well as the theories of 'projects-as-practice' (e.g. Sanderson, 2012), view evaluation largely as an emergent property of project governing, considering that its fate in network governance lies to a great extent beyond the control of any single actor. However, where the actors involved in governance believe that evaluations can indeed influence policy, they seek to control the evaluations and thereby also the governance processes.

Policy actors frequently dispute the credibility and authority of an evaluation, and the control of evaluation design. Likewise, they typically use evaluations strategically, while accusing others of misuse, legitimation and 'symbolic' use of evaluations. Analysing the exercise of power in such situations would help the various involved actors to better understand the evaluation landscape. However, this also raises the question of who indeed could and should evaluate a megaproject, when no single actor has full control over the project governance and the evaluation landscape. One response, in line with the network governance paradigm, is to foster multiple evaluations, conducted by the various partners in a network. This could contribute to greater understanding of not only the megaproject as a network, but also of the evaluation landscape itself.

The questions of power and control likewise raise the issue of the respective vices and virtues of consensus and conflict in megaproject evaluation. Here, the environmental justice literature provides useful insights, similar to those from evaluation practice more generally. Analysis of environmental justice outcomes is commonly expected to help alleviate conflict, by providing a shared cognitive basis for: 1) negotiation on performance measurement criteria; 2) mitigation of harmful impacts; and 3) compensation for the perceived harm. However, for a number of reasons, such an analysis can aggravate rather than mitigate conflict. The analysis may bring into focus previously hidden or unknown unequal distributions of harmful impacts and hence generate dispute and contestation (Walker, 2010: 316). By bringing a new – cognitive – dimension into the existing political conflict, new knowledge enables the contesting parties to broaden their argumentative arsenal and thereby to strengthen their case (Turnhout et al., 2007). Similarly, concrete attempts to deal with the problem of equity and justice in megaprojects, by introducing local 'benefit packages', are often denounced as mere bribery and attempts to 'pay off the opposition' (Cass et al., 2010). The incorporation of environmental justice considerations into assessment procedures (e.g. in the US) led to allegations that such measures are used strategically to legitimise of decisions already made for other reasons (Holifield, 2004: 286). In such contexts, social scientists are increasingly accused of practicing 'acceptology' (Chateauraynaud and Debaz, 2011), i.e. promoting the imposition of *a priori* unpalatable projects and technologies upon a reluctant population, in the spirit of "strong justification" (Stirling, 2006).

Conflict also feeds on the value-laden nature of facts in general, and those relating to the analysis of social justice in particular. Methodological disputes around what constitutes a 'good' or sufficiently robust analysis provide additional tools for different parties to contest the results of analysis; citizen groups frequently denounce the analysis of the social for being underpinned by technocratic expert knowledge (e.g. Foreman, 1998: 29). Finally, the notion of justice is by its very nature contested, and expecting universal agreement on what constitutes a just outcome is unrealistic at best (Walker, 2010: 317).

Summing up, the experience from environmental justice practice and literature echoes the lessons from research on the role of policy evaluation in policymaking: an evaluation or an assessment does not simply and unproblematically contribute to consensus-building, but is itself constitutive of the governance processes. These processes unavoidably also include situations whereby evidence "becomes simply another resource to be utilised, framed and positioned within the strategic interactions of different actors" (Walker, 2010: 317). Whether such processes help to build consensus or instead aggravate conflict is an empirical question and depends on the given decision-making context. Evaluation approaches that seek to reduce conflict are certainly valuable, but if the objective is to enhance learning and reflection, alternative approaches may be more appropriate. Arguably, fostering learning and openness to conflict is challenging in megaproject contexts, not least because project proponents often have an interest to seek premature closure of knowledge and policy options, and thereby retain control over the projects (e.g. Hisschemöller and Cuppen, 2015). Striking a balance between the objectives of, on the one hand, consensus-building in the spirit of 'closing down', and on the other hand, 'opening up' designed to promote learning, is among the key challenges of megaproject evaluation, and requires constant attention to the diverse forms of exercise of power.

Outline of the book

The chapters in the book are divided into two parts. Those in Part I are grounded in particular case studies that critically analyse the existing megaproject evaluation approaches and thereby distance themselves from such narrow perspectives. Part II consists of explorations into specific alternative evaluation approaches that would foster the kind of 'opening up' towards the socioeconomic advocated in this introduction. To varying degrees, they all draw on empirical examples to illustrate the underpinning theoretical and methodological arguments.

The first part of the book draws on empirical experience from megaproject evaluation in order to indicate key issues and shortcomings in current socioeconomic evaluation. In Chapter 2, Saraç-Lesavre presents a critical analysis of the treatment of long-term uncertainties, through an in-depth analysis of the use of economic assessment of the US nuclear waste disposal programme. Chapters 3 and 4 examine transport megaprojects: Dimitriou et al. (Chapter 3) draw on a broad sample of transport sector megaprojects to demonstrate a number of shortcomings in the treatment of risk, uncertainty and complexity in their evaluation, whereas in Chapter 4 Reverdy and Lehtonen analyse the Lyon–Turin high-speed rail project, and illustrate the limits of economic evaluation when faced with powerful vested interests constituted over the years. Chapters 5 to 7 focus on radioactive waste management: Lehtonen, Kojo and Litmanen (Chapter 5) analyse the shifting but always secondary role of socioeconomic evaluation in the management of spent nuclear fuel in Finland. Bergmans and Verhaegen (Chapter 6) explore the opportunities and challenges of citizen participation at the local level in the evaluation of low- and intermediate-level radioactive waste management in Belgium, and in Chapter 7 Litmanen, Kojo, Kari and Vesalainen examine the evolution of the dialogue between two key stakeholders in the Finnish radioactive waste management policy: the nuclear waste management company and the safety regulator.

By exploring evaluations designed to answer the apparently simple question of whether or not adequate fees were collected to finance the US nuclear waste disposal programme, Basak **Saraç-Lesavre** (Chapter 2) shows how economic evaluation tools operate as mediators that involve constant negotiation and reconfiguration of the moral, technical and political dimensions of public policies. In particular, the chapter reveals the changing role of the state over the years, towards an increasing degree of depoliticisation, as a specific response to the increasing uncertainty about the future of the programme. Key political and ethical choices embedded in the evaluations designed to assess the sufficiency of the waste fees were, over time and to an increasing degree, treated as questions of mere technical expertise. This in turn helped to protect these choices against criticism and to exclude them from public debate. These seemingly technical questions entailed implicit choices concerning the ways in which the state defined its role – as either a private or a public investor – and enacted more or less optimistic or pessimistic future states of the society and the economy.

In Chapter 3, Harry T. **Dimitriou**, E. John **Ward** and Phil G. **Wright** present the methodology and conclusions of a five-year international research programme, coordinated under Dimitriou's leadership by the OMEGA Centre at University College London (UCL), on the planning, appraisal and delivery of transport-sector megaprojects. The programme adopted a largely qualitative research approach, entailing narrative analysis, the collection of first-hand experiences of individuals involved in projects, an extensive literature review, and in-depth case studies in ten developed countries. The analysis placed particular attention to risk, uncertainty and complexity, concluding that these issues are largely underestimated by infrastructure and spatial planners but far better understood by managers of megaprojects. On the other hand, there is a tension between the mentality of project managers, geared towards the 'iron triangle' objectives and 'getting things done', and the policy and planning mentality more concerned with sustainability. OMEGA research findings called attention to the crucial importance of the context, the many dimensions of trust, the irreducible uncertainties, the multiple perceptions and definitions of project 'success', the heterogeneity of megaprojects, and the nature of megaprojects as organic, evolving and open systems with fuzzy and constantly shifting boundaries. Furthermore, the findings suggested that the dominance of 'iron triangle' criteria of project success has diverted attention away from the broader sustainable development considerations, especially its institutional dimension, in the governance and evaluation of megaprojects. The authors advocate early stakeholder involvement, but also stronger state leadership as an antidote to the short-termism that frequently plagues megaprojects. Dimitriou et al. argue that active public sector involvement would also be in the interest of the private sector actors, and would constitute a means of ensuring transparency and the accumulation of knowledge gained from different megaprojects.

Chapter 4 presents an analysis by Thomas **Reverdy** and Markku **Lehtonen** of the role of economic evaluation in the Lyon–Turin high-speed railway project. Despite the increasing number of evaluations calling into question its economic viability, the project has continued to advance towards implementation through a stepwise process of decision-making whereby each successive stage strengthens the commitment to the realisation of the project. The case illustrates the weight of an alliance of vested interests and local-level stakeholders constituted over the years, and demonstrates how numerous factors incite these stakeholders to discredit, underestimate or simply ignore critical socioeconomic evaluation. It also points to the dynamics of 'irreversibilisation', whereby the stepwise implementation of the project, e.g. through segmentation and preparatory works along the planned railway trajectory, not only leads to an accumulation of 'sunk costs' but also modifies the outcomes of the evaluation. Interestingly, in the case of the Lyon–Turin railway project the criticism against the opacity and excessive technicality of economic evaluation does not come only from the opponents, but in particular from the supporters of the project.

In Chapter 5 Markku **Lehtonen**, Matti **Kojo** and Tapio **Litmanen** scrutinise the shifting role of socioeconomic evaluation in the governance of what is often portrayed as a success story of nuclear waste policy – the Finnish project of spent nuclear fuel disposal. Since the Finnish parliament gave the green light to the construction of an underground rock characterisation laboratory in 2001, the project has advanced without major difficulties, in a seemingly consensual atmosphere and without the usual problems of local acceptance. While the safety-related technical evaluations have understandably received the bulk of the R&D funding devoted to the project, socioeconomic evaluation – defined here in a broad sense as covering both evaluations proper and social science research on nuclear waste policy – received significant attention during the two-year participatory EIA process organised in 1997–1999 by the waste management company in preparation for the licencing process. The chapter confirms the findings from an abundant body of literature on policy evaluation and 'knowledge use' (e.g. Weiss, 1986; 1999): rather than affecting policy decisions directly, socioeconomic evaluation had a number of indirect impacts that could be labelled as 'conceptual' and 'political'. The waste management company seems to have been the main beneficiary of socioeconomic evaluation. The company used the evaluations to justify siting the facility in Eurajoki – a 'nuclear municipality' already hosting two of the country's four nuclear reactors – and to defend itself against criticism concerning the alleged harmful socioeconomic impacts of the project. The learning effects from the evaluations also seemed to overwhelmingly accrue to the company, which learned more sophisticated ways of managing public opinion and controlling the dialogue processes. The window of opportunity allowing socioeconomic evaluation to influence the project closed down soon after the parliamentary decision of 2001: once local acceptance and official approval for the project was obtained, the company no longer felt a compelling need to commission socioeconomic studies.

Anne **Bergmans** and Marlies **Verhaegen** (Chapter 6) examine the relationships between the long term concerns and citizen participation in megaprojects, through an empirical analysis of the siting process for short-lived, low- and intermediate-level radioactive waste (LILW) in Belgium. They pose the fundamental question of whether wider citizen participation indeed improves the evaluation of the socioeconomic impacts and leads to a more sustainable conception of the project. In line with the observations of Dimitriou et al. (Chapter 3 in this volume), Bergmans and Verhaegen demonstrate how the criteria of *ex ante* evaluation of the project continue to evolve through continuous interaction between citizens and project stakeholders, and how such evolution results from the confrontation of diverse project cultures. Instead of seeking to answer 'what goes wrong' – a key question posed in plenty of the megaproject literature – the chapter concentrates on analysing 'what goes on'. The authors suggest substituting the 'iron triangle' by a 'Velvet Triangle' – an approach characterised by an open and flexible project culture, whereby multiple rationalities would be integrated through qualitative performance criteria, while uncertainty would be confronted by tolerating vagueness and complexity. For example, in contrast with the optimisation underpinning the 'iron triangle' approach, the Belgian case places 'satisficing' at the heart of project management: the financial performance of a project would not be examined against a predetermined project budget, but in the light of long-term financing mechanisms that all key actors would consider fair, feasible and acceptable.

Tapio **Litmanen**, Matti **Kojo**, Mika **Kari** and Jurgita **Vesalainen** (Chapter 7) examine the emerging concerns over copper corrosion in the Finnish spent nuclear fuel disposal project, as an illustration of the challenges involved in long-term governance of megaprojects. Conducting a practice-oriented micro-level analysis in line with the 'projects-as-practice' approach advocated by Sanderson (2012), the authors examine the evolving and long-standing risk dialogue between the nuclear waste management company and the safety regulator. In doing so, the authors bring to the focus a topic seldom explicitly addressed in megaproject literature: the crucial role of the regulator in the governance and evaluation, in a context with safety as by far the overriding concern. The analysis emphasises the constant unplanned adaptations that the highly structured and institutionalised governance of Finnish nuclear waste management project has had to undergo throughout the years. The authors furthermore demonstrate how, as a result of the risk dialogue, the values, mental frameworks and objectives of the two key actors in Finnish nuclear waste policy have gradually converged over the years – thereby risking a blurring of the lines between the developer and the regulator. Where Saraç-Lesavre (Chapter 2) revealed the values and politics embedded in the highly technical financial evaluation tools, Litmanen et al. similarly highlight the political nature and socioeconomic dimensions in risk-related evaluation. The chapter provides a counterpoint to Bergmans and Verhaegen (Chapter 6) in that the intensive dialogue between the Finnish regulator and the waste company has left room for only very limited public participation.

The second part – Chapters 8 to 11 – presents pathways towards broader approaches to socioeconomic evaluation of megaprojects. Lamari, Prévost and Poulin-Larivière (Chapter 8) examine the strengths and weaknesses of four alternative evaluation methodologies, whereas each of the Chapters 9 to 11 focuses on its own specific evaluation methodology: social impact assessment (Chapter 9, Vanclay), collective construction of local well-being indicators (Chapter 10, Renault) and qualitative comparative analysis (QCA; Chapter 11, Verweij).

In Chapter 8, Moktar **Lamari**, Jean-René **Prévost** and Line **Poulin-Larivière** draw on one hundred Canadian megaprojects in order to illustrate the potential and the limitations of four alternative approaches to *ex ante* evaluation in dealing with the multiple risks and uncertainties involved in megaprojects. The Canadian examples largely confirm some of the key findings of megaproject literature, notably the chronic tendencies of delays and budget overruns. The authors identify and systematically analyse risks and uncertainties related to: 1) project design and management of the project; 2) legal and political aspects; 3) construction and exploitation of the infrastructure; 4) economics and finance; 5) anticipated demand for the project; 6) environmental impacts; 7) insertion of the project in the host community; and 8) major disasters. The chapter then examines the ability of four evaluation methods to respond to the challenges raised by these uncertainties: cost–benefit analysis (CBA), social impact assessment (SIA), environmental impact assessment (EIA), and assessment of the socio-political context. In this comparison CBA appears in a relatively favourable light, yet the authors call for a comprehensive and holistic approach to risk and uncertainty. The matrix comparing the four evaluation approaches provides a useful starting point for the search for such a comprehensive framework.

Frank **Vanclay** (Chapter 9) argues that social impact assessment (SIA) has over its forty-year history moved from being merely a regulatory technique towards a "discourse, field of practice and paradigm", emphasising the role of SIA as the "process of managing the social issues". In its focus on 'management' and 'process', Vanclay's chapter echoes much of the literature on megaprojects as well as policy and programme evaluation, but also the call by Lamari et al. (Chapter 8) for greater emphasis on the mitigation and reduction of risk and uncertainty. Vanclay rejects a static "checklist approach" to social monitoring, emphasising the role of SIA as part of adaptive management, the constant attention to indirect second- and third-order impacts, and the need for early and continuous management of 'the social'. Vanclay argues that negative impacts tend to dominate the debate in the developed countries, whereas 'project-induced in-migration' or 'honey-pot effect' often characterise megaprojects in developing countries – as tends to be the case also in economically declining regions in developed countries.

Vanclay identifies neoliberalism and corporate social responsibility as key drivers pushing companies to go beyond mere regulations in dealing with social risks. SIA therefore appears to be elemental in companies' attempts to win a 'social licence to operate', with international NGOs in a pivotal role in such 'licencing' processes. Vanclay mentions the mining industry as one of the first to have recognised the importance of managing social issues.[9] He also discusses the crucial 'impact history' of megaprojects – i.e. the way in which the historically shaped perceptions of a project's local impacts shape its social acceptance: a project may struggle to gain trust and support at the local level, simply because of past bad experiences, including notably the failure of projects to deliver their promised benefits. Yet Vanclay remains relatively optimistic about the ability of SIA to empower local communities and mitigate harmful impacts, and pleads for the extension of the principle of 'free, prior and informed consent' (FPIC) in the appraisal and management of 'the social' to all involved communities.

Michel **Renault** (Chapter 10) draws on his experience from research (ISBET – Societal Indicators of Territorial Wellbeing) into bottom-up, collective and participatory processes designed to develop social indicators of well-being in French municipalities. The project can be seen as a contribution to the current efforts aimed at developing indicators of progress and well-being that would complement, or even replace, the GDP as the leading economic indicator. As opposed to the commonplace approach that sees indicators as direct inputs to policy, Renault's work emphasises their role in generating shared meanings, definitions, objectives, and agreement on the means of achieving these objectives. Drawing on pragmatic philosophy – more specifically, the transactional approach of Dewey and Bentley – Renault stresses the importance of language, communication, words and narratives, challenges the notion that valuation would consist of mere aggregation of individual preferences, and builds on a 'social' conception of value. Renault's contribution speaks directly to attempts at reconciling the 'subjective' and 'objective' aspects of the social, given its emphasis on the construction and continuous redefinition of agents' preferences through communication. Renault stresses that local policies need to be guided by broader human development objectives than merely the growth of GDP, and challenges the dominant expert-led approaches to indicator development. He describes in some detail the concrete steps of the inclusive and participatory indicator development process adopted in the ISBET project, arguing that collective well-being can only be defined and measured through deliberative and interactive approaches – not through surveys aggregating individual judgements and preferences.

Stefan **Verweij** (Chapter 11) argues that there is a gap between the evaluation and implementation of megaprojects, and advocates qualitative comparative analysis (QCA) as a remedy, notably in transport infrastructure research and evaluation. According to Verweij, megaproject evaluation tends to focus excessively on the planning stage, overlooking the complexities involved in the implementation of megaprojects. The open-system nature of these projects means that the project outcomes and their causes cannot be predicted and identified unambiguously, which in turn makes it difficult to evaluate the implementation processes (Rittel and Webber, 1973). Large infrastructure projects face uncertainty and ambiguity, but their evaluations are often informed by a linear-rationalist, objectivist worldview, which compromises the capacity of evaluation to promote learning. Verweij advocates QCA as a complexity-informed evaluation approach, able to account for key phenomena associated with megaprojects, notably their non-decomposability, contingency, non-compressibility and time-asymmetry. Illustrating the arguments by drawing on the Dutch EUR 2 billion transportation infrastructure project A15 Maasvlakte-Vaanplein, the chapter concludes by discussing the applicability of QCA for megaproject research and evaluation.

Chapter 12 pulls together the key lessons, exploring in particular the opportunities and challenges faced in efforts to open up megaproject evaluation to 'the socioeconomic', in ways outlined in the introduction and elaborated in the chapters of this volume. It highlights key challenges and opportunities that relate to various tensions, such as those between learning and accountability as major functions of evaluation, emancipatory and legitimising objectives of public and stakeholder participation, and attempts at control versus flexible adaptation and reflexivity in megaproject governance and evaluation. The chapter highlights lessons that radioactive waste management projects can offer to socioeconomic evaluation, by virtue of their characteristics as a specific type of megaproject.

Notes

1   This book is the fruit of reflections initiated in an international workshop organised in June 2013 by the Institute for Research and Innovation in Society (IFRIS) and the French radioactive waste management agency (Andra), at the headquarters of the latter in the Paris area.
2   Flyvbjerg (2011: 322) subsumes under the term 'megaproject' both 'major projects' – costing USD 100 million or more – and 'major programmes' – a suite of projects whose cost exceeds USD 1 billion.
3   It is worth noting that our definition of the socioeconomic can be considered 'Anglo-Saxon', to the extent that it contrasts with the French definition of 'socioeconomic evaluation' as an assessment of the costs and benefits of a project to society rather than to an individual private actor. Chapter 5 in this book addresses precisely this French conception of the term, in examining the role of economic evaluation in the governance of a railway megaproject.
4   Koppenjan et al. (2010) contrast two approaches to megaproject management and uncertainty – the *predict and control* approach in which "uncertainty is calculated as risk and everything is done to control as many aspects as possible, for instance through time and cost buffers", and the *prepare and commit* approach, which embraces irreducible uncertainty as an inherent part of project management, which should in turn be organised in a manner that allows it to respond to unexpected developments (Giezen, 2012: 784).
5   While "single-loop" learning is defined as learning concerning the best means of achieving predefined objectives, "double-loop" learning entails questioning the broader governance context, whereas triple-loop learning invites the involved actors to question the objectives themselves.
6   The French project of deep geological disposal of radioactive waste, named 'Cigeo', is perhaps the most extreme in that the requirement of reversibility has been inscribed in the country's legislation, through the ACT 2016-1015).
7   Objects of such monitoring typically include demographic impacts, impacts on ways of life and land use, local/regional economy and intra-firm learning, public participation, quality of life and perceptions, and social equity (Gagnon, 2003: 99).
8   Climate policy provides numerous similar examples of 'local solutions to a global problem'.
9   The 'participatory turn' in nuclear waste management policies (Sundqvist and Elam, 2010) attests to a similar rise of awareness in the nuclear sector.

References

Adelle, C., Jordan, A. & Turnpenny, J. 2012. Proceeding in parallel or drifting apart? A systematic review of policy appraisal research and practices. *Environment and Planning C: Government and Policy* 30(3): 401–415.

Albaek, E. 1995. Policy evaluation: Design and utilization. In R.C. Rist (ed.), *Policy Evaluation: Linking Theory to Practice*. Cambridge: Edgar Elgar.

Altshuler, A. & Luberoff, D. 2003. *Mega-projects: The changing politics of urban public investment*. Washington, DC: Brookings Institution Press, co-published with the Lincoln Institute of Land Policy, Cambridge, Massachusetts.

Argyris, C. & Schön, D. 1978. *Organisational learning: A theory of action perspective*. Reading, MA: Addison Wesley.

Ballet, J., Sirven, N. & Requiers-Desjardins, M. 2007. Social capital and natural resource management. A critical perspective. *The Journal of Environment & Development* 16(4): 355–374.

Benjamin, L.M. 2008. Evaluator's role in accountability relationships: Measurement technician, capacity builder or risk manager? *Evaluation* 14(3): 323–343.

Benjamin, L.M. & Greene, J.C. 2009. From program to network: The evaluator's role in today's public problem-solving environment. *American Journal of Evaluation* 30(3): 296–309.

Blowers, A. 2010. Why dump on us? Power, pragmatism and the periphery in the siting of new nuclear reactors in the UK. *Journal of Integrative Environmental Sciences* 7(3): 157–173.

Bornstein, L. 2007. *Community-University Research Alliances (CURA) – Making mega-projects work for communities*. Montréal: Social Sciences and Humanities Research Council of Canada.

Bruzelius, N., Flyvbjerg, B. & Rothengatter, W. 2002. Big decisions, big risks: Improving accountability in mega projects. *Transport Policy* 9(2): 143–154.

Cantarelli, C.C., Flyvbjerg, B., Molin, E.J.E. & van Wee, B. 2010. Cost overruns in large-scale transportation infrastructure projects: Explanations and their theoretical embeddedness. *European Journal of Transport and Infrastructure Research* 10(1): 5–18.

Cass, N., Walker, G. & Devine-Wright, P. 2010. Good neighbours, public relations and bribes: The politics and perceptions of community benefit provision in renewable energy development in the UK. *Journal of Environmental Policy & Planning* 12(3): 255–275.

Chateauraynaud, F. & Debaz, J. 2011. Observer la sécurité sanitaire dans la durée. Leçons cognitives et pratiques d'un observatoire socio-informatique. Socio-informatique et argumentation: sociologie argumentative des controverses, concepts et méthodes socioinformatiques. Available online at: http://socioargu.hypotheses.org/2786 (accessed 30 May 2016).

Collingridge, D. 1980. *The social control of technology*. New York: St Martin's Press; London: Pinter.

Drew, R., Aggleton, P., Chalmers, H. & Wood, K. 2011. Using social network analysis to evaluate a complex policy network. *Evaluation* 17(4): 383–394.

Dryzek, J.S. 2000. *Deliberative democracy and beyond: Liberals, critics, contestations*. Oxford: Oxford University Press.

Flyvbjerg, B. 2007. *Megaproject policy and planning: Problems, causes, cures*. Summary of PhD dissertation, Aalborg University, Denmark. Available online at: www.rucsdigital eprojektbibliotek.dk/bitstream/1800/2727/1/afhandlingBF2007s.pdf (accessed 25 July 2016).

Flyvbjerg, B. 2009. Survival of the unfittest: Why the worst infrastructure gets built – and what we can do about it. *Oxford Review of Economic Policy* 25(3): 344–367.

Flyvbjerg, B. 2011. Over budget, over time, over and over again: Managing major projects. In Morris, P.W.G., Pinto, J.K. & Söderlund, J. (eds.), *The Oxford Handbook of Project Management*. Oxford: Oxford University Press, pp. 321–344.

Flyvbjerg, B., Skamris, H.M.K. & Buhl, S.L. 2002. Underestimating costs in public works projects: Error or lie? *Journal of the American Planning Association* 68(3): 279–295.

Flyvbjerg, B., Bruzelius, N. & Rothengatter, W. 2003. *Megaprojects and Risk: An anatomy of ambition.* Cambridge: Cambridge University Press.

Flyvbjerg, B. & Priemus, H. 2007. Planning and design of large infrastructure projects. *Environment and Planning B: Planning & Design* 34(4): 576–577.

Foreman, C.H. 1998. *The promise and perils of environmental justice.* Washington DC: Brookings Institution Press.

Forester, J. 2001. An instructive case hampered by theoretical puzzles: Critical comments on Bent Flyvbjerg's rationality and power. *International Planning Studies* 6(3): 263–270.

Fortin, M.-J. & Gagnon, C. 2006. Interpreting major industrial landscapes: Social follow-up on meanings, the case of two aluminium smelters, Alcan (Alma, Canada) and Pechiney (Dunkirk, France). *Environmental Impact Assessment Review* 26(8): 725–745.

Gagnon, C. 2003. Les enseignements d'un suivi des incidences sociales d'un changement planifié: le cas du mégacomplexe industriel Alma au Saguenay – Lac Saint-Jean. In *Le GRIR : 20 ans de recherche et d'intervention pour le développement local et régional.* Chicoutimi : GRIR/UQAC, pp. 83–110. Available online at: /www.uqac.ca/msiaa/articlesCG/article06.pdf (accessed 25 July 2016).

Gagnon, C., Simard, J.-G., Tellier, L.-C. & Gagnon, S. 2008. Développeement territorial viable, capital social et capital environnemental: quels liens? *VertigO – La revue en sciences de l'environnement* 8(2): October. Available online at: http://vertigo.revues. org/4983 (accessed 31 May 2016); DOI: 10.4000/vertigo.4983.

Gelatt, H.B. 1989. Positive Uncertainty: A new decision-making framework for counseling. *Journal of Counseling Psychology* 36(2): 252–256.

Gibbons, M., Limoges, C., Nowotny, H., Schwartzman, S., Scott, P., & Trow, M. 1994. *The new production of knowledge: The dynamics of science and research in contemporary societies.* London: Sage.

Giezen, M. 2012. Keeping it simple? A case study into the advantages and disadvantages of reducing complexity in mega project planning. *International Journal of Project Management* 30(7): 781–790.

Hertting, N. & Vedung, E. 2012. Purposes and criteria in network governance evaluation: How far does standard evaluation take us? *Evaluation* 18(1): 27–46.

Hildén, M. 2009. Time horizons in evaluating environmental policies. In M. Birnbaum & P. Mickwitz (eds.), *Environmental program and policy evaluation: Addressing methodological challenges.* New Directions for Evaluation 122: 9–18.

Hirschman A. 1995. *Development projects observed.* Washington, DC: Brookings Institution.

Hisschemöller, M. & Cuppen, E. 2015. Participatory Assessment: Tools for empowering, learning and legitimating? In A.J. Jordan & J.R. Turnpenny (eds.), *The Tools of Policy Formulation: Actors, Capacities, Venues and Effects.* Cheltenham: Edward Elgar, pp. 33–51.

Holifield, R. 2004. Neoliberalism and environmental justice in the United States environmental protection agency: Translating policy into managerial practice in hazardous waste remediation. *Geoforum* 35: 285–297.

Horne, J. & Manzenreiter, W. (eds). 2006. *Sports mega-events: Social scientific analyses of a global phenomenon.* Oxford: Wiley-Blackwell.

Kickert, W.J.M. 2003. Beyond public management. *Public Management Review* 5(3): 377–399.

Kickert, W.J.M., Klijn, E.-H. & Koppenjan, J.F.M. (eds). 1997. *Managing complex networks: Strategies for the public sector.* Thousand Oaks, CA: SAGE.

Klijn, E.-H. & Edelenbos, J. 2007. Meta-governance as network management. In: Sørensen, E. & Torfing, J. (eds.), *Theories of Democratic Network Governance*. London: Palgrave-Macmillan, pp. 199–214.

Koppenjan, J., Veeneman, W.W., Van der Voort, H., Ten Heuvelhof, E. & Leijten, M. 2010. Competing management approaches in large engineering projects: The Dutch RandstadRail project. *International Journal of Project Management* 29(6): 740–750.

Lehtonen, M. 2004. The environmental–social interface of sustainable development: Capabilities, social capital, institutions. *Ecological Economics* 49(2): 199–214.

Littig, B. & Grießler, E. 2005. Social sustainability: A catchword between political pragmatism and social theory. *International Journal of Sustainable Development* 8(1/2): 65–79.

Locatelli, G., Mancini, M. & Scalet, L. 2012. Project controlling in mega events: The Expo 2015 case. *Project Perspectives: The annual publication of International Project Management Association*, pp. 58–65.

Loch, C.H., De Meyer, A. & Pich, M.T. 2006. *Managing the Unknown: A new approach to managing high uncertainty and risk in projects*. Hoboken, NJ: John Wiley & Sons.

Loorbach, D. 2007. *Transition management. New mode of governance for sustainable development*. Utrecht: International Books.

Nowotny, H., Scott, P. & Gibbons, M. 2001. *Re-thinking science: Knowledge and the public in an age of uncertainty*. Oxford: Polity.

OMEGA. 2012. *Mega Projects. Lessons for Decision-makers: An analysis of selected international large-scale transport infrastructure projects*. Executive summary. Bartlett School of Planning, University College London. OMEGA Centre – Centre for Mega Projects in Transport and Development. December 2012. Available online at: www.omegacentre. bartlett.ucl.ac.uk/wp-content/uploads/2014/11/Mega-Projects-Executive-Summary.pdf (accessed 25 July 2016).

Osland, O. & Strand, A. 2010. The politics and institutions of project approval: A critical-constructive comment on the theory of strategic misrepresentation. *European Journal of Transport and Infrastructure Research* 10(1): 77–88.

Perrin, B. 1998. Effective use and misuse of performance measurement. *American Journal of Evaluation* 19(3): 367–379.

Priemus, H. 2010. Mega-projects: Dealing with pitfalls. *European Planning Studies* 18(7): 1023–1039.

Provan, K.G. & Kenis, P. 2007. Modes of network governance: Structure, management, and effectiveness. *Journal of Public Administration & Theory* 18(2): 229–252.

Reed, M.S., Evely, A.C., Cundill, G., Fazey, I., Glass, J., Laing, A., Newig, J., Parrish, B., Prell, C., Raymond, C. & Stringer, L.C. 2010. What is social learning? *Ecology and Society* 15, r1. Available online at: www.ecologyandsociety.org/vol15/iss4/resp1/ (accessed 25 July 2016).

Regeer, B.J., Hoes, A.-C., van Amstel-van Saane, M., Caron-Flinterman, F.F. & Bunders, J.F.G. 2009. Six guiding principles for evaluating mode-2 strategies for sustainable development. *American Journal of Evaluation* 30(4): 515–537.

Renault, M. 2011. Créer un nouvel indicateur de bien-être sur des territoires. In K. Makoto & M. Humbert (eds), *La voie de la décroissance – construire une société conviviale*. Tokyo: Éditions Commons.

Rittel, H. & Webber, M. 1973. Dilemmas in a general theory of planning. *Policy Sciences* 4(2): 155–169.

Roche, M. 2000. *Mega-events and modernity: Olympics and expos in the growth of global culture*. London: Routledge.

Rossouw, N. & Malan, S. 2007. The importance of theory in shaping social impact monitoring: Lessons from the Berg River Dam, South Africa. *Impact Assessment and Project Appraisal* 25(4): 291–299.

Russell, A.W., Vanclay, F.M. & Aslin, H.J. 2010. Technology assessment in social context: The case for a new framework for assessing and shaping technological developments. *Impact Assessment and Project Appraisal* 28(2): 109–116.

Sanderson, J. 2012. Risk, uncertainty and governance in megaprojects: A critical discussion of alternative explanations. *International Journal of Project Management* 30(4): 432–443.

Schlosberg, D. 2013. Theorising environmental justice: The expanding sphere of a discourse. *Environmental Politics* 22(1): 37–55.

Sébastien, L., Lehtonen, M. & Bauler, T. 2014. Can indicators fill the gap between science and policy? An exploration of the (non) use and (non) influence of indicators in EU and UK policymaking. *Nature & Culture* 9(3): 316–343. doi:10.3167/nc.2014.090305.

Sen, A. 1999. *Development as freedom*. Oxford: Oxford University Press.

Shenhar, A.J., Dvir, D., Ofer, L. & Maltz, A.C. 2001. Project success: A multidimensional strategic concept. *Long Range Planning* 34(6): 699–725.

Sørensen, E. 2006. Metagovernance: The changing role of politicians in processes of democratic governance. *The American Review of Public Administration* 36(1): 98–114.

Stark, D. 2000. For a sociology of worth. Working Paper Series, Center on Organizational Innovation, Columbia University. October. Available online at: http://textlab.io/doc/9043216/for-a-sociology-of-worth---center-on-organizational-innov... (accessed 25 July 2016).

Stark, D. 2001. Heterarchy: Exploiting ambiguity and organizing diversity. *Brazilian Journal of Political Economy* 21(1): 21–39.

Stirling, A. 2006. Analysis, participation and power: Justification and closure in participatory multi-criteria analysis. *Land Use Policy* 23 (1): 95–107.

Stirling, A. 2008. 'Opening up' and 'closing down': Power, participation, and pluralism in the social appraisal of technology. *Science, Technology & Human Values* 33(2): 262–294.

Sundqvist, G. & Elam, M. 2010. Public involvement designed to circumvent public concern? The "participatory turn" in European nuclear activities. *Risk, Hazards & Crisis in Public Policy* 1(4): 203–229. doi: 10.2202/1944-4079.1046

Theys, J. 2002. L'approche territoriale du "développement durable", condition d'une prise en compte de sa dimension sociale. *Développement durable et territoires*, Dossier 1: Approches territoriales du Développement Durable. Available online at: https://developpementdurable.revues.org/1475 (accessed 29 January 2013). DOI: 10.4000/developpementdurable.1475

Turnhout, E., Hisschemöller, M. & Eijsackers, H. 2007. Ecological indicators: Between the two fires of science and policy. *Ecological Indicators* 7(2): 215–228.

Vanclay, F. 2004. The triple bottom line and impact assessment: How do TBL, EIA, SIA and EMS relate to each other? *Journal of Environmental Assessment Policy & Management* 6(3): 265–288.

van Marrewijk, A., Clegg, S.R., Pitsis, T.S. & Veenswijk, M. 2008. Managing public-private megaprojects: Paradoxes, complexity, and project design. *International Journal of Project Management* 26(6): 591–600.

van Marrewijk, A. & Veenswijk, M. 2010. Organizing reflexivity in designed change: The ethnoventionist approach. *Journal of Organizational Change Management* 23(3): 212–229.

Vatn, A. 2009. An institutional analysis of methods for environmental appraisal. *Ecological Economics* 68(8–9): 2207–2215.

Verweij, S. & Gerrits, L. 2013. Understanding and researching complexity with Qualitative Comparative Analysis: Evaluating transportation infrastructure projects. *Evaluation* 19(1): 40–55.

Voß, J.-P., Bauknecht, D. & Kemp, R. 2006. *Reflexive governance for sustainable development.* Cheltenham: Edward Elgar.

Wachs, M. 1989. When planners lie with numbers. *Journal of the American Planning Association* 55(4): 476–479.

Walker, G. 2010. Environmental justice, impact assessment and the politics of knowledge: The implications of assessing the social distribution of environmental outcomes. *Environmental Impact Assessment Review* 30(5): 312–318.

Weiss, C.H. 1986. The circuitry of enlightenment: Diffusion of social science research to policymakers. *Knowledge: Creation, Diffusion, Utilisation* 8(2): 274–281.

Weiss, C.H. 1999. The interface between evaluation and public policy. *Evaluation* 5(4): 468–486.

Part I

Socioeconomic evaluation of megaprojects

Critical readings

2 In search of an assessment of the future

The case of the US nuclear waste programme

Başak Saraç-Lesavre

Public policies on topics such as nuclear waste management are implemented through the deployment of a diverse range of evaluation tools, including economic ones. The investigation of those tools – their displacements, and their configurations – offers a novel account of national nuclear waste policies in the making. Furthermore, these tools serve as mediators in processes whereby the moral, technical and political aspects of public policies are negotiated and reconfigured. Nuclear waste indeed implies uncompressible – even incomprehensible – timescales of hazard. Its temporality is located at the margins of calculation, measurement and expertise.

The existing literature on the exceptional temporal schemes associated with nuclear waste seldom directly refers to economic mechanisms, which are thus generally taken for granted, as are instruments that support the accomplishment of the highly sophisticated, extremely long-term technical, political, scientific and legal instruments, procedures, and knowledge production processes. Social scientists have studied decision-making processes associated with the selection of techno-scientific options for the governance of nuclear waste (e.g. Callon et al., 2001; Barthe, 2006), and more broadly, of risks and uncertainties (e.g. Joly, 2001; Stirling, 2008), as they have examined procedures applied to the selection of disposal or storage sites (e.g. Simmons and Bickerstaff, 2006; Blowers and Sundqvist, 2010; Lehtonen, 2010; Bergmans et al., 2015), evaluated risk perception or 'acceptance' levels among citizens on such sites (e.g. Kasperson et al., 1988; Jenkins-Smith and Bassett, 1994; Jenkins-Smith et al., 2011), or shown how techno-scientific knowledge is stretched in an attempt to control and master far futures (e.g. Metlay, 2000; Oreskes, 2000; MacFarlane, 2003; Bloomfield and Vurdubakis, 2005; Shrader-Frechette, 2005).

This chapter takes a different approach, by exploring instead the efforts of governmental institutions to answer a simple, modest and low-profile question: does the project fit within the budget? Or, in other words: are sufficient funds collected in order to finance a specific nuclear waste programme? Answers to these questions call for the evaluation of the performance of megaprojects in relation to their day-to-day execution. Evaluations seeking to answer these questions are concerned with assessing whether the megaproject meets the 'iron triangle' criteria of project success. As the introduction to this volume notes, megaprojects frequently do exceed their budgets and timetables. The common way to approach this is to strengthen efforts to enhance control, transparency and accountability in such projects. This has led to the multiplication of publicly available yet often rather technical evaluation reports that assess the viability of megaprojects. One way to approach those evaluation reports is to categorise them as rationalistic approaches to the governance of megaprojects by concentrating on the motives driving their production. What I propose in this chapter instead is to approach these evaluation reports as an extremely rich resource for empirical investigation.

It is true that evaluations produced to assess the performance of megaprojects do not directly influence the safety and security of future generations, nor do they apparently call the legitimacy or the destiny of those programmes into question. Nevertheless, they do count in megaproject governance. In this chapter, I propose approaching such evaluations by uncovering the complex moral and political rationalities that are embedded in them. Empirically following the deployment of a specific accounting convention in the budgetary evaluations that have been produced throughout the existence of the North American nuclear waste programme allows a description of the evolution of the political and moral role adopted by the federal government vis-à-vis its responsibility towards future generations. In doing so, the analysis will demonstrate how that role has constantly been re-interpreted, re-invented, re-valued and re-appropriated over the years. It also demonstrates the dynamics of responsibility embedded in such evaluations and underlines how these exercises reveal constantly evolving values around which the 'State' is reassembled.

The case

In the United States, the overarching principle of nuclear waste policy is formulated as follows: "The waste generated by nuclear power must be managed so as to protect current and future generations" (Jacob, 1990). The nuclear waste policy has been founded on two principles: that present and future generations could and should be protected from the undesirable consequences of the geological disposal of nuclear waste, and that, in line with the 'polluter pays' principle, the generations who benefit from nuclear energy could and should also be responsible for its waste.[1] The distribution of financial responsibility was conceived around a fee system that ought to feed a Nuclear Waste Fund and that makes the federal government accountable towards those who are responsible for financing the nuclear waste programme. The designed system sought to reassemble "economic efficiency, fairness and effective program management" (CBO, 1982: 31), which required the use of accounting conventions to determine the sharing of burden.

One specific accounting convention that is used to evaluate megaprojects constitutes the centre of interest of this chapter. It is the time value of money, or, in other words, the establishment of a discount rate. Establishing a discount rate means, in a nutshell, considering the future through the gaze of an investor (Miller, 1991; Doganova, 2014; Ortiz, 2014). Time value of money is an integral part of cost benefit analysis, an evaluation method that is used both to determine whether the federal government and its agencies should invest in a project or not, and to assess whether a project evolves on budget. It renders costs and benefits (or costs and revenues) with different temporalities commensurable, once they are translated into monetary values. It is both an extremely contested and yet an almost universally used tool in both policymaking and policy implementation. Depending on its level, discount rates can acquire the power to decide the fate of a public regulation or a governmental project.

The empirical material for this chapter was collected through interviews with relevant actors carried out between 2011 and 2014, archival research and, more specifically, the analysis of the annual fee adequacy evaluations that the Department of Energy has conducted throughout the thirty-year lifetime of the US nuclear waste programme. Each of the annual fee adequacy reviews involved the use of discount rates. The fee began to be collected in 1983 – in other words, well before the Yucca Mountain repository site was first selected for study by Congress in 1987 and then five years later designated, by public law, as the official US deep geological repository site for the disposal of high-level waste and spent nuclear fuel. The calculated nuclear waste fee was supposed to finance the nuclear waste programme, and thereby place the financial responsibility upon those who benefit from nuclear energy. The ratepayers using nuclear electricity are, under the law, financially responsible for the full recovery of the cost of the nuclear waste programme, and the fee shows as a line item on their monthly bills. Due to the high level of uncertainty related to the total cost of the programme, the nuclear waste fee was temporarily fixed at USD 1 million/kWh. The fee mechanism directly related the cost of the repository to the fee collected for the programme and created a calculative space where its adequacy needed to be assessed in relation to many different parameters, such as the projections of growth of nuclear energy production, and estimations of the lifetime of reactors and of their technical efficiency in terms of their burn-up time for nuclear fuel. These were necessary to continuously estimate and re-estimate the life-cycle cost of the nuclear waste programme and calculate how much funding would be necessary to finance it.

In charge of the nuclear waste programme, the Department of Energy was supposed to propose that the fee should be revised if deemed necessary in the annual reviews. These reviews had two purposes: first, to evaluate whether the collected fee was sufficient to cover the estimated total cost of the nuclear waste programme and, if needed, to submit to Congress a proposal for modification of the fee, and second, to justify the continuous collection of the nuclear waste fee from nuclear utilities. In the annual reviews, an assessment report was first issued estimating the total life-cycle cost of the geological repository programme, and then another report evaluating the adequacy of the fee was also issued.

This chapter scrutinises the relationship between calculative practices and political rationalities. It examines which political and moral values are embedded in the calculative practices used to distribute the financial responsibility of the programme among different generations, and analyses how the choice of discount rates embodies specific definitions of the role of the State and of the future states of society. The chapter starts by exploring the initial evaluations of the adequacy of the fee. It enquires about the political and moral role that had been adopted by the Department of Energy vis-à-vis common discount rates recommended by the Office of Management and Budget, the federal agency responsible for setting those rates for all federal agencies. Following the evaluations, the chapter investigates the transformation that the role of the State has undergone, and shows how that role shifted over time from that of a State with an explicit moral and political positioning to one that delegated time-related uncertainty to a multiplicity of rates attributed to the field of technical expertise.

Intergenerational dilemmas of discounting

Choices of discount rates imply different political and moral approaches to intergenerational equity, and generate intense controversies about the moral and political role to be adopted by the State. Several scholars criticize the use of those rates by national governments, and more generally the use of cost benefit analysis in regulatory analysis (e.g. Heinzerling, 1999; 2001; Ackerman, 2008). When the time value of money is used to evaluate projects that are expected to provide long-term uncertain benefits that are difficult to value in monetary terms, this is claimed to unfairly disadvantage long-term projects in comparison to short-term projects with calculable monetary benefits. The predominance of the time value of money calculation is also criticized for encouraging the monetisation of different types of values, considered as mutually incommensurable. Therefore, the method is criticised for its tendency to privilege projects with short-term monetary benefits and to focus on the interests of present generations at the expense of the wellbeing of future generations. For those who oppose long-term discounting, the use of discounting prevents undertaking action in the present for the well-being of future generations (e.g. Goodin, 1978; Heinzerling, 1999; 2001; Ackerman and Heinzerling, 2002).

However, this is not the only suggested ethical perspective. For a long time many scholars in the tradition of neoclassical economics have argued that it is the non-use of discounting that is unethical (e.g. Donohue, 1999; Belzer, 2000). For them, engaging in capital-intensive long-term investments with uncertain future benefits would risk compromising the wellbeing of both present and future generations. This perspective is built on the assumption that future generations would be economically better off, and would possess better technologies, than the present generation. Therefore, undertaking action in the present without the presence of full information about future benefits would result in undesirable irreversible consequences, and would prevent future generations from pursuing better solutions in the future, while at the same time depriving present generations of the possibility to use the currently available resources more efficiently. From this viewpoint, in the absence of discounting, present capital would be displaced at the expense of projects with uncertain future benefits. Following such reasoning, it is precisely the application of a high level of discount that is ethical.

The dilemma is very well illustrated in a historical example that is used by both sides of the debate, namely the controversy over the low discount rates that the US Department of the Interior's Bureau of Reclamation used in its cost–benefit analyses of dam projects in the 1950s and 1960s. To get the projects funded, the Bureau used low discount rates to compensate for the high capital intensity of dam building, rather than using the high discount rates recommended by the federal agency in charge. To illustrate his position, Kip Viscusi, an economist who is an active advocate of the use of high discount rates for governmental projects, took the example of a dam that was built just north of the Grand Canyon, and which caused environmental problems such as flooding of scenic areas, fish kills and salinisation problems. He argued that if the high discount rates recommended by the authority in charge had been used, the dam would never have been built (Viscusi, 2007). He suggested that the use of a high discount rate would have actually implied the adoption of a "pro-environmental approach" (*ibid.*: 215).

In contrast with Kip Viscusi, Lisa Heinzerling, a legal philosopher and one of the fiercest critics of the use of long-term discounting and cost–benefit analysis, argues that discounting has often been used as a means to justify political decisions (Heinzerling, 1999). According to her, the US Corps of Engineers decided to build new dams because it considered these would benefit the future welfare of society, and a low discount rate was used to financially justify that political decision. For Viscusi, setting a high discount rate was the best measure to overcome the irrationality of government and its agencies. For Heinzerling, by contrast, dams were evaluated as beneficial for society, and even though that decision was deficient due to its undesirable environmental consequences, this was not because of the failure to use a high discount rate, nor because of the shortcomings of monetary valuation; rather, it was the outcome of a bad political choice.

This example helps in noting the extent to which the controversy about discounting is also about whether one should delegate the fate of a specific project to an evaluation method that relies on an accounting convention that is standardised for all federal programmes and projects. When it comes to nuclear waste policy, the issue becomes even more complex than the above example suggests. Indeed, nuclear waste policy has been formulated in such a way as to ensure that those who benefit from nuclear energy also carry the financial responsibility for the nuclear waste programme. Seen in this way, generations benefitting from nuclear energy had the obligation to sacrifice a portion of their wellbeing so that future generations would not be burdened by the current use of nuclear energy. Therefore, one could be led to conclude that the reasoning of long-term discounting has been evacuated from the process that led to the definition of the US nuclear waste policy. Yet by examining the history of the US nuclear waste programme in action, this chapter shows how long-term discounting reappears during the implementation of the nuclear waste programme as soon as the federal government starts translating this policy principle into action.

The Office of Management and Budget rates and the political and moral positions of the Department of Energy in the early fee adequacy evaluations

The temporality of the nuclear waste megaproject was not an ordinary one. There was a temporal gap between the collection of the fees and the moment when the costs were incurred. When the nuclear waste programme was launched in 1982, it was expected that making the link between the present revenues and the future costs would be quite unproblematic. The programme was expected to last only until 2033, while the fees that would cover the life-cycle cost were to be collected by 2014. Due to an expected significant increase of nuclear energy generation, the two planned repositories were expected to be full and closed down by 2033. The fee system was designed for a nuclear waste programme lasting fifty years, whilst the fees were supposed to be collected during the first thirty years and the major expenses to be incurred during the same period. Based on those assumptions, using the iterative annual review system, the accuracy, efficiency and fairness of the distribution of financial responsibility could be constantly reassured.

As soon as the nuclear waste policy was enacted into law and the contracts were signed between the federal government and private nuclear utilities for them to charge the fee to their ratepayers, a clear political and moral position was adopted concerning the choice of discount rates to be applied in the fee adequacy evaluations. This position was expressed on the very first pages of the fee adequacy evaluation of 1983:

> Of specific interest to the reader is the specific discount rate used in discounting cash flows of costs and revenues. A real discount rate of 2 percent was used after examination of several alternatives. The Office of Management and Budget prescribed in its Circular A-94 (March 27, 1972) a discount rate of 10 percent to evaluate the measurable costs and benefits of Federal programs and projects extending three or more years beyond their inception dates. That rate was intended to reflect the average rate of return on private investment before taxes and after inflation. That discount rate was not used in this report because: a) the disposal of spent fuel and processed waste is a Federal responsibility for which private investment evaluation criteria do not apply; b) today's market and investment conditions are different from those extant 10 years ago; and c) the discount rate noted in the Circular pertains to the evaluation of newly proposed programs, not to those already authorized by the Congress.
>
> In previous reports on nuclear waste fee calculation the DOE used either 6.5 percent or 7.5 percent as the applicable discount rate. These rates, which reflected average interest rates for marketable U.S. Treasury bills, notes and bonds, were used in pricing the Department's uranium enrichment services. Adjusting for inflation, the rates used in pricing such services correspond to the real interest rate of 2 percent employed in this analysis. Currently, the interest rate for U.S. Treasury bills exceeds the inflation rate by about

4 percent, but the long-term record reveals that the real rate of interest has been 2 to 3 percent. That differential is assumed to continue.

(US Department of Energy, 1983: 7)

But what was Circular A-94 about, and what did the Office of Management and Budget (OMB) rates imply? As a part of the executive branch of the US federal government, the OMB prepares and evaluates the President's annual budget and recommends discount rates for federal regulations and public investments in an annually revised circular.[2] Since the release of its first Circular A-94 in 1972,[3] the OMB has been promoting increased use of cost–benefit reasoning in the evaluation of all government projects and programmes. In Circular A-94 the recommended rate was 10 per cent. The use of this specific rate implied assessing government projects and programmes on the estimation of the average rate of return on private investment before taxes and after inflation, which privileged government investments in short-term projects.

Through its recommended rates, the OMB advised federal agencies to adopt the role of a private investor. In contrast with the position of the OMB, the DOE's fee adequacy evaluations stated that for the nuclear waste programme the role of the State could not be that of a private investor. The report explicitly underlined that the 10 per cent discount rate recommended by the Office was not a rate for government projects and programmes, but for private investments. The statement against the use of OMB-defined rates explicitly suggested that the disposal of spent nuclear fuel fell under the responsibility of the federal government. In order to translate this reasoning into a choice of a discount rate, the DOE officials adopted the rates of US Treasury bills, bonds and notes[4] and defined the role of the federal government as that of a public investor – one that assumes the role of a very long-term guarantor and carries the overall burden of nuclear waste. The report underlined that it had used the same rates as those used for calculating the unit cost of nuclear enrichment services that the federal government provides to nuclear utilities. The US Nuclear Enrichment Company operated as a government corporation. Rather than accepting the discount rate as a purely technical measurement tool to be inserted in the calculation, the evaluation report included an explicit political statement about the role that the federal government should pursue in nuclear waste policy – one that refused to use the OMB-recommended high discount rates, which would equate the role of the federal government to that of a private investor.

As the nuclear waste programme was launched, actors in the field thought through the political and moral ramifications of the different possible uses of an accounting convention. The choice of any specific rate was considered to be the explicit expression of the moral and political role adopted by the State. However, as I will show below, at other times that choice was framed as being the product of pure technical expertise, closing it down to debate and thereby protecting the choice from further questioning.

The State as an optimistic and very long-term investor

Over time, the programme did not remain static. From 1995 on, the timescale of the programme started to expand.[5] Until 1998, discount rates used in the evaluations came from a single source. In 1998, for the first time evaluations integrated new parameters and applied "a series of interest and inflation rates, during the period of 1998 through 2042, for investment of income and reinvestment of maturing securities, as opposed to applying a single average rate as in previous analyses".[6] This increased the degree of sophistication in the choice of discount rates for fee adequacy evaluation.

By 2008 the foreseen operational period of the Yucca Mountain project had expanded to 2133, which required the translation of the fee originally generated only until 2047 (the expected end of the lifetime of the currently operating reactors) to 2133 – and in the 2013 evaluation the duration of the programme extended still further to 2157.[7] The expected programme lifetime had extended from a relatively manageable fifty years, with the fees collected and expenditures made in the first thirty years in 1983, to a long-term programme with its costs predicted in 2013 to stretch over a period of 180 years. The estimated total cost of the nuclear waste programme has increased from USD 36.6 billion in 1998 (in fiscal year 1998 dollars) to USD 96 billion in 2008 (in fiscal year 2008 dollars) (US Department of Energy, 2008). Due to the extended expected lifetime of the programme, there was a moment when the federal government had to rely on the estimations of future costs and future revenues to assess whether the ratepayers would be putting aside enough money so the future generations could complete that policy action and pay for the totality of the expenditures of the programme. Therefore the future of the nuclear waste management programme and all the safety measures to protect future generations for up to one million years from the day of the closure of the repository relied on the capacity of the DOE to accurately estimate the future financial value to be generated by the fees collected in the present. Discounting was to provide a temporal bridge between the present and the distant future, and its rate – whether variable or stable over time – prompted reflection on the role that the federal government should adopt with regard to future generations.

Until 2008 the estimated inflation and interest rates were derived from information provided by one economic forecasting company, DRI/McGraw Inc. The values provided by DRI/McGraw for one- and ten-year Treasury notes, twenty-five-year interest rates and different inflation rates were used. Over time, as the temporality of the programme extended, the evaluation reports became increasingly voluminous. Almost all the extra pages were dedicated to the description of economic scenarios. In 2008 economic parameters used in the reviews were further refined and became increasingly sophisticated. Just before that the DOE submitted to the Nuclear Regulatory Commission (NRC) its licencing application for the Yucca Mountain project in June 2008, wih the evaluations integrating different sources for the first time to estimate the time value of costs and revenues. Highlighting long-term economic uncertainty explicitly, evaluations no longer assumed the capacity of the DOE to continually adjust the fee until the end of the programme, but acknowledged the new temporal relationship generated by the increased temporal discrepancy, and took account of the "uncertainty inherent in projecting long range economic conditions" (US Department of Energy, 2008) using numerous sources. Furthermore, the DOE began to use scenario methodologies to test the future costs (*ibid.*) and revenues under twenty-eight economic scenarios. By 2013 the number of scenarios had increased to forty (US Department of Energy, 2013).

Each scenario began with the year's Nuclear Waste Fund balance, added income expected during that year, and subtracted the spending expected during that year to finally reach a year-end balance. This simulation process was repeated for each year until the end of the programme's lifetime to reach a final balance. In 2008 the future values of collected fees were assessed against future costs, one by one, and tested for twenty-eight economic scenarios, in some of which the fee fell short of covering the future cost of the repository programme. The first set of scenarios came from an econometric forecasting firm and used three economic growth scenarios: low, medium and high. The description of all three scenarios explicitly excluded the possibility of an 'economic crisis'. These scenarios reflected – and in so doing also enacted – an optimistic view of the future of the US economy. Other scenarios were drawn from the historical rates reported in stocks, bills, bonds and inflation (including the two oil crises of the 1970s), the Annual Energy Outlook of the US Energy Information Administration, and the market yield rates, as well as the OMB's inflation and short-term interest rate data that are present in the annual Presidential Budget. All those datasets were used to define a range of rates, which were then applied to the revenues generated from the nuclear waste fee. The 2008 fee adequacy report (US Department of Energy, 2008) demonstrated that the fee "to a great extent" covered the anticipated future costs under different rates. The use of scenarios and how they allowed the DOE to consider different futures were presented in the following way:

> The scenario methodology is intended to examine potential outcomes under a broad range of possible circumstances. Changing economic conditions have the greatest effect on financial outcomes and the Global Insight scenarios cover 90 percent of the paths the economy is likely to take, barring an economic crisis. The historical scenario (Ibbotson) reflects data from the oil shocks of the 1970s.
>
> (US Department of Energy, 2008: 13)

In the reports, the order of priority among different scenarios was not rendered explicitly. The hierarchy was established on the rule of majority. The exclusion of historical scenarios was justified by the fact that historical rates were often crucially shaped by rare and unpredictable events, such as the "oil shocks of the 1970s" (US Department of Energy, 2008: 10). An economic crisis was considered to constitute an extreme case. The scenarios under which the fund showed a positive balance were used to demonstrate the overall adequacy of the fee (Table 2.1). Pessimistic scenarios about the future states of the economy were systematically marginalised.

Table 2.1 Results of the economic scenarios. Source: DOE 2008 Adequacy of the Fee Report (DOE, 2008)

Scenario	Average inflation	Number of cases with	
		Positive balance	Negative balance
Global Insight Optimistic	1.47%	100%	0%
Global Insight Trend	1.96%	100%	0%
DOE Energy Information Administration	2.38%	100%	0%
Office of Management and Budget	2.30%	100%	0%
Market Rates	2.47%	50%	50%
Global Insight Pessimistic	4%	25%	75%
Ibbotson Historical	4.63%	0%	100%

By deciding to undertake action in the present, Congress deliberately discarded the idea of basing nuclear waste policy on assumptions about technological progress or future economic growth. However, fee adequacy evaluations reinterpreted the conditions under which present generations remained responsible for the protection of future ones: a future economy without economic crisis that operates under continuous positive economic growth. Evaluations embodied an optimistic vision of the future of the economy. Moreover, while the evaluations stressed the increased time-related uncertainty, they reduced the responsibility of present generations towards future ones to the mere capacity of 'technical' figures to accurately measure uncertainty. The political and moral roles to be adopted by the federal government in the face of increased uncertainty were no longer explicitly stated. When the programme was launched, the precise ways in which the accounting conventions would be applied were considered to follow from political and moral choices. Over time these choices were to an increasing extent perceived as mere issues of technical expertise. Their political and moral ramifications were no longer rendered visible. Federal institutions in charge of distributing the responsibility of the nuclear waste programme neither explicitly restated the role that the 'State' should adopt vis-à-vis future generations, nor redefined what constitutes a fair, accurate and efficient distribution.

The evolution of Office of Management and Budget rates

The longer the nuclear waste programme followed its course, the more the DOE's moral and political position about time-related uncertainty became invisible. In 1983, when discount rates were selected, there was an explicit political and moral claim about the role and the responsibility of present generations. The 1983 fee adequacy evaluation had voiced an explicit political choice about the role of the State as a public investor, which gave primacy to the federal nuclear waste services to be provided. At the beginning of the programme uncertainties about its future were assumed to decrease over time, including uncertainty about the future costs.

The evaluations entailed an incremental and optimistic approach to time – things were supposed to get easier as time went on. From 1998 onwards, even though the role of public investor was maintained as the starting point, the sources used to estimate the rates were diversified in an effort to account more accurately for time-related uncertainty. The more the temporal discrepancy between the revenues and costs increased due to the project's delay and its constant transformation, the greater was the diversity of the sources used to estimate the discount rates, which would in turn serve to estimate whether the revenues would be sufficient to cover the future costs. The treatment of uncertainty was increasingly reduced to numbers and to sophisticated economic scenarios.

In parallel with the evolution of the nuclear waste programme, in a context of intense debates on the best ways to account for intergenerational welfare (e.g. Bazelon and Smetters, 2001; Newell and Pizer, 2003; Spackman, 2004; Zeckhauser, 2006; Zeckhauser and Viscusi, 2008; Marks, 2011), the OMB's position on discounting has evolved. Even though the Office continued recommending high private investment rates for short-term government projects and programmes, with its 2003 Circular the OMB for the first time recommended that the federal agencies apply sensitivity analysis concerning their long-term programmes and projects in order to incorporate potential implications of intergenerational equity, and using a lower but positive discount rate (Graham, 2007). The integration of the possibility to use such rates in the OMB Circular was a significant change from the OMB's initial position. The new rates embodied a new perception concerning the role of the federal government, moving away from the optimistic expectations of a future economy as constituted by and for short-term investors, while introducing the possibility of the coexistence of a welfare state that accounts for intergenerational equity, while at the same time seeking short-term returns on investment.

Accepting the use of significantly lower discount rates in the analysis, the OMB did not rely on just any old reference to 'intergenerational discounting', but explicitly referred to the work of a respected economist, Martin Weitzman. Weitzman's work has been at the core of an intense debate on the calculation of a discount rate over long timescales. A welfare economist at Harvard University, he was one of the first economists to suggest using a declining discount rate for long timescales. Weitzman was one of several economists who were particularly interested in long-term uncertainty and who adopted a normative stance to adapt the standard theory of discounting to long-term uncertain decisions, with special concern for measures to combat climate change. Weitzman argued that the standard theory of discounting had been designed for short-term investments under certainty, and once applied to long-term uncertain issues like climate change mitigation or nuclear waste management, the use of high discount rates would make any action today seem economically unviable.

Weitzman's suggestion for a way out of this dilemma arrived during a period of vivid debate between the advocates and opponents of discounting. He contested the existing state-of-the-art knowledge on long-term discounting (e.g. Weitzman, 1998; 2001; 2009). Weitzman underlined that a discount rate was not the result of a single technical calculation. According to him, economists also had to think about the type of issue that was at stake.[8] He had a particular perspective on the measurement of risk and uncertainty, notably an approach to long-term uncertainty that took into consideration the possibility of a catastrophic event. Scholars that had adopted a similar approach included Jean-Pierre Dupuy, a philosopher, and Richard Posner, a legal philosopher, both of whom were against basing long-term investment decisions on the standard theory of discounting that adopts Keynes' and Knight's definition of risk and uncertainty, which assume the possibility of exact calculation of probabilities (Posner, 2004; Dupuy, 2004; 2012). However, rather than refuting the use of long-term discounting in line with Dupuy or Posner, Weitzman was determined to integrate deep structural uncertainty and the potential for catastrophes within the standard theory of discounting. This would be achieved by calculating long-term uncertainty through an alternative method, which would nevertheless still rely on probability.

Weitzman suggested that existing definitions of risk and uncertainty fell short of grasping the particular type of probability distribution of uncertainty, and only took into account risks whose probability exceeded a given threshold, which the commonly used probability distribution was unable to calculate. According to him, the major source of the problem was a taken-for-granted assumption, inherent in the existing theory of discounting that is designed for a 'thin-tailed distribution' of probabilities, which is only applicable to short-term decisions under certainty. He suggested that the uncertainty of long-term discounting led all economists who were interested in long-term uncertainty to calculate the 'probability of probabilities', which would, in turn, further accentuate uncertainty, giving a 'fat-tailed' distribution of probability (e.g. Weitzman, 1998; 2001). In order to resolve this problem, Weitzman suggested that "for situations where there do not exist prior limits on damages, CBA [cost benefit analysis] is likely to be dominated by considerations and concepts related more to catastrophe insurance than to the consumption smoothing consequences of long term discounting even at empirically plausible interest rate" (Weitzman, 2009: 2). Weitzman not only argued that long-term discounting was not adapted to issues that had the potential to cause catastrophic consequences, but he also provided a technical demonstration of the consequences from applying the specific assumptions about probability, which underpinned the calculation of short-term discount rates, and that would therefore be inappropriate for the evaluation of projects and policies involving long-term uncertainty.

At first, his findings and methodology generated major controversy. Among others, Christian Gollier, an economist specialised in decision theory from Toulouse School of Economics, challenged his conclusions (e.g. Gollier, 2004). Gollier used a model symmetrical to the one applied by Weitzman, but reached an entirely opposite conclusion: the discount rate had to increase over time. Gollier took Weitzman's criteria and used similar reasoning to calculate the discount rate. However, unlike Weitzman, he considered that the burden of risk should be placed on future, instead of present, generations. Following Weitzman's work, and looking at Gollier's conclusions, other economists joined the debate. For instance; Hepburn and Groom concluded that the definition of the 'future' (time t) or the 'present' (time 0) did not have to be the only potential temporal scales for evaluation – others could be envisaged (e.g. Hepburn and Groom, 2007). Gollier added that the difference between his conclusions and those of Weitzman could result from the difference in the way they accounted for the term that reflects the structure of risk. Later Gollier and Weitzman worked together, and resolved what they called the "Weitzman–Gollier Puzzle", concluding that for long-term decisions under uncertainty, declining discount rates should be used (Gollier and Weitzman, 2010). A declining discount rate slices time into temporal sequences and distributes risk over time, starting with high discount rates which would then decline towards zero. Weitzman and Gollier concluded that very low and very high discount rates could coexist. With Weitzman and Gollier's theory of long-term discounting, the ethically challenged standard theory of discounting not only retained its place but also repositioned its authority on long-term policy decisions. Declining discounts were not only integrated into the OMB's sensitivity analysis, but also became part of the debates on discounting among different national administrations and international organisations.[9]

Integrating this new approach to discounting, the OMB had introduced a new option to the valuation of time-related uncertainty. Following the recommendations of the new OMB Circular, the Department of Energy could include a sensitivity analysis in its evaluation and test the adequacy of the fee for rates that approached zero. However, the fee adequacy evaluations further reinforced the federal government's role as a public investor, and further delegated that role to a diversity of rates provided by different sources. In the evaluations, moral and political responsibility adopted by the federal government towards future generations has never been explicitly re-stated since 1983.

Rates used in the fee adequacy evaluations embedded expectations about the future states of the economy and outlined a framework for what constituted the responsibility of present generations towards future ones. Those rates defined a federal government that continued to operate as a public investor, inside a prosperous future economy that operated under the conditions of a certain level of economic growth. For most of the former scientists and engineers of the Yucca Mountain project that I interviewed, the fee adequacy evaluations, and more particularly discounting, was a convention that had no major moral, ethical or political consequences for the nuclear waste programme; rates were considered as neutral translators. For most of them, the safety and security of future generations relied on techno-scientific measures, whereas the financing of the programme was only an intermediary process needed to execute those measures. One of the retired Yucca Mountain programme managers described the use of rates as follows: "They are not [a safety or security measure]. It is just a number to say whether the waste fund is collecting enough funds or not. Are we collecting enough fee or not?"[10] However, the choice of the discount rate not only defined the conditions under which the federal government could ensure the accuracy, fairness and efficiency of the distribution of responsibility, but also established the responsibilities of present generations by making certain assumptions about the future of existing institutions and about the future of the economy.

Conclusions

This chapter has proposed an alternative reading on megaproject governance and evaluation, one that has not received much attention either in the extant literature or in policy implementation. We saw that by paying attention to the financial evaluations that are conducted throughout the implementation of a long-term public policy, one could observe the dynamic and evolving role that the State adopted throughout the process, and the expectations about the future states of society that thereby became material.

Rather than adopting a normative position on the use of economic evaluation tools, the chapter empirically explored the system of responsibility embedded in the local uses of a specific accounting convention. It demonstrated how actors in the field, instead of making choices between neatly defined moral and political worlds, operate in a dynamic world in which the political and moral implications of their choices are constantly reconfigured. Such reconfigurations could be observed through the exploration of evaluations that were designed to answer the apparently simple question of whether or not adequate fees are collected to finance the programme. In the early stages of the nuclear waste programme the definition of a State that acts as a long-term public investor was explicitly advocated. This State mastered long-term uncertainty and took an explicit political position against the conception of its role as a short-term 'private investor'. However, as the uncertainty associated with the programme increased, moral and political explications of the role of the State were delegated to the instances of technical expertise.

This chapter pointed out how the varying discount rates enabled the State to adopt various alternative self-definitions: it could act as a 'private investor' or 'a public investor', and its actions could enact future states of 'the society' or 'the economy' in multiple ways – as catastrophic, prosperous, stable or stagnant. Initially, political and moral roles embedded in the choice of accounting conventions were made explicit, which in turn made institutions accountable to large audiences and opened up their choices to questioning. However, over time those choices were increasingly delegated to the instances of technical expertise, protecting them against criticism and closing them down to public debate. Opening up the uses of economic conventions to policy and public debate would be an important step towards democratising the government of techno-sciences.

Furthermore, enquiring into the ways in which the notion of 'polluter pays' was translated into practice also showed how the institutions in question designed the margins of their financial responsibility for nuclear waste. This responsibility was associated with the costs of the nuclear waste programme – mainly with the economic costs expected to be incurred during its licencing period – and that responsibility was expected to last only until the closure of the repositories. Should any problem occur beyond the licencing period of the programme, its financial consequences would be transferred to the federal government, which would serve as the de facto ultimate financial guarantor. The distribution of responsibilities for the nuclear waste programme therefore relied on the assumption that the current institutions could successfully confine nuclear waste from the biosphere, while generating the expectation that the financial responsibility for a material that would remain radioactive for a million years could be contained inside a 'fee'.

Notes

1   For normative discussions on the use of discounting for the distribution of the financial responsibility for nuclear waste programmes, see, for instance Ahearne (2000), Kneese, Ben-David, Brookshire, Schulze, and Boldt (1983), Okrent (1999) or Belzer (2000).
2   Office of Management and Budget Circulars A-4 and A-94 (2003 version).
3   At the beginning, the rate determined by the OMB was applied to the cost–benefit analysis for regulations. The evaluation would be conducted in terms of monetary costs and benefits, comparing costs and benefits of commodities traded in markets. From the Reagan administration onwards the OMB started progressively expanding the logic of cost-benefit analysis and discounting further to the monetisation also of non-monetary benefits, including the value of human life or of health-related benefits, as briefly noted above. This extension of cost–benefit analysis to non-monetary benefit values generated a lot of controversy. Morrison (1998: 1333), a legal scholar, describes the evolution as follows: "Although previous administrations issued executive orders encouraging agencies to consider the economic impact of proposed regulations, President Reagan's executive order, EO 12291, 46 Fed Reg 13193, was the first to require cost–benefit analysis. Section 2 of EO 12291 required agencies to ensure that the social benefits of a proposed regulation exceed its social costs. In 1993, President Clinton issued the Executive Order 12866, 58 Fed Reg 51735 (1993), which generally affirms the approach of the Reagan order. Unlike Reagan's order, however, Executive Order 12866 § 1(b) merely endorses cost–benefit analysis as a tool for evaluating regulatory options and does not require that benefits outweigh costs. 58 Fed Reg at 51735-36."
4   These are named 'internal rates', as presented inside a specific section of the OMB's Circular A-94.
5   Field notes from discussions with former DOE officers working on the Yucca Mountain project, Nevada, April 2012.
6   *Ibid.*
7   The DOE was responsible only for the period during which the repository was 'licenced', so the temporality of the project and the responsibility of present and future generations were calculated in terms of the risks that fell within the operational lifetime of the nuclear waste programme.
8   Weitzman first conducted survey research on a large number of PhD economists and on a more restricted number of prominent economists. He categorised futures into four distinct temporalities and then asked them to suggest a suitable discount rate for each period, rather than asking the question "once for eternity". The answers of the economists showed significant uncertainty about long-term discounting: the mean value of the suggested discount rates was about 4 per cent, with a standard deviation of around 3 per cent. Weitzman concluded that discount rates for long timescales were uncertain. Drawing on this analysis, Weitzman created a model where he attributed the same probability to ten different possible future discount rates. The modelling resulted in a discount rate declining progressively over time, with a very low rate to be applied in projects involving very long timescales. Weitzman called this 'gamma discounting': a declining discount rate with the lowest rates applied to the longest-term undertakings. To calculate the discount rate, Weitzman used an 'expected net present value' approach and placed the burden of risk on present generations (Weitzman, 2001). His proposition of hyperbolic (also called declining or gamma) discounting came to constitute an important early step towards a potential reconciliation between the advocates of high and low discount rates.

9 Hyperbolic discounting suggested by Weitzman and later supported by Gollier produced a certain compromise both among economists and among governmental organisations. In 2006, in its analysis of cost–benefit analysis, the OECD started promoting hyperbolic discounting as a way out of the controversy between the advocates of high and low discount rates (Pearce, Atkinson and Mourato, 2006). National commissions, such as those behind the UK Green Book (Her Majesty's Treasury, 2003) and the Rapport Lebègue in France (Commisariat Général du Plan, 2005), worked on the issue of long-term discounting for regulatory analysis. They praised hyperbolic discounting and recommended it to their governments. In the United States the OMB, until recently recommending the use of high discount rates, introduced hyperbolic discounting in its regulatory analysis, even though hyperbolic discounting was recommended for use in sensitivity analysis. In September 2011 the US Environmental Protection Agency (EPA) set up a panel of experts to provide advice on long-term discounting, in particular to respond to the following question: "How should benefits and costs be discounted in an intergenerational context?" Thirteen economists specialised in discounting were appointed to the panel: Arrow, Cropper, Gollier, Groom, Heal, Newell, Nordhaus, Pindyck, Pizer, Portney, Sterner, Tol and Weitzman. The panel recommended the EPA to use hyperbolic discounting for environmental regulations (Arrow et al., 2013).

10 Interview with a retired Yucca Mountain project manager, Las Vegas, Nevada, 25 April 2012.

References

Ackerman, F. 2008. Can we afford the future. *Economics for a Warming World*, London: Zed Books.

Ackerman, F. & Heinzerling, L. 2002. Pricing the priceless: Cost-benefit analysis of environmental protection. *University of Pennsylvania Law Review*, 1553–1584.

Ahearne, J.F. 2000. Intergenerational issues regarding nuclear power, nuclear waste, and nuclear weapons. *Risk Analysis*, 20(6), 763–770.

Arrow, K.J., Cropper, M., Gollier, C., Groom, B., Heal, G.M., Newell, R.G., … Weitzman, M.L. 2013. *How should benefits and costs be discounted in an intergenerational context? The views of an expert panel*. Washington, DC: Resources for the Future. Available online at: www.rff.org/files/sharepoint/WorkImages/Download/RFF-DP-12-53.pdf (accessed 20 July 2016).

Barthe, Y. 2006. *Le pouvoir d'indécision: La mise en politique des déchets nucléaires*. Paris, France: Economica.

Bazelon, C. & Smetters, K. 2001. Discounting in the long term. *Loyola of Los Angeles Law Review*, 35, 277.

Belzer, R.B. 2000. Discounting across generations: Necessary, not suspect. *Risk Analysis*, 20(6), 779–792.

Bergmans, A., Sundqvist, G., Kos, D. & Simmons, P. 2015. The participatory turn in radioactive waste management: Deliberation and the social-technical divide. *Journal of Risk Research*, 18(3), 347–363.

Bloomfield, B.P. & Vurdubakis, T. 2005. The secret of Yucca Mountain: Reflections on an object in extremis. *Environment and Planning D: Society and Space*, 23(5), 735–756.

Blowers, A. & Sundqvist, G. 2010. Radioactive waste management – technocratic dominance in an age of participation. *Journal of Integrative Environmental Sciences*, 7(3), 149–155.

Callon, M., Lascoumes, P. & Barthe, Y. 2001. *Agir dans un monde incertain: Essai sur la démocratie technique*. Paris, France: Editions du Seuil.

Commissariat Général du Plan. 2005. Révision du taux d'actualisation des investissements publics. Available online at: http://temis.documentation.developpement-durable.gouv.fr/documents/Temis/0050/Temis-0050505/15417_rapport.pdf (accessed 20 July 2016).

Congressional Budget Office. 1982. *Financing radioactive waste disposal* (Y 10.2:F 49/2). Washington, DC: US Government Printing Office.

Doganova, L. 2014. Décompter le futur. *Sociétés Contemporaines*, (1), 67–87.

Donohue, J.J. 1999. Why We should discount the views of those who discount discounting. *The Yale Law Journal* 108 (7): 1901–1910.

Dupuy, J.-P. 2004. *Pour un catastrophisme éclairé: Quand l'impossible est certain*. Paris, France: Éditions du Seuil.

Dupuy, J.-P. 2012. *L'avenir de l'économie*. Paris, France: Flammarion.

Gollier, C. 2004. Maximizing the expected net future value as an alternative strategy to gamma discounting. *Finance Research Letters*, 1(2), 85–89.

Gollier, C. 2008. Discounting with fat-tailed economic growth. *Journal of Risk and Uncertainty*, 37(2–3), 171–186.

Gollier, C. & Weitzman, M.L. 2010. How should the distant future be discounted when discount rates are uncertain? *Economics Letters*, 107(3), 350–353.

Goodin, R.E. 1978. Uncertainty as an excuse for cheating our children: The case of nuclear wastes. *Policy Sciences*, 10(1), 25–43.

Graham, J.D. 2007. Valuing the future: OMB's refined position. *University of Chicago Law Review*, 74 (Winter 2007), 51.

Heinzerling, L. 1999. Discounting our future. *Land and Water Law Review*, 34, 39.

Heinzerling, L. 2001. The temporal dimension in environmental law. *Environmental Law Reporter*, 31(9), 11055–11072.

Hepburn, C. & Groom, B. 2007. Gamma discounting and expected net future value. *Journal of Environmental Economics and Management*, 53(1), 99–109.

Her Majesty's Treasury. 2003. *The Green Book: Appraisal and evaluation in central government: Treasury guidance*. London, England: Her Majesty's Stationery Office.

Jacob, G. 1990. *Site unseen: The politics of siting a nuclear waste repository*. Pittsburgh, PA: University of Pittsburgh Press.

Jenkins-Smith, H.C. & Bassett, G.W. 1994. Perceived risk and uncertainty of nuclear waste: Differences among science, business, and environmental group members. *Risk Analysis*, 14(5), 851–856.

Jenkins-Smith, H.C., Silva, C.L., Nowlin, M.C. & DeLozier, G. 2011. Reversing nuclear opposition: Evolving public acceptance of a permanent nuclear waste disposal facility. *Risk Analysis*, 31(4), 629–644.

Joly, P.-B. 2001. Les OGM entre la science et le public? Quatre modèles pour la gouvernance de l'innovation et des risques. *Economie Rurale* 266(1): 11–29.

Kasperson, R.E., Renn, O., Slovic, P., Brown, H.S., Emel, J., Goble, R., ... & Ratick, S. 1988. The social amplification of risk: A conceptual framework. *Risk Analysis*, 8(2), 176–187.

Kneese, A.V., Ben-David, S., Brookshire, D.S., Schulze, W. D. & Boldt, D. 1983. Economic issues in the legacy problem. In R. E. Kasperson (ed.), *Equity issues in radioactive waste management*. Cambridge, MA: Oelgeschlager, Gunn & Hain.

Lehtonen, M. 2010. Deliberative decision-making on radioactive waste management in Finland, France and the UK: Influence of mixed forms of deliberation in the macro discursive context. *Journal of Integrative Environmental Sciences*, 7(3), 175–196.

MacFarlane, A. 2003. Underlying Yucca Mountain: The interplay of geology and policy in nuclear waste disposal. *Social Studies of Science*, 33(5), 783–807.

Marks, S.G. 2011. Valuing the future: Intergenerational discounting, its problems, and a modest proposal. *Boston Univ. School of Law Working Paper*, 11–12.

Metlay, D. 2000. From tin roof to torn wet blanket: Predicting and observing groundwater movement at a proposed nuclear waste site. In D. Sarewitz, R.A. Pielke & R. Byerly (eds.), *Prediction: Science, decision making, and the future of nature*. Washington, DC: Island Press, pp. 199–228.

Miller, P. 1991. Accounting innovation beyond the enterprise: Problematizing investment decisions and programming economic growth in the UK in the 1960s. *Accounting, Organizations and Society*, 16(8), 733–762.

Morrison, E.R. 1998. Judicial reviews of discount rates used in regulatory cost–benefit analysis. *The University of Chicago Law Review*, 65, 1333–1369.

Newell, R.G. & Pizer, W.A. 2003. Discounting the distant future: How much do uncertain rates increase valuations? *Journal of Environmental Economics and Management*, 46(1), 52–71.

Office of Management and Budget Circulars A-4 and A-94 (2003 version).

Okrent, D. 1999. On intergenerational equity and its clash with intragenerational equity and on the need for policies to guide the regulation of disposal of wastes and other activities posing very long-term risks. *Risk Analysis*, 19(5), 877–901.

Oreskes, N. 2000. Why predict? Historical perspectives on predictions in earth science. In D. Sarewitz, R.A. Pielke & R. Byerly (eds.), *Prediction: Science, decision making, and the future of nature*. Washington, DC: Island Press, pp. 199–228.

Ortiz, H. 2014. The limits of financial imagination: Free investors, efficient markets, and crisis. *American Anthropologist*, 116(1), 38–50.

Pearce, D., Atkinson, G. & Mourato, S. 2006. *Cost–benefit analysis and the environment: Recent developments*. Paris, France: OECD.

Posner, R.A. 2004. *Catastrophe: Risk and response*. Oxford, England: Oxford University Press.

Shrader-Frechette, K. 2005. Mortgaging the future: Dumping ethics with nuclear waste. *Science and Engineering Ethics*, 11(4), 518–520.

Simmons, P. & Bickerstaff, K. 2006. *The participatory turn in UK radioactive waste management policy*. Presented at the Proceedings of VALDOR-2006. Stockholm: Congrex Sweden, AB. Available online at: www.iaea.org/inis/collection/NCLCollectionStore/_Public/37/101/37101589.pdf (pp. 529–536) (accessed 20 July 2016).

Spackman, M. 2004. Time discounting and the cost of capital in government. *Fiscal Studies*, 25(4), 467–518.

Stirling, A. 2008. "Opening up" and "closing down" power, participation, and pluralism in the social appraisal of technology. *Science, Technology and Human Values*, 33(2): 262–294.

US Department of Energy. 1983. *Report on Financing the Disposal of Commercial Spent Nuclear Fuel and Processed High level Radioactive Waste* (No. DOE/S—0020/1). Washington, DC: US Department of Energy.

US Department of Energy. 1998. *Nuclear Waste Fund Fee Adequacy: An Assessment*. (US DOE/RW-0509). Washington, DC: US Department of Energy.

US Department of Energy. 2008. *Fiscal Year 2007 Civilian Radioactive Waste Management Fee Adequacy Assessment Report* (No. DOE/RW-0593). Washington, DC: US Department of Energy.

US Department of Energy. 2013. *Secretarial Determination of the Adequacy of the Nuclear Waste Fund Fee*. Washington, DC: US Department of Energy.

Viscusi, W.K. 2007. Rational discounting for regulatory analysis. *The University of Chicago Law Review*, 74, 209.

Weitzman, M.L. 1998. Why the far-distant future should be discounted at its lowest possible rate. *Journal of Environmental Economics and Management*, 36(3), 201–208.

Weitzman, M.L. 2001. Gamma discounting. *The American Economic Review*, 9(1), 260–271.

Weitzman, M.L. 2009. On modeling and interpreting the economics of catastrophic climate change. *The Review of Economics and Statistics*, 91(1), 1–19.

Zeckhauser, R. 2006. Investing in the unknown and unknowable. *Capitalism and Society*, 1(2). Available online at: www.bepress.com/cas/vol1/iss2/art5 (accessed 20 July 2016).

Zeckhauser, R.J. & Viscusi, W.K. 2008. Discounting dilemmas: Editors' introduction. *Journal of Risk and Uncertainty*, 37, 95–106.

3   Megaprojects and mega risks: Lessons for decision-makers of large-scale transport projects

OMEGA Centre lessons derived from European, US and Asia-Pacific case studies[1]

Harry T. Dimitriou, E. John Ward and Philip G. Wright

Introduction

This chapter commences with a broad outline of the research methodology employed by the OMEGA Centre at University College London (UCL) for a five-year international research programme of decision-making in the planning, appraisal and delivery of mega transport projects (MTPs) funded by the Volvo Research and Education Foundations (VREF). It subsequently presents a set of general lessons derived from international case studies, and concludes by summarising the research programme's main observations and findings.

Conducted in association with nine other universities,[2] the Final Report of this international research effort (see Dimitriou et al., 2011) not only incorporates an extensive literature review of the different fields under study but also drew on an examination of the decision-making in thirty MTP case studies in ten developed economies (see Table 3.1). This involved interviews with some three hundred project stakeholders, with particular emphasis given to Narrative Analysis.[3] The Final Report included fifty detailed lessons, which were clustered into nine groups of more general lessons for presentation in an Executive Summary Report (OMEGA Centre, 2012) (see Table 3.2) discussed and outlined in the following text.

Table 3.1 OMEGA 2 project case studies. Source: OMEGA Centre (2012: 4)

Country	Mega Transport Project	Date Finished	Final Costs US$ (billions)[1]	Project Type
UK	Channel Tunnel Rail Link (CTRL)	2007	9.6	High-speed rail
	Jubilee Line Extension	1999	6.8	Metro rail (subway)
	M6 Toll Road	2003	1.7	Inter-urban toll motorway
France	Météor Rail: Saint Lazare – Olympiades, Paris	1998	1.8	Metro rail (subway)
	TGV Med: Valence – Marseille	2001	6.6	High-speed rail
	Millau Viaduct: Millau, southern France	2004	0.5[2]	Road bridge (on motorway)

Greece	Rion-Antirion Bridge: Rion – Antirion	2004	1.3	Road bridge
	Athens Metro: Sepolia – Dafni and Monastiraki – Ethniki Amyna, Athens	2003	4.6	Metro rail (subway)
	Attiki Odos, Athens	2004	5.4	Inter-urban toll motorway
Germany	Neubaustrecke: Cologne-Rhine/Main	2001	8.6	High-speed rail
	Tiergarten Tunnel: Berlin	2006	9.0	Urban motorway and rail tunnel
	BAB20 Motorway: Brandenburg, to Schleswig-Holstein	2005	2.7	Motorway
Netherlands	HSL Zuid: Amsterdam Zuid to Schiphol Airport, Rotterdam and Connections to Antwerp, Brussels and Paris	2009	9.8	High-speed rail
	Randstadrail: The Hague to Rotterdam and Zoetermeer	2007	1.6	Light rail and bus
	Beneluxlijn: Extension of Rotterdam Metro Network	2002	1.0	Metro rail (subway)
Sweden	Øresund Road, Rail, Bridge/Tunnel Link: Malmo – Copenhagen	2000	4.1	Road and rail, bridge and tunnel
	Södra Länken Road Tunnel: Stockholm	2004	1.3	Urban motorway tunnel
	Arlanda Rail Link: Stockholm Airport to Stockholm	1999	1.1	Airport express rail link
USA	Airtrain: JFK Airport: New York City	2003	2.2	Light rail airport link
	Alameda Rail Link: Los Angeles (port – downtown)	2002	2.8	Freight rail line
	Big Dig Road and Tunnel Links: Boston	2007	15.5	Urban road tunnel and bridges
Australia	City Link, Melbourne	2000	2.5	Urban toll motorway
	Metro Rail, Perth	2007	1.7	Inter-urban rail line
	Cross City Tunnel, Sydney	2005	1.1	Tolled urban road tunnel
Hong Kong	Western Harbour Crossing: Hong Kong Island – Kowloon	1997	0.9[3]	Tolled urban road tunnel
	Airport Rail Links: Hong Kong Central – Chek Lap Kok International Airport	1998	4.4	Airport express rail link
	KCRC West Rail Link: Tsuen Wan – Yeung Long	2003	5.9	Urban rail line
Japan	Metropolitan Expressway: Nishishinjuku Junction – Kumanocho Junction, Tokyo	2007	5.5	Tolled urban road tunnel
	Shinkansen High-Speed Rail Link: Kagoshima - Chuo – Nakata	2004	7.5	High-speed rail
	Oedo Metro: Hokomae – Hikarigaoka Tokyo	2000	11.4	Metro rail (subway)

1 Adjusted to 2010 prices.
2 While this project did not meet OMEGA's cost criteria, it was included in view of its iconic status and range of key impacts.
3 Again, while this project did *not* strictly meet the minimum cost criteria set, it was considered to be close enough to be included, on the grounds that it represented a critical piece of infrastructure for the territory.

Background to the research

The OMEGA Centre in the Bartlett School of Planning at UCL is a Global Centre of Excellence in the study of Mega Projects in Transport and Development,[4] funded from 2005 principally by VREF and other research and consultancy contracts. Having undertaken twelve such contracts at the time of writing, the investigations reported here (otherwise referred to as the OMEGA 2 project) examined the very rudimentary but important question of "what constitutes a 'successful' MTP?" These projects are defined as large-scale, typically complex, land-based transport infrastructure projects costing in excess of USD 1 billion (at 1999 prices) built within urban/metropolitan areas or linking such areas, often viewed as iconic symbols of modernisation (Dimitriou et al., 2011).

Much of the conceptual spadework for the OMEGA 2 project was carried out as part of the Centre's first research study (the OMEGA 1 project) also funded by VREF (Dimitriou et al., 2008) (see Figure 3.1). This sought to identify transferable lessons in major project decision-making from sectors and disciplines *outside* MTP studies where risk and uncertainty are seen much more to be at the centre of complex megaproject planning, appraisal and delivery. The OMEGA 2 project adopted as its working premise the assumption that infrastructure and spatial planners understand far less about the treatment of risk, uncertainty and complexity of megaproject decision-making in their planning and appraisal than do project managers in project delivery, and that this shortcoming has major implications for the 'effectiveness' of the outcomes of such projects, in whichever way this effectiveness may be defined. In support of the OMEGA 1 project, the

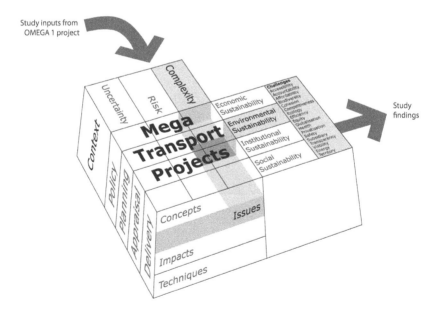

Figure 3.1 Relationship of OMEGA 2 project study themes.
Source: Dimitriou et al. (2011).

Centre commissioned papers prepared by a number of leading experts from different fields of megaproject development where risk and uncertainty in decision-making has long been at the heart of their planning, appraisal and management experiences. These included contributions (to mention but a few) from perspectives of the military (Stone, 2008), earthquake engineering (Rossetto, 2008), banking (Lemmon, 2008), insurance (Gibson, 2008), public health (Dora et al., 2008) and agriculture (Mumford, 2008).

The findings of the OMEGA 1 project proved very important for the OMEGA 2 research on several fronts. First and most importantly, the significance of the context of decision-making emerged as all important: the notion that 'context is everything' and that 'context is frequently more important than content' repeatedly emerged as critical in the interdisciplinary set of findings. The concept of trust similarly came out as very significant. In infrastructure planning, the focus on trust rarely goes beyond the tight boundaries of concerns regarding stakeholder project management, whereas many or most of the OMEGA 1 project contributions *also* alluded to wider policy and social corporate responsibility dimensions of trust.

Another difference identified between the findings of the OMEGA 1 research and the practices of traditional infrastructure planning concerned the importance placed by the former on the role of strategy in coping with risk and uncertainty in complex decision-making, especially when decision-making environments are complex, fluid and turbulent. This emphasis on strategy and irreducible uncertainty contrasts with the practice (as opposed to the rhetoric) of infrastructure planners and project managers, who tend to suggest (and believe) that their master plans and project management schemes *can* reduce uncertainty to more manageable levels than is possible in reality (Dimitriou and Thompson, 2007).

Findings of the OMEGA 2 project

Past and current notions of 'success' for most MTPs have been presented *largely* as being about delivering projects 'on time, on budget and to prescribed specifications', as reflected in the early work of Merrow (1988) and more recently the work of Flyvbjerg et al. (2003). Often collectively termed as 'iron triangle' considerations of project management (Weaver, 2007), these have preoccupied most major project promoters and investors keen to ensure that the economic, financial and physical outcomes of such projects comply closely with their plans and forecasts. Iron triangle criteria have also frequently been employed by the media, politicians and opposition groups to promote and/or criticise such projects – as in the case of the Big Dig Project in Boston, USA (Brecher and Nobbe, 2010) and the recent High Speed 2 Rail project in the UK (*FT*, 2013). Of late there has been such a crescendo of negative press in many parts of the world regarding megaprojects (concerning what are considered 'excessive' project delays and cost-overruns, and failures to meet declared project objectives) that this cacophony has led some governments (as in the UK) to introduce measures that seek to counter the 'optimism bias' in appraisals, seen to be the main underlying source of such miscalculations (HM Treasury, 2003).

Notwithstanding these developments and trends, the findings of the OMEGA 2 project *strongly* suggest that iron triangle considerations are in fact all too frequently (and ultimately) *not* the overriding determinants of project 'success'. The research reveals, for example, that in judging a project's 'success', it is *very* significant to differentiate between the objectives set at the outset of the project from those that 'emerged' over time – particularly for MTPs with long gestation periods and those that are conceived, appraised and/or delivered in turbulent times. Findings from case studies undertaken as part of the OMEGA 2 project showed that of the thirty projects, *only* one-third achieved more than 75 per cent of their original project objectives, whereas for those thirteen projects where 'emergent objectives' were identified, the success rate was *much* higher, with more than three-quarters achieving 100 per cent of their 'emergent objectives', thereby *totally* transforming judgements of 'project success'. In some instances, it was noted that the amendments to the original project objectives were so great that one could legitimately argue that 'the project' had fundamentally changed its nature, scope and *raison d'être*.

The above finding reflects yet another conclusion of the OMEGA 2 project, namely that MTPs are essentially *not* static engineering artefacts but organic phenomena if one includes the impacts (both negative and positive) on the territories, communities and economies they traverse and serve (see discussion to follow). Taken in these wider geographical and sectoral terms, particularly over long time periods of thirty years or more, it is rational *not* to judge project outcomes against the first set of objectives or the first set of costs when the contexts, if not the very functions of such projects may have altered dramatically. Societal, political and environmental visions, values and priorities alter over time, as do the composition and influence of the project stakeholders. Different project stakeholder values, priorities and expectations – in different cultural contexts – translate over time (and location) into a myriad of perceptions of 'success'. This finding reinforces earlier conclusions of Friend and Jessop (1969) and subsequently Hall (1980), which explain why in certain circumstances 'failed' megaprojects of the past have been re-classified as 'successes' today and *vice versa*.

What is most important here is to appreciate that different infrastructure sectors have *very* different expected megaproject lifespans. In the transport sector, for example, the lifespan of such projects *prior* to any major retrofits is within a one-hundred-year period, typically fifty years or so. Where very much longer time frames are advocated, as in the case of the nuclear industry where mention is made of the use of a million year time frame for dealing with radioactive waste (NRC, 1995), one can reasonably argue that it is *impossible* to judge whether the 'success' of such projects can be sustained given our current inabilities to reliably predict futures beyond thirty years, much less one hundred years, let alone a million years! A caveat regarding the generic value of the OMEGA 2 research findings has to do with the fact that the case studies reviewed are *not* current and thus reflect the outcomes of *past* contextual constraints and opportunities, which may or may not replicate themselves.

While it is common practice to conduct interviews in support of research that is hypothesis-led and to question interviewees regarding specific themes and topics gleaned from earlier supporting literature reviews of material in the public domain, the OMEGA 2 project also conducted non-hypothesis-led investigations at an early stage of the research programme. In effect these encouraged interviewees to

Megaprojects and mega risks 49

story-tell their project experiences. They proved *in all cases* to be a huge source of additional knowledge that would otherwise *not* have been obtained via more traditional hypothesis-led questionnaire methods. Such storytelling also complemented the knowledge acquired from publications and reports in the public domain.

As indicated earlier, the OMEGA 2 project interviewed some three hundred key stakeholders in ten countries, involving thirty MTPs (three in each study country). Advised and trained by Cognitive Edge Pty, a knowledge-management consultancy firm that is expert in the application of story-telling analysis to decision-making in the corporate world, the OMEGA 2 project team encountered a number of challenges when undertaking the narrative analyses. The most prevalent related to cultural and language issues, since both the interviewers and interviewees often came from cultures different to the Anglo-Saxon background that primarily underpins the rationale of narrative analysis. In most cases, furthermore, the parties interviewed conversed in a language (and belonged to a culture) that was *not* English; some were Asian (Japanese and Hong Kong Chinese) and others European (speaking French, German, Dutch, Swedish or Greek). Even among English-speaking parties, there were numerous subtle cultural differences (among those from the UK, USA and Australia).

The narrative of each party was found to be conditioned in some way by their cultural perceptions about how narratives should be presented, their attitudes toward transparency, their sense of loyalty to past employers, and their sense of national pride in terms of how the narrative might (or might not) have boosted or undermined this. Notwithstanding these differences, the OMEGA team considered the findings of the narrative analysis of the OMEGA 2 case study respondents as both intriguing and compelling. The OMEGA interviewees, in all cases, were invited to story-tell *before* being asked to respond to hypothesis-led questions about their project experiences, with common and contrasting patterns of knowledge highlighted from each interview process as a basis for lesson identification. As may be appreciated from Figure 3.2, the knowledge gathered and analysed from these two interview exercises was also compared/contrasted with that extracted from public domain material and websites, government documents, consultancy reports, case study material and academic literature.

As earlier indicated, the lessons derived from both the international case studies and other material reviewed by the OMEGA 2 project were grouped around the nine important general lessons/themes (see Table 3.2) as follows:

- MTPs as agents of change
- MTPs as open systems
- MTPs as organic phenomena
- MTPs as projects that need to be framed differently
- the power of context on decision-making
- engaging with MTP stakeholders
- the role of sustainable development visions
- institutional policy and legislative support, and
- MTP lesson-learning and lesson-sharing.

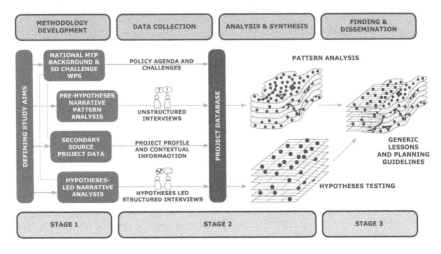

Figure 3.2 Overall study methodology of the OMEGA 2 project.
Source: Dimitriou et al. (2011).

Table 3.2 Key findings of the OMEGA 2 project. Source: OMEGA Centre (2012)

MTPs as 'Agents of Change'	There is a need for a change of mindset concerning the way in which MTPs are positioned, framed and planned.
MTPs as 'Open Systems'	Planning, appraisal and delivery agents need to recognise that MTPs are phenomena that require 'open systems' treatment in light of their complex and fluid relationship with the areas/ sectors/communities they serve, traverse and impact upon.
MTPs as 'Organic' Phenomena	MTPs are 'organic' phenomena (rather than static engineering artefacts) that often need 'time to breathe'. This time for reflection can present special opportunities that should be seized and exploited by key decision-makers.
The Framing of MTPs	The changing demands placed on MTPs can make it excruciatingly difficult to judge their successes and failures. This makes it imperative to ensure proper project framing so as to enable their appraisal to be based upon a fair and transparent foundation.
The Power of Context	Context-awareness and sensitivity to context on the part of project decision-makers is vital for both successful planning, appraisal and delivery of MTPs and suitable treatment of contextual risks, uncertainties and complexities.
The Role of Sustainable Development Visions	The lack of a clear and shared vision of the meaning of 'sustainable development' threatens to seriously undermine the potential for, and use of, MTPs to make a positive contribution to its achievement.
Engaging with MTP Stakeholders	Effective and early engagement with key stakeholders is seen as critical in MTP planning, appraisal and delivery.
Institutional, Policy and Legislative Support	MTPs are unlikely to be able to deliver the full range of agent of change benefits unless accompanied by a suitable institutional, policy and legislative framework that remains in place throughout the project lifecycle.
Lesson Learning and Sharing	It is apparent that systematic, widespread lesson-learning and sharing is not currently a significant feature of MTP planning, appraisal and delivery, and that there are few examples in the public domain of post-project evaluation that go beyond time/cost/specification assessments of project performance.

MTPs as 'agents of change'

The first general lesson is that there is an *urgent* need for a change of mindset concerning the way in which MTPs are positioned, framed and planned. This is critical, since the OMEGA 2 research findings confirmed that many (if not most) such projects employ objectives that allude to 'agent of change'[5] aims and aspirations that are much wider than those addressed by the iron triangle project management criteria. Given that many MTPs are in fact marketed as potentially transformational projects, the OMEGA 2 research team sees the inclusion of multiple criteria that incorporate spatial, economic, social, environmental, institutional *and* other wider non-project management considerations as *critical* – hence the subsequent advocacy by the OMEGA Centre of the use of policy-led multi-criteria analysis (PLMCA) approaches to project appraisal[6] (see Dimitriou, 2016). Any omission of such considerations is seen to be a partial, if not completely, biased assessment of the performance of MTPs at best – and a misleading assessment at worst. One can, for example, have a major toll road project that is completed 'on time', 'within budget' and 'according to specifications', but which services a privileged group (of high income-earning motorists) at a high cost to the public purse, addressing the needs of the least fuel-efficient means of travel, incurring unsustainable environmental costs in areas that are already environmentally fragile and the home of the poor and thus of the least influential.

MTPs as 'open systems'

The second general lesson concerns the question of whether and when MTPs should be seen as 'open' or 'closed' systems.[7] The findings of the OMEGA 2 project revealed that while the prevailing project management mentality for MTPs *essentially* treats them as 'closed systems' (in an effort to contain risks and ensure greater certainty), evidence suggests that greater risks and uncertainties can lurk *outside* the project's 'closed system' boundaries. By way of illustration, for all the sophisticated project planning and management practice in Singapore, what happens in Indonesia (in terms of forest fires and resultant air pollution) severely compromises the impacts of these exemplary Singaporean project management efforts. Similarly, however prudent the efforts of the Hong Kong administration are in controlling its water and air pollution, what happens in south China overall in terms of water and air pollution mitigation matters a great deal to Hong Kong. In other words, there is a need to look at megaprojects as both closed systems *and* open systems. Open systems analysis was found to be a prerequisite of effective MTP planning and appraisal, and for post-construction monitoring, whereas 'closed-systems' thinking is essential at times of project implementation and construction.

MTPs as 'organic' phenomena

The preceding findings reinforce the third general OMEGA 2 lesson, namely that MTPs are 'organic' phenomena (rather than engineering fixed assets alone). They are deemed organic on account of the fact that (as earlier acknowledged) MTP functions, features and even dimensions can radically alter over time, in response to changes in contexts, demands, values and priorities that prevail over time and space. Efforts to adapt to such forces of change can lead to delays and periods of inactivity which in certain circumstances can offer periods for reflection ('times to breathe') in decision-making. Such periods, it is contended, present special opportunities that key decision-makers should seize and exploit rather than waste. The OMEGA 2 team further argues that MTP developments can also enhance innovative thinking about how best in the future to retrofit them to twenty-first century needs.

The framing of MTPs

Following on from the above, the fourth general lesson concerns the very difficult matter of where the boundaries of a MTP *should* be drawn, and the fact that this very much matters when judging the 'success' of such projects. This follows from the changing demands frequently placed on MTPs over time and in different locations by different stakeholders – making it excruciatingly difficult to judge the full extent of their merits and costs. For the transportation planner or operator, for example, the project may be confined to a linear corridor extending 800 metres on either side of the track/road (line-haul link) together with terminals and other hubs, with traffic volumes, capacity provision and rates of return being all that truly matters. For central, regional and local governments, by contrast, the boundaries of interest are typically far broader. These typically involve more strategic development dimensions and wider economic interests, including those shared by other stakeholders, such as real estate parties, which are especially interested in sites and property with easy access to the transport facility that are likely to enjoy an uplift in land and property values as a result of the new major transport investment.

In the case of the CTRL/HS1, the conscious expansion of the project boundaries by the UK government under the political leadership of Michael Heseltine was part of the evolving nature of the project's scope – from merely a rail link connecting London to Europe to *also* representing a transportation spine for an urban regeneration corridor that was to become part of a sub-regional strategy for London and the south-east. *Ultimately*, this helped London win the rights to host the 2012 Olympic Games. In this sense, the CTRL acted as a catalyst for additional megaprojects and thus fundamentally functioned as a transformational agent of development that went way beyond its initial purpose. Given these circumstances, when we talk about the 'success' or 'failure' of MTPs, the question that really needs to be asked is: which of the project's aims are we passing judgement on, and on this basis, which boundaries of the megaproject are we talking of, and which among them are the most relevant?

The power of context

The fifth general lesson presented by the OMEGA 2 project concerns 'the power of context' on decision-making. OMEGA 2 research findings suggest that context awareness and sensitivity to context on the part of project decision-makers is *vital* to the ultimate success of MTPs – as is the suitable treatment of contextual risks, uncertainties and complexities. This can be especially significant when new knowledge comes to light during those planning and appraisal phases of a project that present 'game-changing' economic, environmental, social and political risks (and prospects), which can alter the viability of the project in both the long and the short term. This is reinforced by earlier conclusions of the OMEGA 1 project, which also point to the need to have a *much* greater regard and respect for the context(s) of project decision-making – both in terms of the impacts that (changing) contexts have on the values that surround judgements and the importance of acknowledging the fuzzy and dynamic characteristics of project boundaries beyond their physical parameters. Together, these contextual concerns incidentally highlight the significance of acknowledging the existence (and influence) of multiple stakeholder perceptions and definitions of 'success' – which in turn depend on stakeholder interests and the temporal and locational characteristics of the contexts of such judgements.

A further dimension of the understanding of the power of context on project decision-making, first alluded to by Johnson (1972), has to do with the politics (with a small 'p') of the different professional cultures that come into play at different stages of the project lifecycle. In the case of MTPs, the city and regional planner is highly influential *up to* the point of the approval of the project. Behind the scenes, meanwhile, potential project investors lobby hardware providers and potential construction firms for prospective participation in the project. Professions representing project investors vie for influence in the economic appraisal phase, while project managers and prospective project operators are all-powerful at the project implementation and delivery stage. The role of politicians (national and local), however, can be potentially *very* significant in all phases of the project (depending on who they are and what power they wield) – either in championing the project's promotion or in leading or lending support to its opposition.

The role of sustainable development visions in MTPs

The *sixth* general lesson of OMEGA 2 research is that a low priority is given to sustainable development concerns in MTP investments, and that the identified lack of a clear and shared vision of the meaning of 'sustainable development' threatens to seriously undermine the potential for, and use of, MTPs as agents of sustainable development. As a result of current developments, the OMEGA 2 team identified (as already mentioned) that retrofitting the MTPs of today for tomorrow's needs could well become a major industry for the future. To explain why sustainable development dimensions of MTPs were rarely top appraisal concerns in the reported case studies, it needs to be appreciated that the OMEGA 2 project looked at MTPs that were completed between 1997 and 2010. In the early planning years of such projects, many in the field did not yet see 'sustainability' as a mature concept. Since then, it has been increasingly acknowledged (see UN-Habitat, 2013) that sustainability needs to be built on four rather than the three traditional pillars of sustainable development (i.e. economic, social and environmental), the fourth being 'sustainable institutions'. This is argued on the basis that economic, social and environmental sustainability can *only* be delivered if projects are promoted, governed and regulated by institutions and governance systems that are themselves sustainable, and share the common visions of sustainability.

Notwithstanding the above development, and despite the extensive rhetoric that has prevailed among many governments, investors and international development agencies indicating that the promotion of sustainable development is high on their agendas, the past international praxis of MTP developments suggest a very different reality (see Head, 2008). Hajer (1996) puts this down to the lack of a shared understanding of the meaning of sustainable development among politicians, technocrats and the public, while Zegras (2011) attributes it to the failure to operationalise many of the sustainable development objectives into meaningful appraisal criteria and performance indicators. The findings of the OMEGA 2 project confirm both these explanations as major contributors to the current knowledge deficit regarding what MTPs do (and can do) for sustainable development.

Engaging with MTP stakeholders

The seventh general lesson that emerged from the OMEGA 2 research has to do with public engagement in MTP developments. Scandinavian transport megaproject experiences suggest that early effective engagement by government with key project stakeholders (public and private, as well as third sector parties[8]) is *highly* advantageous, potentially reducing friction and subsequent delays. An approach of this kind suggests that there is room for views *outside* the realm of the 'expert' to be taken on board by project promoters (even at the earliest stage of project development) and that these may merit modifying expert views about how the project should be conceived, appraised and delivered. Pursuing an approach of this type, however, requires periods of time that are not typically afforded to megaprojects such as the Olympic Games. Here the completion date is fixed, final and sacrosanct, even if this means increased costs. This contrasts with other projects that are more organic in their development and which offer greater time for reflection and participation.

Notwithstanding the very different circumstances cited above, if MTPs are to be built, all *eventually* arrive at a stage (through compromises or otherwise) when the fate of project 'winners' and 'losers' are finally determined. By engaging stakeholders early, the OMEGA team contends that one is in a better position to reduce the number of project 'losers', increase the number (and spread) of project 'winners', and be more transparent about who the 'real' stakeholders are. In so doing, there is also a greater chance of the MTP being transformed from a project that is coveted by the engineers, economists and politicians, to one that is more widely owned by the public benefiting from the 'wisdom of crowds' (Surowiecki, 2004).

Institutional, policy and legislative support

The eighth and penultimate general lesson of the OMEGA 2 research suggests that MTPs are unlikely to be able to deliver the full range of agent of change benefits unless accompanied by a suitable institutional, policy and legislative framework that remains in place throughout the project lifecycle. All too often (but not inevitably), many private sector investors see the prevailing processes of framing MTP policies and planning, as presented by government, as *obstacles* to what they are trying to achieve and/or to the pace at which they wish to achieve progress. In the UK and elsewhere, this tension has frequently led to the establishment of special legislation and delivery vehicles designed to minimise or overcome these perceived difficulties and speed up MTP delivery. In current neo-liberal climates of public sector austerity and increased dependence on private sector finance (and expertise), some politicians and many project promoters increasingly accuse governments of promoting excessive red tape bureaucracy in the form of, for example, environmental and social safeguards that add to the delay and monetary costs of projects.

There is then friction, to say the least, between the project management mentality of 'getting things done' on time and within budget and according to given specifications, and the policy and planning mentality that looks to the project delivering broader sustainability – that is, outcomes that are environmentally friendlier, more equitable, and economically sound. Some consulting engineers and project managers see this disjoint between policy and planning on one hand and project delivery on the other as a failure by policymakers and planners to come to grips with the logistics and importance of basic resource management principles (Allport, 2011). To address these perceived shortcomings they advocate extending project management principles into policymaking and planning in what some have called front-loaded strategic project management (Edkins et al., 2013). We contend that this is counterproductive as it imposes closed-systems thinking to early stages of the project development, which is better served by open-systems thinking as advocated in OMEGA lesson 2 and revealed by OMEGA research findings.

Lesson-learning and lesson-sharing

The final general lesson derived from the OMEGA 2 project concerns the significance of learning and sharing lessons concerning decision-making experiences in the planning, appraisal and delivery of MTPs. In conducting its research the OMEGA 2 research team discovered that systematic, widespread lesson-learning and sharing of experiences was *not* a significant feature of MTP planning, appraisal and delivery, and that few examples could be found in the public domain of post-project evaluation that would have gone beyond time/cost/specification assessments of project performance and impact. In addition, the research team frequently encountered difficulties in *formally* accessing key reports and data that were in the possession of private sector parties involved in such projects. This lack of transparency was justified on the grounds that access to such material would – or at least might – compromise the commercial interests of these parties by divulging information that would otherwise offer a competitive advantage. As the public sector increasingly relies on the private sector to help fund and deliver MTPs, we argue that this lack of transparency will become increasingly problematic to lesson-learning and lesson-sharing, thereby restricting knowledge-building. This has potentially profound implications for possibilities to investigate in any meaningful way what is a 'successful' MTP.

Notwithstanding the fact that the collection of insights and information by the OMEGA 2 project (as earlier acknowledged) is biased towards key stakeholder sources (i.e. those involved in promoting and delivering MTPs as opposed to those impacted by such projects), the OMEGA 2 project team contend that the findings of the research are nonetheless *very* significant beyond the interests of these privileged parties. This is because the insights and generic lessons identified were *not* derived from an ivory-tower academic scouring exercise of theoretical literature, but to a very significant extent also report on first-hand insights and experiences of those who are *actually* involved in MTP decision-making, thereby making the lessons more 'evidence-based'.

Other observations regarding treatment of risk, uncertainty and complexity

As regards one of the OMEGA 2 project's overall research questions – namely, how well was the treatment of risk, uncertainty and complexity dealt with in MTP planning, appraisal and delivery – the research concluded that 'the success' of a project ultimately very much depends *not only* on how well these issues are dealt with in the decision-making process, but *also* (as earlier alluded) on the impact of contextual forces at play (i.e. 'the power of context') on this decision-making. These findings have informed recent work completed by the OMEGA Centre for the European Investment Bank (EIB) (OMEGA Centre, 2014) which incorporates all four criteria (i.e. the treatment of risk, uncertainty, complexity, and the power of context) as important parameters of a PLMCA approach to the appraisal of potential major urban and regional investment projects. An approach of this kind is seen to be useful as offering (as a minimum) a 'risk-register' of what traditional Cost Benefit Analysis (CBA) may fail to register as significant. The approach is seen as particularly useful for large-scale, complex, multi-sectoral urban projects, where there is widespread recognition that a much broader appraisal approach is needed to inform investment decision-making – albeit with CBA informing this wider assessment.

We acknowledge, however, that retaining in MTP development some level of inherent strategic flexibility and resilience to address challenges such as dealing with risks, uncertainties and complexities is not easy. This is particularly the case when influential private-sector stakeholders look to 'lock-in' the public sector to commitments that substantially reduce their risks, while simultaneously providing themselves with flexibility that keeps their options open for as long as possible. It should be emphasised that these public/private sector dynamics and frictions are very different for fixed-date projects such as those associated with forthcoming Olympic Games – in the sense that the 'lock-in' for such projects has essentially all but been established from the outset. Such projects are a form of 'megaprojects on steroids', possessing high risks but also high certainty concerning their end date for completion, requiring full commitment by all parties to very tight fast-track schedules and (ostensibly) to firm budgets, with any divergence from this guaranteed to catch the attention of the press and thus be potentially exposed to negative publicity.

Conclusions

In order to oversee the development of MTPs in line with the lessons outlined earlier in this chapter, it would appear that governments need to put in place institutional planning, appraisal and delivery frameworks that guide the parties involved through a passage of decision-making that is more transparent, inclusive and broader in scope than traditional approaches have hitherto typically offered. It is in this context especially, however, that strong political leadership and/or political champions become important. For where public sector strategic leadership is compromised by fragmented institutional arrangements of planning, approval and delivery and/or short-term perspectives on project costs and gains, this neither allows any real continuity of decision-making nor does it foster holistic decision-making. This, in turn, erodes any shared and co-ordinated efforts at knowledge-building from past megaproject development experiences that could otherwise prove invaluable for future projects.

It was noted in the UK OMEGA 2 case studies that these less strategic and holistic developments have tended to favour a situation in which specialist knowledge about MTP planning, appraisal and delivery has increasingly resided within the private sector, while the public sector's knowledge base of such projects has been, by contrast, increasingly eroded by austerity cut-backs and the privatisation of public services. Although less true in other countries such as Sweden, Germany, France and Japan – which have to a much greater degree (at least for the present) retained their traditions of a strong public sector and strategic and more integrated thinking – this transfer of leadership and knowledge about megaproject developments has subsequently made the dialogue between the public and private sector in the UK very one-sided, with the latter being increasingly more disadvantaged. Significantly, several private sector stakeholders engaged in megaproject developments interviewed for the OMEGA 2 research expressed similar concerns regarding these developments and consider that the imbalance poses a serious risk to their industry. They fear that the public sector will ultimately be left with insufficiently qualified, experienced and knowledgeable staff, unable to adequately work with them, and thereby jeopardising project outcomes on all fronts.

Responding to the above concerns, the OMEGA 2 team concludes that in order to continue offering innovative solutions for MTP developments, private sector stakeholders should actively encourage and promote the development of a strong public sector counterpart with which to dialogue – one that draws from past public sector and partnership experiences and is competent and knowledgeable about the best ways of representing the public interest.

In light of these sentiments, it is odd, to say the least, that despite the billions of US dollars, Euros, Pounds Sterling, Yen, Yuan etc. spent all over the world on MTPs and made available for future projects, researching what constitutes a 'successful' project and what efforts are required to generate comprehensive lesson-learning and lesson-sharing should have received so little attention until recently. The hypothesis that this lack of adequate lesson-learning and lesson-sharing (especially in industry) can be attributed to limited R&D funds or is an 'oversight' on the part of all concerned is suspect. Apart from the fear by the private sector of sharing commercially advantageous knowledge mentioned earlier, what the OMEGA 2 research uncovered was that a more likely explanation lies in a combination of the extensive path-dependency of many MTP development practices (Low et al., 2005) and the prevailing short-term interests and attitudes of many involved in the MTP industry, despite the long-term nature of the business. The OMEGA 2 team suspects that such parties have fallen victim to the kind of criticism levelled at many international corporations by the McKinsey Consulting Group (see Baghai et al., 1999). This analysis saw too many of such businesses focusing excessively on current lucrative business models rather than investing significantly in innovative practices likely to be more open to future opportunities and be more resilient to twenty-first century risks and uncertainties posed by challenges such as climate change, energy shortages, global funding restrictions and rising social unrest, to mention but a few.

OMEGA 2 research findings also conclude that as a result of the perpetuation of current MTP development practices, dominated as they are by the rhetoric of project management iron-triangle concerns of project delivery, the private sector is becoming much more influential and powerful, employing essentially the iron-triangle template as a basis for judging MTP successes globally. This reliance on what is a closed-systems understanding of the complexity of MTP decision-making challenges ahead, coupled with the timid use of new technologies for fear of increasing project risks, will have the added disadvantage of making such decision-making less transparent and the future scrutiny of such projects nearly impossible. These outcomes will not only compromise any aspirations in academia or practice regarding learning and sharing past mistakes and successes, but also restrict access to the information needed to benefit from such lessons, thereby limiting our knowledge of where MTP risks and opportunities ultimately lie and how best to judge their successes and failures.

Notes

1   This text has been derived from a forthcoming book jointly authored by the same authors entitled *Mega Transport Projects: Decision-making beyond the iron triangle,* to be published by Routledge in 2017.

2   The following university departments were involved: Australia: University of Melbourne, The Faculty of Architecture, Australasian Centre for the Governance and Management of Urban Transport (GAMUT); France: Ecole Nationales Ponts et Chaussees, Paris – Laboratoire Technique Territoires et Societes (LATTS); Germany: Free University of Berlin, Institute for Geographical Studies, Urban Studies Section; Greece: University of Thessaly, School of Engineering, Department of Planning and Regional Development; Hong Kong: University of Hong Kong, Faculty of Architecture, Department of Real Estate and Construction; Japan: Tokyo Institute of Technology, Graduate School of Science and Engineering, Department of Built Environment; Netherlands: University of Amsterdam, Graduate School of Social Sciences, Institute for Metropolitan Studies; Sweden: Lund University, Faculty of Engineering, Department of Technology and Society; and USA: New York University, Wagner School of Public Policy, Rudin Centre for Transportation Policy and Management.

3   This denotes an approach whereby stakeholders' stories concerning MTP decision-making derived from non-hypothesis-led interviews were analysed using a combination of 'sense-making' software developed by Cognitive Edge Pty. The Narrative Analysis was complemented by a more traditional examination of responses to hypothesis-based questions to determine key patterns of knowledge. Hypothesis-led investigations comprised structured interviews with a similarly diverse range of typically ten to fifteen key stakeholders, who were requested to respond directly to the OMEGA overall research questions and overall hypotheses, as well as a range of project-related hypotheses. Again, narrative data was analysed to determine patterns of responses to the OMEGA overall research questions and research hypotheses, plus other important insights.

4   See www.omegacentre.bartlett.ucl.ac.uk (accessed 20 July 2016).

5   'Agents of change' in the context of MTPs allude to the transformational powers that large-scale transport projects may possess given the widespread and long-term impacts upon the spatial, economic, social, environmental, institutional and other aspects they potentially present to the development of the areas they traverse and serve.

6   PLMCA as applied to project appraisal can be defined as "an eclectic framework and attendant set of processes for undertaking multiple project stakeholder analysis and trade-offs in decision-making (led by policy guidelines) that facilitate key decision-makers to arrive at more integrated and sustainable investments that are more strategic, comprehensive, robust and transparent in character than those primarily reliant on traditional project appraisal methods" (Dimitriou, 2013).

7   MTPs are seen as 'open systems' as a result of their continuous interaction and interdependency with the changing 'context(s)' they serve, traverse and impact upon – including environmental, social, economic, physical, institutional and political contexts. Megaprojects can be regarded as 'closed systems' when they fail to interact with the above contexts.

8   The term 'third sector' is used to emphasise the separation from the public and private sectors. Other common terms used to designate these non-government advocacy and service association organisations include 'voluntary', 'non-profit', 'community' and 'civil society' (Casey, 2004).

References

Allport, R.J. 2011. *Planning Major Projects*. London: Thomas Telford.

Baghai, M., Coley, S. and White, S. 1999. *The Alchemy of Growth: Kick-starting and sustaining growth in your company*. London: Texere.

Batty, M. (2008) Complexity and Emergence in City Systems: Implications For Urban Planning. Section 3.2 in Working Paper 3, OMEGA 1 Project, *Review of past and contemporary treatment of complexity, uncertainty and risk in city and regional planning, transport, and project development*, OMEGA Centre, University College London, London.

Brecher, C. and Nobbe, P. 2010. *Boston Artery Tunnel Case Study Report.* Rudin Centre for Transportation Policy and Management, New York University, New York City.

Casey, J. 2004. Third sector participation in the policy process: A framework for comparative analysis. *Voluntas: International Journal of Voluntary and Non-profit Organizations*, 32(2), 241–257.

Dimitriou, H.T. (ed.). 2016. The application of policy-led multi-criteria analysis to megaproject transport infrastructure appraisal. *Journal of Research in Transportation Economics*, Special Issue Number 55.

Dimitriou, H.T. 2013. Multi-criteria analysis: policy inputs and targets. *MIPAD MSc Lecture Notes on 21st Century Toolkit for Mega Project Planning, Appraisal and Delivery.* Bartlett School of Planning, University College London, London.

Dimitriou, H.T. and Thompson, R. 2007. Strategic thought and regional planning: The importance of context. In H.T. Dimitriou and R. Thompson (eds), *Strategic Planning for Regional Development in the UK: A review of principles and practices.* London: Routledge.

Dimitriou, H.T., Oades, R.S., Wright, P.G. and Ward, E.J. 2008. *Generic Lessons for Improving the Treatment of Risk, Uncertainty and Complexity of Mega Urban Transport Projects.* Working Paper 4, OMEGA 1 Project, OMEGA Centre, Bartlett School of Planning, University College London, London.

Dimitriou, H.T., Wright, P.G. and Ward, E.J. 2011. *Mega Projects and Mega Risks: Lessons for decision makers through a comparative analysis of selected large-scale transport projects in Europe, USA and Asia Pacific.* Final Report, OMEGA 2 Project, OMEGA Centre, Bartlett School of Planning, University College London, London.

Dimitriou, H.T., Wright, P.G. and Ward, E.J. 2017. *Mega Transport Projects: Beyond the iron triangle*, London: Routledge (forthcoming).

Dora, C., Vickers, C. & Walker, K. 2008. Scientific Uncertainty and Complexity in Public Health. Section 2.7 in H.T. Dimitriou, R.S. Oades and E.J. Ward (eds.), *The Contemporary Treatment of Risk, Uncertainty and Complexity in Decision-making in Selected Disciplines.* Working Paper 2, OMEGA 1 Project, OMEGA Centre, University College London, London.

Edkins, A., Geraldi, J., Morris, P. and Smith, A. 2013. Exploring the front-end of project management. *Engineering Project Organization Journal*, 3(2), 71–85.

Flint, J. and Raco, M. (eds). 2011. *The Future of Sustainable Cities*, Bristol: Policy Press.

Flyvbjerg, B., Bruzelius, N. and Rothengatter, W. 2003. *Megaprojects and Risk: An anatomy of ambition.* Cambridge: Cambridge University Press.

Friend, J.K. and Jessop, W.N. 1969. *Local Government and Strategic Choice: An operational research approach to the process of public planning.* London: Tavistock Press.

FT. 2013. Internal Treasury concerns mount over HS2. *Financial Times*, Available online at: www.ft.com/cms/s/0/1f331cde-0988-11e3-8b32-00144feabdc0.html#axzz2qvbbeC3J (accessed 19 January 2014).

Gibson, L. 2008. Complexity, Uncertainty and Risk-taking in General Insurance and the Role of the Actuary. Section 2.5 in H.T. Dimitriou, R.S. Oades and E.J. Ward (eds.), *The Contemporary Treatment of Risk, Uncertainty and Complexity in Decision-making in Selected Disciplines.* Working Paper 2, OMEGA 1 Project, OMEGA Centre, University College London, London.

Hajer, M. 1996. Politics on the move: The democratic control of the design of sustainable technologies. *The International Control of Knowledge and Utilization*, 8(4).

Hall, P. 1980. *Great Planning Disasters.* London: Weidenfeld and Nicolson.

Head, P. 2008. *Entering the Ecological Age – the engineer's role*, Brunel International Lecture Series, Institution of Civil Engineers, London. Available online at: http://publications.

arup.com/publications/e/entering_the_ecological_age_the_engineers_role (accessed 4 April 2016).

HM Treasury. 2003. *The Green Book: Appraisal and evaluation in central government*. London: HMSO.

Johnson, T.J. 1972. *Professions and Power*, Studies in Sociology, British Sociological Association. London: Macmillan Press Ltd.

Lemmon, M. 2008. The Treatment of Risk, Uncertainty and Complexity in Project Finance: A banker's perspective. Section 2.4 in H.T. Dimitriou, R.S. Oades and E.J. Ward (eds.), *The Contemporary Treatment of Risk, Uncertainty and Complexity in Decision-making in Selected Disciplines*. Working Paper 2, OMEGA 1 Project, OMEGA Centre, University College London, London.

Low, N., Gleeson, B. & Rush, E. 2005. A multivalent conception of path dependence: the case of transport planning in metropolitan Melbourne, Australia. *Environmental Sciences*, 2(4), 391–408.

Merrow, E.W. 1988. *Understanding the outcomes of megaprojects: A qualitative analysis of very large civilian projects*. Santa Monica: RAND Corporation.

Mumford, J. 2008. Agricultural Pests and Diseases: Complexity, uncertainty and risk. Section 2.6 in H.T. Dimitriou, R.S. Oades and E.J. Ward (eds.), *The Contemporary Treatment of Risk, Uncertainty and Complexity in Decision-making in Selected Disciplines*. Working Paper 2, OMEGA 1 Project, OMEGA Centre, University College London, London.

National Research Council. 1995. *Technical Bases for Yucca Mountain Standards*. Washington, DC: National Academy Press, cited in 'The Status of Nuclear Waste Disposal,' *The American Physical Society*, January.

OMEGA Centre. 2012. *Mega Projects – Executive Summary: Lessons for decision-makers of selected large-scale transport infrastructure projects*. OMEGA Centre, Bartlett School of Planning, UCL, London.

OMEGA Centre. 2014. *Multi Criteria Analysis Methodology for Project Appraisal*. Final Report prepared for Regional and Urban Development Division (REGU), Projects Directorate, European Investment Bank (EIB), Luxembourg.

Rossetto, T. 2008. Earthquake Engineering and Seismic Risk. Section 2.3 in H.T. Dimitriou, R.S. Oades and E.J. Ward (eds.), *The Contemporary Treatment of Risk, Uncertainty and Complexity in Decision-making in Selected Disciplines*. Working Paper 2, OMEGA 1 Project, OMEGA Centre, University College London, London.

Stone, J. 2008. Strategy: Military Planning Under Conditions of Uncertainty, Complexity and Risk. Section 2.7 in H.T. Dimitriou, R.S. Oades and E.J. Ward (eds.), *The Contemporary Treatment of Risk, Uncertainty and Complexity in Decision-making in Selected Disciplines*. Working Paper 2, OMEGA 1 Project, OMEGA Centre, University College London, London.

Surowiecki, J. 2004. *The Wisdom of Crowds: Why the many are smarter than the few*. London: Little Brown.

UN-Habitat. 2013. *Planning and Design for Sustainable Urban Mobility: Policy Directions*, Global Report on Human Settlements 2013. London: Earthscan-Routledge.

Weaver, P. 2007. The Origins of Modern Project Management. Paper submitted to *Fourth Annual PMI College of Scheduling Conference*, April, Vancouver.

Zegras, C. 2011. Mainstreaming sustainable urban transport: Putting the pieces together. In H.T. Dimitriou and R. Gakenheimer (eds.), *Urban Transport in the Developing World*. Cheltenham: Edward Elgar.

4 The Lyon–Turin high-speed railway project and the escalation of commitment

Thomas Reverdy and Markku Lehtonen

Introduction

The Lyon–Turin train project consists of a plan to build a new high-speed train line for both passenger and freight traffic, including the construction of numerous tunnels through the French–Italian Alps. The planning of the project began over twenty-five years ago, and has gathered speed since the turn of the century. According to its promoters, the project would require an estimated EUR 24–26.1 billion of investments (Cour des Comptes, 2012a). This project is ambitious, not least because of the numerous tunnels to be constructed, including a cross-frontier section consisting of a 57 km base tunnel (at an expected cost of EUR 8.5–10.5 billion). The French and the Italian governments, as well as many local authorities, are highly committed to the project. The investments in the cross-frontier section are expected to come mainly from public sources. Financing of EUR 1 billion has already been either committed or invested in the construction work and preparatory studies.[1] The arguments put forward to justify the construction of the train line primarily relate to its expected economic benefits and to the alleged insufficiency of the existing capacity to support the predicted increasing volumes of freight and passenger traffic.

The project faces strong opposition in Italy, because of its impacts on the local environment in the densely populated valleys along the planned line. In France, the contestation concerns primarily the estimated economic benefits of the project, and its place among the public spending priorities. The Green Party in the region of Rhône-Alpes openly opposed the project in its campaign for the 2015 regional elections, the City of Grenoble recently took a position against the project (Conseil municipal de Grenoble, 2016: 6), and some conservative local politicians have also raised doubts about its relevance. Furthermore, many transport economists, as well as the National Court of Auditors, contest the traffic forecasts and the estimations concerning the economic benefits of the project. Even within the state apparatus the project is anything but consensual, in the context of constant pressure to reduce public debt and to modernise the existing railway network.

The difficulties encountered during the planning phase have a lot to do with the temporal dimensions of the project: numerous successive transport plans have in the past included Lyon–Turin, yet implementation has been repeatedly postponed because the project is deemed costly and its economic benefits more modest than those from many other high-speed train line projects. Over time, successive commitments to the realisation of Lyon–Turin have accumulated, thereby making the project increasingly irreversible. Detailed analysis and site investigations, as well as new safety requirements, have considerably pushed up the cost estimates. At the same time, freight traffic growth estimates, which had thus far been a primary argument justifying the project, have been revised downwards over time. It has become increasingly difficult to justify the doubling of current transport capacity on the grounds of an expected growth in freight transport, not least because past predictions have repeatedly proven false. In fact, both rail and road freight traffic in the existing tunnels have decreased since 1999 (Société Française du Tunnel Routier du Fréjus, 2013). Moreover, many of the recently completed rail projects in France have proven highly uneconomic in operation, which has further eroded the credibility of the estimations and the relevance of this type of project (e.g. Cour des Comptes, 2014).

In this technically and economically evolving context, the project proponents have sought new ways in which they present the project, in order to justify its viability in an increasingly unfavourable environment. Four changes merit being highlighted. First, the project, initially designed to serve primarily passenger traffic, is now mainly justified by the objective of promoting a modal shift of freight from road to rail. Second, while the project was previously presented as a single whole, it is now conceived of as a series of independent sub-projects, the most important of which would be the cross-frontier 'base' tunnel. Third, the promise of a massive financial contribution from the EU (40 per cent of the total investment cost of the base tunnel) has essentially put an end to the debate on the economics of the project in France, which would only have to finance 25 per cent of the EUR 8.5 billion estimated cost of the base tunnel, Italy financing the remaining 35 per cent. Fourth, the project proponents no longer argue on the basis of full economic evaluations (of costs and benefits), but prefer simply highlighting the expected economic benefits, without addressing the details concerning the cost, financing and economic viability of the project.

The project therefore appears to be highly resilient, as demonstrated by its ability to adapt to the declining transport volumes and to renew its justifications and support networks. This resilience has allowed the project to survive, despite the accumulating evidence about its economic unviability. In order to explain the rather extraordinary resilience of the project, we shall draw on the concept of "escalation of commitment" used by Ross and Staw (1993) to examine the decision-making processes that led to the construction of the Shoreham nuclear power station near New York by the Long Island Lighting Company. Despite the more than USD 5 billion invested, the power station was never put into operation. Ross and Staw suggest four mechanisms to explain the seemingly absurd decisions concerning the plant. The first hypothesis refers to the "objective aspects of a project" (Ross and Staw, 1993: 702), including notably its economic costs and benefits. The authors evoke the practice of sequencing of the economic calculations, which makes each incremental cost increase to appear relatively modest. Hence, even when a comprehensive cost calculation would demonstrate the project to be unviable, each individual decision during the process can be justified by seemingly reasonable economic calculations that compare the needed future investments with their expected benefits. Such calculations exclude past investments, considering these as irrevocable 'sunk costs'. This project was able to survive for a long time, because despite its progressively worsening overall cost–benefit ratio it remained profitable in the light of each individual new investment needed.

The second hypothesis suggested by Ross and Staw (1993) is akin to what Flyvbjerg (2011: 325–327) calls "optimism bias". It draws on psychological explanations for the limited rationality of decision-makers, who tend to systematically ignore internal difficulties and blame external factors for the successive cost increases.

The third hypothesis emphasises the political context and the interdependencies in which the enterprise is embedded. All through the process the project proponents must persuade external stakeholders of the benefits of the project. As the proponents repeatedly have to downplay the uncertainties and come up with new arguments in support of the project, they become increasingly imprisoned by their need to maintain a coherent argumentation, and remain credible. This mechanism is similar to the findings of van Marrewijk et al. (2008: 592): "getting megaprojects off the ground and keeping them going, presents ample opportunity for participants to make claims about qualities or convictions they do not necessarily have, in other words, for the organisation of hypocrisy. Facing demands for certainty while confronting much that is unknowable and undecidable may well make hypocrisy the norm."

The fourth hypothesis concerns factors internal to the project organisation. For example, the teams participating in the realisation of the project come to constitute, over time, a powerful coalition able to exert significant influence on decision-makers. In the most extreme case, the prospect of abandoning the project might endanger the very survival of the implementing organisation.

In contrast with the private-sector-driven nuclear power project analysed by Ross and Staw, the forces behind the Lyon-Turin project consist of a coalition of public and private actors at the European, national and local levels. In this chapter we argue that the cumulating political commitments – at local, national and European levels, and together with the participation of the private sector – have resulted in a series of increasingly irrevocable decisions allowing the project to carry on, despite the increasingly evident weaknesses of its economic justifications.

This chapter builds on document analysis and a series of interviews conducted with project advocates (the French national rail network company – Réseau Ferré de France – and the multi-stakeholder partnership set up to promote the project – la Transalpine[2]), as well as environmentalists, transport economists and a Court of Auditors representative who oppose the project. The interviews were conducted between June 2014 and December 2015.

The transformations of the project: adaptation to the context or escalation of commitment?

The Lyon–Turin infrastructure project has been in preparation for twenty-five years. It was envisaged to connect Lyon and Turin by a 235 km high-speed railway through the Alps, thus replacing the existing line which passes through Saint-Jean-de-Maurienne and Modane, and has only one tunnel section crossing the French–Italian border (see Figure 4.1). On the steepest slope of 3 per cent along this cross-border tunnel, three locomotives are needed to pull freight trains up the hill at a maximum speed of not higher than 30 km/h. This obviously limits the capacity of the connection. A further bottleneck is located near Chambéry, where the existing line has a single track.

The plans for constructing a new line have constantly shifted over time, with changes in routing, the definition of what should be maximised (high speed or high capacity), and whether the line should primarily serve freight or passenger transport. Initially passenger transport was given the highest priority, whereas today the emphasis is on freight. Two elements have remained stable: the construction of a 57 km cross-border tunnel through the Alps, and the intention to serve both passenger and freight transport.

For a long time presented as a complete and unique whole, the project is ever more frequently portrayed as divisible into a series of elements to be implemented in a stepwise manner. Only the new cross-border tunnel is designated to receive EU funding, and it has thereby become the central, primary and most urgently needed strategic element in the efforts to reinvigorate rail freight transport in France. The cross-border tunnel would be directly connected to the existing train line, and could therefore be used immediately, while the other tunnels and legs of the railway would still be awaiting construction.

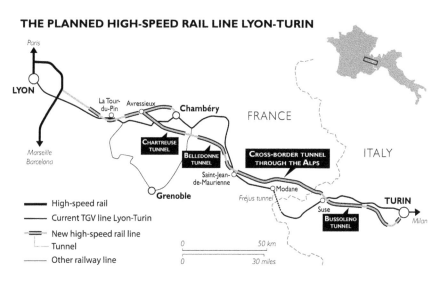

Figure 4.1 The existing and planned railway connections between Lyon and Turin.

An intergovernmental Lyon-Turin commission[3] was created in 1996 in order to facilitate collaboration and decision-making between France and Italy. Freight transport has taken priority in project planning after an accident in the Mont Blanc tunnel in 1999, and due to the increasing awareness among the region's politicians concerning the harmful impacts of road traffic in the valleys, but also because the tunnel would make only a modest contribution to the supply of passenger transport. The possibility of a combined freight and passenger line was therefore envisaged for the French part of the project, also to provide a connection to the line with the high-speed line at the Lyon-Saint-Exupéry airport.

The Lyon–Turin project is governed by a complex network of multiple actors operating at multiple governance levels. An agreement between France and Italy in 2001 confirmed the commitment of the two countries to the implementation of the project. Since then a French–Italian summit has been organised each year, to demonstrate the continuing commitment from both partners. The project is also part of the Trans-European Transport Network (TEN-T), and the EU has over the years progressively stepped up its commitment in support of the project.

Two recent key milestones deserve attention. In August 2013 the French government granted to the project a Déclaration d'Utilité Publique, thereby declaring the section between Lyon and Saint-Jean-de-Maurienne as being in the public interest (Journal Officiel, 2013a), and in November of the same year the country's parliament ratified the French–Italian agreement from 2012 concerning the international section of the project (Journal Officiel, 2013b).

Until 2015, the French section of the project was operated by the national rail network company RFF (Réseau Ferré Français), whereas LTF (Lyon Turin Ferroviaire) was responsible for the cross-border part. In January 2015 a new company, TELT (Tunnel Euralpin Lyon Turin), replaced LTF. TELT is owned half-and-half by the French state and the Italian national railway company FS (Ferrovie dello Stato). The new company will be responsible for the construction and operation of the 65 km cross-border leg of the railway.

On 23 February 2015 the two heads of state signed a protocol confirming the realisation of the project, and handing the responsibility for its completion to TELT (Transalpine, 2015b). The protocol is due to be ratified by the parliaments of the two countries.

The project also receives significant financial support from the EU. The Lyon–Turin connection is part of the Algeciras–Budapest 'corridor' of the TEN-T central network approved by the European Commission. This connection could absorb a part of the current road transit from the Iberian Peninsula through France and Italy to the countries of Eastern Europe. The EU would contribute 40 per cent of the EUR 8.6 billion total cost of the cross-border tunnel. The agreement concluded on 30 January 2012 in Rome concerning the construction of the cross-border tunnel foresees the following distribution of burden: the EU – 40 per cent (EUR 3.44 billion); Italy – 35 per cent (EUR 2.935 billion); and France – 25 per cent (EUR 2.225 billion) (Transalpine, 2015a).

For the period from 2007 to 2013, the EU Commission allocated EUR 672 million (Premier Ministre, 2012) for background studies and for the first steps towards the construction of the base tunnel. However, the actual amount of the payments will depend on the ability of each of the two beneficiaries to respect their deadlines, as established in the application for co-financing as part of the TEN-T.

France and Italy submitted to the EU Commission, on 26 February 2015, a financing application in response to a call for projects within the "Connecting Europe Facility". The European Innovation Networks Agency (INEA), responsible for managing and evaluating transport infrastructure projects in the EU, suggested that the EU would allocate EUR 814 million for the construction of the first project section, with an estimated total cost of EUR 1981 billion (Transalpine, 2015a). Presumably, Italy has already included its own contribution in the state budget, whereas the French contribution still awaits the approval of Parliament.

Two members of the French parliament, Michel Destot and Michel Bouvard, have called for the introduction of an 'ecotax' levied on all heavy goods vehicles circulating on the Alpine motorways (Destot and Bouvard, 2015). This tax would bring in EUR 40 million per year – not enough to cover the loans that TELT could obtain from the European Investment Bank (EIB) or from the French Caisse des Dépôts et des Consignations. Funding from the state budget would therefore be needed (*ibid.*).

The deputy-mayor of the city of Chambéry, Louis Besson, has become somewhat of an emblem of local political support for the project. Besson has always defended the view that the project would be the best means of ensuring that a high-speed rail connection would indeed be constructed between Lyon-Saint-Exupéry airport and Chambéry. The local politicians focus their attention on job opportunities, local revenue distribution, and reduction of the harmful impacts of road transport. A transport users' association, la Fédération Nationale des Associations d'Usagers de Transport (FNAUT), is likewise in favour of the project.

Compared with this broad mobilisation of resources and actors in favour of the project, the opponents appear weak. Key critics include Yves Crozet, a renowned economist and member of the Board of Directors of RFF, as well as a handful of Green Party regional council candidates and elected officials (Olivier Cabanel, Pierre Mériaux and Daniel Ibanez) and at the EU Parliament (Michèle Rivasi). In April 2016, soon after taking office, the new green–left municipal council of the City of Grenoble declared its opposition to the project. The French Court of Auditors has raised doubts concerning the financing and economic profitability of the project (e.g. Cour des Comptes, 2012a). Some local environmental groups have joined forces with the local residents that would be directly affected by the construction work.

Apart from a few citizens living near the future construction site, none of the actors has a sufficient economic interest to defend that would spur them to protest. On the French side, as is typical with megaprojects in general, the high cost of the project would be shouldered by all French taxpayers, who are obviously not organised with a view to contesting the project. The opposition against the project is dispersed, devoid of a supportive network, and lacking in legitimacy. Nevertheless, the ability of this fragile and fragmented ensemble of critics to deconstruct virtually every argument presented in favour of the Lyon–Turin project has given rise to a highly mediatised opposition. Recent media appearances of this opposition include the coverage of the project in a TV programme "Pièces à conviction",[4] an article in the professional rail industry journal "Le Rail" (Dulez and Gélarond, 2015), as well as numerous texts published in the social media.

The opponents also use legal recourse in order to stop the project. In December 2014, Michèle Rivasi, together with Karima Delli, her party colleague at the EU Parliament, appealed to the European anti-fraud office (OLAF), highlighting in particular the alleged links of the two Italian companies involved in the project with the Mafia (e.g. Barbière, 2015; Gradt, 2015). To further back up their claim, they also pointed out the inexplicably high costs of computer equipment on the Italian side. On the French side, the claimants argued that the president of the Lyon Turin Ferroviaire company had a conflict of interest in the project. OLAF examined the claims put forward by Delli and Rivasi, but in the end rejected them as unfounded.[5]

In March 2014, a coalition composed of national and regional nature protection associations (France Nature Environnement and the Fédération Rhône-Alpes de protection de la nature – Frapna), municipalities, and hundreds of individual citizens brought a legal challenge against the decree of 23 August 2013, which granted to the project a 'Public Utility Declaration' and highlighted the urgent need to start construction (e.g. Collet, 2014). On 9 November the Council of State rejected the challenge, concluding that the organisation of a public consultation ('public debate') would not be required by law, because the main contours of the project had been decided upon in 1994, a year before the creation of the National Commission of Public Debate (CNDP),[6] and because the project had not significantly changed since then (Conseil d'Etat, 2015).

The Council of State also deemed that the planned project was in the general interest, because it would allow the development of transalpine rail freight transport between France and Italy, while at the same time enabling faster passenger transport, improved safety and reduced pollution. The Council furthermore noted that neither the potential harmful impacts on privacy and on the environment nor the high economic cost would put the project at odds with the general interest – in particular when taking into account the measures already undertaken to minimise these impacts.

Uncertainties concerning traffic growth forecasts

Most of the debate and controversy over the project concern the predictions for future rail freight volumes. Only growth in rail freight transport would justify the doubling of the existing capacity. Two hypotheses underpin the predictions of increasing rail freight: the growth in the transport of goods – on both road and rail – and the increasing share of rail freight in the total transport of goods.

When the first plans for Lyon–Turin were prepared a quarter of a century ago, goods transport between France and Italy was expanding rapidly on both rail and road. This traffic grew by 14 per cent between 1994 and 2004, and therefore seemed to justify the construction of new rail infrastructure that would encourage modal shift towards rail (Sutto, 2009). In 2001, estimations foresaw a quadrupling of traffic from 10 million tonnes to 40 million tonnes by 2025–2030. However, only a few years later these predictions were already subject to significant controversy (*ibid.*). In the following section, we shall examine in more detail how new facts have come to partly undermine these estimations, leading to increasing contestation.

The recent decline of goods transport through the Alps

The estimations invoked by RFF, LTF and the Transalpine in 2012 predict that goods transport in Europe will continue along the historically observed growth trend. Indeed, the freight traffic forecast that RFF presented as part of the documentation it submitted to the public inquiry in 2012 (RFF, 2012) assumes that the total transport demand will continue to increase at the rate observed between 1987 (72 million tonnes) and 2004 (144 million tonnes). Even in its most pessimistic scenario, RFF anticipates a significant increase of total transport volume from 217 million tonnes in 2020 to 296 million tonnes in 2035.

However, in 2014, new statistics (CE and OFT, 2015) showed that the total goods transport through the Alps reached only 141 million tonnes in 2012, in other words, less than the 150.8 million tonnes in 2005. The rapid growth of goods transport observed in the 1990s had indeed begun to slow down at around the turn of the century, well before the economic crisis of 2008. Also, the French share of goods transport through the Alps had been in decline since 2000, and the amount of freight passing through the French Alps had also begun to diminish. From 49.7 million tonnes in 2000, its total volume had fallen to 40.3 million tonnes in 2012, and further to 39.8 million tonnes in 2013. According to a study conducted in preparation for the Public Utility Declaration of 2012 (RFF, 2012), the transport volumes in tonnes of freight in the Northern Alps (Mont Blanc/Fréjus for road and Modane for rail) had been in decline since 1994. The volume decreased by 18 per cent between 1994 and 2007 (from 26.5 million to 21.7 million tonnes per year). Measured in tonnes transported, the traffic in 2007 equalled its 1990 level in Mont Blanc and Fréjus, but the number of heavy goods vehicles had declined slightly from 1.56 million in 1994 to 1.46 million in 2007. The annual reports of the Société Française du Tunnel Routier du Fréjus (2014) confirm these trends: in the seven years between 2007 and 2014, the number of heavy goods vehicles passing through the Fréjus tunnel each year decreased by 24 per cent, from 876,000 to 666,000.

In the light of these figures, the doubling of the transport volumes through the Alpine region in thirty years (from 2005 to 2035) therefore seems highly unlikely. In Western Europe, a decoupling of the volume of goods transport (road and railway) from the growth of GDP seems to have started (e.g. Raynard and Vielliard, 2014: 8), whereas the positive correlation between the two still persists in Eastern Europe (Reverdy, 2016). The difference can be explained by the fact that industrial activities in Western Europe are already sufficiently integrated or are being delocalised outside of Europe – thereby increasing the share of maritime transport between Asia and Europe – whereas the Eastern European economies are still in the process of being integrated with those of the West (Reverdy, 2016).

The decline of rail freight

The advocates of the project (Destot and Bouvard, 2015) explain the diminishing share of rail on the present transalpine route by operational difficulties such as lack of reliability and timeliness, degradation of the quality of the infrastructure, and the obstruction caused by construction works (modernisation, and adjustment to the European GB1 standard gauge) realised between 2002 and 2011. Once these improvements had been completed, the capacity of the connection was estimated at 14 million freight tonnes per year (RFF, 2012). The operation of the line faces a number of particularly severe constraints, such as the steep slopes, a single-tube tunnel, and the general unpredictability associated with the operation of a mountain railway line. The project advocates also argue that the stagnation of traffic volumes has been partly provoked by the economic crisis of 2008–2009.

However, the modal shift to the detriment of rail follows the trend observed in France over the past two decades, and cannot therefore be explained by the 2008 crisis. The share of goods transported by rail fell from 15 per cent in 2000 to 10 per cent in 2012 (Eurogroup Consulting, 2012). The decline of the share of freight rail in Europe (especially in France and in southern Europe) is partly a result of changed production and consumption patterns. The spatial and temporal fragmentation of goods transport and the rapidly growing traffic penalise rail freight, whose competitive advantage lies in concentrated traffic flows – the ability to transport large volumes of goods on a single journey.

The most important European traffic flows are channelled through the transport axes that lead from the large ports in the north of Europe towards the south and the east. The massive transport volumes from ports such as Antwerp and Rotterdam account for a significant proportion (almost 50 per cent of the traffic flows) of transit and international rail transport in Germany, whereas in France they represent a far lower proportion of rail traffic flows. The relatively high modal share of rail in Austria and Switzerland (36 per cent and 39 per cent, respectively) is explained primarily by the transit flows between the ports of northern Europe and Italy (CE and OFT, 2016).

The hypothesis of accelerating modal shift

In its documentation submitted to an enquiry in 2012, RFF predicts that 45 per cent of the goods transport passing through the Northern Alps would be carried by rail (RFF, 2012). The plans presented by the enterprise in charge of the project since February 2015 assume an even higher modal share of 55 per cent for rail through the French–Italian part of the Northern Alps (Destot and Bouvard, 2015). The supporters of the project take the 65 per cent modal share of rail in Switzerland as an example, to defend their argument that through determined action, France could reach as high as an 80 per cent share of rail in freight transport. The critics retort that the modal share of rail in France has been in constant decline throughout the past fifteen years: this share decreased from approximately 20 per cent in 1999 to 9.3 per cent in 2013, but remained constant in Austria (32 per cent) and Switzerland (68 per cent). In response to this criticism, and to help France catch up with the Swiss and the Austrians, the defenders of the project suggest implementing a 'rolling motorway' (transport of heavy goods vehicles by train) (Destot and Bouvard, 2015).

To better explain the difference between France and Switzerland, the critics of the project point to the estimates of traffic flows through the Swiss Alps, of which international transit constitutes 78 per cent (CE and OFT, 2015). The goods in transit consist primarily of containers originating from the ports in the North Sea or from the large industrial centres in Germany. By contrast, this type of transport makes up only 12 per cent of journeys through the French Alps (*ibid.*).

The hypothesis of redirecting the East–West traffic flows

The defenders of the project rely, in their estimations of the total volume of goods transport, on the rates used to calculate the total traffic flows passing through the French Alps from Mont Blanc to the Mediterranean, including the road traffic that currently passes through Ventimiglia. The volume of heavy goods vehicle traffic through Ventimiglia today reaches 17.7 million tonnes per year (Destot and Bouvard, 2015). The project defenders postulate that this traffic, as well as the flows passing through the tunnel of Fréjus, could be transferred to rail once the new tunnel comes into operation.

The critics of the project contest the credibility of such a hypothesis, pointing out that the Spanish transport operators are even less inclined than the French and the Italians to move freight to rail: the modal share of rail in Spain is only 4.6 per cent, compared to 15 per cent in France and 13 per cent in Italy (Eurogroup Consulting, 2012). Furthermore, maritime transport between Spanish and Italian ports could be further stepped up. The volume of freight passing each year through the two largest Spanish ports (Barcelona and Valencia) is 90 million tonnes, while Italy's largest ports (Genoa and Trieste) handle 94 million tonnes/year (Commission Européenne, 2013).

The Mediterranean East–West corridor that the European institutions wish to promote exists currently in the form of a railway tunnel. The capacity of this tunnel can be doubled by constructing a 'motorway of the sea' between Barcelona and Genoa – another project currently supported by the European TEN-T "West Med Corridors" initiative (EC, n.d.). Ports already represent 37 per cent of intra-European freight traffic and the concept of a 'motorway of the sea' foreseen in the TEN-T could rapidly increase the share of maritime traffic in European goods transport flows. Furthermore, Italy is already constructing a EUR 6 billion Genoa–Milan rail link, which would connect Genoa and the Mediterranean directly to the East–West corridor (Commission Européenne, 2013).

Hence, the critics argue that given the decline in traffic volume through the French Alps between 2000 and 2012, and in the absence of new factors that would reverse this decline, it is highly unlikely that the total volume of freight traffic would increase from its current level (22.2 million tonnes) on the roads between Mont Blanc and Fréjus and on the Montcenis railway. Taking as the basis the optimistic hypothesis of an increase of modal share of rail to 45 per cent, the goods volume would reach 10 million tonnes – well below the current capacity of the railway line, which the RFF (2012) estimates at 14.6 million tonnes. According to Bernard Reverdy (2016), an economist who produced the first counter-expertise on the issue in 1997 (Depagneux, 1997), even in the most optimistic scenario, the modal share captured by the planned new rail tunnel would not exceed the current capacity of the tunnel.

To refute these claims, Lyon–Turin Ferroviaire (LTF) responded by attempting to denigrate the predictions based on recent empirical observations, and by referring to long-term tendencies. On its website LTF affirms: "The predictions of future economic growth rely on recognised methodologies and on the official hypotheses adopted by the EU. Therefore, given that the infrastructures in question would have a lifetime of several hundreds of years, the predictions are extrapolated on the basis of long-term trends, and not merely on the basis of erratic observations from the past few years. The resulting prediction therefore foresees an increase rather than a stagnation of transport volumes" (LTF, n.d.). These expectations of long-term trends are based on the belief in an indefinitely increasing goods transport volume, whereas empirical observations instead suggest that the increase of goods transport is tapering off.

Economic expertise, counter-expertise and the problematic relationships between economics and politics

The French law requires that the Lyon–Turin project must be subjected to an analysis of its economic value for society. Article 14 of the domestic transport framework act (LOTI) from 1982 and the associated decree (1984) stipulate that the choice of infrastructure projects must be based on their economic efficiency and on an evaluation of their cost–benefit ratio. In addition, the laws on air quality and the rational use of energy – LAURE (1996) – and on regional planning and sustainable development (1999) require a monetary evaluation of the external costs, as part of the overall economic evaluation.

The project promoters indeed conducted an evaluation of the expected economic and environmental benefits of the project. A summary of the results was presented in the report produced in preparation for the public utility declaration (RFF, 2012). The economic evaluation presented in the documentation submitted to the public inquiry in 2012 treats the project as a single whole. The outcome of this analysis is highly dependent on predictions of transport growth – whose weaknesses and uncertainties we described in the preceding sections, and which have not been truly taken into account in decision-making. However, the proponents of Lyon–Turin have adopted a strategy of getting the project financed step by step and not as a single large project – in a manner similar to the Shoreham nuclear power plant, as described by Ross and Staw (1993).

Moreover, the evaluation gives the results in aggregate terms, making it difficult for the reader to fully grasp the underlying reasoning. The positive impacts for passenger and goods transport are grouped under a single heading – "users, including the quality of the service" – and are estimated at EUR 24.79 billion. Likewise, the different components of the economic revenue reaped by the rail operators are not distinguished from each other. This makes it impossible to judge whether the operational costs and revenues (excluding the depreciation of capital) are in equilibrium, for both passenger and freight services. It is worth keeping in mind that the project relies on the hypothesis of modal shift from road to rail, which in turn can only be achieved if the planned 'rolling motorway' indeed becomes operational. However, it is far from self-evident that a financial equilibrium could be achieved; for instance, two existing rolling motorways – the Luxemburg–Perpignan 'plateau' and the Aiton–Orbassano mountain line – have a negative operating cost–benefit ratio (Cour des Comptes, 2012b).

In an interview conducted as part of our research, a counsellor at the French Court of Auditors (Cour des Comptes) underscored the difficulty of assessing the costs objectively: "Since almost all consultancy firms in Europe have been involved in the studies concerning the Lyon–Turin project, it is very difficult to obtain neutral expertise on the subject. They all have an interest in the project going ahead as planned, because of the contracts they have signed with the project developers."[7] Neither the Court of Auditors nor the Ministry of Finance have the financial and technical means necessary for producing counter-expertise of the same level of detail as the expertise produced by the project proponents. The counsellor further explained the procedure adopted by the Court of Auditors: "In fact, we look at the coherence of the studies produced as part of the economic evaluation. Then we check whether there are obvious biases, whether costs are manifestly underestimated or the traffic volumes manifestly overestimated. We conduct approximations, in order to see whether all that appears as coherent. And we then check the estimations of the Ministry of Finance."

The confidentiality of the models and of the underlying data renders counter-expertise virtually impossible. The RFF justifies the confidentiality clause by referring to the strong competition between the rail operators, and argues that the modelling results are based on long experience and accumulation of data. In its October 2014 report on high-speed railways, the Court of Auditors repeated the message it had expressed ten years earlier in a report concerning the 'Mediterranean' high-speed railway project: "the concerns with regard to business secrecy are fully legitimate, yet they cannot be used to justify the gaps in the information provided to the state" (Cour des Comptes, 2014: 57).

The project opponents therefore demand that a new economic evaluation be carried out in order to take into account the changes in the context, in particular the evolution of transport volumes and the uncertainties involved in estimating future transport trends. They also call for proper counter-expertise, yet the obligation to carry out such analysis does not apply to Lyon–Turin, which obtained its Public Utility Declaration before December 2013, when a decree from the

General Commissariat for Investment (Commissariat Général à l'investissement, 2013) made counter-expertise mandatory.

The most contestable hypotheses underlying the economic profitability calculations of Lyon–Turin concern the expected modal shift and volume of goods transport. Yves Crozet, a university economist and member of the Board of Directors of RFF, explained in an interview conducted as part of our research: "The traffic volume estimates are completely distorted, they are totally false. We'll never have those transport volumes, we'll never have 40 million tonnes – a multiplication by eight from the present level. Even in the Channel Tunnel, we don't have them. Hence, to reach those levels of traffic, there would really have to be a miracle. So, there we go, they use completely distorted figures, and indeed, that way they arrive at a result that makes the project seem profitable." On the basis of the currently known freight supply, Crozet also estimates that if the infrastructure were constructed and brought into use, the line would operate at a loss.

Since it is hard to get an idea of the costs without conducting a full-fledged economic evaluation – which in turn is made difficult by the lack of access to data – the project's opponents have compared it to the Channel Tunnel. According to Yves Crozet, Lyon–Turin would cost twice as much to construct, but attract only a fifth of the amount of passengers. It is difficult to imagine that the volume of freight carried would exceed that of the Channel Tunnel, which connects urban and industrial centres far more significant than those along the Lyon–Turin connection.

For the project proponents, economic calculations have become a problem rather than a tool that would help them to argue their case. A representative of the contractor on the French side conceded to us in an interview: "One must be very careful with the hypotheses made at any given point in time". For him, "if the balance is positive, all the better, and if the balance is negative, it suggests there may be other, slightly different, ways of proceeding. (...) No-one has ever said that the truth lies in this book. It is an exercise in prediction, simulation – and has a value as such. And one should not try, at any point in time, to try and make it say other things than what it actually says." According to his view, a calculation primarily outlines a long-term trend and constitutes only one, amongst many elements in decision-making.

As we advanced with our interviews, we noticed that those in favour of the project placed strong emphasis on the uncertainty of the outcomes of the economic evaluation. Their discourse primarily seeks to discredit this instrument, and highlight instead political decision-making as the only possible means of managing uncertainty concerning the future. "Economic calculation is incomplete. It is at odds with the long-term challenges. And that is why Lyon–Turin is above all a political project. And if politicians perceive the project as such, it is because behind a project of this type there is the political choice of constructing Europe in the long run, a choice for the economy…"

The supporters of the project remind us that, for the public and for politicians, economic evaluation appears as a complex, obscure and technocratic method. In her doctoral thesis Lisa Sutto (2009) describes how this sentiment appears whenever economic calculations become a subject of public discussion: "In reality, the sporadic attempts to evoke economic calculations or their results have been perceived in a highly negative manner by the public, which sees in them above all as an opaque instrument, and quickly accuses them of playing into the hands of the technocracy. The primary conclusion from this point of view is that of an absence: economic calculations are rarely evoked in participatory procedures." Indeed, all of the local authority representatives that we consulted for this research expressed their lack of interest in this type of calculations as well as in the hypotheses underpinning them. In the words of one of these interviewees: "It's a brave man who seeks to explain them, because I myself tried to delve into them, but did not understand much. (…) It is not something that one can elaborate on as part of an argumentation, and I've never talked about the economic rate of return even to politicians, because that's not what will enable us to explain and justify Lyon–Turin."

In a way, the Lyon–Turin project has witnessed a reversal of the habitual roles of defenders and critics, since it is the former who most vehemently criticise economic evaluation. Those in favour of the project seek to simply ignore and set aside the economic evaluations, in the hope of avoiding the constraints that the results of these evaluations might impose upon them. Indeed, if economic analyses were based on more reliable foundations, they would narrow down the range of choice available to politicians.

These dynamics resonate with the work of Harold Mazoyer (2012), focused on the opposition and tensions between economists and politicians in the transport sector. In the interviews that Mazoyer conducted, engineer-economists sometimes described their relationships with professional politicians as eminently conflictual. Indeed, elected officials do not like economic studies, which tend to restrict their freedom to decide, whereas engineer-economists tend to adopt an attitude of loyalty towards politicians and declare their willingness to ultimately accept decisions made in the political sphere. According to Delphine Dulong (1997), "economics tends to neutralise politics by reducing it to a mere rational management technique."

Julien Dehornoy (2011) argues that the entire transport policy is marked by a tension between on one hand the ideal of objectivity, presumably incarnated by the economist, and on the other hand the inclination of the decision-makers to seek compromise. Dehornoy maintains that the results of economic calculations are accepted only when they lend support to those decisions that politicians wish to make – or have, de facto, made already. By contrast, when an economic calculation does not offer the expected results, it is either discredited or concealed.

The new argumentation of the project proponents: the base tunnel and the implementation of a heavy-vehicle charge designed to impose a modal shift

The defenders of Lyon–Turin have become the prime advocates of a policy designed to achieve a radical modal shift in goods transport through the Alps. They call for the implementation of a charge on heavy goods vehicles that pass through the Alps. Such a charge would finance the base tunnel and the policies needed to trigger a modal shift, while at the same time discouraging truck traffic.

The charge would have to be levied on all routes, including the one that goes via Ventimiglia, which currently has no tunnel. Indeed, increasing the road toll levied on vehicles that travel through the currently existing tunnels would shift truck traffic to the route through Ventimiglia, thereby aggravating congestion on the motorways and causing serious harmful environmental impacts in the cities along this route. To be equitable, the charge would therefore need to apply to all traffic, regardless of the route taken. The charge should not penalise local cross-border traffic. It should also be proportional to the distances covered, in order to incite long-haul carriers to choose rail.

According to the promoters of the project, the legitimacy of this charge primarily depends on the proposed alternatives – in other words, on the provision of rail transport services. Only by offering modern, efficient and high-quality rail services can the authorities justify this charge on heavy goods vehicle transit. The EU Eurovignette Directive would allow France to implement this type of charge, at a rate of about 15 per cent of the current motorway charge (Destot and Bouvard, 2015). As a result, the state would gain approximately EUR 40 million per year, which would cover about one fifth of the French share in the financing of the tunnel.

The argumentation of the defenders (Destot and Bouvard, 2015) of Lyon–Turin therefore increasingly consists of advocating the construction of the base tunnel alone, justified by a significant modal shift. The construction of a base tunnel and the implementation of a charge on heavy goods vehicles would allow phasing out the current subsidies to the existing 'rolling motorway'. At present, the cost to the public purse is estimated at EUR 10 million for each 1 million tonnes of goods transport transferred from road to rail. In the absence of a new tunnel, this subsidy would therefore continue to increase in proportion with the rate of modal shift towards rail, and could exceed the value of amortisation of the base tunnel. In other words, the project advocates maintain that by providing a considerably more modern and efficient alternative to the existing tunnel, the base tunnel would enable the elimination of the subsidies currently paid to finance the 'rolling motorway'. Moreover, the charge would make the modal shift more attractive to transport operators.

Critics disparage this scenario, which combines the base tunnel with modal shift and a charge on road transport. Some contend that it is not realistic to imagine a scenario that would foresee a significant modal shift, if the project would only entail the construction of the base tunnel. Indeed, modal shift is only possible for transport over long distances. However, a significant modal shift would further increase the already significant goods traffic (180 trains per day) on the rail section between Chambéry and Montmélian. The capacity of this leg could quickly reach its limits. In the absence of significant investments in other rail lines, modal shift therefore has only limited potential (Dulez and Gélarond, 2015).

In an interview conducted as part of this research, Yves Crozet contested the idea that infrastructure choices alone could radically redirect the transport flows.

Instead, he advocated modal shift through a 'rolling motorway' on the existing line, which has been modernised for precisely this purpose, and which in fact offers a quality of service equal to that provided by the Swiss tunnels. The modal shift could be financed via the charge on heavy goods vehicles.

Splitting the project between a base tunnel and a series of supplementary legs is largely motivated by the desire to obtain financing step by step. Local politicians, such as Michel Destot, defend the high-speed rail project not only as a means to reduce truck traffic in the Alpine valleys, but also and above all to improve the quality of rail transport between Lyon and Chambéry. This is the portion of the project which presents the greatest potential at the local level. After the completion of the base tunnel it would be more difficult to obtain support for the other sections, even though these would allow the utilisation of the base tunnel while at the same time improving the quality of passenger rail service to Chambéry.

Conclusions

The Lyon–Turin rail project constitutes a perfect example of "escalation of commitment" (Ross and Staw, 1993). The project faces a situation similar to that of the Shoreham nuclear power station. On the one hand, new critical evaluations of both economic costs and benefits foster learning, and thereby fuel criticism against the underlying justifications of the project, while on the other hand the stepwise investments in economic and political capital narrow the space for decision-making, lead to accumulating commitment and render the project increasingly irreversible.

The Shoreham and Lyon–Turin projects have two key common elements in common: the optimism bias among the project proponents, and the necessity for project proponents to appear coherent in their decisions. In the case of Lyon–Turin, the dynamics of escalating commitment rest on the systematically overestimated estimates of goods transport volumes, combined with the highly optimistic, politically established hypotheses concerning modal shift. These forecasts are considered credible because they appear congruent with the collective belief still shared by many politicians: that investing in new transport infrastructure is a primary means of fostering economic development, spurring economic activity and mobility in the region, and thereby contributing to economic revival. However, at least academic scholars increasingly call into question this dominant belief – especially its applicability in highly developed societies with mature and abundant infrastructure. Nothing proves, either, that goods transport will continue to increase apace with economic growth in the future. When giving oral evidence in Parliament on 14 October 2014, Yves Crozet[8] denounced what he called "infrastructure fetishism": obtaining an infrastructure project for one's own constituency area as the best way for a local politician to earn a place in the small and privileged group of those who have left a trace in history.

The defenders of the project prefer a strategy of stepwise investment, as a means of consolidating the project by making it increasingly irreversible over time. By obtaining an authorisation first for the base tunnel and then separately for each supplementary leg, they exercise a strategy whereby the costs of each individual sub-project would be compared with the expected benefits of the entire project. Ten per cent of the investments (our calculation) needed for the base tunnel have indeed already been committed. The project proponents, in turn, consider that the decision to construct the new connection has already been made, and see no reason to reopen the discussion.

However, today it appears clear that the base tunnel alone would not satisfy the established objectives (a modal shift), and that it should be complemented by new investments in the other sections of the railway line. Nevertheless, the new investments have yet to be financed: the cost for the French state will greatly exceed that of the base tunnel alone. The Court of Auditors has therefore noted that "the quality of the project management is not in phase with the financial stakes in question". The Court of Auditors Counsellor that we interviewed for this project explained that as decisions are successively avoided, the project is left to live its own life, and in fact becomes irreversible: "with this policy of small steps, after a while you end up saying that since we've already spent more than a billion euros, we might just as well continue." Moreover, the representatives of the project promoters highlighted in our interviews that the current level of financing (EUR 50–100 million per year) could easily be brought to a level of up to EUR 200 million per year, which would enable the project to be completed.

The case of Lyon–Turin has also demonstrated the complex and sometimes ambiguous role of economic expertise in megaproject planning, management and evaluation. Economists have been vital as 'whistleblowers' who expose the alleged flaws in economic calculations underpinning the decisions. This critique follows the logic of 'speaking truth to power', largely in line with Flyvbjerg's analysis of key problems in megaproject evaluation. On the other hand, economists – in particular those working within consultancy firms and other organisations participating in project planning and management – have contributed to the escalation of commitment. While privately critical of the economic calculations, these economists refrain from expressing their concerns, because of the strong vested interest they have in the project going ahead as planned.

The powerlessness of the state-level actors in general, and the Court of Auditors in particular, illustrates another argument put forward by Flyvbjerg (2009: 352–353): as compared to the state, the local-level actors enjoy the double benefit of better knowledge and greater interest in fighting for 'their' project. What further accentuates this asymmetry is that the bulk of the benefits accrue to a limited number of local and private actors, whereas the costs spread out over the entire population and over a long period of time. The local political actors in favour of the project have managed to build a powerful international coalition promoting the project, and obtained the crucial financial support from the European Commission. Hence, the controversies over Lyon–Turin are not only about a juxtaposition between the local and the national: as one of the few – if not the only – infrastructure project in France eligible for EU support, Lyon–Turin has to a certain extent become a question of national interest and prestige.

In terms of the role of expertise and the arguably necessary 'opening up' of procedures of evaluation (see Chapter 1 in this volume), the Lyon–Turin project underscores the difficulties of producing legitimate counter-expertise when knowledge-production is concentrated into few hands and when key actors have considerable vested interests to defend. The escalation of commitment continues, in the absence of actors with sufficient interest, skill and power to not only produce counter-expertise, but also to ensure that such expertise gets taken seriously in decision-making. A key dividing line goes between the powerful 'insiders', with strong interests built up throughout their long-term engagement in the project, and the 'newcomers', who are less constrained by previous decisions and hence might be more able and willing to produce counter-expertise, but who lack direct access to decision-making.

Finally, the politics around Lyon–Turin has illustrated the importance of the temporal dimensions and the associated uncertainties – omnipresent in megaproject planning, management and evaluation in general. The advocacy for the Lyon–Turin project greatly relies on the uncertain promise of long-term benefits that would presumably override the far more certain and easy-to-calculate short-term costs. Second, the relevance and power of evaluation largely depends on its timing in relation to the escalation of commitment. This, however, presents a dilemma. The earlier an evaluation is conducted, the less time there has been for the commitment to escalate, and hence the greater the chances that the evaluation will influence decisions. However, an evaluation conducted early in the process necessarily carries with it greater uncertainties concerning the long-term trends – uncertainties that can be used in order to downplay the the importance of evaluation results. As is the case with many other megaprojects, the Lyon–Turin experience illustrates the ultimate challenge of evaluation: in a constantly evolving policy context, what chances does an evaluation have of preventing premature closure and irreversibility that result from the escalation of commitment?

Notes

1   Interview with the Counsellor at the National Court of Auditors responsible for the preparation of the evaluation report.
2   Both countries have their own partnerships, *Comité pour la Transalpine* in France, and *Comitato Transpadana* in Italy.
3   La Commission Intergouvernementale franco-italienne (C.I.G.).
4   Available at www.youtube.com/watch?v=SM5BCal2qiE (accessed 20 July 2016).
5   Available at www.transalpine.com/breves/lyon-turin-rejet-plainte-fraude-loffice-lutte-antifraude-europeen-olaf (accessed 20 July 2016).
6   CNDP is an independent public organisation created in 1995, with a mandate to organise public debates and ensure public participation in infrastructure projects of national interest, which have significant socioeconomic or environmental impacts or implications for land use planning. The CNDP is a consultative body without decision-making power, and it does not give recommendations.
7   All citations from interviews and published French-language sources are translated by the authors.
8   Statement of Yves Crozet at Parliament, 14 October 2014, www.youtube.com/watch?v=bp7lsX488jI (accessed 18 May 2016).

References

Barbière, C. 2015. EU launches fraud probe into Lyon–Turin rail link. *Euractiv*, 9 February 2015. Available online at: www.euractiv.com/section/transport/news/eu-launches-fraud-probe-into-lyon-turin-rail-link/ (accessed 8 May 2016).

CE & OFT. 2015. Observation et analyse des flux de transports de marchandises transalpins: Rapport annuel 2013. Commission européenne, DG MOVE & Office fédéral des transports (OFT). 24 March 2015. Available online at: http://ec.europa.eu/transport/modes/road/doc/2014-annual-report-covering-the-year-2013.pdf (accessed 8 May 2016).

CE & OFT. 2016. Observation et analyse des flux de transports de marchandises transalpins: Rapport annuel 2014. Commission européenne, DG MOVE & Office fédéral des transports (OFT). 29 January 2016.

Collet, P. 2014. Lyon–Turin: FNE et la Frapna déposent un recours contre la déclaration d'utilité publique. *ActuEnvironnement.com*, 13 March 2014. Available online at: www.actu-environnement.com/ae/news/tgv-lyon-turin-fne-frapna-recours-utilite-publique-21063.php4 (accessed 8 May 2016).

Commissariat Général à l'investissement. 2013. Décret n° 2013-1211 du 23 décembre 2013 relatif à la procédure d'évaluation des investissements publics en application de l'article 17 de la loi n° 2012-1558 du 31 décembre 2012 de programmation des finances publiques pour les années 2012 à 2017. Available online at: www.legifrance.gouv.fr/affichTexte.do?cidTexte=JORFTEXT000028379985&categorieLien=id (accessed 8 May 2016).

Commission Européenne. 2013. Ports maritimes européens à l'horizon 2030. Mémo 13/448. Available online at: http://europa.eu/rapid/press-release_MEMO-13-448_fr.htm (accessed 8 May 2016).

Conseil d'Etat. 2015. Décisions, le 9 novembre 2015, société France nature environnement et autres, M. G...et autres, commune de Chimilin et autres. Nos 375322, 375672, 375673. Available online at: www.conseil-etat.fr/Decisions-Avis-Publications/Decisions/Selection-des-decisions-faisant-l-objet-d-une-communication-particuliere/CE-9-novembre-2015-societe-France-nature-environnement-et-autres-M.-G-et-autres-commune-de-Chimilin-et-autres (accessed 8 May 2016).

Conseil municipal de Grenoble. 2016. Compte-rendu de la séance du Conseil municipal du lundi 18 avril 2016. Service de l'Assemblée, Bureau du conseil municipal, Grenoble. Available online at: www.grenoble.fr/416-les-comptes-rendus-des-conseils-municipaux.htm#par4215 (accessed 8 May 2016).

Cour des Comptes. 2012a. Référé sur le projet de liaison ferroviaire Lyon–Turin, soumis au premier ministre le 1er août 2012. Référé numéro 64174. Available online at: http://lyonturin.eu/documents/docs/courdescomptesRefereLyonTurin20121105.pdf (accessed 31 May 2016).

Cour des Comptes. 2012b. Les autoroutes ferroviaires en France: premiers enseignements et enjeux pour l'avenir, Rapport public annuel (pp. 360–404).

Cour des Comptes. 2014. La grande vitesse ferroviaire: un modèle porté au-delà de sa pertinence. Rapport public thématique de la Cour des Comptes. Available online at: www.ccomptes.fr/Publications/Publications/La-grande-vitesse-ferroviaire-un-modele-porte-au-dela-de-sa-pertinence (accessed 8 May 2016).

Dehornoy, J. 2011. La politique des transports suit-elle les recommandations des économistes? *Tracés. Revue de Sciences Humaines* 11, 199–211.

Depagneux, M.-A. 1997. TGV Lyon–Turin: 70 milliards, c'est trop cher. *Les Echos*, 1 December 1997. Available online at: www.lesechos.fr/01/12/1997/LesEchos/17533-

095-ECH_tgv-lyon-turin---70-milliards--c-est-trop-cher.htm#4D6KVCeugfyY4EEQ .99 (accessed 20 July 2016).

Destot, M. & Bouvard, M. 2015. Liaison ferroviaire Lyon–Turin: Examen de nouvelles sources de financement pour les travaux de la section transfrontalière. Rapport au Premier ministre. Assemblée nationale & Sénat. Paris. 13 juillet 2015. Available online at: www.actu-environnement.com/media/pdf/news-25009-rapport-financement-tunnel-lyon-turin-eurovignette.pdf (accessed 20 July 2016).

Dulez, R. & Gélarond, D. 2015. Lyon–Turin: arrêtez la gabegie financière! *Le Rail* 221–222, 26–30.

Dulong, D. 1997. *Moderniser la politique. Aux origines de la Vᵉ République.* Paris: L'Harmattan.

EC. n.d. European Commission. *Infrastructure – TEN-T – Connecting Europe: Mediterranean Core Network Corridor.* Available online at: http://ec.europa.eu/transport/themes/infrastructure/ten-t-guidelines/corridors/med_en.htm (accessed 8 May 2016).

Eurogroup Consulting. 2012. Le fret ferroviaire, un mode d'avenir pour l'Europe? Regards croisés de chargeurs, opérateurs, commissionnaires, gestionnaires d'infrastructures et pouvoirs publics. The European rail freight days. Puteaux. Mars 2012. Available online at: www.eurogroupconsulting.fr/sites/eurogroupconsulting.fr/files/document_pdf/jeff_-_etude_situation_fret_ferroviaire_mars_2012_-_vfinale-ok.pdf (accessed 20 July 2016).

Flyvbjerg, B. 2009. Survival of the unfittest: Why the worst infrastructure gets built – and what we can do about it. *Oxford Review of Economic Policy* 25(3): 344–367.

Flyvbjerg, B. 2011. Over budget, over time, over and over again: managing major projects. In P.W.G. Morris, J.K. Pinto & J. Söderlund (eds), *The Oxford Handbook of Project Management.* Oxford: Oxford University Press, pp. 321–344.

Gradt, J.-M. 2015. L'Office anti-fraude européen va enquêter sur la LGV Lyon–Turin. *Les Echos*, 6 February 2015. Available online at: www.lesechos.fr/06/02/2015/lesechos.fr/0204139878465_l-office-anti-fraude-europeen-va-enqueter-sur-la-lgv-lyon-turin.htm (accessed 20 July 2016).

Journal Officiel. 2013a. Journal Officiel de la République Française. Décrets, arrêtés, circulaires. 25 août 2013. Texte 12 sur 58. Available online at: www.transalpine.com/sites/default/files/documents/decret_du_23_08_2013_-_dup_lyon-turin.pdf (accessed 8 May 2016).

Journal Officiel. 2013b. Journal Officiel de la République Française. Lois. December 3, 2013. Texte 1 sur 103. Available online at: www.transalpine.com/sites/default/files/documents/publication__loi_approbation_lt_jo_03-12_2013.pdf (accessed 8 May 2016).

LTF. n.d. Lyon Turin Ferroviaire – LTF. En savoir plus sur le Lyon-Turin: La future liaison ferroviaire en questions clés. Available online at: www.ltf-sas.com//wp-content/uploads/d%C3%A9pliant-final-FR.pdf (accessed 8 May 2016).

Mazoyer, H. 2012. La construction du rôle d'ingénieur-économiste au ministère des Transports. Conseiller le politique, résister au comptable et discipliner le technicien (1958–1966). *Gouvernement et action publique* 4(4): 21–43. Available online at: www.cairn.info/revue-gouvernement-et-action-publique-2012-4-page-21.htm (accessed 20 July 2016). DOI: 10.3917/gap.124.0021.

Premier Ministre. 2012. Réponse au Référé Projet de liaison ferroviaire Lyon–Turin de la Cour des Comptes. 8 Octobre 2012. Available online at: www.ccomptes.fr/index.php/Publications/Publications/Le-projet-de-liaison-ferroviaire-Lyon-Turin (accessed 31 May 2016).

Raynard, C. & Vielliard, F. (sous la direction de Gressier, C.). 2014. *La politique européenne des transports: quatre enjeux pour la nouvelle mandature.* France Stratégie. Paris. December

2014. Available online at: www.strategie.gouv.fr/sites/strategie.gouv.fr/files/atoms/files/ rapport_politique_europeenne_des_transports_17122014.pdf (accessed 8 May 2016).

Reverdy, B. 2016. Lyon–Turin: L'inutilité du projet est à nouveau confirmée. Available online at: https://bernardreverdy.wordpress.com/2016/03/27/lyon-turin-linutilite-du-projet-est-a-nouveau-confirmee/ (accessed 20 July 2016).

RFF. 2012. Enquête préalable à la Déclaration d'Utilité Publique pour la création d'une nouvelle liaison ferroviaire entre Grenay (Isère) et Saint-Jean-de-Maurienne (Savoie) dans le cadre du projet Lyon–Turin (itinéraires d'accès au tunnel franco-italien).

Ross, J. & Staw, B.M. 1993. Organizational escalation and exit: Lessons from the Shoreham nuclear power plant. *The Academy of Management Journal* 36(4): 701–732.

Société Française du Tunnel Routier du Fréjus. 2004/2013. Annual reports. Available online at: www.sftrf.fr/doc/general/rapportannuelsftrf2013.pdf www.sftrf.fr/doc/general/ rapport%20annuel%20SFTRF%202004-2005.pdf (accessed 20 July 2016).

Société Française du Tunnel Routier du Fréjus. 2014. Annual report. Available online at: www.sftrf.fr/doc/general/rapportannuelsftrf2014.pdf (accessed 20 July 2016).

Sutto, L. 2009. Rôle de l'expertise économique dans l'élaboration des politiques alpines de transport et du projet Lyon–Turin: vers l'émergence d'un espace alpin? Doctoral thesis, Economics and Management. Université Lumière – Lyon II & Politecnico di Milano.

Transalpine. 2015a. Les données-clés de la section transfrontalière et de son financement – fiche de synthèse – 2 octobre 2015. Available online at: www.transalpine.com/sites/ default/files/document2015/synthese_rapp_bouvard_destot_donnees_cle_ financement_lt_octobre2015_1.pdf (accessed 20 July 2016).

Transalpine. 2015b. Communiqué de presse: Constitution du nouveau promoteur en charge de la section transfrontalière de la liaison Lyon–Turin. Available online at: www. transalpine.com/sites/default/files/documents/cp_nouveau_promoteur_lyon_ turin_23_02_2015.pdf (accessed 20 July 2016).

Van Marrewijk, A., Clegg, S.R., Pitsis, T.S. & Veenswijk, M. 2008. Managing public-private megaprojects: Paradoxes, complexity, and project design. *International Journal of Project Management* 26(6): 591–600.

5 The Finnish success story in the governance of a megaproject

The (minimal) role of socioeconomic evaluation in the final disposal of spent nuclear fuel

Markku Lehtonen, Matti Kojo and Tapio Litmanen

Introduction

The history of the management of radioactive waste and spent nuclear fuel (SNF)[1] goes back to the beginning of the development of civilian and military nuclear power programmes in the 1940s (Jacob, 1990; Berkhout, 1991; de la Bruheze, 1992; Shrader-Frechette, 1993). Finland and Sweden are today the countries with the furthest advanced radioactive waste management programmes, and are often highlighted in international debate as 'success stories' – examples for other countries to follow. This chapter examines the disposal of SNF in Finland, focusing specifically on the role of socioeconomic evaluation in explaining the relatively rapid and smooth advancement of the project.

In the 1970s Finland was implementing its nuclear power programme (the country's four currently operating reactors were constructed between 1971 and 1980), but research on nuclear waste management was at that time practically non-existent in the country (e.g. Nikula et al., 2012: 76–84). The country's nuclear waste policy relied on the idea of international nuclear fuel cycle management, at the time essentially operated and controlled by the USA and the Soviet Union. However, changes in context (e.g. the hostility of the Carter administration in the US towards reprocessing and the collapse of the Soviet Union) and the high cost of reprocessing spurred Finland to change policy. The premises were anything but good, because a small country with few resources and limited expertise in nuclear technology had to start almost from point zero (e.g. Jåfs, 2009; Särkikoski, 2011; Nikula et al., 2012).

This is in stark contrast with today's situation, when the nuclear waste company, Posiva, has become an internationally distinguished player in its field. The Finnish programme of SNF management got a 'flying start' as the country benefited from determined technology transfer in the 1970s and 1980s, when the power company Teollisuuden Voima (TVO) began developing a company-specific policy of technology transfer in the area of nuclear waste management.[2] This was supported by an R&D policy approach emphasising pragmatism, flexibility and cost-awareness. Both the company and the Finnish authorities considered that a country with a small nuclear power programme needed to be adaptive. Gradually, TVO established national and international networks with organisations in other countries, especially with the Swedish SKB. In the mid-1980s Finland adopted the Swedish KBS-3[3] method, which has remained the reference concept for the Finnish waste management policy ever since.[4]

The successful realisation of this highly complex nuclear waste disposal project requires constant evaluation of not only its technical feasibility, but also of its various socioeconomic dimensions. In this chapter we shall focus on the role of socioeconomic evaluation in the governance of a project strongly dominated by technical, engineering and safety-related considerations. We define socioeconomic evaluation as composed of the two dimensions described in Chapter 1 of this book, denoting the evaluation of the socioeconomic impacts but also a broader 'non-rationalistic' approach to evaluation. Moreover, in this chapter we adopt a broad definition of evaluation, encompassing socioeconomic 'studies' conducted or commissioned by Posiva, as well as social science research on radioactive waste management. The chapter draws on extensive empirical and theoretical research by the authors over the years concerning the Finnish disposal project (e.g. Kojo and Oksa, 2014a; 2014b; Kojo, 2005; 2009; 2014; Kojo and Litmanen, 2009; Lehtonen, 2010a; 2010b; Litmanen, 2008; Litmanen and Kaunismaa, 1999). In addition to an analysis of the documentation produced by the nuclear industry, Posiva, Finnish Radiation and Nuclear Safety Authority (Säteilyturvakeskus – STUK), the ministry in charge of energy policy, and various research and citizen organisations, interviews addressing specifically the role of socioeconomic evaluation were conducted with representatives of these key actor groups in the period from 2012 to 2014.

We shall first present the nuclear waste disposal megaproject and briefly describe its evolution in the two subsequent sections. This is followed by an examination of the role of socioeconomic evaluation in three phases of the project: the initial phase leading towards site selection; the choice of the site – in particular the crucial environmental impact assessment process; and the period from site selection to the approval of the construction licence in 2015. We then analyse the ways in which key actors perceive socioeconomic concerns today. The concluding section focuses in particular on the role of socioeconomic evaluation in the governance of the Finnish SNF disposal project.

Disposal of spent nuclear fuel in Finland – a megaproject?

Finland's SNF disposal project qualifies as a megaproject on several counts. First, it has parallels in the history of science, in research projects that can be qualified as "Big Science" (e.g. Weinberg, 1961; Galison and Hevly, 1992; Lambright, 1998). The term was coined in the post-war era and denotes projects that are exceptionally large in terms of their budgets, personnel, and the size of the necessary equipment and laboratories. Second, with its estimated total cost of EUR 3.3 billion (Posiva, 2012a: Annex 13), the project exceeds the one-billion-dollar minimum limit usually set for a project to qualify as a megaproject. As with other high- and intermediate-level radioactive waste disposal projects, it also fulfils a number of other megaproject criteria, such as the very long timescales, complexity, dynamism, high political stakes, and lack of precedents. Radioactive waste management nevertheless differs from conventional megaprojects notably by its main objective and underlying rationale: solving a major societal problem – with safety as the overriding concern – rather than producing added value and prosperity for society.[5] Delivering the project on time and within budget are important performance criteria, but they are secondary and subordinated to safety as the primary objective.

Although the project certainly constitutes a major industrial undertaking in Finland, especially in socioeconomic terms, its character as a megaproject should be put into perspective.[6] When compared with the French radioactive disposal project – estimated to cost EUR 25 billion and generate up to 4,000 direct, indirect and induced jobs during its construction time until 2025, and up to 1,000 jobs during the operational phase of the facility (Andra, 2013: 85; SDIT, 2013) – the Finnish project is expected to generate socioeconomic impacts that are significant, but not of truly 'mega' scale. For instance, according to the socioeconomic impact studies commissioned by Posiva, even during the peak construction period the employment effects in the host municipality would not exceed about 220 new jobs in the labour catchment area of the host municipality, Eurajoki, which contains about 20,000 employed people in total (Posiva, 2008: 115–116). Today, the facility itself employs just over 100 persons (Posiva, 2015: 18). The timescales involved are substantial: planning has been under way for more than thirty years, the construction and operation period will span over a century, and the post-closure time involving potential radiation hazards ranges from tens of thousands to a million years (Posiva, 2012a: Annex 8, 22). Some in Finland therefore consider final disposal of SNF as an environmental protection project of several centuries, while others have seen it a Faustian pact throwing open the floodgates for the construction of more nuclear power (Malaska et al., 1989a: 49–59; Malaska et al., 1989a: 47–57; Malaska et al., 1989b; see also Malaska, 1991; Malaska and Kasanen, 1987).

History of SNF disposal planning in Finland: advancing towards implementation, with determination and perseverance

The decision adopted by the Council of State in 1983 is often evoked as the key starting point for the subsequent process of planning for SNF disposal in Finland. The decision outlined a timetable for stepwise decision-making, planning and research on the project. The government's timetable was based on the schedule presented by TVO (Raumolin, 1982: 5–7) for the final disposal of spent fuel (see Box 5.1).

However, by 1983 much had happened already. The four nuclear power plant (NPP) units currently in operation were built in the 1970s. In 1978 an amendment to the 1957 Atomic Energy Act made the licence holder of an NPP unit responsible for all measures and costs relating to nuclear waste management. Detailed stipulations concerning waste management were incorporated into the licences issued to NPP units (Posiva, 1999: 3).

Box 5.1 Timetable from 1982 for spent fuel final disposal by TVO

1980–1982 Suitability study with safety analyses
1983–1985 Preparation for the preliminary site characterisation
1986–1992 Preliminary site characterisation in five to ten selected sites
1993–2000 Additional siting studies (two to three sites)
2001–2010 Detailed studies of chosen disposal site and preplanning of the siting and the encapsulation plant
2011–2020 Planning and construction of the disposal site and the encapsulation plant
2021–2050 Final disposal facility is operational
2050–2060 Closure of the disposal site

At the time, the state-owned company Imatran Voima Ltd. (IVO) exported its waste to the Soviet Union, whereas the privately-owned TVO was searching for a management solution for its SNF. TVO was negotiating on a reprocessing contract with the British company British Nuclear Fuels and the French company COGEMA, but it abandoned reprocessing plans in the early 1980s for financial reasons. In 1990 reprocessing was reconsidered but rejected again, largely for economic and financial reasons (Posiva, 1999: 12–13).

The two companies had also collaborated, in particular within the Nuclear Waste Commission of Finnish Power Companies (Ydinjätetoimikunta, YJT), to coordinate their R&D activities. However, it took until 1995 before the utilities established a joint company, Posiva, for spent nuclear fuel management,[7] in reaction to the legislative change that put an end to nuclear waste exports to Russia.

Apart from Posiva and the two energy companies, key actors in the Finnish nuclear waste policy include the Ministry of Employment and the Economy (formerly the Ministry of Trade and Industry), responsible for overall policy development and monitoring, and STUK, subordinated to the Ministry of Social Affairs and Health.[8] Until the site selection, the candidate municipality can exercise significant influence through its right of veto over the proposal to construct a facility in its area, whereas Parliament ultimately approves the Decision-in-Principle. The VTT Technical Research Centre of Finland is the main research organisation in nuclear matters. In 2007 a new player, the Fennovoima consortium, entered the field, planning to construct a new nuclear power station in the north of the country. As Fennovoima is not a shareholder in Posiva, it has been negotiating with Posiva on the possibility of disposing of its SNF at Olkiluoto, but the negotiations have so far proven fruitless (Kojo and Oksa, 2014a).[9]

In the following, we shall present the changing role of socioeconomic evaluation at the various stages of the evolution of the project.

Socioeconomic evaluation of the project

We shall here divide the advancement of the project into three periods. The first precedes the final site selection, spanning the period from the DiP of 1983 to the mid-1990s, when Posiva started preparing in earnest for what it called the "EIA of the century" (e.g. Hokkanen, 2001; Rasilainen, 2002: 137), concerning the disposal facility in four candidate municipalities (Eurajoki, Kuhmo, Loviisa and Äänekoski). The second period represents the 'golden era' of socioeconomic evaluation, beginning with the preparatory studies for the EIA and ending in 2001 with parliamentary approval for siting the project at Eurajoki. This principled approval for the project marked the starting point for the third phase, which entailed preparatory work by Posiva, from 2001 onwards, for a construction licence application, which it submitted in 2012. The government approved the application in November 2015.[10] The licencing process is to culminate in the submission by Posiva of an application for an operation licence, scheduled for 2020.

The beginnings: 1980s to the mid-1990s

The idea behind Finland's SNF solution has its origins at the international level, yet it was from Sweden that Finland ended up 'importing' its waste disposal concept. In 1980, a working group established by the Ministry of Trade and Industry advocated heavy reliance on foreign research, especially on other than site-specific topics. To be a credible partner, Finland should also have something to offer, but as a small country with limited ability to influence international waste management policies, it would also have to be ready to adapt (Nuclear Waste Working Group, 1980).

During this period, evaluation of the project focused on technical and safety-related aspects, but the economic and financial dimension was also recognised (e.g. Raumolin, 1983; Suunnittelukeskus, 1987). Research and studies were conducted by VTT, at the request of TVO (Anttila et al., 1982; Peltonen et al., 1985; Vieno et al., 1992; Vieno and Nordman, 1996; 1999), which also initiated collaboration with consultants and research institutions, notably the Geological Survey of Finland (GTK), the Department of Radiochemistry at the University of Helsinki, and the Helsinki University of Technology. This partly government-funded research mainly aimed at satisfying the requirements relating to waste management stated in the operating license, and in this way at ensuring that TVO could continue operating its NPP (Kojo and Oksa, 2014b). TVO also sought information from abroad and participated in international research projects. In particular, the participation of TVO, IVO and the Ministry of Trade and Industry in the STRIPA (1977–1992) project – initially a Swedish–American bilateral effort, but from 1980 onwards coordinated by the OECD-NEA – was crucial for the development of know-how in Finland (Nikula et al., 2012: 85). In the end, the collaboration with the Swedes turned out to be the most fruitful, leading to the adoption of the Swedish KBS concept as the reference model.

Socioeconomic aspects were already gradually gaining importance during this period, partly because of legislative changes and partly as part of TVO's efforts to prepare for site selection (see e.g. Suunnittelukeskus, 1987). In 1987 the Nuclear Energy Act granted to the host municipality a veto right on the siting decision, and waste management financing arrangements independent of government budget and policies were established. Moreover, the authors of the history of TVO portray the company as a forerunner in "open communication" in Finland (Björklund et al., 1994: 184). According to these authors the company leadership had learned their lessons, notably as a result of a few problematic area acquisitions the company had undertaken in the preceding years, and therefore they demonstrated unprecedented openness in their communication strategy when preparing for the siting of the NPP in the early 1970s (*ibid.*). The first public hearings were organised in two candidate municipalities – Bromarv and Eurajoki (*ibid.*).

The first steps towards what could be called socioeconomic evaluation were taken as TVO gradually shifted its strategy, from one that would seek to identify the 'best' site towards a more 'pragmatic' approach (Kojo, 2005). As in several other countries at the time, strong local opposition in many of the candidate municipalities spurred the industry to change strategy and adopt a more dialogical and participatory approach in their search for a site (e.g. Sundqvist, 2002; Kojo 2009; 2014).

TVO's initially declared ambition was to survey the entire country, and progressively exclude areas geologically unsuitable for hosting the facility (McEwen and Äikäs, 2000: 33). To support this work, the company commissioned studies from the GTK and the consultancy company Saanio & Laine. However, socioeconomic aspects emerged on the agenda when TVO ranked the investigation areas in an order of preference: selection criteria included not only geology, but also population density, transportation conditions and land ownership (McEwen and Äikäs 2000: 43–46). Hence, out of the 102 rock blocks that TVO presented in 1985 as suitable for future investigations, all but one were the "result of the systematic selection and elimination process" (Vieno et al., 1992: 22). As it appears, the 102nd was Olkiluoto in Eurajoki, a choice motivated primarily by the possibility of minimising waste transport, thereby reducing both risks and costs. TVO approached the sixty-six municipalities it considered potentially suitable, to get an idea of the general acceptance and willingness in these municipalities to volunteer. In 1987, TVO began preliminary site characterisation work in five municipalities. By the end of 1992, only three were still in the race: Eurajoki, as a 'nuclear community' expected to be favourable to the project; Kuhmo, a sparsely populated and relatively poor municipality in the northeast of the country; and Äänekoski, an industrial town undergoing a transformation due to the decline of its hitherto dominant pulp and paper industry.

Kojo (2005) has described the phases in the evolution of TVO's strategy: at the initial stage, during 1984–1986, the company did not consult municipal authorities prior to the choice of candidate sites, whereas the years 1986–1987 were precisely characterised by negotiations with municipal authorities. During 1987–1992 TVO concentrated primarily on one-way communication to remedy what it perceived as a knowledge deficit among the local inhabitants.

Throughout these early years, a limited amount of socioeconomic evaluation was conducted on issues such as transport connections, the service capability of the locality and the cost of the excavation work (Kojo, 2014: 171–172). These evaluations guided the choice of the candidate municipalities for detailed site investigations (*ibid.*). The ministry had not yet included social sciences in its nuclear waste management R&D programmes. Very little academic social science research was carried out on nuclear waste policy in Finland until the early 1990s (Kojo, 2014: 58).

1994–2001: The 'EIA of the century' and the golden era of socioeconomic evaluation

In 1994, two legislative decisions fundamentally moved the goalposts of Finnish nuclear waste policy. First, an amendment to the Nuclear Energy Act in 1987 banned any import or export of nuclear waste as of 1996, which meant that IVO could no longer export its waste to Russia, since nuclear waste produced in Finland must "be handled, stored and permanently disposed of in Finland" (Nuclear Energy Act 990/1987). Second, the Environmental Impact Assessment (EIA) procedure became a mandatory phase in the decision-making process. TVO and IVO hence felt compelled to establish a joint company, Posiva, to develop an SNF disposal method. This also meant that the disposal plans and R&D activities would need to accommodate the fuel from the Loviisa NPP, which was of a slightly different nature than the TVO waste. The capacity needed for the disposal facility was estimated at about 2,600 tU (Kojo and Oksa, 2014b).

The newly-established Posiva embarked on preparations for an ambitious EIA, a two-year participatory process designed to examine not only environmental but also socioeconomic aspects of the project. At the same time the site selection process evolved, Loviisa – the host to two of IVO's NPP units – was added to the list of candidate municipalities in 1997. In its search for a site, Posiva had by this time already shifted the focus to Eurajoki and Loviisa, largely because it believed that social acceptance would be the highest in these already 'nuclearised' municipalities.[11]

In 1999 Posiva submitted its application for a Decision-in-Principle (DiP), suggesting Eurajoki as the only candidate with Loviisa as the fallback option. A DiP is to determine whether the project in question is in line with the overall good of society, as defined in the Nuclear Energy Act. Eurajoki had indeed given its approval to the project on the condition that other municipalities would be already excluded from the 'race' at this stage of decision-making (Kojo, 2009). The choice of Eurajoki was confirmed in a succession of decisions, beginning in December 2000 when the Council of State adopted the DiP, followed by a favourable vote in the Eurajoki municipal council in January 2001, and finally culminating in the approval of the DiP by Parliament in May 2001. It is noteworthy that, unlike in many other countries, in Finland the licencing of a repository and an underground bedrock research facility were merged into a single process. Indeed, several statements made during the parliamentary debates on the DiP in 2001 reduced the issue to a mere decision on a 'research licence', whereas especially after the adoption of the DiP, the approval was portrayed as a green light for a disposal facility (Raittila and Suominen, 2002; Lammi, 2009). In practice, the merging of the two processes meant that the excavation of the repository got under way as soon as the construction of the research laboratory began in 2004.

Socioeconomic evaluation: studies commissioned by Posiva and social science research funded by public sector research programmes

Technical and safety-related research has throughout the years constituted the overwhelming majority of the research on SNF disposal (e.g. Rasilainen, 2002; Vuori, 2014: 11–36; MEE, 2011; MEE, 2012; MEE, 2015a). However, during this second period, socioeconomic evaluation attracted far more attention, both in the activities of Posiva, in public sector research programmes, and in Posiva's decision-making, than during the preceding and subsequent periods. Hence, the share of social sciences in the public sector research programme reached 20 per cent during the period 1997–2001 – an order of magnitude greater than the 2–3 per cent in the period 2011–2014 (Rasilainen, 2002: 121, 258; MEE, 2015a: 9).[12]

Posiva had conducted socioeconomic studies in the 1980s, years before the EIA process, on a limited number of themes, focusing notably on the evolution of the socioeconomic conditions and public opinion in the candidate municipalities. However, the bulk of the socioeconomic studies were conducted in 1997–1999, as part of the mandatory EIA process. Crucially, the EIA process is designed as the main opportunity for public participation and analysis of the socioeconomic impacts in project planning and decision-making. However, the conclusions of the EIA are not binding, and have no direct bearing on the licencing decisions.

Legal obligations were not the only reason why Posiva decided to embark on a highly ambitious and participatory EIA process. The company also wanted to avoid the kind of problems encountered in other countries. Experience from the 1980s and opinion surveys had revealed that the issue was controversial and prone to conflicts at the local level. The municipal veto further reinforced the need for dialogue especially with local authorities and politicians.

As part of the EIA process, Posiva commissioned socioeconomic impact studies in the four candidate municipalities. In order to maximise the credibility of these studies, it called upon academics and consultants who would appear to be as independent as possible in relation to the company and to the nuclear industry. This effort mobilised dozens of researchers and experts – exceptional in a country of just over five million inhabitants, although obviously modest compared to the investment in technical and engineering research in the area. The socioeconomic impact studies were, according to Posiva, conducted with an equal degree of attention to detail in all four municipalities, although the application for a Decision-in-Principle only mentioned Eurajoki as a potential host municipality.[13]

The studies financed by Posiva focused on the impacts on employement and demography, municipal economy, the image of the municipality, the local opinions concerning the disposal project, and the psychosocial effects from the possible installation of a disposal site (Posiva, 1999). The analyses demonstrated that the employment impacts – and therefore also many other socioeconomic impacts (concerning e.g. demography, health, environment, and transport) – would be modest. This not only provided Posiva with 'scientific evidence' that was useful in its efforts to reduce public concerns about potential harmful impacts, but also enabled the company to tone down the most unrealistic expectations concerning the benefits from the project.[14] For example, the interest of Kuhmo in hosting a disposal facility declined further once the studies showed how the benefits from increased tax revenues would be largely outweighed by a corresponding loss of state subsidies, as the municipality would become wealthier.

The expected impacts on the image of the host municipality generated plenty of debate, and provided the municipal leaders with useful information for their decision-making. The image studies further reinforced Posiva's resolve to focus on Eurajoki, where the negative image impact would be modest. The surveys suggested that Finns in fact had a very vague knowledge of the municipality of Eurajoki, and did not easily associate the well-known Olkiluoto 'nuclear island' with its 'mother municipality' (Kankaanpää et al., 1999). Having until the early 1990s been opposed to the disposal project, the municipality now strived to base its socioeconomic development upon the nuclear industry, and thereby fully assumed its image as a 'nuclear community'. In Loviisa opinions were more divided, partly as a result of the past memories concerning the arrival of nuclear power in the 1970s and 1980s, when the balance between the Swedish- and Finnish-speakers shifted in favour of the latter and the population became divided between the Finnish-speaking 'incomers' who were in favour of nuclear energy and the predominantly Swedish-speaking original population who were against it (e.g. Rosenberg, 1999). The situation was further aggravated by the fact that the construction of the two nuclear reactors in the 1970s led to a steep increase in house prices, followed by an equally abrupt fall and an economic stagnation once the reactors were completed and the workers had gone (Ridell and Raak, 1997).[15]

In turn, Kuhmo wished to attract prospective new tourists and residents by developing its image as a destination 'close to nature' – an image that would be difficult to reconcile with a nuclear waste disposal site. Finally, Äänekoski found the project unattractive because hosting a waste disposal facility would compromise its attempts to get rid of its image as an industrial town – one of the most well-known pulp paper cities in the country. However, at least some in Posiva felt that, precisely thanks to this industrial past, the municipal leaders and local population in Äänekoski would be more positive towards the disposal project than in Kuhmo.

During the second half of the 1990s the authorities responsible for nuclear waste policy were concerned about the possibility that Posiva would become the only actor commissioning social science research on nuclear waste management (Litmanen, 2008: 436; Rasilainen, 2002: 14). A multi-stakeholder steering group on social science research, chaired by the Ministry of Trade and Industry, was therefore established to decide upon research priorities and manage R&D programmes in the area. The group also included representatives of STUK, TEKES (the Finnish Funding Agency for Innovation), Posiva, as well as the two nuclear power companies TVO and Fortum. The programmes were managed and for the most part financed by the MTI, with STUK as the second-most important contributor (Rasilainen, 2002: 258).

Outcomes of the socioeconomic research and studies

Plenty of social science research and studies were commissioned and financed by the government and by Posiva.[16] The research themes closely followed the evolution of the Finnish nuclear waste policy. In the early 1990s research focused on the controversies over nuclear waste management, and was conducted primarily by researchers at the University of Jyväskylä, while from 1995 onwards the preparation of the EIA process attracted most of the attention (Nurmi et al., 2012). One line of research sought to provide a theoretical basis for EIA and draw lessons from other countries, whereas other streams focused on monitoring the EIA process itself and on evaluating its quality. Projects not directly related to the EIA process analysed the socioeconomic and political characteristics of the candidate municipalities, the media coverage of nuclear waste disposal, and the role of the media in this policy.

The NGOs were not integrated in the management of the research programmes, but the ministry provided, outside of the programme, a limited amount of funding to NGOs. In April 1999, as the EIA process approached its conclusion, the MTI granted to NGOs a modest sum of EUR 34,600. More than 80 per cent of this funding went to one single organisation – the Finnish Association for Nature Conservation – more than ten times more than the sums granted to any single local citizens' group (Kojo, 2005).

The central role of the MTI in Finnish nuclear waste policy has provoked criticism, especially concerning the independence of the research. The ministry prepares and frames the research programme, commissions the research, and potentially uses the results (Sandberg, 1999: 236; Litmanen, 2008: 440). Perhaps most importantly, the EIA process had a very modest impact on public debate and political decision-making (e.g. Hokkanen and Kojo, 2003; Hokkanen, 2007; Strauss, 2010). Indeed, crucial decisions concerning the compensations from Posiva and TVO to Eurajoki were made behind closed doors between the companies and the local politicians (Kojo, 2009).

From principles to construction – and the return of the technical (2001–2015)

Once Posiva had completed the extensive EIA process and obtained the crucial political approval and local acceptance for the disposal project, it no longer felt any particular need to analyse the socioeconomic aspects associated with nuclear waste management. Technical and safety-related issues regained their absolute dominance in the minds of both Posiva and authorities, given that safety and technical implementation would be crucial for the acquisition of a construction licence, the second of the three steps in the licencing process. In October 2003, the Ministry of Trade and Industry stipulated that by the end of 2009 Posiva should submit an interim report on the advancement of the project, while the final construction licence application should be submitted by the end of 2012. In December 2012 Posiva duly submitted the application. Following a statement by STUK on the safety review and assessment the government granted the licence in November 2015. The licence covers a maximum of 6,500 tonnes of uranium, i.e. the SNF produced by five NPP units – two in Loviisa and three in Olkiluoto (STUK, 2015; MEE, 2015b).[17] Posiva plans to submit the operation licence application in 2020.[18]

Socioeconomic evaluation: monitoring and updating of the existing information

As most of the socioeconomic studies have been conducted in the context of the EIA process, the work during the past ten to fifteen years has primarily consisted of updating the existing information, in keeping with the EIA legislation. As the developer, Posiva is obliged to prepare monitoring programmes, submitted to the Ministry of Employment and the Economy for verification. The ministry also approves Posiva's annual reports that contain the results from the actual monitoring. To fulfil these duties, Posiva commissioned studies from consultants on topics such as the impact of the facility on local and regional economy, employment, the image of the municipality, as well as attitudes and trust among local people and TVO's employees towards the facility and towards Posiva (e.g. Posiva, 2008). However, the scope and ambition of the analysis were considerably more modest than in the EIA conducted for the DiP process in 1998. Slightly more precise estimates of socioeconomic impacts (e.g. employment impacts estimated at a maximum of 45 person-years in Eurajoki and 220 person-years in the catchment area) were provided, and the updated information allowed a comparison of attitudes with those that had prevailed fifteen years earlier.

The declining priority given to monitoring can be seen by comparing the various reports published by Posiva over the years. In its EIA report of 1999 the company had outlined possible monitoring activities, which would be "limited mainly to the potential impact of repository development on the surface environment" (Posiva, 2003b: 7). Following the comments by the ministry, in 2003 Posiva published a programme for monitoring the effects of the construction of the repository. Apart from monitoring the site characteristics and safety-related aspects, monitoring of "anthropogenic and social effects" was foreseen as part of environmental impact monitoring (*ibid.*: 4, 69). As topics to be addressed, the report specifically mentions changes in land ownership, settlement, land use, water supply, and food resources. Five years later, in the 2008 EIA report Posiva mentioned three socioeconomic issues as part of a tentative list of topics to be included in the monitoring programme: the image of Eurajoki, the occurrence of radiation fears, and socioeconomic impacts (Posiva, 2008: 164). Finally, in the updated programme for monitoring, covering the period 2012–2018 but also intended as a generic outline for monitoring during repository operation, socioeconomic issues were no longer mentioned.[19] Monitoring would focus "solely on technical and scientific measurements motivated by the long-term safety and environmental impact of the disposal facility" (Posiva, 2012c: 27).[20] Hence, issues such as following progress in nuclear waste disposal projects abroad or follow-up studies of public attitudes would not be included in monitoring, but would be "treated separately" (*ibid.*).

Interviews that we conducted confirmed the declining status of socioeconomic monitoring. Both the Posiva representatives and the officials at the ministry considered monitoring as something of a routine, without any significant bearing on decision-making. For the ministry, the priority is to ensure that Posiva has the necessary technical human and other resources for adequate implementation and safety monitoring of the project.

Monitoring of public opinion concerning nuclear issues has a long tradition in Finland, and will certainly be carried forward to the future. **At the national level**, the attitudes of Finns towards Posiva's project have become clearly more positive over the years (Kari et al., 2010). In the early 1980s there was significant mistrust towards the final disposal model: in 1983–1988 some 60 per cent of respondents disagreed with the statement that final disposal in the Finnish bedrock was safe. Since the mid-1980s the share of these negative views has declined steadily although slowly, while the proportion of those expressing trust in the disposal concept has seen a corresponding increase. It is noteworthy that those with a negative attitude still dominate: in 2015, 44 per cent of those polled disagreed with the statement "It is safe to dispose of nuclear waste in the Finnish bedrock", whereas 34 per cent agreed (Finnish Energy Industry, 2015).

Local opinion surveys have, throughout all of the stages of the project described above, constituted one of the main topics of socioeconomic evaluation, and a key theme of interest for Posiva (e.g. Yli-Kauhaluoma and Hänninen, 2014). These surveys revealed a slight degradation of the company's image among local residents during the first years following the 2001 Decision-in-Principle. A Posiva representative interviewed for this research attributed this decline to the disappointment among the local citizens concerning the true socioeconomic benefits from the project. According to this line of reasoning, the strong visibility of Posiva during the EIA process had generated unrealistic expectations concerning the short-term benefits of the project. Nevertheless, the 2008 EIA report states that the majority of citizens considered Posiva to be a trustworthy and competent actor (Posiva, 2008). In a study carried out by Kari et al. (2010: 41) among citizens in Eurajoki municipality, trust in Posiva as a reliable source of information on nuclear matters was equally divided between 'trustful' and 'untrustful' (32 per cent each), while 37 per cent had no opinion.

Social science research in preparation for the DiP and the construction licence

Social science research in this period can be divided into three phases, with the following key research themes (Nurmi et al., 2012; MEE, 2014; MEE, 2015a):

1 2000–2004:
    - media reporting on the decision-making processes, including the role of the EIA in decision-making

2   2005–2010:
  •   research focused on Eurajoki, including analysis of the socioeconomic
       aspects and impacts of the disposal facility on the image of the municipality
  •   broader issues concerning democracy and knowledge
3   2012–2016[21]
  •   socio-technical aspects, nuclear waste issues in the national print media,
       comparisons with Sweden.

An amendment to the Nuclear Energy Act in 2004 strengthened the security of
the financing within the public sector research programmes by obliging the nuclear
energy companies to pay an annual charge corresponding to 0.08 per cent of their
estimated liabilities. In 2012, this funding reached EUR 1.7–1.9 million, of which
only 0.04 per cent was designated to social science research. Interestingly, the
2014 public research programme nevertheless outlined three general orientations
for R&D, giving the false impression that the three were roughly equal in terms of
funding: 1) new technologies and alternatives for nuclear waste management; 2)
safety; and 3) sociological research (MEE, 2010: 17).

   A novelty in this most recent, and ongoing, period has been the integration of
two new social science topic areas into the research programme: ethical aspects
and the specific challenges relating to the long-term nature of waste disposal. Most
of the social science research is conducted by independent academics, to a large
extent also within European research projects. In this advanced stage of the
disposal project, the role of social science research in its governance is uncertain.
Technical and safety-related research seems to have further strengthened its
dominance – a tendency observed already in the immediate post-DiP phase.

Socioeconomic concerns today

Current key concerns relating to the disposal project, as expressed by the various
actor groups, focus mostly on safety and engineering challenges, yet the
socioeconomic aspects have not totally disappeared from the radar. Key actors and
stakeholders[22] in Finnish nuclear waste politics appear to be more concerned about
socioeconomic issues than the citizens participating in public hearings. Finnish
nuclear experts interviewed for a recent research project evoked challenges relating
to issues such as social acceptability, the generation and maintenance of know-how
over generations, the flexibility necessary to respond to emergent issues in the
future, the reliability of information (especially of the models and tests), the risk of
human intrusion into the disposal facility, and the need for political consensus and
stability in energy policy (Litmanen et al., 2012; Nurmi et al., 2012: 29–30).

   By contrast, the citizens participating in the public consultation processes in
2008 concerning the extension of the facility were mainly concerned about the
long-term safety of the facility. Some socioeconomic matters were mentioned,
notably the inextricable link between the policies on nuclear power[23] and nuclear
waste, and the information needs and citizen participation at the municipalities
(Nurmi et al., 2012: 18–19; see also Litmanen et al., 2012).[24]

While it is understandable that, once the siting decision was made, concerns relating to the image of the host municipality faded into the background – after all, it would be difficult to significantly influence the image of the host municipality – the virtually complete lack of concern for the cost and financing of the project seems surprising. The final disposal is estimated to cost EUR 3,305 million (2009 prices), spread over a period of more than a hundred years of operational lifetime of the repository.[25] The authorities and the nuclear industry have no doubts about the sufficiency of the funds collected in the face of the funding needs; for them, the risk that the taxpayer would have to foot the bill is practically non-existent.[26] The financing system obliges the nuclear industry (TVO and FHP) to set aside the necessary funds for the implementation of the project. Should the developer fail to complete the repository, this guarantee fund would ensure the financing. The fund should contain, at any point in time, the resources necessary for the completion of the project. Each time a phase in the construction of the disposal facility is completed, the fund returns the corresponding sum of money back to the industry. The fund would hence be exhausted when the project is completed. The Ministry of Employment and the Economy assesses, once a year, the sufficiency of the fund, and the National Audit Office conducts ad hoc analyses of the operation of the system. However, no regular and institutionalised system of external control and evaluation is in place.

Virtually the only criticism towards this financing system has come from a small number of social science researchers who have pointed out that decision-making surrounding the fund depends heavily on information provided by the nuclear industry (Auffermann et al., 2015). They have further criticised the procedure that allows a company to borrow back, at a highly favourable interest rate, up to two-thirds of the money it has deposited to the fund, provided that it sets aside a corresponding amount as a guarantee, which is independent of the industry (*ibid.*). As a matter of comparison, in Sweden the funding system has been under close scrutiny for some years, and even the National Council for Nuclear Waste has expressed concerns about the sufficiency of the country's nuclear waste fund, in case nuclear plants are closed down ahead of schedule due to declining profitability (Kärnavfallsrådet, 2016; Reuters, 2016).

One might therefore conclude that our interviewees and the general public do not perceive the disposal project as a true megaproject – or that they are unaware of the potential megaproject 'pathologies'. The latter explanation seems unlikely, especially in view of the recent problems concerning other megaprojects in Finland, including the delays and cost overruns in the construction of the EPR (European Pressurised Reactor) NPP unit at Olkiluoto. The Swedish concerns over the sufficiency of funding do not seem irrelevant for Finland either, as the problems with the Olkiluoto 3 EPR unit probably contributed to a recent fall in TVO's credit rating (TVO, 2016), after having led the company to abandon its plans to build a fourth reactor at Olkiluoto (TVO, 2015).

Another possible explanation for the lack of interest could be that Finns have taken particularly seriously the specificity of the SNF disposal project as an atypical megaproject, whose justification rests on the need to solve a societal problem, rather than on the added benefits it promises to generate for society. Under such conditions, cost indeed does not matter in the same way as it does with typical megaprojects.

Conclusions: the role of socioeconomic evaluation in the 'Finnish model' of governance

In this chapter we have defined evaluation broadly, to include *ex ante* assessment and *ex post* policy evaluation, but also socioeconomic studies and social science research concerning the disposal project. Indeed, the Finnish SNF project has not been subjected to policy evaluation in the proper sense of the term (for a definition, see e.g. Vedung, 1997). Between 1990 and 2010 almost 120 social science articles, reports or books were published on nuclear waste management (Litmanen and Kaunismaa, 1999; Litmanen, 2008; Nurmi et al., 2012). This volume of research of course pales in comparison to the extensive literature in the natural sciences and technology, but nevertheless serves to illustrate the scientific activity generated by the project.

The reasons for the heightened interest in social sciences by key actors in Finnish nuclear waste policy since the 1990s relate to both legislative–institutional factors and the need to build and maintain public support – especially at the local level – for the planned disposal project (Litmanen, 2008: 446). Social science research was expected to help manage public opinion in general, and opposition and criticism in particular, whereas the new EIA Act and the municipal right of veto introduced slightly more democracy into the planning of the project.

Weak direct impacts of socioeconomic evaluation on decision-making

Unsurprisingly, technical and safety-related evaluation occupies a privileged position both in public debate and in the public concerns relating to nuclear waste management in Finland. Especially at the national level, socioeconomic evaluation, most of which was conducted in support of the EIA process 1997–1999, played a very minor role in decision-making. Not only did the socioeconomic aspects receive little attention in the parliamentary debate preceding the 2001 DiP, but – despite its long duration and high degree of ambition – the entire EIA process had a minimal impact on the final decisions concerning the project (Hokkanen and Kojo, 2003; Hokkanen, 2007). Reasons included the confusion generated by the overlapping of the EIA and DiP application processes, the fact that the application presented only one waste management option in detail, and particularly the agreement negotiated behind closed doors between Posiva and the host municipality concerning a nearly EUR 7 million compensation package to Eurajoki (Hokkanen, 2001: 37). The main contribution of the EIA and the socioeconomic evaluations was to improve the general knowledge basis for decision-making (*ibid.*: 38–39).

At the **local level**, the studies of socioeconomic impacts received more attention. Since other possible socioeconomic effects were estimated to be modest, the debates preceding the site selection concentrated on the potential impacts of the disposal facility on the image of the municipality. The image studies reinforced the existing views and attitudes in the municipalities, and further consolidated Posiva's perception of Eurajoki as the only viable candidate.

Posiva as the main user of socioeconomic evaluation

Indeed, Posiva seems to have been the main user of socioeconomic evaluation. As explained by a company representative interviewed for this project, Posiva used these studies to better communicate and justify its project, by grounding its arguments in research perceived as independent, reliable and 'scientific'. They helped Posiva to manage local opinion, build acceptance for the project, obtain a more accurate idea of local opinion and atmosphere in the candidate municipalities, predict possible local reactions, and identify means of maximising the local socioeconomic benefits while minimising the harmful impacts. With 'scientific evidence' at hand, the company could demonstrate the likely socioeconomic benefits of the project to the host community, refute the claims concerning the possible negative impacts, and address the 'fears' that the studies had revealed. Posiva's EIA process also operated as a 'safety valve', allowing the citizens to express their views, even though these views might not affect the final decision.

The socioeconomic studies helped to persuade Posiva that it was best to concentrate their efforts on the already 'nuclearised' communities – Eurajoki and Loviisa – where citizens were already familiar with nuclear power and enjoyed the socioeconomic benefits of this industry. Siting a disposal facility in these relatively wealthy communities would present only modest socioeconomic challenges, in contrast with megaprojects situated in remote and less prosperous areas. Questions of justice and (regional) equity would not have the same acuteness as in 'peripheralised' communities (Blowers and Leroy, 1994) – of which the French, German and British radioactive waste disposal projects provide typical examples (Blowers, 2016). The studies helped Posiva to discover the divisions among the local population and local politicians in Loviisa on nuclear issues in general, and waste disposal in particular.[27] They also helped to bring more realism to expectations about the local socioeconomic benefits, and thus refocused the public and political debate on safety-related questions – a topic on which Posiva certainly felt itself more competent than the somewhat unpredictable socioeconomic issues.

With Eurajoki as its only negotiating partner, the company could focus on two lines of action: continued general public communication, and informal closed-door negotiations with one single municipality (Kojo, 2005: 94). Opponents in Loviisa criticised Posiva for using the image studies as yet another justification for the project; a disposal facility could at least not further deteriorate the prevailing image of Loviisa as a 'nuclear community' (Rosenberg, 1999).

In terms of the conventional functions of policy evaluation (e.g. Valovirta, 2002; Lehtonen, 2005), these socioeconomic studies allowed Posiva to *learn* how to better communicate about its project (e.g. Rosenberg, 1999), as well as to *improve and develop* its activities – by strengthening the viability and legitimacy of the project in the eyes of the local populations and elected officials. To the extent that the municipalities could influence the framing of the studies commissioned by Posiva and by the public sector research programmes, the studies also helped the local politicians to formulate their positions and to better target their communication efforts. The ultimate function of the studies was, however, *political*: the studies allowed Posiva to **legitimise** and **justify** the project, defend itself against criticism, and **persuade** the authorities that Eurajoki indeed was the best – and *de facto* the only feasible – siting alternative.

Finland as an example? Independence and credibility or passivity and credulity?

The smooth progress of the Finnish final disposal project has attracted considerable curiosity and admiration abroad, as a potentially risky megaproject which has nevertheless been exceptionally well received by local populations. We do not suggest that socioeconomic evaluation would explain this success – rather, our analysis reveals potential 'success factors' relating to the Finnish governance style. The defenders of the project like to stress the scientific and technological rigour supposedly characterising the project implementation, including continuous monitoring and evaluation by the authorities of the technical and safety performance of the project. Critics concentrate their arguments on the alleged vested interests behind the project, including the firm commitment by the state, the trade unions and the business at large (especially the forest industry) to supporting nuclear energy (Kojo and Litmanen, 2009; Litmanen and Kojo, 2011). Even the critics seldom draw on socioeconomic evaluation to back up their arguments.

Finland's success is often described as a manifestation of the 'Nordic model' of final disposal of SNF. Indeed, close technical collaboration between the Swedish and Finnish waste management companies around the shared KBS-3 technology has been established over the years. However, the term 'Nordic model' would appear inappropriate in the socioeconomic area. In particular, civil society organisations play a very different role in the regulation and governance of the projects in these two respective countries (Litmanen et al., forthcoming). In contrast with the close collaboration in engineering-related R&D and technology transfer, Posiva and SKB have little cooperation in the area of socioeconomic evaluation and social science research. As possible reasons, the Posiva representative interviewed for this research suggested language barriers (few Finnish speakers are comfortable speaking Swedish – the second official language of the country), and the diversity of socioeconomic conditions in different contexts. The differences in the conceptions and institutions of democracy in Finland and Sweden[28] may partly explain why transfer of knowledge has been less visible and frequent in socioeconomic evaluation than in the technical areas.

The great emphasis placed by both Posiva and the government on the independence and credibility of socioeconomic evaluation raises the question of the stark concentration of power into the hands of a few key actors in the Finnish nuclear sector. More surprising than this concentration as such is that it seems to remain largely uncontested. For both Posiva and the government, it was crucial that the public and the stakeholders would perceive the socioeconomic studies as competent and totally independent of the nuclear industry. Posiva clearly perceived the need and lamented the lack of external criticism, pluralist expertise, and mechanisms enabling NGOs to carry out their own research and evaluations. It seems symptomatic of the high asymmetries of power in the Finnish nuclear waste policy that Posiva would perceive its hegemonic role as a potential threat to the legitimacy of the project.

The interviewed Finnish authorities and nuclear industry mouthpieces underlined the virtues of the 'Finnish model' of financing social science research and studies, arguing that this ensures true independence. Yet, the central role of the ministry responsible for energy policy – simultaneouly an advocate of the disposal project, a commissioner of social science research and studies, and the potential user of these studies – puts this claim into a different perspective. Decisions concerning both the independence of and priorities in the area of social science research are firmly in the hands of the ministry and the industry (Martell and Van Berendoncks, 2014). In the Finnish legal–administrative system, the developer has significant control over the framing and execution of the EIA procedure (Rosenberg, 1999; Hokkanen, 2007; Strauss, 2010). Critics have further argued that social scientists, in agreeing to conduct research on opinions in the candidate municipalities, in reality end up legitimising the project (Rosenberg, 1999). Finally, the representatives of the management of the publicly funded nuclear waste research programme wished to ensure that the social science research conducted would be of 'the right kind' and 'useful' – an attitude that chimes poorly with the ambition of 'opening up' and reflexivity (Litmanen, 2008: 441–443).

The fact that no separate underground research laboratory was constructed in Finland but the licencing of the laboratory and the disposal site were merged into one process also reflects the 'policy style' in the Finnish nuclear waste governance, and perhaps Finnish governance more broadly. How did the power companies manage to avoid the potentially costly and time-consuming extra step of constructing a separate research laboratory? Again, tentative explanations can be suggested: the lobbying power of companies, pragmatism of the authorities, high trust and confidence among decision-makers and citizens in Finnish experts and industry, and the relative weakness of a critical civil society in the country (e.g. Litmanen, 2009; Lehtonen, 2010a; 2010b).

The future of socioeconomic evaluation

Once the political approval for the project had been obtained in 2001, the interest in socioeconomic evaluation declined sharply, since the project proponents no longer needed to compare siting alternatives and demonstrate the socioeconomic benefits of the facility in the prospective candidate communities. Today, a key question concerns the role of the monitoring of socioeconomic impacts: what should be monitored, why, and by whom? Posiva will certainly continue to monitor local opinions and attitudes towards the company and the facility, as required by the EIA legislation, but the fate of broader monitoring of socioeconomic trends, beyond the minimum legal requirements, is uncertain. Who indeed would have both the interest in and the needed resources for conducting such monitoring? It seems symptomatic that Posiva (2012c: 27) has made the explicit choice of focusing only on the strictly technical and safety-related issues in its monitoring plans, while socioeconomic issues such as public attitudes and international progress in the area would be held separately from the monitoring programme. In a small country, the pool of independent and sufficiently competent evaluators is limited. Eurajoki municipality has limited resources, and may not have an interest in conducting any socioeconomic evaluation and monitoring of a project that is in the municipality 'to stay'. The number of academic researchers working in the area is small and their role in public debate on nuclear power is limited, whereas the country in general lacks a tradition of 'counter-expertise'. The strong trust in authorities and 'official' sources of knowledge on matters related to nuclear power may further reduce demand for socioeconomic evaluation and monitoring. There does not seem to be outright resistance and reluctance towards evaluation, but there is no strong demand for alternative perspectives either (e.g. Kojo, 2014: 104). The profound lack of interest in the financing of the disposal project further consolidates the image of a population highly trustful of its civil service and expert community.

A final question relates to the nature of the Finnish SNF project as a megaproject – whether the project fulfils the criteria of a megaproject, and whether it is perceived as such by the population. Posiva has described the socioeconomic impacts of the project as modest. It admits the pervasive uncertainties typical to megaprojects, but seems to have made little attempt to use socioeconomic evaluation to help it deal with such uncertainties. As for its governance arrangements, the SNF management project also differs from similar megaprojects (e.g. the French radioactive waste disposal project) in that the roles and responsibilities of different actors are – at least in principle – clearly defined, the number of key actors involved is limited, local and regional authorities play virtually no role in the governance of the project, and the challenge of dealing with waste from military nuclear installations is absent in Finland. One secret of the Finnish 'success' may therefore lie in the combination of exceptionally strong trust among Finns in their official institutions and experts, and in the ability of the government and the industry to avoid the project from taking up true 'mega' dimensions.

Notes

1   In this chapter we use the terms 'spent nuclear fuel' and 'nuclear waste' interchangeably, given that unlike in countries that have opted for reprocessing of spent fuel, in Finland SNF is considered as waste.
2   The other of the two Finnish companies currently operating nuclear power plants, the state-owned IVO, had a waste export agreement with the Soviet Union, and therefore felt no pressing need to develop its skills and capacities in waste management.

3   The Swedish nuclear industry's waste management organisation, SKB, had been developing its own KBS-method since the late 1970s (Sundqvist, 2002). The KBS-3 concept entails placing spent fuel in isolating copper canisters with a high-strength cast iron insert. The canisters are then surrounded by bentonite clay, and placed in individual deposition holes at approximately 500 m depth in granitic bedrock.

4   Especially at the beginning, the Swedish partners were somewhat concerned about the imbalanced relation, as Finns could simply draw on the benefits of work done by their western neighbours. Over time, the relationship grew more balanced as the Finns gradually built up their skills and capacities.

5   Obviously the Finnish disposal project brings vital benefits for the nuclear industry and creates jobs and prosperity in the host community, yet these are ancillary benefits that alone would not suffice to justify the implementation of the project.

6   The 'mega' character of the project can also be measured in terms of its capacity in tonnes of waste to be deposited. The planned capacity of the Finnish project has varied over the years. In 1999 Posiva applied for a licence for a capacity of 9,000 tU, but subsequently decreased the capacity to 4,000 tU in November 2,000 in order to exclude the waste to be produced by the new NPP units that the owners of Posiva were planning. The disposal capacity of 4,000 tU corresponds to the amount of SNF produced by the four operational NPP units during their sixty-year lifetime, because some politicians did not wish to send a positive signal for nuclear new builds by approving in advance the disposal of SNF from the planned new NPP units (Nurmi et al., 2009: 14–15). In terms of the volume of packaged waste, the Finnish project, with its 60,000 m^3 of total waste (Auffermann et al., 2015: 235) represents just under one-sixth of the French disposal project, whose planned total capacity is estimated at 380,000 m^3 (Andra, 2013: 15).

7   In February 2008, TVO argued on economic grounds as it rejected the vision of reprocessing as a part of Finnish nuclear waste management in coming decades (Satakunnan Kansa, 20 February 2008). However, Jukka Laaksonen, the then director general of Radiation and Nuclear Safety Authority, STUK, argued in a newspaper interview that SNF disposal would not be a sustainable solution, and predicted the return of reprocessing, for environmental and economic reasons (Loviisan Sanomat, 15 February 2008; Satakunnan Kansa, 23 April 2010). Thus the possible revival of nuclear power programmes in Europe and elsewhere, and rising uranium prices, might pose new challenges for Finnish nuclear waste policy in the form of a global nuclear fuel cycle (see Kojo, 2009: 167–168).

8   The department for monitoring nuclear waste and materials at STUK employs 31 people, of whom 17 are assigned to nuclear waste management.

9   In June 2016 Fennovoima signed an agreement with Posiva Solutions, a subsidiary of Posiva, on providing expertise on final disposal of SNF. However, Posiva and Fennovoima have not agreed on a joint final disposal at Olkiluoto.

10   www.tem.fi/ajankohtaista/tiedotteet/tiedotearkisto/vuosi_2015?119950_m=119283 (accessed 6 May 2016).

11   Interview with a Posiva offical, 12 August 2013.

12   During 2011–2014, the share of social science research was 1.7–2.6 per cent of the just under EUR 7 million total budget of the government-run nuclear waste research programme (MEE, 2015a: 9). This can be compared, for example, with R&D funding in Sweden: the budget of the Swedish SKB's social science research programme (2004–2010) alone was SEK 23 million (Berner et al., 2011: 12), i.e. about EUR 2.5 million.

13   The Ministry of Trade and Industry approved Posiva's approach to examine only one main option – which goes against the fundamental EIA principle of comparison between alternatives – on the grounds that in view of the complexity and difficult nature of the question, it would be in vain to keep in the 'race' municipalities in which the project would be likely to generate conflict and resistance (interview with a STUK official, 15 August 2013).

14   Observations in this paragraph all come from an interview with a Posiva official on 12 August 2013.
15   Most of the observations in this paragraph come from an interview with a Posiva official on 12 August 2013.
16   By 1999, a total of forty-five studies and social science research projects had been financed, either by Posiva or by the publicly funded research programmes. Posiva had commissioned studies from seventeen organisations, including universities and other establishments of higher education, research centres, consultants, and local employer organisations. Research funded by the state-run research programmes, in turn, were conducted by researchers at the VTT Technical Research Centre, the universities of Tampere and Jyväskylä, and one private consultant (Litmanen and Kaunismaa, 1999: 167–169).
17   In 2008 Posiva submitted an application for a DiP for an extension to the repository for SNF produced by the Olkiluoto 4 NPP unit. The favourable DiP given in 2010 to a fourth unit in Olkiluoto led Posiva to increase the disposal capacity of the repository to 9,000 tU. In 2015, the government rejected TVO's application to extend the 2010 DiP for Olkiluoto 4 beyond the legally stipulated five-year period, which meant that the application to extend the disposal capacity also lost its relevance.
18   Posiva website, available online at: www.posiva.fi/en/final_disposal/general_time_schedule_for_final_disposal#.Vu_mL01f1jo (accessed 22 May 2016).
19   The updated monitoring programme was divided into five sub-programmes as follows: 1) Rock mechanics, 2) Hydrology and hydrogeology, 3) Geochemistry, 4) Foreign materials, and 5) Environmental monitoring.
20   Posiva (2012c: 27) defined monitoring as follows: "*Continuous or periodic observations and measurements of engineering, environmental or radiological parameters, to help evaluate the behavior of components of the repository system, or the impacts of the repository and its operation on the environment, and to help in making decisions on the implementation of successive phases of the disposal concept.*"
21   In 2011 the publicly funded research programme did not finance social science research.
22   The interviewees were from the Radiation and Nuclear Safety Authority, the Ministry of Employment and the Economy, Posiva, Fennovoima, Greenpeace, and the Ministry of the Environment (Nurmi et al., 2012).
23   A decision to build new nuclear power plant not only increases the need for waste disposal capacity, but the specific reactor technology also has a qualitative impact on the disposal method. Another connection between energy and waste policies – the government's decision, in 2002, to approve nuclear new-build – was greatly facilitated by the approval to the repository given in 2001, which entailed the perception that the 'waste problem' was now 'solved'.
24   These research findings were based on an analysis of the twenty-one statements submitted on the extension of the final disposal facility. These statements were selected amongst a larger sample, because they touched on interesting socio-technical challenges (Nurmi et al., 2012).
25   The calculation is based on the assumption that the repository would receive waste produced by the four existing Finnish NPPs (two units in both Loviisa and Olkiluoto) and Olkiluoto 3 (still under construction) during their expected lifetimes, amounting to a total of 5,550 tU. The estimated construction costs amount to EUR 700 million, while the running costs would reach EUR 2,405 million, and the closing of the final disposal space EUR 200 million (Posiva, 2012a: Annex 13, 3). These costs include research work, administration, taxes and monitoring by officials (*ibid.*).
26   In fact, it would be more accurate to say that the system seeks to avoid making the consumer pay twice, given that the project would be financed – in line with the polluter-pays principle – by the electricity producers, who would then add the cost to the price of the electricity.
27   Interview with a Posiva official, 1 June 2009.

28 For instance, relying on results from the World Values Study (Pettersson and Nurmela, 2007: 22–26), Swedes place greater value on a democratic leadership and administrative style than Finns, who also show less resistance against undemocratic governance options.

References

Andra. 2013. *Projet cigéo – Centre industriel de stockage reversible profound de déchets radioactifs en Meuse/Haute-Marne.* Le dossier do maître d'ouvrage. Déebat public du 15 mai au 15 octobre 2013.

Anttila, M., Halonen, O., Holopainen, P., Korhonen, R., Kätkä, M., Meling, K., Noro, H., Peltonen, E., Rasilainen, K., Savolainen, I. & Vuori, S. 1982. *Safety analysis of disposal of spent nuclear fuel.* Helsinki, Nuclear Waste Commission of Finnish Power Companies, Report YJT-82-41.

Auffermann, B., Suomela, P., Kaivo-Oja, J., Vehmas, J. & Luukkanen, J. 2015. A final solution for a big challenge: The governance of nuclear waste disposal in Finland. In A. Brunnengräber, M.R. Di Nucci, A.M. Isidoro Losada, L. Mez & M.A. Schreurs (eds.), *Governance of nuclear waste management: An international comparison.* Wiesbaden: Springer, pp. 227–247.

Berkhout, F. 1991. *Radioactive waste: Politics and technology.* London: Routledge.

Berner, B., Drottz Sjöberg, B.-M. & Holm, E. 2011. *Social Science Research 2004–2010. Themes, results and reflections,* SKB. Available online at: www.skb.se/upload/publications/pdf/socialscienceresearch2004_2010webb.pdf (accessed 9 May 2016).

Björklund, N.G., Westerholm, W. & von Bonsdorff, M. 1994. Ydinsähköä. Teollisuuden Voima Oy 1969–1994. Helsinki: Teollisuuden Voima Oy.

Blowers, A. 2016 (forthcoming). *The legacy of nuclear power.* London: Routledge.

Blowers, A. & Leroy, P. 1994. Power, politics and environmental inequality: A theoretical and empirical analysis of the process of 'peripheralisation'. *Environmental Politics* 3(2): 197–228.

de la Bruheze, A.A.A. 1992. *Political construction of technology: Nuclear waste disposal in the United States, 1945–1972.* Delft: WMW-publikatie 10, Eburon Press.

Eurobarometer. 2008. *Attitudes towards radioactive waste.* Special Eurobarometer 297, Wave 69.1. TNS Opinion & Social. European Commission. Available online at: http://ec.europa.eu/public_opinion/archives/ebs/ebs_297_en.pdf (accessed 24 April 2013).

Finnish Energy Industry. 2015. *Finnish energy attitudes 2015.* Available online at: http://energia.fi/sites/default/files/energia_asenteet_2015.pdf (accessed 15 April 2016).

Flam, F. 1992. Europeans confident in the battle of the big machines. *Science* 256(5056): 466–467.

Flyvbjerg, B. 2005. Machiavellian megaprojects. *Antipode* 37(1): 18–22. DOI: 10.1111/j.066-4812.2005.00471.x.

Flyvbjerg, B., Bruzelius, N. & Rothengatter, W. 2003. *Megaprojects and risk: An anatomy of ambition.* Cambridge: Cambridge University Press.

Galison, P. & Hevly, B. (eds.). 1992. *Big Science. The growth of large-scale research.* Stanford: Stanford University Press.

Hämäläinen, K. 2010. Olkiluodon ja Loviisan voimalaitosten ydinjätehuollon tutkimus- ja kehitystyön sekä teknisen suunnittelun ohjelma 2010-2012. STUK:n esittelymuistio, 4.10.2010, diaarinumero 5/H48112/2009.

Hevly, B. 1992. Reflections on Big Science and Big History. In P. Galison & B. Hevly (eds), *Big Science. The growth of large-scale research.* Stanford, CA: Stanford University Press, pp. 355–363.

Hewlett, R.G. & Anderson, Jr., O.E. 1962. *Volume I: A History of The United States Atomic Energy Commission. The New World, 1939/1946*. Pennsylvania: Pennsylvania State University Press.

Hodge, G. & Greve, C. 2013. Public-private partnership in developing and governing mega-projects. In Priemus, H. & van Wee, B. (eds), *International handbook on mega-projects*. Cheltenham: Edward Elgar, pp. 182–208.

Hokkanen, P. 2001. EIA and decision making in search of each other. A case study: EIA of the final disposal nuclear waste in Finland. In T. Hilding-Rydevik (ed.), *EIA, Large development projects and decision-making in the Nordic countries*. Nordregio R2001:6, Stockholm: Nordregio, pp. 95–152.

Hokkanen, P. 2007. *Kansalaisosallistuminen ympäristövaikutusten arviointimenettelyssä*, Acta Electronica Universitatis Tamperensis: 683. Tampere: Tampere University Press.

Hokkanen, P. & Kojo, M. 2003. Ympäristövaikutusten arviointimenettelyn vaikutus päätöksentekoon, Suomen ympäristö 612, Ympäristöministeriö, Helsinki. Available online at: https://helda.helsinki.fi/bitstream/handle/10138/40473/SY_612.pdf?sequence =1 (accessed 6 May 2016).

Irwin, A. 1995. *Citizen Science: A study of people, expertise and sustainable development*. London: Routledge.

Jacob, G. 1990. *Site unseen: The politics of siting a nuclear waste repository*. Pittsburgh: University of Pittsburgh Press.

Jåfs, D. 2009. *Introduktionen av kärnkraften I Finland: en undersökning med focus speciellt på vår verkstadsindustris roll*. Åbo: Akademisk avhandling, Åbo Akademi University Press.

Kankaanpää, H., Haapavaara, L. & Lampinen, T. 1999. Tutkimus loppusijoituslaitoksen vaikutuksista kuntien imagoon. *Energiaosasto*, Kauppa- ja teollisuusministeriön tutkimuksia ja raportteja 1/1999, Kauppa- ja teollisuusministeriö, Helsinki.

Kari, M., Kojo, M. & Litmanen, T. 2010. *Community divided. Adaptation and aversion towards the spent nuclear fuel repository in Eurajoki and its neighbouring municipalities*, University of Jyväskylä, University of Tampere, Jyväskylä. Available online at: http:// urn.fi/URN:ISBN:978-951-39-4149-9 (accessed 23 April 2013).

King, F., Ahonen, L., Taxen, C., Vuorinen, U. & Werme, L. 2002. *Copper corrosion under expected conditions in a deep geologic repository*, POSIVA 2002-01, Posiva Oy, Helsinki. Available online at: www.posiva.fi/files/2620/POSIVA-2002-01_web.pdf (accessed 26 April 2013).

Knapp, A. 2012. How much does it cost to find a higgs boson? *Forbes* 7/05/2012. Available online at: www.forbes.com/sites/alexknapp/2012/07/05/how-much-does-it-cost-to-find-a-higgs-boson/ (accessed 15 April 2013).

Kojo, M. 2005. Changing approach: local participation as a part of the site selection process of the final disposal facility for high-level nuclear waste in Finland. *The 10th International Conference on Environmental Remediation and Radioactive Waste Management – ICEM'05*, 4–8 September, Glasgow, Scotland. ICEM05-1239.

Kojo, M. 2009. The strategy of site selection for the spent nuclear fuel repository in Finland. In M. Kojo & T. Litmanen (eds), *The renewal of nuclear power in Finland*. Basingstoke: Palgrave Macmillan, pp. 161–191.

Kojo, M. 2010. Ydinjätepolitiikassa kamppaillaan vallasta. *Kanava* 38(8): 38–41.

Kojo, M. 2014. *Ydinjätepolitiikin osallistava käänne* (The public engagement turn in nuclear waste policy), PhD thesis, Acta Electronica Universitatis Tamperensis 1474, Tampere University Press. Available online at: http://urn.fi/URN:ISBN:978-951-44-9605-9 (accessed 6 May 2016).

Kojo, M. & Litmanen, T. 2009 (eds). *The renewal of nuclear power in Finland*. Basingstoke: Palgrave Macmillan.

Kojo, M., Kari, M. & Litmanen, T. 2010. The socio-economic and communication challenges of spent nuclear fuel management in Finland: The post site selection phase of the repository project in Eurajoki. *Progress in Nuclear Energy* 52(2): 168–176.

Kojo, M. & Oksa, A. 2014a. *The second repository for disposal of spent nuclear fuel in Finland: An analysis of the interests, resources and tactics of the key actors*. Tampere: InSOTEC working paper, University of Tampere. Available online at: http://urn.fi/URN:ISBN:978-951-44-9514-4 (accessed 6 May 2016).

Kojo, M. & Oksa, A. 2014b. *Adaption of the Swedish KBS disposal concept to Finland: A technology transfer case study*. Tampere: InSOTEC Working paper, University of Tampere. Available online at: http://urn.fi/URN:ISBN:978-951-44-9515-1 (accessed 6 May 2016).

Kärnavfallsrådet. 2016. *Swedish National Council for Nuclear Waste 2016*, Nyhetsblad från Kärnavfallrådet, Nr 2016:5. Available online at: www.karnavfallsradet.se/sites/default/files/nyhetsblad_2016_5.pdf (accessed 31 May 2016).

Laaksonen, J. & Varjoranta, T. 2010. Säteilyturvakeskuksen alustava turvallisuusarvio Posiva Oy:n käytetyn ydinpolttoaineen loppusijoituslaitoksen periaatepäätöshakemuksesta. STUK, statement 11.1.2000. Available online at: www.stuk.fi/ydinturvallisuus/ydinjatteet/fi_FI/pap_lausunto/_print/#yleis (accessed 25 April 2013).

Lambright, H.W. 1998. Downsizing Big Science: Strategic choices. *Public Administration Review*, 58(3): 259–268.

Lammi, H. 2009. Social dynamics behind the changes in the NGO anti-nuclear campaign during 1993–2002. In M. Kojo & T. Litmanen (eds), *The renewal of nuclear power in Finland*. Basingstoke: Palgrave Macmillan, pp. 69–87.

Lehtonen, M. 2005. OECD Environmental Performance Review Programme: Accountability (f)or Learning? *Evaluation* 11(2): 169–188.

Lehtonen, M. 2010a. Opening up or closing down radioactive waste management policy? Debates on reversibility and retrievability in Finland, France, and the United Kingdom. *Risk, Hazards and Crisis in Public Policy* 1(4): 135–175.

Lehtonen, M. 2010b. Deliberative decision making on radioactive waste management in Finland, France and the UK: Influence of mixed forms of deliberation in the macro discursive context. *Journal of Integrative Environment Sciences* 7 (3): 175–196.

Lehtonen, M. 2014. Evaluating megaprojects: From the 'iron triangle' to network mapping. *Evaluation* 20(3): 278–295. DOI: 10.1177/1356389014539868.

Litmanen, T. 2008. The changing role and contribution of social science to nuclear waste management in Finland. *Energy and Environment*, 19(3+4): 427–453.

Litmanen, T. 2009, The temporary nature of societal risk evaluation: Understanding the Finnish nuclear decisions. In M. Kojo & T. Litmanen (eds), *The renewal of nuclear power in Finland*. Basingstoke: Palgrave Macmillan, pp. 192–217.

Litmanen, T., Kari, M., Kojo, M. & Solomon, B. (in review). Is There a Nordic Model of Final Disposal of Spent Nuclear Fuel? Governance Insights from Finland and Sweden. Forthcoming in *Energy Research and Social Science*.

Litmanen, T. & Kaunismaa, M. 1999. *Ydinjäte yhteiskuntatieteilijän silmin. Tutkimuksia käytetyn ydinpolttoaineen loppusijoituksen sosiopoliittisista kysymyksistä*, Jyväskylän yliopiston sosiologian julkaisuja 64. Jyväskylä: Jyväskylän yliopisto.

Litmanen, T. & Kojo, M. 2011. Not excluding nuclear power: the dynamics and stability of nuclear power policy arrangements in Finland. *Journal of Integrative Environmental Sciences* 8(3): 171–194.

Litmanen, T., Kojo, M. & Nurmi, A. 2012. The socio-technical challenges of Finland's nuclear waste policy. The technoscientific community's discussion on the safety of the geological disposal of spent nuclear fuel. *Risk, Hazards, and Crisis in Public Policy* 3(3): 84–103.

McEwen, T. & Äikäs, T. 2000. *The site selection process for a spent nuclear fuel repository in Finland – Summary Report*. Posiva 2000–15. Posiva Oy, Helsinki.

Malaska, P. 1987. *Ydinvoima – Kohtalon kysymys?* Kauppa- ja teollisuusministeriö, Energiaosasto, Sarja B:63, Helsinki.

Malaska, P. 1991. Faustinen kaupankäynti ydinvoimalla. In O. Lindfors, E. Paakkola & K. Pylkkänen (eds), *Yhteisödynamiikka: ihminen muuttuvassa työyhteisössä ja kulttuurissa*. Jyväskylä: Atena, pp. 243–263.

Malaska, P., Kantola, I. & Kasanen, P. 1989a. *Energiapolitiikan arvoristiriidat*, Turun kauppakorkeakoulun julkaisuja. Turku: Sarja A – 1.

Malaska, P., Kantola, I. & Kasanen, P. 1989b. Arvot, moraalinen harkinta ja rationaalisuus. In P. Malaska, I. Kantola & P. Kasanen (eds.), *Riittääkö energia – Riittääkö järki*. Helsinki: Gaudemus.

Malaska, P. & Kasanen, P. 1987. Ydinvoima – Kohtalon kysymys? Kauppa- ja teollisuusministeriä, energiaosasto, Sarja B:63, Helsinki.

Martell, M. & Van Berendoncks, K. 2014. *Integrating societal concerns into research and development (R&D) on geological disposal at the national level*, InSOTEC Deliverable 3.2. Available online at: https://docs.google.com/viewer?a=v&pid=sites&srcid= aW5zb3RlYy5sdXxpbnNvdGVjfGd4OjJkZTNiY2YwZjkyMjdmY2M (accessed 9 May 2016).

Ministry of Employment and the Economy. 2010. *Finnish Research Programme on Nuclear Waste Management KYT 2014. Framework programme for the Research Period 2011-2014, MEE Publications*, Energy and the Climate 68/2010, Ministry of Employment and the Economy, Helsinki. Available online at: http://kyt2014.vtt.fi/docs/puiteohjelma_TEM_68_2010_netti.pdf (accessed 6 May 2016).

Ministry of Employment and the Economy. 2011. *KYT2010 Finnish research programme on nuclear waste management 2006–2010, Final report*. Publications of Ministry of Employment and the Economy, Energy and the climate 22/2011. Available online at: www.tem.fi/files/30191/TEM_26_2011_netti.pdf (accessed 6 May 2016).

Ministry of Employment and the Economy. 2012. *Report of the committee for nuclear energy competence in Finland*. Publications of Ministry of Employment and the Economy, Energy and the climate 14/2012. Available online at: www.tem.fi/files/33402/Report_of_the_Committee_for_Nuclear_Energy_Competence_in_Finland.pdf (accessed 9 May 2016).

Ministry of Employment and the Economy. 2014. *Finnish research programme on nuclear waste management KYT2018: Framework programme for the research period 2015–2018*. Publications of the Ministry of Employment and the Economy, Energy and the climate 51/2014. Helsinki: MEE.

Ministry of Employment and the Economy. 2015a. *KYT2014 Finnish research programme on nuclear waste management 2011-2014 – Final report*. Publications of Ministry of Employment and the Economy, Energy and the climate 60/2015. Ministry of Employment and the Economy, Helsinki. Available online at: www.tem.fi/files/44329/TEMjul_60_2015_web_19112015.pdf (accessed 6 May 2016).

Ministry of Employment and the Economy. 2015b. *Posiva receives a construction licence for a spent nuclear fuel disposal facility*. Ministry of Employment and the Economy, Press release on 12 November 2015. Available online at: www.tem.fi/en/energy/press_releases_energy?89521_m=119285 (accessed 13 November 2015).

NASA. 2011. *Mars Science Laboratory/Curiosity*. Available online at: http://solarsystem. nasa.gov/missions/profile.cfm?InFlight=1&MCode=MarsSciLab&Display=ReadMore (accessed 15 April 2013).

Nikula, A., Raumolin, H., Ryhänen, V., Seppälä, T., Vira, J. & Äikäs, T. 2012. *Kohti turvallista loppusijoitusta. Ydinjätehuollon neljä vuosikymmentä.* Eurajoki: Posiva Oy.

Nuclear Waste Working Group. 1980. *Kauppa- ja teollisuusministeriön ydinjätetyöryhmä. Ydinjätehuoltoon liittyvien tutkimusten suorittaminen* (The Nuclear Waste Working Group of the Ministry of Trade and Industry. Conducting studies in the nuclear waste management), Kauppa- ja teollisuusministeriö, Helsinki, 1980-02-25.

Nurmi, A., Kojo, M. & Litmanen, T. 2009. *Yleisökysymyksiä vailla vastauksia, Käytetyn ydinpolttoaineen loppusijoituslaitoksen laajennushankkeen yleisötilaisuudet Eurajoella 2008– 2009*, Yhteiskuntatieteiden ja filosofian laitos, Sosiologian työraportteja, Jyväskylän yliopisto, Jyväskylä. Available online at: http://docplayer.fi/9219774-Yleisokysymyksia-vailla-vastauksia.html (accessed 23 May 2016).

Nurmi, A., Kojo, M. & Litmanen, T. 2012. *Identifying remaining socio-technical challenges at the national level: Finland.* InSOTEC, European Commission, Community Research. Working paper (WP 1 – MS 5), University of Jyväskylä & University of Tampere. Available online at: https://jyx.jyu.fi/dspace/handle/123456789/38353 (accessed 24 April 2013).

Peltonen, E., Vuori, S., Anttila, M., Hillebrand, K., Meling, K., Rasilainen, K., Salminen, P., Suolanen, V. & Winberg, M. 1985. *Käytetyn ydinpolttoaineen loppusijoituksen turvallisuusanalyysi: perustapaus*, YJT-85-22, Voimayhtiöiden ydinjätetoimikunta, Helsinki.

Pettersson, T. & Nurmela, S. 2007. *Eri tapoja kohdata suuri elefantti. Suomalaisen ja ruotsalaisen kulttuurin vertaileva tutkimus.* Helsinki: Suomalais-ruotsalainen kulttuurirahasto.

Posiva. 1999. *The final disposal for spent nuclear fuel: Environmental impact assessment report*, Posiva Oy, Helsinki. Available online at: www.posiva.fi/en/databank/publications/eia_reports#.VzCQak1f1jo (accessed 6 May 2016).

Posiva. 2003a. *TKS-2003. Nuclear waste management of the Olkiluoto and Loviisa power plants: Programme for research, development and technical design for 2004–2006.* Available online at: www.posiva.fi/files/344/TKS-2003.pdf (accessed 24 April 2013).

Posiva. 2003b. *Programme of monitoring at Olkiluoto during construction and operation of the Onkalo.* Posiva Report. Posiva 2003–05. Available online at: www.posiva.fi/files/335/ Posiva_2003-05web.pdf (accessed 15 April 2016).

Posiva. 2006. *TKS-2006. Nuclear waste management of the Olkiluoto and Loviisa power plants: Programme for research, development and technical design for 2007–2009.* Available online at: www.posiva.fi/files/345/TKS-2006web.pdf (accessed 24 April 2013).

Posiva, 2008. *Expansion of the repository for spent nuclear fuel – environmental impact assessment report 2008.* Eurajoki: Posiva Oy. Available online at: www.posiva.fi/ files/519/Posiva_YVA_selostusraportti_en_lukittu.pdf (accessed 6 May 2016).

Posiva. 2010. *TKS-2009. Nuclear waste management at Olkiluoto and Loviisa power plants review of current status and future plans for 2010–2012.* Available online at: www.posiva. fi/files/1078/TKS2009_Eng_web_rev1_low.pdf (accessed 24 April 2013).

Posiva. 2011. *Vuosikertomus 2011.* Available online at: www.posiva.fi/files/1523/ Vuosikertomus_2010_FI.pdf (accessed 24 April 2013).

Posiva. 2012a. *Hakemus. Olkiluodon kapselointi- ja loppusijoituslaitoksen rakentamiseksi käytetyn ydinpolttoaineen loppusijoitusta varten.* Available online at: www.posiva.fi/ files/2923/Posivan_rakentamislupahakemus.pdf (accessed 25 April 2013).

Posiva. 2012b. *YJH-2012. Olkiluodon ja Loviisan voimalaitosten ydinjätehuollon ohjelma vuosille 2013–2015.* Posiva, Eurajoki. Available online at: www.posiva.fi/files/2844/YJH-2012-ohjelmaFinal.pdf (accesed 23 April 2013).

Posiva, 2012c. Monitoring at Olkiluoto – A programme for the period before the repository operation. Posiva Report. Posiva 2012–01. Available online at: www.posiva.fi/files/3012/POSIVA_2012-01_web.pdf (accessed 6 May 2016).

Posiva. 2015. *Annual Report 2014*. Available online at: www.posiva.fi/files/4004/Annual_Report_2014.pdf (accessed 6 May 2016).

Raittila, P. & Suominen, P. 2002. Keskustelu ydinjätteen loppusijoitusta koskevasta periaatepäätöksestä eduskunnassa ja mediassa. In P. Raittila, P. Hokkanen, M. Kojo & T. Litmanen (eds.), *Ydinjäteihme suomalaisittain*. Tampere: Tampere University Press, pp. 92–113.

Rasilainen, K. (ed.). 2002. *Nuclear waste management in Finland: Final report of public sector research programme JYT2001 (1997-2001)*. Helsinki: Ministry of Trade and Industry. Available online at: www.vtt.fi/inf/julkaisut/muut/2002/final-jyt2001.pdf (accessed 6 May 2016).

Raumolin, H. 1982. *TVO:n ydinjätehuollon toimintaohjelma ja aikataulut*, Raportti YJT-82-55, Voimayhtiöiden ydinjätetoimikunta, YJT, Teollisuuden Voima Oy, Helsinki.

Raumolin, H. 1983. *Ydinjätehuoltoon liittyvät taloudelliset kysymykset eri maissa*, Raportti YJT-83-08, Teollisuuden Voima, Helsinki.

Reuters. 2016. *Vattenfall puts pressure on Swedish government to cut nuclear tax*. Available online at: www.reuters.com/article/vattenfall-nuclear-idUSL5N17V5HN (accessed 31 May 2016).

Ridell, H. & Raak, S. 1997. Selvitys kiinteistöjen hintakehityksestä Loviisan alueella. Posiva, Työraportti 97-48. Helsinki. Available online at: www.posiva.fi/files/2421/POSIVA-97-48_Tyoraportti_web.pdf (accessed 27 May 2016).

Rosenberg, T. 1999. Turhauttavaa teatteria, Loppusijoitus-YVA Loviisa-liikkeen näkökulmasta. In T. Litmanen, P. Hokkanen & M. Kojo (eds), *Ydinjäte käsissämme, Suomen ydinjätehuolto ja suomalainen yhteiskunta*. Jyväskylä: SoPhi, pp. 266–282.

Sandberg, J. 1999. Päättikö eduskunta geologisesta loppusijoituksesta jo vuonna 1994? Käytetyn ydinpolttoaineen huoltoa koskeva lainsäädäntö ja viranomaispäätökset. In T. Litmanen, P. Hokkanen & M. Kojo (eds.), *Ydinjäte käsissämme: Suomen ydinjätehuolto ja suomalainen yhteiskunta* (Nuclear waste in our hands: the Finnish nuclear waste management and the Finnish society), University of Jyväskylä, Department of Social Sciences and Philosophy, SoPhi 44, pp. 43–64.

Särkikoski, T. 2011. Rauhan atomi, sodan koodi. Suomalaisen atomivoimaratkaisun teknopolitiikka 1955–1970. Suomen ja Pohjoismaiden historia. Filosofian, historian, kulttuurin ja taiteiden tutkimuksen laitos. Historiallisia tutkimuksia Helsingin yliopistosta XXV. Helsingin yliopisto, Helsinki. Available online at: http://urn.fi/URN:ISBN:978-952-1-7287-1 (accessed 21 July 2016).

Schwartz, S.I. 1998. *Atomic audit: The costs and consequences of US nuclear weapons since 1940. Cumulative costs in millions of dollars as of December 31, 1945*. Available online at: www.brookings.edu/about/projects/archive/nucweapons/table1-1 (accessed 15 April 2013).

Shrader-Frechette, K.S. 1993. *Burying uncertainty: Risk and the case against geological disposal of nuclear waste*. Berkeley: University of California Press.

Strauss, H. 2010. Involving the Finnish public in nuclear facility licensing: Participatory democracy and industrial bias. *Journal of Integrative Environmental Sciences* 7(3), 211–228.

STUK. 2013a. *Ensimmäinen vaihe Posivan rakentamislupahakemuksen viranomaiskäsittelyssä valmis*. Available online at: www.stuk.fi/stuk/tiedotteet/fi_FI/news_840/?utm_source=twitterfeed&utm_medium=twitter (accessed 29 April 2013).

STUK. 2013b. *Olkiluodon kapselointi- ja loppusijoituslaitoksen rakentamislupahakemuksen STUKille toimitetun aineiston kattavuustarkistus.* Available online at: www.stuk.fi/stuk/tiedotteet/fi_FI/news_840/_files/89568069157261459/default/paatos-kattavuustarkastus22042013.pdf (accessed 29 April 2013).

STUK. 2015. Statement of the Radiation and Nuclear Safety Authority on the construction of the Olkiluoto encapsulation plant and disposal facility for spent nuclear fuel. Statement 1/H42212/2013. Available online at: www.stuk.fi/documents/88234/176831/stuk_lausunto_posivan_rl-hakemuksesta12022015en.pdf/5a4dc60d-b40d-4462-bdd2-3efac2d33da2 (accessed 13 November 2015).

Sundqvist, G. 2002. *The bedrock of opinion: Science, technology and society in the siting of high-level nuclear waste.* Dordrecht: Kluwer Academic Publishers.

Suunnittelukeskus. 1987. The economical impact of final disposal of spent fuel – siting alternative Kuhmo. Work report 87-10, Teollisuuden Voima Oy, Helsinki.

Tripp, S. & Grueber, M. 2011. *Economic impact of the Human Genome project. How a $ 3,8 billion investment drove $ 796 billion in economic impact, created 310,000 jobs and launched the genetic revolution.* Batelle Memorial Institute. Available online at: http://battelle.org/docs/default-document-library/economic_impact_of_the_human_genome_project.pdf (accessed 15 April 2013).

TVO. 2015. *TVO will not now apply for construction license for OL4.* Press release, 24 June 2015. Available online at: www.tvo.fi/news/1615 (accessed 31 May 2016).

TVO. 2016. *Standard & Poor's downgraded TVO's credit rating from 'BBB-' To 'BB+'; Outlook Stable.* Press release, 23 May 2016. Available online at: www.tvo.fi/news/1737 (accessed 31 May 2016).

Valovirta, V. 2002. Evaluation utilization as argumentation. *Evaluation* 8(1): 60–80.

Vedung, E. 1997. *Public policy and program evaluation.* New Brunswick: Transaction Publishers.

Vieno, T. et al. 1992. Käytetyn ydinpolttoaineen loppusijoituksen turvallisuusanalyysi TVO-92. Raportti/Voimayhtiöiden ydinjätetoimikunta, YJT. Imatran Voima.

Vieno, T. & Nordman, H. 1996. *Interim report on safety assessment of spent fuel disposal TILA-96.* Posiva, Helsinki. Available online at: www.posiva.fi/files/2643/POSIVA-96-17_web.pdf (accessed 23 April 2013).

Vieno, T. & Nordman, H. 1999. *Safety assessment of spent fuel disposal in Hästholmen, Kivetty, Olkiluoto and Romuvaara TILA-99,* Posiva-99-07, VTT Energy. March 1999. Posiva, Helsinki.

Vuori, S. 2014. *Research and development activities related to management and disposal of spent nuclear fuel in 2001-2013,* VTT Technology 190. Available online at: www.vtt.fi/inf/pdf/technology/2014/T190.pdf (accessed 6 May 2015).

Warrack, A. 1993. *Megaproject decision making: Lessons and strategies.* Western Centre for Economic Research, University of Alberta. Edmonton, Alberta, No. 16/May 1993. Available online at: https://business.ualberta.ca/-/media/business/centres/cibs/documents/publications/16.pdf (accessed 27 November 2015).

Weinberg, A.M. 1961. Impact of large-scale science on the United States. *Science* 134(3473): 161–164.

YLE. 2013. Ydinjätteen loppusijoituksen keskeinen ongelma ratkaisematta. Uutiset, Kotimaa. 5.4.2013 klo 6:28 | päivitetty 5.4.2013 klo 11:15. Available online at: http://yle.fi/uutiset/ydinjatteen_loppusijoituksen_keskeinen_ongelma_ratkaisematta/6563686 (accessed 24 April 2013).

Yli-Kauhaluoma, S. & Hänninen, H. 2014. Tale taming radioactive fears: Linking nuclear waste disposal to the "continuum of the good". *Public Understanding of Science* 23(3): 316–330.

6 How stakeholder and citizen participation influences evaluation criteria for megaprojects

The case of the Belgian LILW repository

Anne Bergmans and Marlies Verhaegen

Introduction

Resistance to the planning of large-scale utilities or megaprojects, or to the way they are decided upon and carried out, has led scientists and policymakers to believe that participation is a precondition for such projects to succeed (e.g. Armour, 1991; Hage et al., 2010; OMEGA, 2012; Lehtonen, 2014). When advocating participatory mechanisms for their democratic merits, for putting stakeholders in control (and not because participation circumvents public concern or leads towards acceptance – Sundqvist and Elam, 2010), we should ask ourselves if and how participation in megaprojects brings about a more thorough evaluation of the socioeconomic impact and a more sustainable conception of the project at hand.

While the notion of sustainability is a relatively vague concept with many possible interpretations, it does stress the importance of finding a balance, a 'triple bottom line' (Elkington, 1997), between the social, the environmental and the economic impact of any given human activity. Elkington's notion of the triple bottom line holds a notion of measuring, above and beyond the financial bottom line of the profit and loss account. This resonates well with the challenges of evaluating megaprojects. Only by measuring or making visible or explicit the potential economic, environmental and social impacts of such projects will it become possible to take into consideration all the dimensions and the challenges of developing a sustainable project.

However, experience with sustainability reporting and assessment has shown that these three accounts demand different ways of measuring. Such separate accounts are not easily added up, and the usual solution of translating the measuring of people and planet aspects in monetary terms ignores the specificity of these aspects (Hindle, 2008). As Vanclay (2004) argues, the trouble with triple bottom line accounting, as with any interpretation of impact assessments (whether they be social, environmental or other) as decision algorithms, is that not all things that count can be measured. This is particularly the case for social impacts, as they are difficult if not impossible to define precisely, and can therefore never be entirely grasped in a quantitative manner. Alternatively, as Scrase and Sheate (2002: 277) put it: "*assessments do not usually deal just in facts, but with objectives, preferences and value judgements. These are not simply 'out there' … but are actively constructed in historically specific processes of negotiation and conflict, including in the course of assessment processes".*

Specific for nuclear waste repositories as megaprojects is that they span over several decades, even several generations, of active planning, construction and operation. From a purely economic and financing perspective (even within the assumption that after closure of the facility the system will perfectly hold as planned and not require any further attention), one can hardly expect that the cost estimates of projects of such scale and longevity could be fully accurate. Neither will it be possible to set aside enough money to cover all eventualities and all possible changes in scenarios over the total lifetime of the facility, from construction to closure. How to manage this type of uncertainty and how to assess criteria of fairness and equity among stakeholders with varying interests spread out over both space and time?

In this chapter we will consider the siting process for short-lived, low- and intermediate-level radioactive waste (LILW) in Belgium as a case where the criteria for an ex-ante evaluation or assessment of the project have been – and continue to be – constructed throughout the assessment and decision-making process. We hold a preference for the term assessment, as the notion of evaluation is often reserved for ex-post analysis of the performance of a policy or a programme. Given the long time frames involved in the development and implementation of a radioactive waste repository, we find it more appropriate to think in terms of continuous (re)assessment of the situation, rather than in terms of strictly separable ex-ante assessment and ex-post evaluation. We will touch on both dimensions of 'the socioeconomic' as described in the introductory chapter to this volume by trying to capture if and how the opening up of the assessment processes has allowed multiple interpretations and rationales to contribute to decision-making in this particular case.

We do not aim to propose a practical stakeholder management method or promote the process as it unfolded in this particular case. Nor will we dissect the full range of related stakeholder engagement activity. Instead, what we will do is to highlight the particularity of bringing one, albeit very homogenous, type of stakeholder, namely the local host community, into the planning and decision-making process. In doing this, we will focus on (particular) stakeholder interests and influences. We are aware that this holds the risk of paying "*a disproportionate amount of attention to the two-way relational ties between the focal firm* [in our case the national radioactive waste management agency] *and particular stakeholders*" (Mok et al., 2015: 455). However, while a full network analysis of the relations between all stakeholders in the project – as promoted by Neville and Menguc (2006) – would certainly bring additional understanding, the focus in this chapter is on the specific challenge of bridging (at least to some extent) internal and external factors by engaging local stakeholders in the project's management, thus redrawing the boundaries between the inside and outside of project management. In that respect, we take an "*internally focussed, contextually-grounded view of actual practice*" (van Marrewijk et al., 2008: 592) rather than aiming to evaluate project performance from an outsider's perspective. The latter we consider in any case as value laden and dependent on the viewpoint taken. Therefore we do not see this as a role that we as researchers should take up.

To build our argument, we will start with a brief introduction to the case and clarify how we obtained the data for our empirical analyses. Then we will focus our analysis on how multiple rationales have contributed to decision-making and to what extent the assessment process has been opened up. From this we will derive a number of lessons learned, fully aware that these single case study findings are only a hypothesis for further research.

Radioactive waste repositories: the cAt project as a particular type of megaproject

As explained above, the case analysed here is a LILW repository project in Belgium. LILW consists of operational waste from the nuclear industry, other industrial activity, hospitals and research, and of decommissioning waste from nuclear installations.[1] Although Belgium depends for about 50 per cent of its electricity production on nuclear energy[2] the country's nuclear programme is relatively small in scale (seven reactors and a total capacity of 6000 MW). Originally the LILW was to be disposed of in the sea (IAEA, 1999) and it was only after the international ban on sea burial in 1993[3] that the Belgian authorities fully focused on disposal on land. A surface repository was judged by the responsible agency, ONDRAF-NIRAS,[4] to be the best option, as disposal in abandoned coal mines was dismissed for reasons of safety and deep disposal in clay was too expensive (NIRAS, 1990). After some failed attempts to identify the most suitable location in the light of mainly technical and economic criteria, the federal government[5] gave ONDRAF-NIRAS in 1998 the mandate to investigate the possibility to site a final repository for the country's LILW with the following criteria: safe, well integrated at the local level, technically feasible and progressive in nature, while remaining flexible and reversible (NIRAS, 2008). As a consequence, a process was launched in which potential host communities were given a role in the feasibility studies. These feasibility studies were to consider various aspects of the repository facility, including the choice of technical concept and its environmental and social impact (for a more extensive account of this process, see: Bergmans, 2005; Bergmans et al., 2006; Bergmans, 2008). Participatory processes were organised at the municipal level, by means of a platform named 'Local Partnership'. Between 1999 and 2003 three such Partnerships were established, of which two (STORA and MONA, in the neighbouring communities of Dessel and Mol) continued their operations after selection of the site in Dessel in 2006.[6] Through this process, local stakeholders (including civil society organisations, politicians, socioeconomic actors[7] – e.g. business and labour union representatives, local merchant organisations – and individual citizens) were involved in designing the repository and in setting the conditions under which their community would be willing to host the repository facility as part of an integrated project (Bergmans, 2008). At a later stage, after the site selection, a regional dialogue platform was put in place to specifically address socioeconomic and environmental impacts on a wider scale. The aim of this platform was to detect regional opportunities linked to the advent of the repository. From 2011 onwards, round tables for regional stakeholders were organised addressing themes such as social economy, tourism, education, nature and sustainability.[8]

We have been involved in this project as action researchers from the very start. At the outset we acted as facilitators, bringing the parties together in a structure that was considered fit for purpose. Once the project was up and running it was left to the actors in the field to manage their own process. Members of our research team have continued to follow up the Partnerships' activity through participatory observation during working group meetings of both Partnerships still active today, planning meetings between the Partnerships and ONDRAF-NIRAS, and various (public) meetings organised within this process. Our role today is an advisory one: we keep an eye on the participatory process and, on a regular basis, provide feedback on our impressions and evaluations to the Partnerships, the waste management agency and the municipality, who can subsequently act upon that information as they see fit.

The empirical findings elaborated on in this chapter were gathered through this process of participatory observation, as well as through formal and informal contacts with concerned actors and analysis of written communications (minutes of meetings, reports etc.) between 1999 and 2015. We will focus in particular on the period of more concrete project development since the siting decision in 2006.

The following sections describe the Belgian LILW repository project – or cAt project[9] as it is known today – as a megaproject. Long-term LILW behaviour is in itself a well-researched topic, leaving relatively few persistent scientific uncertainties. However, the particularity of the local situation in which to implement the repository facility does leave a good number of technical, environmental and societal (including political, institutional, legal and socioeconomic) uncertainties and complexities. We will outline these for our case, thus highlighting the similarities to the characteristics of megaprojects put forward in the introductory chapter to this volume.

A multitude of concerned parties

Key players in each stage of the process include in particular the government agency, ONDRAF-NIRAS, responsible for radioactive waste management and acting as implementer of the disposal project; the regulatory body, AFCN-FANC;[10] the municipality hosting the waste and its neighbouring communities, represented via the Partnerships; and the project funders. Based on the 'polluter pays' principle, the financing comes from the industrial waste producers[11] and the Belgian state as the party with financial responsibility for nuclear liabilities. Further key actors include the nuclear research centre SCK-CEN in Mol, providing various conceptual studies for ONDRAF-NIRAS as well as input for the licence application, and ONDRAF-NIRAS' subsidiary company Belgoprocess, active in the decommissioning of obsolete nuclear facilities and responsible for the processing and storage of radioactive waste in its central storage facility in Dessel.

A range of additional consulting, design, planning and building companies are involved in the concrete implementation of the project, in some cases with a very specific type of expertise (e.g. the concrete walls for the repository require a particular type of composition, demanding a very careful pouring technique). Also, various local and regional organisations and levels of government play a role, for example in relation to urban planning, mobility, environmental impact (from other than nuclear activities)[12] etc.

Such a diversity of concerned parties obviously implies a widely varying range of interests and opinions concerning various aspects of the project. Over the course of the years of negotiation and project development there have been many examples of conflicting and mutual interests, both within each Partnership and between the Partnerships and their surroundings. Safety, for example, has always been an obvious mutual interest. Nonetheless, as we shall see below, the modifications that one Partnership requested to the original repository design demonstrate that safety can have different meanings for different actors. Other examples include the different preferences regarding the methodology for an economic impact assessment of the project; conflicting opinions and expectations regarding the access to information as well as the physical accessibility of the site (e.g. demands for transparency and monitoring clashing with security regulations); and the most appropriate forms of compensation for harmful impacts on nature (e.g. legal constraints to compensate the cutting of exotic pine trees on traditional moorland).

A continuing quest

Looking at the timeline of the search for a solution for Belgian LILW, one can observe a long horizon during which the approach of the Belgian radioactive waste management organisation has changed due to uncertainties in its environment (Bergmans, 2005). By and large, we can distinguish a geology-focused approach from the early 1980s until the mid-1990s, after which the focus shifted to addressing the problem as a societal question with technical implications instead of the other way round. Instructed by the 1998 government decision and with the support of social scientists, ONDRAF-NIRAS attached greater importance to communication and dialogue, which led to the setting up of the Partnerships. This participatory turn was witnessed across several countries with a nuclear waste programme (Sundqvist and Elam, 2010; Bergmans et al., 2015).

In 2010, ONDRAF-NIRAS hoped construction would start in 2013 and operations would begin in 2016 (NIRAS, 2010). However, it is still waiting to obtain a licence: the licence application – only submitted in 2013 – is still under review by the regulator. Almost ten years after the government decision to opt for surface disposal in Dessel, crucial elements are still being negotiated between the host communities, ONDRAF-NIRAS as the implementer, the regulatory body AFCN-FANC, and the waste producers as funders of the project. The repository itself is estimated to take at least thirty years to fill up after construction, and several years to be closed off and covered with concrete and several layers of natural materials and soils (NIRAS, 2010). After this an institutional control phase is to be initiated, for a period whose length is to be decided by AFCN-FANC (NIRAS, 2008).

Given the widely varying interests and perceptions highlighted above, full consensus regarding the various aspects of such a project is hard if not impossible to achieve. Nonetheless, it is clear that some form of middle ground must be found, and that integrating to the extent possible the criteria perceived as necessary by all stakeholders is fundamental, if the project is to be 'sustainable' in the meaning described above. Involving affected citizens through the Partnerships offered the local community the possibility to safeguard its own interests by setting the terms under which it considered the repository to be acceptable. This breakthrough supports the postulate that there is no place for waste disposal 'outside of society' (Landström and Barbier, 2012). The result, in this particular social context, is an integrated repository project; a patchwork of several megaprojects (as visualised in Figure 6.1) with the repository (tangible), safety and participation (intangible) at its core, surrounded by a host of side projects that respond to the specific demands of the local community.

Complex budget estimates

Building a radioactive waste repository facility is a costly activity. However, the actual cost is not something that can be easily estimated in advance, as it depends on a variety of factors that are likely to shift over space and time. In the case of the Belgian LILW facility, initial estimates were based on a generic surface repository

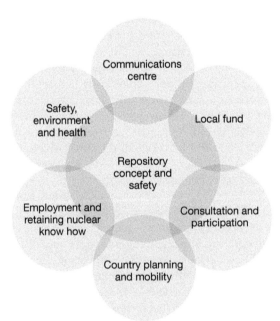

Figure 6.1 The main components of the cAt project (after NIRAS, 2010: 29).

concept, with a minimum of engineered barriers, to be implemented in a geologically optimal environment, taking primarily the technical infrastructure aspects into account (NIRAS, 2008). However, all three sites investigated at the time had certain geological shortcomings for which engineered solutions needed to be sought (Bergmans et al., 2006). Furthermore, by reopening the technical choice of the repository concept (e.g. by adding an inspection gallery, a feature to which we will return later) and giving the potential host community the possibility to set additional conditions regarding location, (environmental) safety and socioeconomic impact of the facility, budget estimates were in flux during the phase of the feasibility studies and are only stabilised to some extent today.

Neither of the two Partnerships still in operation, MONA and STORA, provided a budget estimate at the end of their feasibility studies. In preparation for its final report MONA conducted a multi-criteria analysis to decide which option (surface or subsurface disposal) they would support. The outcome was a tie on all accounts except for the budget, which the Partnership judged not to be for them to decide, as long as all safety criteria and local conditions were met (MONA, 2005). A similar reasoning can be found in the final report of their Dessel colleagues, who also limited themselves to describing in relatively general terms their conditions, and pointed out that the federal government was responsible for raising the appropriate funds for a project that serves the national interest (STOLA, 2004). In its 2006 report to the government, ONDRAF-NIRAS also refrained from making a full cost estimate. Some reference was made to the order of magnitude difference between surface and subsurface disposal mentioned in previous reports. The report further stated that more concrete estimates needed to be made at a later stage, and the emphasis was put on the need for securing an appropriate funding mechanism for the newly-developed approach of an integrated repository project (NIRAS, 2006).

Permitting changes and organising flexibility

Several aspects of the cAt project have not been firmly carved in stone. In 2010, the project blueprint was consolidated in a Masterplan (NIRAS, 2010), for two reasons: first, to establish how the requirements set out by both Partnerships in 2005 were to be integrated (as requested by the government in its 2006 siting decision[13]) and to reassure the local communities that their conditions were not forgotten; and second, to establish a more detailed budget baseline in order to start funding negotiations.

The repository project had by then exceeded the boundaries of the technical project initially foreseen, both in scope (including socioeconomic conditions of its host environment) and in technical concept design (safety conditions due to the nature of its host environment). For obvious reasons, the funders were not prepared to write a blank cheque, and a more precise cost estimate for both the repository facility, its auxiliary infrastructure and the additional project components was called for.

While the estimates for the technical infrastructure was left largely in the hands of ONDRAF-NIRAS, assessing the necessary budget for the additional project components became a joint effort to which the waste management organisation, both Partnerships and external parties contributed. The most striking example of such a collaborative assessment is the way in which an agreement was reached on the budget needed for the Local Fund. The Local Fund was seen as a way to make sure that not only current but also future generations would be able to benefit from the municipalities' 'sacrifice' to offer a solution for a national problem (STOLA, 2004; MONA, 2005). As it was described in the 2010 Masterplan: "*A fund is a suitable instrument to create a continuum of socioeconomic values: it ensures a permanent source of funds for many generations. Furthermore, a fund allows for anticipation of changing needs in society. After all, it is neither possible nor desirable at this moment to make an estimate of the types of projects and activities that will provide added value to local communities a few decades from now*" (NIRAS, 2010). Thus it was argued that enough capital should be raised to allow for the fund to yield a reasonable net amount each year to fund local initiatives, but also to reinvest, so as to absorb inflation rates and to keep the fund stable over the long term. But how to decide how much is 'enough' and what is 'reasonable'?

As a basis for the discussions on this question three studies were commissioned, with each study having its own advocate: a 'classical' cost–benefit analysis (ordered by ONDRAF-NIRAS and STORA), an eclectic multi-criteria analysis – EMCA (ordered by MONA), and a comparative study of 'community benefits' accompanying nuclear waste facilities elsewhere in the world (ordered by ONDRAF-NIRAS and the International Association for Environmentally Safe Disposal of Radioactive Materials – EDRAM) (NIRAS, 2010). The latter study was used as a benchmark. The former two provided a basis for calculating the basic capital needed for the Local Fund. From the cost–benefit analysis a minimum value for the Local Fund was drawn, whereas the EMCA study presented a bottom end and upper end multiplier to quantify the differences in social preferences for certain alternatives (e.g. surface disposal versus deep disposal with economic development above ground) (NIRAS, 2010). The combination of the real annual compensation (following from the cost–benefit analysis), an added value index (based on the multipliers drawn from the EMCA) and an interest rate, expected to fluctuate over the years within a certain range, led to a figure which was considered by all parties involved to be fair and reasonable, and which was expected to be defensible in negotiations with the project funders.

While various aspects at the time still needed further detailing (in particular the aspects of the project that were outside the core competence area of ONDRAF-NIRAS remained relatively sketchy), the 2010 Masterplan presented a total overall cost estimate for the project of between 844 and 1008 million euros (in euro March 2010): 734 to 878 million euros for the repository and all directly related aspects, and 110 to 130 million euros for the additional local conditions or 'community benefits' (NIRAS, 2010). This subsequently became the basis for budget negotiations with the government and the main waste producers.

Since the publication of the cAt Masterplan there have been further developments: initiatives were taken for necessary changes in urban planning prescriptions (e.g. for implementing the communication centre), an overall budget estimate was consolidated (see above) and a licence application prepared and submitted to AFCN-FANC in 2013.[14] Given that sixteen years have passed since the start of the feasibility studies, and more than ten years since the Partnerships issued their proposals, some of the specifications set out for certain requirements are being revised (e.g. regarding the modalities of an interactive communications platform integrating data on repository development – and in a later stage repository behaviour – with citizen journalism and community storytelling). Some aspects, such as the request for continuous participation throughout the repository lifetime, are bound to be in need of continuous revision over time, as both the project and society evolve. Also, however, more material aspects of the project may change. We already mentioned that the facility will not be closed until thirty years after the start of operations. While the design and plans for the way the facility will be covered after closure have been prepared in view of the licence application, both ONDRAF-NIRAS and the Partnerships have explicitly stated that the stakeholders at that time will need to have a say on these issues (MONA, 2005; STOLA, 2004; NIRAS, 2010). Therefore, budget estimates are likely to remain somewhat in flux over the course of the project implementation.

In order to be able to cover all costs of the integrated project, an already existing funding mechanism, the Long Term Fund (LTF), was supplemented by a second mechanism, a Medium Term Fund (MTF). According to the 'polluter pays' principle, both the LTF and the MTF are established through contributions from the waste producers (NIRAS, 2010). They differ in that the LTF is based on fees paid for services provided by ONDRAF-NIRAS to the waste producers, and serves first and foremost the financing of the repository as a technical facility.[15] The MTF is based on contributions for funding all project components that benefit the local community and "*aim at safeguarding public support for the disposal now and in the future and which do not constitute a direct service for the waste producers*" (NIRAS, 2010: 122).[16]

We explicitly refer to these funding mechanisms, as we see them as a means of building flexibility into the project management and for dealing with uncertainties in budget calculations. The 2010 Masterplan provides an overview of project components and mechanisms through which they should be funded (see Table 6.1). For a number of components, both the LTF and the MTF are expected to contribute. While the MTF is constituted as a closed funding envelope, the LTF has a somewhat more flexible structure as the tariffs are recalculated on a regular basis, based on the cost estimates for disposal at that time. Furthermore, the possibility of additional third party funding is foreseen.

Widening modes of project governance

Broadening the scope from a mere waste repository to an integrated project has made ONDRAF-NIRAS responsible for a range of tasks (e.g. the optimisation of nuclear emergency planning, a regional health study, the supervision of the local fund, and the design of a communication centre) that go beyond the agency's core competencies and certainly beyond its initial purely technical approach. The list

120   *Anne Bergmans and Marlies Verhaegen*

Table 6.1 Funding mechanisms for the various components of the cAt project (source: NIRAS, 2010: 125)

Project component	Funding mechanism
Project management	LTF
Construction and operation of the quay	LTF
Construction and operation of the caisson plant	LTF
Construction and operation of the MPF*	LTF
Construction and operation of the disposal modules	LTF
Construction and operation of the peripheral provisions	LTF
Prototypes	Specific contract for the project phase and LTF
Communication centre	LTF, MTF, communication budget, ONDRAF-NIRAS and third party funding
Local Fund	MTF
Participation	LTF, MTF, ONDRAF-NIRAS budget, third party funding (to be examined)
Retention of nuclear know-how	Third party funding
Safety, environment and health	LTF and MTF

* Monolith production facility

of subcontractors, local partners, governmental levels and departments involved with various parts of the project has grown substantially. These subcontractors and parties communicate directly with the Partnerships or through ONDRAF-NIRAS about their tasks and progression, which requires both an adapted pace of meetings and decision-making and a flexible management style, in order to ensure the synchronisation of the various project components and the people working on them.

Long-term engagement in a process such as the one described above inevitably turns local people into some form of experts. Over the years, participatory settings such as the Partnerships therefore risk becoming a closed community responding defensively towards new actors that emerge along the way. The extensive interaction with ONDRAF-NIRAS in a process of collaborative research and development, and the ability to influence the project, gave the local participants a feeling of ownership of the project (Bergmans, 2008). From a sharing of expertise, the relationship between the waste manager and its local 'partners' evolved to one of cherishing a shared project. One of the reasons for linking a continuation of the Partnerships to the acceptance of hosting a repository was that people wanted to make sure that the project was implemented in the way described in the Partnership reports. In that respect, certain technical features of the repository design became symbolic for all local conditions and the local ownership of the project. The 'Dessel inspection gallery' is a good example of this.

The inspection gallery was a feature that was explicitly added on request of the STORA Partnership in Dessel. Given the importance of the broader area around the potential site as a crucial freshwater reservoir for the whole Flanders region, the local people wanted guarantees that any contamination (either radiological or chemo-toxic) of the groundwater because of a leakage from the facility could be detected and contained as quickly as possible. Thus an inspection gallery was introduced, intended to serve as a monitoring area and as a 'drip tray' in order to allow for swift detection of potential contamination in case of a water flow through the repository. This gallery, initially a cave-like, accessible structure, was part of the Partnership report and in that respect was indirectly 'approved' by the government siting decision of 2006. However, the regulator had refused to take part in the feasibility studies leading up to the Partnership reports, arguing that this could compromise its independence when judging a licence application. No specific guidance or requirements for repository design were provided at the time, either (Bergmans, 2005). With the publication of the Masterplan in 2010, AFCN-FANC raised the first formal objection against the inspection gallery in its original design. While the Dessel Partnership acknowledged the regulator's concerns regarding stability (too little) and accessibility (too much), they nevertheless insisted there were very good reasons (also from a safety perspective) for maintaining the principle of an inspection gallery in the design of the repository. Further amendments to the design were made in order to satisfy the regulator. However, in response to the safety report filed by ONDRAF-NIRAS in 2013 as part of the licence application, AFCN-FANC raised 293 additional questions, but only after a delay of about a year. This has raised doubts that the regulator might intentionally seek to postpone the whole endeavour; as some sort of mutual antagonist of both the implementer and the affected community. Where one could expect Partnership members to perceive the regulatory agency as a natural ally when it comes to guaranteeing the safety of the facility, we now see them reproaching the regulator for not providing clear standards and taking too much time to formulate its arguments. AFCN-FANC in turn defends itself by arguing that evaluating the safety case takes time, because a project of this kind and magnitude is unprecedented in Belgium.

A first of its kind

The cAt repository will indeed be a first of its kind in Belgium. Even when compared with similar facilities in other countries, the Belgian repository remains unique in a number of ways. First, it will have to rely more strongly on engineered barriers, as the geology and water table in the designated area are considered suitable, but not optimal. Second, the population density around the designated site is rather high, particularly when compared to similar facilities in other countries, as illustrated in Table 6.2. Third, the integration of an inspection gallery underneath the facility poses a relatively unprecedented technical challenge.

The Belgian cAt project has moved beyond being a clearly circumscribed project. Therefore it is probably better described as a 'programme' addressing a complex public problem and being carried by *"networks of people and organizations that work more or less coherently and purposefully"* (Benjamin and Greene, 2009: 297),

Table 6.2 Population density around five radioactive waste disposal/storage sites (figures collected in 2009; Bergmans, 2010)

	Type of facility	Host community (population – size)		Population density (inh./km²)	Closest neighbours at …
Spain – El Cabril	SD LILW & CIS	4,678	906 km²	5.2	10 km
France – Soulaines	SD LILW	267	21 km²	12.7	4 km
Canada – Kincardine	GD LILW	11,173	538 km²	20.8	3 km
Switzerland – ZWILAG	CIS	4,000	9.4 km²	425.5	1 km
Belgium – cAt	SD LILW & CIS	8,865	27 km²	328.3	350 m

Legend: SD = Surface Disposal; GD = Geological Disposal; CIS = Central Interim Storage.

as put forward in the introductory chapter of this volume. This 'mega-programme' is actually comprised of a number of components (see Figure 6.1), of which some could be considered megaprojects on their own (e.g. the repository facility and its auxiliary technical infrastructure, but to some extent also the communication centre, including various functions such as a science centre). Other programme components are more fluid (e.g. the conservation of nuclear know-how or ensuring participation throughout the life time of the cAt project) and thus even more difficult to pin down, plan and budget up front for the whole duration of their assumed need. Not all concerned actors – including the waste manager as project implementer – are directly involved in all programme components, or involved to the same degree. For example, the same company will not be solicited to construct the repository and the communication centre; the local community will take a leading role in the management of the local fund, with ONDRAF-NIRAS as observer, whereas for repository operation the roles will be reversed.

Continuously constituting and reconstituting the project and its governance

In this section we will further analyse how multiple interpretations and rationales have contributed to decision-making and to what extent the assessment process has been opened up.

Much of the literature on megaprojects takes their underperformance as a given, and subsequently aims to understand the reasons for and ways of avoiding such underperformance. Authors such as Flyvbjerg (2007; 2009) even include these problems, mainly described in terms of 'cost overruns and/or benefit shortfalls', as a characteristic in their definition of what constitutes a megaproject. Very large-scale projects delivering "*a substantial piece of physical infrastructure or a capital asset with a life expectancy measured in decades*" (Sanderson, 2012: 432) of the type analysed in this chapter may indeed be highly likely to overrun initial cost estimates and take a lot longer to complete than originally anticipated or hoped for. However, whether or not they will eventually 'perform' as expected and provide the promised benefits to society is not something that can be assessed in a simple and straightforward manner.

To develop a better understanding of the performance assessment taking place in the context of the cAt project, we will make use of the notions of 'decision-maker cognition as guided by satisficing' (as described by Sanderson, 2012), of 'ambiguous project culture' (as interpreted by van Marrewijk et al., 2008), and of 'managing uncertainty through flexibility and tolerance of vagueness' (as put forward by Atkinson et al., 2006) in a context of bounded rationality.

Drawing on Winch and Maytorena (2011), Sanderson (2012) distinguishes three types of **cognition** that impute conscious decisions in relation to project management or project governance. These are: optimising (choosing the best alternative among a known range of options), optimising within limits (utility maximisation given existing restrictions in time, availability of information and cognitive capacity), and satisficing. With reference to Simon (1955) and Selten (2001), the latter is described as "*taking into account the organizational complexity within which decision-makers are operating, embracing the complexities and conflicts of organizational life*" (Sanderson, 2012: 434).

From van Marrewijk et al. (2008) we adopt a focus on **project culture**, understanding it in the case of megaprojects as ambiguous, because of the various perspectives, ambitions, interests and practices of the actors involved in the project. This ambiguity comes in addition to the complexity of the context within which the project operates and the multiplicity of views and perspectives from various stakeholders 'around' the project. Given the scope and potential impact of a megaproject on its social environment, the boundary between both the elements and actors that are inside or outside the project also tends to become blurred. In that respect it would seem more appropriate to talk about 'project cultures' rather than of a single project culture.

Managing uncertainty is at the core of all project management. However, megaprojects entail high levels of uncertainties that are often difficult or impossible to quantify – also referred to as socialised uncertainty (Sanderson, 2012: 436) – which calls for different management processes that are "*associated with building trust, sense-making, organisation learning, and building an appropriate organisational culture*" (Atkinson et al., 2006: 688). Such an approach calls for flexibility and a certain degree of 'tolerance' towards uncertainty. Whereas Atkinson et al. (2006: 697) portray vagueness as "*one possible method of reducing uncertainty*", we prefer to phrase it as **handling uncertainty**, thus recognising that not all uncertainty can and needs to be fully reduced.

Decision-making as a process of 'satisficing': beyond 'Iron Triangle' thinking

Cases such as the cAt project clearly illustrate the need to take a broader approach to megaproject evaluation than the conventional "Iron Triangle" considerations of "*on time, on budget and within prescribed specifications*" (OMEGA, 2012: 2). This is particularly because of the lack of clear criteria – often due to the sheer impossibility of fully prescribing all aspects of the project at a certain point in time, after which the project is to unfold according to a predefined plan – but also because of inevitable differences in the appreciation of the performance of such a project by various concerned actors or 'stakeholders'. Furthermore, the multiplicity of stakeholder perceptions makes it difficult to distinguish between exogenous and internal management factors, which Sanderson (2012) characterised as opposing strands in the megaproject evaluation literature.

Overoptimistic schedules have certainly been a feature of the process of developing the cAt project, and project timing has been continuously reassessed. Overall, this does not appear to have caused too much concern so far, and the urgency of constructing a repository has been counterbalanced by extending interim storage capacity. From an efficiency perspective, this situation may not be ideal and could increase the costs of the overall radioactive waste management programme (even if not of the repository in itself). However, seen from a safety perspective, for example, it would appear fully justified that the regulator takes the time required for a thorough evaluation. As we have seen, at the local level some tension has been building up, as ten years after the siting decision not much of the project that was co-developed and to a large extent appropriated by the local community has been accomplished. However, some of this delay has resulted from the time taken to (re)negotiate host community conditions.

With regard to the budget, perceptions of what is considered acceptable obviously vary between the concerned actors. For the repository facility, for example, the local actors – represented by the Partnerships and municipal councils (STOLA, 2004; MONA, 2005) – and the regulator[17] take the same position: the criterion of safety must prevail. However, a greater priority for the local actors in particular, but also for the implementer and for decision-makers at the federal level – as defenders of the public interest – was that adequate funding mechanisms must be put in place to make sure the required funding could be raised.

The cAt project evolves continuously, as new concerned actors emerge and become integrated into the process along the way, even though the core group remains relatively stable over time. This resonates well with the view of a (mega) project being "*the constantly renegotiated sum of the activities of the individuals involved*" (Hällgren and Söderhol, cited in Sanderson, 2012: 441). The cAt project clearly is not a predefined object, but one that is "*continuously constituted and reconstituted through the socially situated activities of all of the practitioners involved, however tangentially*" (Sanderson, 2012: 441).

However, since time and budget are not the main criteria, and a fully detailed project description against which to measure outcome is not available, which criteria, if any, do we see being deployed in the assessment of the cAt project? Considering the coming into being of this project as a specific case of decision-making as a process of 'satisficing' rather than 'optimising' (Sanderson, 2012), what elements are at play in deciding this is a satisfactory answer to the question of solving the long-term management problem for the country's LILW?

As mentioned in the introductory chapter, **safety** is the primary concern in megaprojects where the aim is to find a solution for the problem of radioactive waste. The cAt project is no exception in this respect. Still, safety as a criterion remains vague and is a concept that has different meanings for different people, as extensive research on risk perception has long since shown (Fischhoff et al., 1981; Slovic, 1987; Kasperson et al., 1988; Renn, 1992). Therefore, in the continuous performance assessment of cAt to date safety has served as a general guideline, but its exact implementation has been left open to interpretation and discussion.

Furthermore, our account makes clear that it was the search for a sustainable solution, in this case one discussed with the host community, that paved the way for alternative performance criteria such as **local acceptability**. This, again, is a broad criterion, open for interpretation and hard to capture through standard evaluation checklists or quantifiable figures, unless it is reduced to regular opinion polls. The local conditions (continuous participation, the Local Fund, the communications centre etc.) set out in the Partnership reports and consolidated in the 2010 Masterplan could be seen as steps towards fleshing out this high-level criterion of local acceptance in more detail.

The call for continuous participation also reveals two implicit criteria applied by the local actors: **transparency** in the decision-making process and a **willingness to adapt** to the pace of each partner.

While we stated above that the requirement that the repository be finalised 'on budget' has so far not been a major issue, this does not mean that **financing** has not been considered important or that project management is ruled by the credo of 'anything goes'. Rather, the emphasis has not been on fixing a specific project budget but on securing broad envelopes and financing mechanisms that guarantee long-term funding, and which are considered fair, feasible and acceptable to all the key actors involved.

Our account shows that rather than quantifying these criteria or specifying in all cases how to meet them, it was the Partnership's role to introduce them, to make space for them and to keep open – or to reopen – negotiations, if it felt that its criteria were not being met and the proposed alternative was not considered satisfactory. We consider this a clear example of *bringing in 'the socioeconomic' through performance criteria* – or at the very least through a change in approaching performance criteria in a **qualitative**, rather than a quantitative way.

Blurred lines: adding local colour to project culture

The cAt project is described by most of its partners as unique and innovative, particularly with regard to the strong engagement of the local community through the Partnership structures. The choice of incorporating local community representatives into the project management structure has made the classical inside and outside distinction of the project management fluid and ambiguous. As a result, the distinction between project "governing" and project "governance" (Sanderson, 2012) has become less explicit. While the ONDRAF-NIRAS project team is central in the coordination of conceptual design, project planning and development, it could not be regarded as the "*single centre of calculation and control*" (van Marrewijk et al., 2008: 592). Partnership members take part in monthly project meetings in which they systematically discuss planning and the state of affairs of the different components, while decision-making at the project level is shared between ONDRAF-NIRAS and both Partnerships in the form of a Steering Committee.

This could be seen as a way of **bringing in 'the socioeconomic' into evaluation approaches or processes**. Emerging project goals were incorporated along the way. For instance, Partnerships where created when it was necessary to give a role to host communities, due to earlier failures and to the 1998 government decision; informing the public by means of a communications centre and long-term participation became a key feature of the project; and the implementer negotiated an inspection gallery with the regulator on behalf of its local project partners. The most explicit change in project goals was perhaps introduced when the technical approach of finding a geologically optimal solution was exchanged for a societal approach of finding out what a potential host community considers a feasible solution. However, after the main boundaries for the project were set (a surface repository in Dessel, as part of an integrated project that meets both STORA and MONA requirements) and a Masterplan consolidated, new insights have prompted numerous smaller adaptations (e.g. changes to the original design of the repository; the creation of the MTF). This continuous adaptation results to a large extent from the long trajectory covered so far and the multiple stakeholders involved.

This case shows that decision-making is not only steered in response to a context of 'bounded rationality', that is to say, operating "*within constraints of limited time, information and cognitive capacity*" (Sanderson, 2012: 433). It also illustrates that satisficing is additionally being guided by the need to recognise and reconcile various perceptions, interests and rationalities within the project organisation, and to subsequently open up the project management structure to a broader range of stakeholders.

The above-mentioned willingness of the professional members of the project management to adapt to the pace of the local volunteers – a willingness encouraged by repeated gentle, and sometimes firm, reminders to do so – and an emphasis on taking the time to resolve disputes among key partners, seems to have engendered trust in the process. All partners give testimony of a mutual feeling of striving for the good of the project and the well-being of the local community, even if opinions sometimes differ on the exact meaning and ways of achieving well-being.

Managing uncertainty through flexibility

Throughout the various stages of the development of the cAt project, project management has taken different forms. Initially foreseen to last for about two years (the estimated time to conduct feasibility studies), the Partnerships have been in place for over fifteen years. During this period, their role and relationship with the implementer – but also with other actors, such as the regulator, the municipal council and the other Partnership – has changed and adapted according to the project management stage. This flexibility, learning and adaptation appear to become more present, though in a more incremental way, as the project develops and becomes more complex. Once the site in Dessel was chosen and the work of both Partnerships was recognised as the basis for further project development, conscious steps were taken to adapt the governance mode of the project once more. Added elements of this new governance mode included shared decision-making in the Steering Committee, continuous revisions of each subproject resulting in a Masterplan, the installation of ad hoc working groups when specific issues arose, and the creation of a regional dialogue platform.

It therefore seems appropriate to conclude that uncertainty management in this project entails flexibility as well as tolerance to a certain level of vagueness and complexity, rather than attempts to reduce uncertainty at all costs. Further elements to corroborate this could be discerned from our analysis, such as the room left for dialogue and (re)negotiation; the sharing of expertise and various forms of collaboration (e.g. ONDRAF-NIRAS and STORA ordering one type of socioeconomic impact study and MONA commissioning another); the preparation of prototypes (a demonstration test, a subsidence test and a test cover, the latter to be monitored and studied during several decades); and flexibility in timing and financial provisions.

Uncertainty management in relation to the financing of the whole project is of particular interest here, because it demonstrates how retaining a certain level of vagueness and complexity could prove to be key in guaranteeing that the necessary funding will be available. In order to overcome a possible legal dispute on whether the status of the LTF would entitle it to be applicable to all aspects of the integrated project, a second funding mechanism, the MTF, was created. By indicating certain project components to be financed through both funds without defining exactly how costs will be divided between the two (see Table 6.1), some room was created for eventually dedicating costs to a particular funding structure.

Lessons learned from the cAt project

We have presented here a single case study. Therefore we can only formulate a number of hypotheses, which we consider to be of interest for further in-depth studies, drawing on different cases in megaproject research. Our focus has been on megaproject management: not on 'what goes wrong', but on 'what goes on'. We have looked at what impact – if any – a widening of the notion of project management may have on project culture, on managing uncertainty and on assessing performance at different stages in the project's development. In the previous sections we have tried to capture if and how the opening up of the assessment processes has allowed for multiple interpretations and rationales to contribute to decision-making in this particular case.

It is our understanding that the enlarged project management structure of the cAt project and the way it operates could be seen as an example of what van Marrewijk et al. (2008) describe as the *"ambiguous culture and bounded rationality"* of megaprojects. Like them, we did not find evidence of a systematic and deliberate underestimation of costs, but rather a situation that is *"managed to the best of their abilities, by professionals and civil servants in the context of very complex operations, paradoxes, uncertainties and ambiguities which surround these projects"* (van Marrewijk et al., 2008: 597).

'Iron triangle thinking' does not seem to dominate the project culture in this particular case, nor did we see any evidence of outsider pressure in this regard, at least at this stage in the project development. A strong focus on project content (a safe repository concept within a broader project answering to the conditions set by the host community) and a relatively relaxed attitude towards project timing by most partners, created space for reflection and negotiation. There is no doubt this has led in some instances to additional uncertainty, agitation among certain partners and even unnecessary stalling of decisions. However, it is our understanding that the inclusion of local community representatives in the project management, an overall absence of excessive pressure and an emphasis on taking time to resolve disputes among key partners, has contributed to a feeling of trust in the process and to a mutual feeling of collaboration within the project, for the benefit of the local community.

Our case suggests a need to complement the notion of bounded rationality with that of multiple rationalities. The latter is often depicted as part of the former (e.g. Atkinson et al., 2006; Sanderson, 2012; and to a lesser extent van Marrewijk et al., 2008). However, our case illustrates that they both play a role, but in different ways. The more complex the project and the more actors involved, the greater the tendency of these two types of rationality to reinforce each other.

The more inclusive the structure of project management, the more ambiguous is the project culture – or the more diverse are the project cultures – shaping the project's development. However, even the most inclusive project management will always be confronted with an outside reality, again with different rationalities, perceptions and interests. Flexibility to deal with that type of uncertainty and the ability to deal with changes in stakeholder 'morphology' over time are thus important.

The cAt project already has a relatively long history, but the Belgian LILW repository project is technically still in a planning phase, as no licence has yet been obtained for its central component. Nevertheless, some components are already being launched (e.g. the governing body for the Local Fund will be put in place in June 2016), thus making the transition from plan to project more fluid. In spite of Masterplans and detailed technical licence applications, many project components remain relatively open and difficult to describe in tangible and measurable outcome criteria. Therefore, a continuous process of (re)assessment, particularly regarding the socioeconomic impacts of the project, appears to have unfolded, guided by mainly qualitative performance criteria. These criteria remain rather vague, thus allowing them to act as boundary concepts or boundary objects (Star, 1989; Star and Griesemer, 1989). Boundary objects are arrangements that allow collaboration without consensus: they are "at once temporal, based in action, subject to reflection and local tailoring, and distributed throughout all of these dimensions" (Star, 2010: 603). Moving back and forth between a "vaguer identity as a common object" and a more specific interpretation or form of the object by each of the concerned actors, a certain dynamic develops which can turn the boundary object into a standard or a process (Star, 2010: 604–605). In our case, this could lead to more specifically defined performance criteria. However, even if that stage is not reached, meaning and appreciation can be attributed and qualitative assessments made on the basis of 'overlapping interpretations'. As Fox (2011: 82) puts it, these performance criteria as boundary objects thus become active "elements that encapsulate the broader social meaning of a concept, theory, technology or practice, and the underlying relations that surround its development and adaption".

In our analysis, we focused on the enlarged project management, including its structure, with local stakeholders representing the host community. It was within that broadened group of directly involved organisations and individuals that this continuous (re)assessment process developed, based on qualitative performance criteria. The question now remains whether a complete outsider (e.g. the Belgian State Audit Office) that would evaluate the project would be able and willing to appreciate the necessary dynamic created through this organised flexibility or whether they would primarily question the money and time invested in a solution that is still not operational and remains permanently open to discussion and changes. From an iron triangle point of view, this project is not yet ready for evaluation or would fail completely if put to the test at the moment. An evaluator having an eye for values advanced in the introductory chapter, such as learning, reflexivity and dynamism, would probably come up with a different appreciation.

Conclusions

The history of the project management of cAt shows that complexity should not necessarily be seen as a negative attribute. Projects of this magnitude are characterised by a variety of project cultures and understandings, both within and around their management structure. Acknowledging complexity creates room for negotiation and a more conscious way of approaching megaprojects as being continuously (re)constituted through the actions of all concerned parties, within a context of multiple bounded rationalities leading to socialised forms of often irreducible uncertainty.

Far from claiming that the approach taken with the cAt project is an ideal model, we feel that the absence of a preconceived idea of what the project or its management structure should look like at the outset actually contributed to the robustness of the project governance. It is hard to predict whether or not the project, when fully implemented, will effectively be judged as sustainable. However, it appears to us that a flexible and inclusive management culture and a certain vagueness resulting from the application of mainly qualitative performance criteria has been constructive in managing and handling uncertainty in this particular case.

Further research is obviously needed, but based on our case study and broader literature analysis, we would suggest that in megaproject assessment, the time is nigh for replacing the iron triangle considerations by a '*velvet triangle*' thinking in terms of adopting an open and flexible project culture, fostering multiple rationalities through qualitative performance criteria, and managing uncertainty through tolerating vagueness and complexity.

Notes

1   www.niras.be/content/classificatie
2   In 2014, 47.5 per cent of the 67.6 TWh total net electricity production in Belgium was provided by the nuclear power plants of Doel and Tihange (www.febeg.be/statistiek-elektriciteit).
3   By means of the 1993 amendment to the London Convention of 1972 on the Prevention of Marine Pollution by Dumping of Wastes and Other Matter (www.imo.org/en/OurWork/Environment/LCLP/Pages/default.aspx).
4   The acronym of the Belgian Agency for Radioactive Waste and Enriched Fissile Materials is NIRAS in Dutch and ONDRAF in French.
5   Decision by the Cabinet Ministers of the Federal Government of January 16, 1998.
6   All three Partnerships had advised positively, provided the repository project would be developed according to the technical requirements and additional conditions outlined in their final reports. Only the municipal councils of Dessel and Mol subsequently agreed to become official candidates for host community (Bergmans et al., 2006). As the 'opting out' of the third candidate site is not of relevance for the aspects discussed in this chapter, we will only focus on the Partnerships in Dessel (STORA – originally named STOLA, the Partnership changed its name in 2005) and Mol (MONA).
7   Belgium has a strong tradition of dialogue and engagement with the so-called social or socioeconomic partners with regard to labour relations at policy and company level. These socioeconomic partners include labour unions, the union of independent workers, business and industry confederations, farmers associations, etc.
8   www.niras-cat.be/nl/getpage.php?i=125
9   The classification and corresponding abbreviations that are internationally used are low- and intermediate-level waste (LILW) and high-level waste (HLW). The Belgian waste managing agency has separate programmes for these two types of waste. LILW is called category A waste (hence the cAt project) whereas two categories are distinguished within HLW: B waste and C waste.
10   The acronym for the Belgian Federal Authority for Nuclear Safety is FANC in Dutch and AFCN in French.
11   The most important among the industrial producers are Electrabel, which operates the nuclear power plants, and its subsidiary company, Synatom, responsible for managing the nuclear fuel chain.
12   In Belgium the Federal Government is responsible for nuclear safety, with the regulator AFCN-FANC, while environmental safety in general is a regional matter. In the case of Dessel and Mol, the Flanders Environment Agency is responsible for environmental protection.
13   Decision by the Cabinet Ministers of the Federal Government of June 23, 2006.
14   www.niras-cat.be/en/getpage.php?i=77
15   "This fund should cover all costs and investments necessary to store the radioactive waste and to build, operate and close a final disposal facility, and to ensure its institutional control after closure, as subscribed in the appropriate licenses" (Law of December 29, 2010 regarding various stipulations (I) art. 181 – Moniteur Belge 31/12/2010 – authors' own translation).
16   "This fund should cover all costs related to the additional conditions endorsed by on the one hand the municipal council(s) of the municipality or municipalities having created and maintaining societal support for the disposal facility, through a continuous participatory process, and on the other hand the federal government" (Law of December 29, 2010 regarding various stipulations (I) art. 181 – Moniteur Belge 31/12/2010 – authors' own translation).
17   www.fanc.fgov.be/nl/news/berging-afval-van-categorie-a-het-fanc-vraagt-niras-om-zijn-vergunningsaanvraag-aan-te-vullen/626.aspx

References

Armour, A.M. 1991. The siting of locally unwanted land uses: Towards a cooperative approach. *Progress in Planning* 35: 1–74.

Atkinson, R., Crawford, L. & Ward, S. 2006. Fundamental uncertainties in projects and the scope of project management. *International Journal of Project Management* 24(8): 687–698.

Benjamin, L.M. & Greene, J.C. 2009. From program to network: The evaluator's role in today's public problem-solving environment. *American Journal of Evaluation* 30(3): 296–309.

Bergmans, A. 2005. Van "de burger als beleidssubject" naar "de burger als partner": de Belgische queeste naar een langetermijnoplossing voor het beheer van het laagradioactief en kortlevend afval (*From "citizens as policy subjects" to "citizens as partners": The Belgian quest for a long term solution for the management of low and intermediate level radioactive waste*). PhD dissertation, Antwerp: University of Antwerp – Faculty of Social and Political Sciences.

Bergmans, A. 2008. Meaningful communication among experts and affected citizens on risk: Challenge or impossibility? *Journal of Risk Research* 11(1–2): 175–193.

Bergmans, A. 2010. *International benchmarking of community benefits related to facilities for radioactive waste management*, EDRAM Research report. Available online at: www.edram.info/uploads/media (accessed October 2015).

Bergmans, A., Van Steenberge, A. & Verjans, G. 2006. *CARL Country Report Belgium*, CARL Research Report, Antwerp: University of Antwerp. Available online at: http://uahost.uantwerpen.be/carlresearch/docs/20070914152818OZSV.pdf (accessed October 2015).

Bergmans, A., Sundqvist, G., Kos, D. & Simmons, P. 2015. The participatory turn in radioactive waste management: Deliberation and the social-technical divide. *Journal of Risk Research* 18(3): 347–363.

Elkington, J. 1997. *Cannibals with forks: The triple bottom line of 21st century business*. Oxford: Capstone.

EURIDICE. 2015. *Research on geological disposal of radioactive waste*. Information brochure. Available online at: www.euridice.be (accessed September 2015).

Fischhoff, B., Lichtenstein, S., Slovic, P., Derby, S.L. & Keeney, R.L. 1981. *Acceptable Risk*. Cambridge: Cambridge University Press.

Flyvbjerg, B. 2007. *Megaproject policy and planning: Problems, causes, cures*. Summary of PhD dissertation, Aalborg University, Denmark. Available online at: www.rucsdigitaleprojektbibliotek.dk/bitstream/1800/2727/1/afhandlingBF2007s.pdf (accessed July 2015).

Flyvbjerg, B. 2009. Survival of the unfittest: Why the worst infrastructure gets built – and what we can do about it. *Oxford Review of Economic Policy* 25(3): 344–367.

Fox, N.J. 2011. Boundary objects, social meanings and the success of new technologies. *Sociology* 4 (1): 70–85.

Hage, M., Leroy, P. & Petersen, A.C. 2010. Stakeholder participation in environmental production. *Futures* 42(3): 254–264.

Hindle, T. 2008. *The Economist guide to management ideas and gurus*. London: Profile Books.

IAEA. 1999. *Inventory of radioactive waste disposals at sea*, IAEA-TECDOC 1105, Vienna: International Atomic Energy Agency. Available online at: www-pub.iaea.org/MTCD/publications (accessed July 2015).

Kasperson, R., Renn, O. & Slovic, P. 1988. The social amplification of risk: A conceptual framework. *Risk Analysis* 8(2): 177–187.

Landström, C. & Barbier, J. 2012. The challenge of long-term participatory repository governance. *Technikfolgenabschätzung – Theorie und Praxis* 21(3): 66–72.

Landström, C. & Bergmans, A. 2015. Long-term repository governance: A socio-technical challenge. *Journal of Risk Research* 18(3): 378–391.

Lehtonen, M. 2014. Evaluation of "the social" in megaprojects: Tensions, dichotomies, and ambiguities. *International Journal of Agriculture, Engineering and Construction* 3(2): 98–109.

Mok, K.Y., Shen, G.Q. & Yang, J. 2015. Stakeholder management studies in mega construction projects: A review and further directions. *International Journal of Project Management* 33(2): 446–457.

MONA. 2005. *MONA, een weg naar de aanvaardbaarheid van een berging van categorie A-afval in Mol?*, Final report, available online at: www.monavzw.be/sites/monavzw.be/files/mona_eindrapport_jan_2005_-_lage_res.pdf (accessed July 2015).

Neville, B.A. & Menguc, B. 2016. Stakeholder multiplicity: Toward an understanding of the interactions between stakeholders. *Journal of Business Ethics* 66(4): 377–391.

NIRAS. 1990. *De berging van laagactief afval*. Stand van zaken en vooruitzichten, NIROND 90-01, Brussels: ONDRAF-NIRAS.

NIRAS. 1994. *De oppervlakteberging op Belgisch grondgebied, van laagactief afval en afval met korte halveringstijd*. Synthese en aanbevelingen, NIROND 94-04, Brussels: ONDRAF-NIRAS.

NIRAS. 2006. De berging, op Belgisch grondgebied, van laag- en middelactief afval met korte levensduur. Afsluitend rapport van NIRAS betreffende de periode 1985-2006, waarbij de federale regering verzocht wordt te beslissen over het gevolg dat moet worden gegeven aan het bergingsprogramma. NIROND 2006-02N mei 2006, Brussels: ONDRAF-NIRAS. Available online at: www.niras.be/content/publicaties-volgens-thema (accessed September 2015).

NIRAS. 2008. Het geïntegreerd project van oppervlakteberging in Dessel voor het Belgisch laag- en middelactief afval met korte levensduur. *Rapport van NIRAS over de periode vanaf de beslissing van de ministerraad van 23 juni 2006 tot november 2008*, NIROND 2008-01 N November 2008, Brussels: ONDRAF-NIRAS. Available online at: www.niras.be/content/publicaties-volgens-thema (accessed September 2015).

NIRAS. 2010. *The cAt project in Dessel – A long-term solution for Belgian category A waste*. NIROND 2010-02, Brussels: ONDRAF-NIRAS. Available online at: www.niras-cat.be/downloads/cAt_masterplanENG.pdf (accessed October 2015).

OMEGA. 2012. *Mega projects. Lessons for decision-makers: An analysis of selected international large-scale transport infrastructure projects*. Executive summary, Bartlett School of Planning, University College London, OMEGA Centre – Centre for Mega Projects in Transport and Development, December 2012. Available online at: www.omegacentre.bartlett.ucl.ac.uk/publications/reports/mega-project-executive-summary/ (accessed January 2015).

Renn, O. 1992. Concepts of risk: A classification. In S. Krimsky & D. Golding (eds), *Social Theories of Risk*. Westport: Praeger.

Sanderson, J. 2012. Risk, uncertainty and governance in megaprojects: A critical discussion of alternative explanations. *International Journal of Project Management* 30(4): 432–443.

Scrase, J.I. & Sheate, W.R. 2002. Integration and integrated approaches to assessment: What do they mean for the Environment? *Journal of Environmental Policy and Planning* 4(4): 275–294.

Selten, R. 2001. What is bounded rationality? In G. Gigerenzer & R.Selten (eds.), *Bounded Rationality: The Adaptive Toolbox*. Cambridge, MA: MIT Press.

Simon, H.A. 1955. A behavioural model of rational choice. *Quarterly Journal of Economics* 69: 99–117.

Slovic, P. 1987. Perception of Risk. *Science* 236: 280–285.

Star, S.L. 1989. The structure of ill-structured solutions: Boundary objects and heterogeneous distributed problem solving. In L. Gasser & M.N. Huhns (eds), *Distributed artificial intelligence: vol 2*. Menlo Park, CA: Morgan Kaufman Publishers.

Star, S.L. 2010. This is not a boundary object: Reflections on the origin of a concept. *Science, Technology & Human Values* 35(5): 601–617.

Star, S.L. & Griesemer, J.L. 1989. Institutional ecology, translations and boundary objects: Amateurs and professionals in Berkeley's Museum of Vertebrate Zoology 1907–1939. *Social Studies of Science* 19(3): 387–420.

STOLA. 2004. *Het Belgisch laagactief en kortlevend afval: Thuis in Dessel?* Final Report, available online at: www.stora.org/sites/stora.org/files/Documents/bergingsproject%2520nlds.pdf (acessed July 2015).

Sundqvist, G. & Elam, M. 2010. Public involvement designed to circumvent public concern? The "participatory turn" in European nuclear activities. *Risk, Hazards & Crisis in Public Policy* 1(4): 203–229.

Van Marrewijk, A., Clegg, S.R., Pitsis, T.S. & Veenswijk, M. 2008. Managing public-private megaprojects: Paradoxes, complexity, and project design. *International Journal of Project Management* 26 (6): 591–600.

Vanclay, F. 2004. The triple bottom line and impact assessment: How do TBL, EIA, SIA and EMS relate to each other? *Journal of Environmental Assessment Policy & Management* 6(3): 265–288.

Winch, G.M. & Maytorena, E. 2011. Managing risk and uncertainty on projects: A cognitive approach. In P.W.G. Morris, J.K. Pinto & J. Söderlund (eds), *The Oxford Handbook of Project Management*. Oxford: Oxford University Press.

7 Does technical risk dialogue entail socioeconomic evaluation?

The case of scientific dispute over copper corrosion in a spent nuclear fuel disposal project

Tapio Litmanen, Matti Kojo, Mika Kari and Jurgita Vesalainen

Among the proponents of nuclear power, the project for the safe and secure disposal of spent nuclear fuel (SNF) in Finland is often deemed as a success story. Opponents have had difficulties getting publicity for their claims about the risks of the project. Their most powerful arguments have been mostly ethical, but on technical issues the opponents have been in a weaker position than the proponents. However, recently the risk of corrosion in oxygen-free water has become subject to scientific controversy, possibly threatening even the realisation of the final disposal of spent nuclear fuel (Andersson, 2014: 2; Wallace, 2010). In Sweden, this issue has been intensively debated since 2007 (Andersson, 2014; SNCNW, 2013), but only recently has this debate taken off in Finland (Lempinen and Silvan-Lempinen, 2011; Nurmi et al., 2012; Litmanen et al., 2012; FANC, 2013; Klötzer et al., 2013).

While the main dispute is about the ability of copper canisters to resist corrosion in nearly oxygen-free geological conditions after the closure of the repository, there is also some controversy regarding other types of corrosion related to these canisters. The theme of copper corrosion has long since been addressed from a scientific perspective in the context of the Swedish KBS-3 method (King et al., 2002: 137). These canisters, containing SNF, are to be buried in the bedrock, at a depth of approximately 500 metres, and surrounded by bentonite clay. The current scientific assumption is that copper corrodes at an extremely slow rate in such an environment and that no corrosion will take place in oxygen-free conditions (see e.g. King, 2010; Posiva, 2013: 434–436). However, as Andersson (2014) has indicated, this assumption has been challenged by experimental results of researchers working at the Swedish Royal Institute of Technology. The researchers are suggesting that, even in an oxygen-free environment, copper could corrode by taking oxygen from water molecules. This continuation of general corrosion could mean that the canister would not withstand the conditions prevailing throughout the hundred-thousand-year foreseen lifetime of the final disposal, if the thickness of the copper were five centimetres, as planned (Hultquist, 1986; Szakálos et al., 2007). Despite Posiva's announcement in 2015 that the issue of copper corrosion had been brought to a conclusion and that the investigations had confirmed that copper will not be significantly corroded in oxygen-free conditions (Posiva, 2015: 6), the scientific dispute continues.

The focus of this chapter is on the risk dialogue over copper corrosion between the nuclear waste company, Posiva, and the Finnish Radiation and Nuclear Safety Authority, STUK; especially the ways in which these organisations deal with the challenge that copper corrosion presents to final disposal. The study of the copper corrosion dispute in the final disposal of SNF will shed light on how socioeconomic evaluation issues of a megaproject are intertwined both with institutional arrangements allowing and preventing evaluation, and with technical risk dialogue, where socioeconomic evaluation is excluded from the agenda, and would not be touched during the later stages of decision-making. Regardless of the seeming political neutrality of risk assessment, larger socioeconomic valuations frame the dyadic risk dialogue between the implementer and the regulator. Our aim is to illustrate: 1) how technocratic risk assessment functions; but also 2) how this risk assessment is embedded in the broader societal-institutional setting, which to a large extent predetermines the outcome.

Conventionally risk assessment and safety regulation are assumed not to entail socioeconomic evaluation, but on closer examination they can be seen to reflect changing societal-institutional goals. The collaborative arrangements between the enterprise and the supervising authority constitute a unique form of socioeconomic evaluation whose objective is, in addition to safety, also to ensure that the megaproject advances according to the originally set timetable, and does not call into question the outcomes of the initial socioeconomic evaluation (conducted as part of the DiP procedure).

The structure of the chapter is as follows. First we discuss the Finnish regulatory culture in its institutional settings and the problematic nature of socioeconomic evaluation in the chosen case. In the following section, we then describe our methodological choices. The main empirical findings are presented in five sections covering each of the phases of risk dialogue studied: 1) setting the stage (2003–2004); 2) focus on future projections (2006–2007); 3) intermingling of two processes (2009–2010); and 4) crisis in the relationship (2012–2013). The final section of the chapter discusses the findings and draws conclusions about whether the power to define the 'common good' is handed over to the parties of the risk dialogue.

Institutional settings behind the regulatory culture

Posiva's and STUK's risk dialogue takes place in legally and institutionally defined regulatory settings (Heinonen et al., 2014), which comprise two major elements: the Finnish Nuclear Energy Act (990/1987)[1] and Regulatory Guides on nuclear safety (YVL).[2] In accordance with the Act, the power companies Teollisuuden Voima Ltd (TVO) and Fortum Power and Heat Ltd (FPH) are responsible for their own waste. For managing SNF, the power companies have established a joint company, Posiva, which is procedurally connected to STUK, for a number of reasons: 1) STUK regulates the safety of the handling, storage and disposal of nuclear waste; 2) the authorities have issued reporting obligations to the producers of nuclear waste and STUK's role is to monitor the companies; 3) STUK reviews Posiva's studies and technical plans for final disposal with the aid of other expert organisations and gives feedback to Posiva;[3] 4) STUK conducts the safety review at each stage of the licencing process;[4] 5) STUK is given powers of search and entry, access to records, the right to take samples and install monitoring devices, to require reports from the operator, and to issue guidelines concerning the manufacture of equipment; 6) STUK can also require Posiva to make changes to the physical structure of a nuclear facility and to operating practices and procedures; and 7) all STUK's regulatory costs are recovered from the licencees (OECD, 2008; Laaksonen, 2006).

This institutionally defined, decades long risk communication between the implementer and STUK has created a special relationship between the parties. As in Sweden (Wärnbäck, 2012; Wärnbäck et al., 2013), in Finland, too, the implementer and the regulator have been engaged in a series of conversations on the advancement of research, planning, and technical design related to disposal of SNF, and the interaction has affected their relationships (see also Elam and Sundqvist, 2009: 973). The Finnish regulatory framework and the relationship between the implementer and the safety authority are somewhat similar to those in Sweden, but there are also differences – mostly of historical origin (Wahlström, 1999; Litmanen et al., forthcoming). In Finland the main actors were in close dialogue already before the beginning of the construction licencing (CLA) process, i.e. during the pre-licence phase (see Figure 7.1). As argued by Wärnbäck et al. (2013), close cooperation over a long period of time might change the way the actors perceive themselves and others, as well as how they formulate their goals and aims. Therefore the roles and responsibilities are not always as clear as claimed. For instance, STUK perceived Posiva's preliminary licence documentation submitted in 2009 (see Figure 7.1), required by the Ministry of Employment and the Economy (MEE) as an exercise for the actual licence application review (Heinonen et al., 2014: 3–4). In general, the aim of the exercise was to improve actual performance, in view of learning and reflection designed to potentially transform the regulatory approach or some aspects of it.

Even though it is difficult to identify pure national regulatory styles in Finland and Sweden (Wahlström, 2007: 353; Melber and Durbin, 2005; Litmanen et al., forthcoming), Finnish regulatory culture has been seen as flexible, development-oriented and, as such, oriented towards gradual learning and refinement (NEA, 2003). Gradual learning refers to a process where the development of regulation is related to the current phase of decision-making, starting from very general principles and ending with the guidance applicable to a licencing review (NEA, 2003: 12). The regulatory philosophy of gradual learning is characterised as one that provides plenty of opportunity for a constructive dialogue between the regulator and the implementer, but not with civil society actors (Litmanen et al., forthcoming). A strange paradox is that this development-oriented regulatory style can be beneficial for the development of technical procedures and it also leaves room for interpretation and control by the authorities (NEA, 2003: 12–13; see also Laaksonen, 2006)[5], while at the same time closing the door to initiatives coming from other societal actors, such as civil society organisations (Litmanen et al., forthcoming).

This Finnish model of dialogue between implementer and regulators has been seen to require: 1) strong social trust in the regulatory authorities; and 2) a well-defined interaction process that earns public confidence and ensures that decision-making in regard to licencing is not subsequently constrained or compromised in the legal or "quasi-judicial" sense (NEA, 2003: 10). The Finnish nuclear regulation culture can also be characterised in Renn's (2008) terms as a mixture of fiduciary and consensual approaches (Renn, 2008: 359); because of the close-knit relations of the prominent actors (STUK, the nuclear industry and the MEE), little or no opportunity for public participation remains (Litmanen et al., forthcoming). Informal communication between the parties (Laaksonen, 2006: 59–60) is significant as it creates an interactional culture and some sense of togetherness. In general, STUK has to balance between three sometimes conflicting roles in its regulatory tasks. STUK operates simultaneously as: 1) an expert, with dialogue, cooperation, self-criticism and reflectivity as key attributes; 2) an authority, whose work is shaped by independence, mediated control and perceptions; and 3) in a public role where reporting, informing and openness are important (Reiman and Norros, 2002: 188).

The time and place of socioeconomic evaluation of SNF final disposal

Recently there has been much interest in studying emergent and prospective technologies from the perspective of social expectations and experiences (Konrad, 2006; Geels and Raven, 2006; Borup et al., 2006). Applying these kinds of socioeconomic evaluation perspectives to the study of nuclear power is rather difficult, because the technology is not new and innovative. One option would be to follow current megaproject governance and evaluation approaches such as conventional rational evaluation schemes or megaproject pathologies approaches (Flyvbjerg et al., 2003; Flyvbjerg, 2005) or their rivals such as the projects-as-practice approach (Sanderson, 2012) or reflexive and learning-oriented evaluation[6] (Lehtonen, 2014a). Instead of conducting any such large-scale socioeconomic evaluation exercises, this chapter aims to make a novel contribution to research on megaproject governance. As both Sanderson (2012) and Lehtonen (2014a) have indicated, the features of megaprojects are far from simple. Both authors have characterised megaprojects more as programmes of projects, networks or organic open systems with both substantive and institutional complexity and a multiplicity of rationalities, all producing serious difficulties for governance and evaluation. As Lehtonen (2014b: 98) has indicated, the ambiguities related to 'the social' also produce problems for the socioeconomic evaluation. Conventional ways of measuring 'the social' through quantitative indicators tend to overlook the more qualitative elements, and in so doing, objectify 'the social' (Lehtonen, 2014a: 98).

One way to start deconstructing the socioeconomic evaluation of megaprojects in the field of nuclear technology is to focus on time. The temporal scales involved in nuclear technology projects are huge, due to the longevity of radioactive material. If we leave out ex post evaluation due to the long-term legacy[7] of SNF and concentrate on ex ante evaluation questions, we have to ask when ex ante evaluation is done. In the case of nuclear technology projects, socioeconomic evaluation is normally conducted in the planning and decision-making phases. The Finnish case of final disposal of SNF will illustrate the continuous and dynamic nature of the ex ante evaluation process despite the main actors' efforts to confine it to the crucial decision-making phases.

In the three-step Finnish licencing process for nuclear facilities, socioeconomic questions are discussed mostly in the first phase, which is called the Decision in Principle (DiP).[8] During this decision phase socioeconomic issues are debated widely at different spatial levels, because, for instance, a proposed host municipality can use its veto right before the government makes the decision and Parliament ratifies the Decision in Principle. The DiP is seen as the Government's answer to the main political question, i.e. whether the proposed nuclear facility is in line with the overall good of society (The Nuclear Energy Act 1987/990, Section 1).[9]

As Strauss (2011; see also Hokkanen, 2007 and Kojo, 2014) has indicated, the process of socioeconomic evaluation of the project is separated into two tracks. The first track, based on the Nuclear Energy Act, is more decisive, because socioeconomic considerations are then decisive, whereas the second track is based on the Finnish Act on Environmental Impact Assessment (EIA) Procedure.[10] The EIA Act gives citizens an opportunity to participate, but in a way that does not in a real sense affect the decisions taken in track one. According to Strauss (2011: 150) the function of track two is to channel citizen participation into a smooth and efficient administrative process, which compromises the critical potential of civil society and ensures that the overall goal of acceptance is reached in a quasi-democratic manner. Besides these two institutionally regulated socioeconomic evaluation tracks, also informal socioeconomic evaluation by, for example, the anti-nuclear movement can affect both the dominant socioeconomic evaluation outcomes and also the ongoing technical risk assessment and safety regulation.

Strauss' (2011) study of public participation in the siting of nuclear and hydro projects in Finland, concluded that politicians and authorities have sought to avoid the politicisation of licencing and decision-making procedures. This has been the case especially after the acceptance of the DiP. Both STUK[11] and Posiva deemed that the political phase of the licencing procedure ended when the Finnish Parliament ratified the DiP in 2001 (Äikäs, 2013; Isaksson, 2007).[12] The interpretation is that after the ratification of the DiP, the process, which is expected to lead to a construction licence and an operating licence, is essentially technical, and does not leave much room for political or socioeconomic considerations (Isaksson, 2007: 177; Äikäs and Sundell, 2014: 8–9).

Both STUK and Posiva seem to advocate a clear division between the 'technical' and the 'political'. They frame the last two steps of the licencing procedure as forums for technical expertise, thereby dismissing political considerations and fostering depoliticisation. During the second and third licencing phases, the spectrum of socioeconomic issues to be taken into account in the evaluation is narrow, given that the decision is taken only by the Government on the basis of safety and technical considerations. The necessary prerequisite for issuing construction and operation licences is a positive safety evaluation by the Finnish Radiation and Nuclear Safety Authority (STUK). In this sense, socioeconomic issues are bracketed out from these decision-making phases, but the political reality is that every time the Government handles nuclear facility applications, national political debates over the use of nuclear power proliferate.

Instead of analysing how different stakeholders present the socioeconomic impacts of the SNF disposal project and what kinds of results their socioeconomic evaluation schemes produce in different phases of the project, this study focuses on dyadic risk dialogue[13] between the main actors in the SNF disposal project. The study design is similar to that of Wärnbäck's (2012) extensive analysis of expert dialogue between the Swedish Nuclear Fuel and Waste Management Company (SKB), the regulatory authorities and the Government.

We have chosen the actor-centred projects-as-practice approach, which has three basic methodological components: 1) a micro-analytic focus upon the day-to-day activities of management practitioners and their meaning in a specific social setting; 2) a focus on the wide range of actors both formally and informally engaged in a project; and 3) emphasis on the relevance and importance of emergent, non-programmed work activities for an understanding of how a project develops (Sanderson, 2012: 441). Our analysis focuses on the risk dialogue over copper corrosion between the nuclear waste company, Posiva, and STUK, and the ways in which these organisations deal with the challenge that copper corrosion presents to final disposal. While the project-as-practice approach emphasises the importance of analysing different actors involved in the project, our analysis highlights the country-specific features of the Finnish regulatory system of SNF disposal and the nature of the long-standing risk dialogue between the parties. Even though MEE has the general regulatory power in nuclear waste policy,[14] the study of dyadic interaction between STUK and Posiva is important, because these two organisations negotiate risks regarding the disposal of SNF, and their risk dialogue is framed by the Finnish legislation. Though the project-as-practice approach stresses the need to analyse the relevance and importance of emergent, non-programmed work activities, our approach focuses on institutionally channeled work activities, which can be interrupted by unplanned changes. Research design, which covers a long time period, did not allow us to observe the day-to-day activities of management practitioners and their meaning construction in a specific social setting. We concentrate solely on the official written exchanges of information – even here there was plenty of material to examine (Litmanen et al., 2014: 13). The minutes of the face-to-face interactions between Posiva and STUK were not available for investigation.

Data and method of the analysis

The empirical material for this study was obtained by examining key documents concerning the risk dialogue as part of the regulatory process between Posiva and STUK, namely the Research, Development and Technical Design (RTD) review process and the CLA process. RTD related to the KBS-3 concept[15] has been underway for over thirty years,[16] but there are still some uncertainties. As the KBS-3 concept is originally Swedish, Posiva has been cooperating closely with its Swedish counterpart, SKB (Kojo and Oksa, 2014). Because of the similarities in the technical plans and safety cases the two companies have had 'extensive research cooperation covering the whole disposal technology' (Posiva, 2010a: 12–13).[17]

We examined Posiva's RTD programmes published in 2003,[18] 2006 and 2009, and their successor, the Nuclear Waste Management (NWM) programme published in 2012.[19] The RTD programmes describe the progress and the management of the radioactive waste activities that Posiva undertakes on behalf of its owners, TVO and FPH, and other stakeholders. Regarding the purpose of the reports, an important change has taken place. The focus of the reports has been on the development of the SNF disposal programme, but the documents from 2003 to 2009 reflect the steps taken to prepare for the construction licence application and aim to show the feasibility of the repository (Posiva, 2006: 11).[20] Therefore we also examined the pre-CLA. This data, which consists solely of the official written exchanges of information, can obviously only illuminate a part of a more complex picture of risk dialogue between the actors.

When examining STUK, we analysed the statements that the regulator submitted to the MEE concerning Posiva's reports. We also examined the appendices of the statements[21] that give more detailed background information on the issues raised in the statements. In these documents STUK, together with its subcontractors, evaluates the RTD efforts and the adequacy of the company's application material, comments on the planned research, development and technical design of the spent fuel repository system and the state of the application material, and makes recommendations regarding further development.

The analysis focused on copper corrosion, because the copper canister is one of the main barriers in the KBS-3 final disposal concept. In the data analysis, both copper corrosion and the corrosion issue in general were taken into account. However, forms of corrosion unrelated to copper (e.g. the corrosion of iron inserts, reinforcement materials or some of the metal parts of the fuel assemblies) were excluded from the research, as they did not fit into the frame of the present study.

The design of our study follows the sequence of the dialogue between Posiva and STUK (see Figure 7.1). We investigated both the RTD review process and the CLA authorisation process as part of the regulatory process. The progress of Posiva's RTD concerning the possibility for a deep geological nuclear waste repository is influenced by the continuous exchange of information with STUK as well as the official statements of the authority (both indicated in the figure with arrows) that were developed on the basis of the RTD reports. STUK's were influenced by the risk communication it conducted with Posiva. Statements by the MEE following STUK's review statements are not included in the data and are not mentioned in Figure 7.1. As Figure 7.1 indicates, it was only after 2009 that the CLA review began to affect the RTD review process. STUK's pre-CLA review influenced STUK's own 2010 RTD review and Posiva's new NWM-2012 programme. STUK's pre-CLA review also affected Posiva's 2012 CLA. The

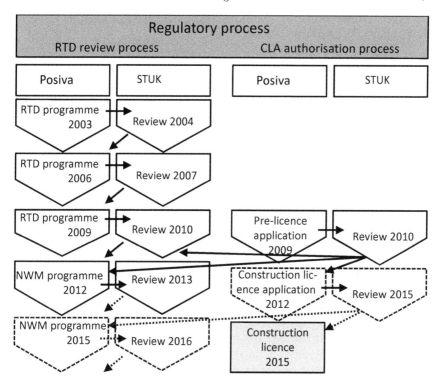

Figure 7.1 The flow of risk dialogue between Posiva and STUK as part of the regulatory process.

Finnish Government granted the licence to construct an SNF encapsulation plant and disposal facility at Olkiluoto in November 2015. The maximum disposal capacity of the facility is 6,500 tonnes of uranium (MEE, 2015).

Years 2003 and 2004: setting the stage

The stage for the copper corrosion dialogue between Posiva and STUK was set in 2003, two years after the first step of the authorisation process and the ratification of the DiP by Parliament. In the RTD report of 2003, Posiva described their own and their cooperative research on corrosion, as well as their thoughts concerning aspects needing further research. To complement its own expertise, STUK hired external experts to review the RTD. These reviews led STUK to demand further consideration, clarification and research on several issues.

During this period many uncertainties were identified regarding copper corrosion. Nevertheless, Posiva seemed to remain optimistic, while hoping for favourable results from future studies and improved insight into unclear matters related to copper corrosion. On the other hand, STUK (2004: 2) considered Posiva's RTD report of 2003 to be a general overview of the situation at that time and expected answers to many questions and concrete technological choices to be given in the near future.

With respect to the specifications of the canister for the isolation of SNF, Posiva (2003: 36) argued that canister design rests on the assumption that it is 'watertight and airtight, corrosion resistant and mechanically solid'. According to the company, a great deal of research that the company had conducted over a period of twenty years, both by Posiva and by its counterpart and collaborator, SKB, proved the suitability of copper. Posiva stated that 'available evidence supports' the claim that the canister can hold the waste for more than a hundred thousand years. Nevertheless, it simultaneously admitted the need for further research (Posiva, 2003: 119).

At the time, Posiva and SKB, together with some Canadian partners, were engaged in a joint project aimed at developing a model for predicting long-term corrosion in sulphide-containing compacted bentonite. Posiva and SKB also investigated issues such as general corrosion in oxygen-free and saline conditions, localised corrosion, the impact of redox conditions on corrosion, and the effects of methane and high-pH conditions on corrosion (Posiva, 2003: 119–120).

Some of the above-mentioned issues were also presented in Posiva's RTD report. With respect to general corrosion in oxygen-free conditions and salinity, the company cited a couple of contradictory studies and concluded that the issue still needed further research in conditions as similar as possible to those of the repository. Further research would also be needed on the possibility of localised corrosion that could cause an early failure of the copper shell. The impact of redox conditions on corrosion, with an unclear duration in the initial toxic period as well as estimates regarding the relevant chemical, electrochemical and microbiological processes was recognised as another area of uncertainty (Posiva, 2003: 120–121). On the effects of methane, Posiva argued that according to the literature reviewed, methane had no negative effect on copper (Posiva, 2003: 121). Finally, with respect to the effects of high-pH conditions, Posiva (2003: 121) stated that a high pH would lead to the passivation of the canister surface, which would increase the stability of the canister and its ability to prevent local corrosion. Although Posiva's 2003 RTD report provided a detailed overview in which the main issues concerning copper corrosion were thoroughly and logically addressed (Read, 2004: 8), STUK and its reviewers raised numerous comments, questions and requirements about further research on how to determine the corrodibility of the copper canister. In relation to Posiva's estimate of the lifetime of the canister, Hänninen (2003: 2) highlighted that the isolation of the waste in the canisters for more than a hundred thousand years was a much longer time span than 'the operation time of any other industrial product', whereas Apted et al. (2004: 11) believed that Posiva minimised numerous concerns. Therefore, Posiva was urged to consider, for instance, the manufacture of the canisters, the materials to be used, and their mechanical characteristics, in order to be able to address all forms of corrosion and other risks (Hänninen, 2003: 2).

STUK, together with its reviewers, required more research on various issues and highlighted some aspects that Posiva should consider. For example, Apted

(2004: 10) noted that temperature might play a role in mineralogical alteration for some designs. Changes in volume due to the corrosion of the canister had to be taken into account while studying chemical interactions between the backfill and the buffer. Hänninen (2003: 2) agreed with Posiva that a thinner copper shell would be advantageous, but he also pointed out the need for proof that such a shell would withstand corrosion. STUK (2004: 5) pointed out that groundwater conditions were more prone to facilitate corrosion in the bedrock of Olkiluoto than in the operating waste cave, and this would have to be kept in mind when interpreting the results of copper corrosion research. Hänninen (2003: 8) and Apted et al. (2004: 11–12) demanded that the representative creep behaviour of the copper canister be tested to avoid canister corrosion. That said, Read (2004: 9) expressed his full support for the joint Posiva and SKB project, focusing on the development of 'a corrosion model for copper in sulphide media containing compacted bentonite'.

Years 2006 and 2007: focus on future projections

During the second round of the dialogue, the issue of copper corrosion gained both breadth and depth. The increased coverage of the corrosion issues in the RTD of 2006 indicated both improved knowledge and remaining uncertainties. STUK recognised Posiva's efforts at enhancing its knowledge, but nevertheless identified weaknesses and pointed out areas in need of further research.

In this period, the discussion between Posiva and STUK extended to the future prospects of and the possible concerns related to the long-term corrosion behaviour of copper in changing repository conditions. The increasing attention given to copper corrosion in Posiva's 2006 RTD report suggested that during this three-year period the company gained more information and clarity on the issues, but was simultaneously confronted with continuing uncertainties. STUK acknowledged the advances in Posiva's knowledge, but once again required more information about certain issues related to corrosion processes. STUK and its consultants deplored the lack of a coherent picture of the research, of evidence on the long-term properties of the canister design, and of research on the possibility of early failure of the canister due to creep or stress corrosion. STUK required clarifications and further consideration of a number of other matters as well.

Posiva's 2006 RTD report delineated the requirements, reviewed the steps taken during the previous three years and outlined further RTD issues for the upcoming period. The document dwelled on 'technical performance of the disposal concept and of the engineering components in site-specific conditions'. Since the deadline for the submission of the CLA was approaching, the focus of this report shifted towards the 'operational and long-term safety of the system' (Posiva, 2006: 11).

Posiva (2006: 49) had collected a substantial amount of knowledge regarding the corrosion of copper, and argued that such potential forms of corrosion in repository conditions had been extensively studied already, but information was still lacking on microbially induced corrosion. Stress corrosion cracking was deemed unlikely because of the low concentration of elements that induce stress corrosion cracking and the remarkably low corrosion potential values (Posiva, 2006: 49, 197). In the report, Posiva (2006: 49–50, 71, 238) also described what it had learned about the interaction between forms of copper corrosion mentioned earlier (including uniform and pitting corrosion) and the constantly evolving repository environment, with a focus on oxygen-free, saline, chlorine and alkaline conditions, together with the effects of temperature and pH. Moreover, the possible impacts of alien materials on copper corrosion were considered in the report (Posiva, 2006: 257).

Posiva also paid attention to the changing repository conditions and to the expected corrosion processes during the planned lifespan of the repository. Posiva's examination took into account both the repository construction phases (e.g. early post-closure, the post-closure saturated phase) and climate change periods including, for example, permafrost and glacial melting (Posiva, 2006: 196–201). Despite the lack of clear insight into upcoming changes, the document stated that the investigations carried out supported earlier findings, which have tended to corroborate the hypothesis that the copper canister concept is safe and feasible (Posiva, 2006: 208). However, because of numerous uncertainties concerning long-term corrosion in the repository environment, Posiva (2006: 62) stated that it would continue to research the issue. In addition, the future RTD efforts of the company were to be directed towards the investigation of, for instance, corrosion in anoxic and saline conditions as well as compacted sulphide-containing bentonite (Posiva, 2006: 50). Also, the company planned to continue studies on the potential for corrosion due to welding, as well as on the effects of acetates (Posiva, 2006: 57–58, 140).

STUK (2007a: 2) stated that together with a group of external experts, it would continue to engage in dialogue with Posiva on research into the repository and the construction of ONKALO. The safety authority gave positive feedback on the reporting and technical development that had taken place during the preceding three years, but also identified weaknesses and areas for further investigation. STUK (2007b: 2) criticised the RTD report for failing to give a clear picture of the research and for a lack of evidence concerning the long-term properties of the canister design, and argued that the risk of an early failure of the canisters due to creep or stress corrosion had received too little attention in the document. Other uncertainties had to do with the relationship between groundwater and copper corrosion (STUK, 2007b: 4; Bath et al., 2007: 20). STUK also required further explanation regarding the worst-case scenario of copper corrosion caused by sulphate-reducing bacteria (Read et al., 2007: 30). Finally, Hänninen et al. (2007: 27) noted that information was lacking about stress corrosion cracking under reducing and oxidising conditions.

STUK and its reviewers required more RTD efforts on numerous copper-corrosion related issues. According to the authority, extensive research and mathematical modelling were still needed to ascertain the long-term durability of the technical barriers, and special attention would need to be paid to the interaction between the copper canister and bentonite. STUK also stated that the remaining questions concerning the processes affecting the corrosion behaviour of copper had to be investigated (STUK, 2007a: 2). Finally, STUK's subcontractors (Bath et al., 2007: 18–19, 20) asked for more investigation concerning the biogeochemical inputs into the engineered barrier system that impacts copper corrosion of the canister as well as into the effects of sulphate on redox stability.

Years 2009 and 2010: intermingling of two processes

At this stage the authorisation process brought up difficulties in the fairly simple regulatory review process. As indicated in Figure 7.1, the regulatory review process, i.e. the RTD review, was affected by the authorisation process, i.e. the CLA review. This intermingling of two processes increased STUK's criticism, and the approval of the CLA no longer seemed self-evident.

In this period, in addition to its RTD report Posiva also had to submit material for the so-called pre-construction licence application (pre-CLA) required by the MEE. Interestingly enough, different perceptions of the pre-CLA by Posiva and STUK affected both of STUK's reviews. Finding the pre-CLA material lacking in many ways, STUK extended its criticism to the RTD report, looking at it in the light of its assessment of the pre-CLA material. The criticism voiced by STUK was essentially twofold. On the one hand, it expected a more comprehensive approach from Posiva, and on the other, it still required more attention to corrosion. Having expected a more holistic view in the pre-CLA, STUK now expressed harsh criticism. It deplored the lack of coherence, justifications and conclusions, but also Posiva's inability to keep up with its timetables (STUK, 2010a; 2010b).

Notably, at this time Posiva and STUK focused on almost the same themes related to copper corrosion as in earlier documents. This suggests that all the known strictly copper-corrosion related issues had probably been identified by that time.[22] Nevertheless, Posiva's discussion of the corrosion behaviour of copper in the RTD of 2009 was more extensive than before and paid considerably more attention to comments made by STUK. However, in its statements STUK demanded a more comprehensive picture from Posiva and at the same time continued to demand answers to outstanding strictly corrosion-related questions before the next milestone – the CLA in 2012.

From STUK's comments it is obvious that Posiva and STUK were not on the same page regarding the pre-CLA material. Posiva had submitted a compilation of research accomplished, whereas STUK had expected a more holistic view on what Posiva would present later in the actual CLA. STUK found Posiva's material to be lacking in coherence, justifications and conclusions, and excessively concentrated on individual issues. STUK considered that some delayed and unfinished ongoing tasks had become critical to the schedule, and stated that the RTD programme concurrently in review would be assessed with the findings of the pre-licence review in mind (STUK, 2010a).

As one would expect, given that the pre-licence material[23] and the RTD programme were submitted at roughly the same time, these two sources did not significantly differ in the ways that they addressed the strictly copper-corrosion related issues. In its last actual RTD programme report in 2009, Posiva (2010b:

13) addressed the topic of SNF disposal presented research as well as technical development and design work. For example, in the document, the company (Posiva, 2010b: 292, 297–298, 309) discussed the ability of the bentonite buffer that would surround the copper canister to protect it from corrosion and from other risks. Moreover, in relation to the chemical composition of groundwater, Posiva (2010b: 302–304) considered the potential for chloride corrosion as well as the unfavourable impact of solutes and other corrosive agents on the copper canister. Posiva's research and formulation of scenarios also addressed corrosion processes caused by the influx of oxygen into the repository along with glacial meltwater (Posiva, 2010b: 307, 358). In response to an earlier review by STUK, the document discussed various forms of copper corrosion (e.g. general corrosion, metal corrosion, localised corrosion, the inter-granular corrosion of copper in the welds, and microbially induced corrosion), and did so with reference to different phases of the disposal of the canister (Posiva, 2010b: 356–357).

Posiva had also identified some areas of concern that still needed further research. Although the company deemed stress corrosion cracking to be unlikely under the expected conditions, it admitted to the remaining uncertainties with respect to evolving changes in climate as well as repository conditions (Posiva, 2010b: 358–359). Posiva also stated that it would continue research on, for instance, possible material defects in the copper canister shell and weld as well as the adverse impacts of residual stresses that might increase the risk of stress corrosion cracking (Posiva, 2010b: 208–209, 211–212, 239–240, 345–346, 358–359). Moreover, Posiva planned to investigate the potential for stress corrosion cracking due to the presence of oxygen, certain redox potential values, sulphide ions and sulphide impacts under anaerobic conditions (Posiva, 2010b: 359, 362). With respect to canister evolution, the company said it was also going to study unlikely but possible scenarios related to uniform corrosion induced by sulphide ions (Posiva, 2010b: 362, 411).

STUK and its reviewers acknowledged the substantial progress that Posiva had managed to make with respect to copper corrosion and other issues (STUK, 2010b; STUK, 2010a: 2). Nevertheless, the regulator still required some clarifications because it considered that the material provided was incomplete on numerous safety issues related to the canister's corrosion properties. Although Posiva's further analyses of copper corrosion indicated that the SNF would be safely isolated for ten thousand years in the canister, once again STUK suggested taking into consideration the possibility that, for instance, some canisters might suffer from manufacturing flaws deficiently and would therefore not necessarily last the entire required period (Hämäläinen, 2010: 4). Furthermore, stress corrosion, copper corrosion in pure oxygen-free water as well as possible changes in the repository due to environmental conditions (e.g. groundwater or glacial meltwater penetrating the repository) were safety issues that would require more research (Hämäläinen, 2010: 5; Heinonen, 2010: 10, 14, 22; STUK, 2010b: 4).

STUK's broader criticism related to the inadequate extent of the safety analysis and the lack of a plan on how the performance targets would be reached, and in some cases even how the targets would be established (2010b: 2–4). STUK considered that Posiva had a lot of work to do in order to improve the coherence of its presentation, notably of the conclusions and justifications. It noted that the schedule for the CLA would be very tight, as a sizeable part of the long-term research was to be done after 2012. STUK also stated that if safety-related research and conclusions were presented after the submission of the licence application, this could delay the safety case review (2010b: 1–2, index 18).

Years 2012 and 2013: crisis in the relationship

At this stage, during the last regulatory review round before the CLA, the existing tensions between the parties increased further. As in previous stages, here too, the two processes of regulatory review and authorisation (Figure 7.1) intersected with and affected each other, creating a somewhat confusing situation. Both the NWM 2012 programme and the official CLA were under review. In the NWM 2012 review process Posiva referred in many cases to material that was to be included in the CLA. The documents indicate that STUK was intensifying its criticism, because Posiva had not taken earlier criticism seriously enough. One major argument by STUK was that Posiva would need more time for some of its studies. It estimated that some studies would be completed only after the CLA review by STUK. Thus, after an initial rejection, STUK only accepted Posiva's NWM after the company had submitted clarifications and amendments in reaction to STUK's initial review.

In this period the themes related to copper corrosion again remained much the same. In its first NWM report, Posiva (2012c) tried to respond to the criticism by updating its safety plan with extra care, taking into account the feedback from STUK. In fact, Posiva claimed that it had compiled the comments into detailed lists accompanied by a plan on how it would take the comments into account. In the report Posiva identified research done, for example, regarding the suitability of the site, the future evolution of the system, barriers and the canister (Posiva, 2012c: 34–35, 46–98, 120–170). The report was to include future plans up to 2015, but Posiva had chosen to make an account of plans up to 2018. The list of aspects needing further research still appeared extensive and included many issues similar to those that had been under investigation already; however, most of them were not strictly related to copper corrosion.

While the themes of the period had not really changed, the tone of STUK's criticism did, as it considered that Posiva had not taken its earlier criticism seriously enough. STUK argued that although Posiva planned in many instances to continue its research on the basis of projects started earlier, in many of these cases Posiva had neither made clear their relationship and contribution to safety nor outlined a timeline for conducting these projects. Also, according to STUK, Posiva had overestimated the time available for Posiva to conduct its studies in order to complement the application afterwards. STUK stated that the report contained little new information on long-term safety and that it had already criticised the RTDs of 2006 and 2009 for having been insufficient in this regard. STUK also reiterated its earlier criticism on the lack of a plan for implementing the measures needed to reach the performance targets (STUK, 2013: 1–5).

After STUK's rejection Posiva complemented the NWM programme with more comprehensive plans regarding the schedules for the intended R&D. With regard to the issues concerning long-term safety, in its response Posiva frequently referred to material intended for the CLA. At the time, Posiva had already submitted the CLA, but expected to supplement it while STUK would be reviewing it. STUK deemed the amended NWM acceptable, but stated that the plans for ensuring long-term safety would have to be evaluated as part of the CLA review.[24]

Conclusions

In this study, we focused on the dialogue between the nuclear waste management company, Posiva Ltd, and the nuclear safety authority, STUK, with particular attention to copper corrosion as one of the key challenges in the final disposal of SNF. The starting point of the study was that technical risk dialogue is not apolitical or asocial, but rather takes place in institutional settings and therefore entails socioeconomic evaluation.

Our empirical findings suggest that the need for an SNF repository pushed Posiva to adopt an optimistic view on safety issues right from the first RTD report in 2003, yet the company admits its lack of knowledge on many aspects related to copper corrosion. The results suggest that Posiva's programmes evolved from a mere description of the situation towards more focused and extensive discussions. Meanwhile, the primacy of the ultimate safety of SNF disposal seems to determine how STUK frames the copper corrosion as a significant challenge to be dealt with in a way that leaves no room for error, but at the same time, as safe final disposal is seen as the goal, it supports Posiva in pushing ahead in its RTD work, recognising the company's advancements and identifying the areas that need further research.

Since the dyadic risk communication between the organisations is determined by Finnish legislation, STUK exercised its right to demand information, while the implementer, Posiva, was compelled to comply with the requirements. Nevertheless, the organisations appeared to operate on an equal footing in that they both pursued the common goal of successful development of a safe repository for SNF. The results show that under the normal steady flow of interaction, the risk governance process is oriented towards mutual learning and improvement; however, at the time of crucial decision-making, extra tensions entered the relationship. This mixture of two processes, the RTD review process and CLA authorisation process, enabled an explicit discussion on socioeconomic issues when STUK rejected Posiva's NWM programme.

The results of this research support the assumption that long-lasting interaction between the implementer and the regulator tends to shape the regulatory style. Both the existing literature on the Finnish nuclear regulatory culture and the case studied indicate that the regulatory culture is a mixture of fiduciary and consensual approaches due to the prominent roles of the main actors, STUK and Posiva, and the total absence of or very limited opportunity for public participation. The stepwise decision-making and implementation process affected the regulatory process, which is also stepwise. The Finnish nuclear regulatory culture can be characterised as flexible, development-oriented and, as such, oriented towards gradual learning and refinement. This regulatory philosophy provides plenty of opportunities for a constructive dialogue between the regulator and the implementer, which can be beneficial for the development of technical procedures but this straightforward dyadic dialogue both neglects interaction with other parties and hampers more open socioeconomic evaluation. Ideally, the respective roles of the implementer and the regulator should be clearly defined and separate from each other, but this study of long-standing interaction indicates that engagement in dialogue has transformed STUK's role towards greater attention to development, thus shifting STUK's input towards the advancement of the project and giving it a consultative role of sorts. However, at the time of the pre-licence application and actual CLA, STUK reviewed Posiva's RTD and pre-licence application primarily from the point of view of a regulator.

Even though the regulator may have enough regulatory power and it may enjoy powerful institutional status, the long-standing interaction may also create convergence between the organisations. Wärnbäck et al. (2013) warn of the tendency of the values and priorities of the implementer and the regulator to converge over time due to prolonged social interaction. In the Finnish case, this rapprochement of values and priorities could be seen in the three RTD phases – 2003, 2006 and 2009 – but the analysis of the 2009 pre-CLA and NWM 2012 showed the withdrawal of STUK from a consensual regulatory style to a more independent and critical regulatory role, probably because of the intersection of two processes, namely the normal regulatory process RTD and the construction licence authorisation process. The diffusion of these two processes caused confusion for the implementer in 2009, as it produced a pre-CLA which did not meet the expectations of STUK. In the next phase, in 2012, STUK's increasing dissatisfaction with Posiva's work led to a crisis in the relationship. STUK rejected Posiva's NWM programme and accepted the new programme only after Posiva had provided a supplement. Yet, STUK underlined that the new NWM 2012 programme would once again be evaluated as part of the CLA review. The consensus and shared understanding achieved in earlier phases of interaction seemed to vanish in the pre-CLA and official CLA review processes.

In addition to the regulatory culture, interesting questions concern the regulatory object. The study indicated that from 2003 to 2006 STUK's main regulatory object was the R&D process and the studies related to the advancement of the disposal project, whereas from 2009 to 2012, due to the approaching licencing procedure, STUK shifted its focus towards a broader understanding of safety. These two issues are of course connected, but during the regulation process the emphasis seemed to change.

Both Posiva and STUK state that the DiP ratified by Parliament in 2001 consolidated the dominance of the scientific–technical approach over socioeconomic evaluation. Both parties adhered to the view that the DiP closed the gates to political intervention, legitimating fiduciary regulation, with a small number of directors obliged to make the 'common good' the guiding principle in their actions, and excluding public involvement (see Renn, 2008: 358–361).

These company and regulatory directors were de facto given the freedom to define what was meant by the 'common good' or 'the good of the society'.

Acknowledgements

This research is a part of the EURATOM InSOTEC project and the Finnish Research Programme on Nuclear Waste Management (KYT) 2011–2014. The authors also acknowledge the support of the Academy of Finland (research project no. 253332). The authors want to thank all partners in the InSOTEC project for providing constructive feedback on earlier versions of the chapter. We appreciate the constructive criticism given by Juhani Vira of Posiva and the insightful comments of Anne Bergmans (University of Antwerp), the InSOTEC project coordinator. In gathering the data, the help of Jaana Avolahti of the Ministry of Employment and the Economy and Jussi Heinonen and Risto Paltemaa of STUK is also appreciated.

Notes

1   The legislation regarding nuclear activities in Finland includes three main instruments: 1) the Nuclear Energy Act 1987 (990/1987); 2) the Radiation Protection Act 1991 (592/1991); and 3) the Nuclear Liability Act 1972 (484/1972 & 588/1994) (OECD, 2008). However, the legislation was updated in 2008. As part of the legislative reform, a number of the relevant Government Decisions were replaced with Government Decrees (GDs). The Decrees entered into force on 1 December 2008. The Government Decision (478/1999) regarding the safety of the disposal of spent nuclear fuel, which particularly applied to the disposal facility, was replaced by the Government Decree 736/2008, issued on 27 November 2008 (Posiva, 2012a: 15).

2   These YVL regulatory guides are issued by STUK. The STUK mandate to issue detailed technical and administrative guidance is rooted in the Nuclear Energy Act.

3   Posiva is obliged to prepare triennial programmes for research, development and technical design (RTD), which STUK must review. STUK also has to publish an expert evaluation of the programme report. However, before it became obligatory, Posiva compiled the 2003 RTD voluntarily.

4   For major nuclear facilities, including spent fuel storage and disposal facilities, the nuclear legislation defines a three-step authorisation process: 1) Decision-in-Principle: the Government makes the licencing decision, prior approval by the host municipality and ratification by Parliament are required; 2) Construction licence, issued by the Government; 3) Operating licence, issued by the Government. STUK is obliged to conduct a safety review in each of these licencing processes and the MEE prepares the licencing decisions.

5   The example given by NEA gives is the reply by STUK's former Director General Jukka Laaksonen to a question concerning the knowledge base of their review of the Decision-in-Principle (DiP) for the final disposal project of radioactive waste. Laaksonen's pragmatic response was to point out that in the DiP stage, no definitive conclusion on the safety of the proposed disposal concept was required. What was needed at this stage was only a preliminary safety appraisal stating that nothing had been found that would raise doubts about the feasibility of achieving the required safety level (NEA, 2003: 12–13).

6   In concrete terms, the learning approach would mean: 1) charting the network and its boundaries; 2) defining the accountability structures; 3) clarifying the goals and

objectives of the network, and 4) exploring the role of evaluation and the evaluator in project governance (Lehtonen, 2014a: 287).

7 In a narrow sense, socioeconomic expectations and evaluations are related to each project's life cycle. The initial design lifespan of a nuclear power plant (NPP) is usually thirty to forty years. Purely economic evaluation entails financial depreciation of the investment in the plant and also the return for investments during the initial lifespan. Usually socioeconomic evaluation in the planning phase also includes indirect economic benefits to the local, regional and even the national economy, but in the evaluation, the actors should also pay attention to the expected impacts on sociocultural factors such as quality of life, lifestyles and values. However, the long-term hazards from the radiotoxicity of the spent fuel extend to tens of thousands and even hundreds of thousands of years. This risk of radiotoxicity requires isolation from the biosphere and implies substantial challenges for socioeconomic evaluation. The dilemma is how to anticipate such distant futures and assess socioeconomic impacts in a future which cannot be imagined.

8 As part of the procedure for the first step in the authorisation process, the DiP, which was issued in 2000, the Radiation and Nuclear Safety Authority (STUK) made a preliminary safety appraisal (Ruokola, 2000). According to the Finnish timetable for nuclear waste management (originally set out in the Government's policy decision of 1983), Posiva submitted a CLA for a final repository for spent nuclear fuel, including a safety case, at the end of 2012 (cf. Posiva, 2010c; 2012a; 2012b; 2013). The construction licence for the final disposal facility was granted in November 2015. Before that STUK conducted a safety appraisal of Posiva's CLA safety case, as part of the procedure leading to the construction licence. According to the Nuclear Energy Act (990/1987, §55), STUK is responsible for the supervision of safe use of nuclear energy, and participates in the processing of licence and operation applications.

9 Indeed, the Finnish legislation regulating nuclear power includes a general socioeconomic assessment principle. The very first section of the Nuclear Energy Act indeed (1987/990) states that the objective is "To keep the use of nuclear energy in line with the overall good of society…" The crucial socioeconomic evaluation question of nuclear megaprojects in Finland tends to crystallise in the question: "Is this project in line with the overall good of society?"

10 Within environmental impact assessment (EIA), socioeconomic impact assessment (SEIA) can have a formal status and follow standardised procedures. For instance, the Mackenzie Valley Environmental Impact Review Board has defined that 'SEIA is the systematic analysis used during EIA to identify and evaluate the potential socioeconomic and cultural impacts of a proposed development on the lives and circumstances of people, their families and their communities' (Mackenzie Valley, 2007: 6). The impacts can be defined as potential changes caused by industrial development activities (Mackenzie Valley, 2007: 6) or policy action (Michigan Sea Grant, 2009: 23).

11 STUK is obliged to control the safety of nuclear facilities in Finland. This control has two dimensions: 1) the evaluation of plans and analyses pertaining to the plant; and 2) the inspection of plant structures, systems and components as well as operational activity.

12 STUK's former director Tero Varjoranta has described the importance of this DiP by saying that in the eyes of STUK, the DiP gave Posiva the additional dimension of a construction organisation, while its earlier role had been limited to research and development (Nikula et al., 2012: 73).

13 Dyadic risk dialogue is seen here as an interactional communicative co-construction, where: 1) central institutional risk governance organisations define safety priorities, negotiate agendas for scientific–technological research programmes and advance a socio-technical project set out in official political decision-making; 2) the importance, relevance, sufficiency and validity of scientific research on the safety of SNF disposal plans are negotiated and co-produced; and 3) certain aspects of scientific findings or

technological risks are accentuated and others downplayed in order to gain the support of target stakeholders, convince the decision-makers, fulfil the priority set in advance for the overall project and reach governmental permission to implement the plans (Dewulf et al., 2004; 2009; Fairman et al., 2012; Risley, 2011). Although there is a tendency to involve many stakeholders in risk-related decision-making, we share the view of those researchers who argue that the institutionalisation of risk governance has given risk professionals and expert organisations a powerful role in risk regulation (Renn, 2008: 203–204; Beck, 1992; OECD, 2002). In many cases, powerful expert organisations have significant power to frame issues and to conceptualise debates (Dewulf et al., 2009: 166). However, risk communication is not free of constraints, because it takes place within given institutional settings (Renn, 2008: 215–217) and sociocultural contexts (Kasperson et al. 1988; Kasperson et al. 2001).

14 The MEE decides on the principles and sets the timetables that the power companies follow. Construction permits and operating licences for nuclear facilities in Finland are issued by the Government, and the MEE receives applications and prepares decisions for the Government. This involves collecting and summarising the statements and views on the application, preparing the licence text with appropriate conditions, and presenting the case to the Government for decision. A prerequisite for any licence is safety (Laaksonen, 2006: 50).

15 The final disposal of SNF in Finland is based on the Swedish KBS-3 concept. The basic concept for the disposal of SNF rests on its encapsulation and emplacement in crystalline rock at a depth of about 500 m. Spent nuclear fuel is to be encapsulated in spheroidal graphite cast iron canisters that will have an outer shield made of copper. The surface of the canisters is to be protected by a clay buffer isolating it from the rock. The canisters are to be placed in individual deposition holes in deposition tunnels. Tunnels are to be backfilled with materials of low permeability and closed.

16 The disposal concept proposed in the DiP application has been the focus of research and development work conducted in Finland over the past thirty years. The target schedule and the objectives were originally defined in the Government Decision of 1983: 1) interim progress reporting in 1985 and 1992; 2) preparedness for the selection of a disposal site by the end of 2000; 3) preparedness for the construction licence application by the end of 2010; and 4) preparedness for the commencement of disposal operations as of 2020 (Ruokola, 2000: 9).

17 SKB and Posiva have also sought to jointly promote pan-European cooperation in the field of geological disposal. The technology platform "Implementing Geological Disposal" was established to enhance this cooperation.

18 The reason for focusing on the period 2003–2012 rests on two facts: 1) in 2003, the Ministry of Trade and Industry (MTI, nowadays MEE) decided to postpone the deadline for Posiva's construction licence application to the end of 2012 because it was expected that the timetable would be too tight for Posiva; and 2) in 2003 Posiva started to publish triennial RTD programmes instead reporting annually to the supervising ministry, MTI. According to the Nuclear Energy Act 1987 (990/1987) and the Nuclear Energy Decree, which regulate the nuclear waste management of Finnish nuclear power plants, the owners of NPPs have to report at regular intervals to the MTI/MEE on how the companies in charge of SNF have planned to implement and prepare the nuclear waste management actions. According to the Nuclear Energy Act, Posiva was obliged to submit these reports yearly to the MTI/MEE, but changes in the law in 2009 formalised the practice that Posiva and MEE had followed since 2003. The MEE hence allowed Posiva to report on its research, planning and technical design every three years instead of annually.

19 YJH-2012 stands for 'Nuclear Waste Management at Olkiluoto and Loviisa Power Plants: Review of Current Status and Future Plans for 2013–2015' (in Finnish: Olkiluodon ja Loviisan voimalaitosten ydinjätehuollon ohjelma vuosille 2013–2015) (NWM, 2012; Posiva, 2012c).

20 The triennial programme was renamed as the "NWM programme" following the amendment of the Nuclear Energy Act that came into force in 2009.
21 STUK's archive record numbers: 5/H48112/2009 tks2009 lausunto; Y811/123 tks2006 lausunto; Y811/43 tks2003 lausunto.
22 As Heinonen et al. (2014) explain, the MEE required Posiva to submit preliminary (draft) licence documentation by the end of 2009. It is not known what originally triggered this improvisation in the official timetable, but STUK noted that the reasoning was: 1) to have a regulatory review of the status of the construction licence application; 2) to use it as an exercise for the actual licence application review; and 3) to test the review process, review organisation and assessment of preliminary safety case status (Heinonen et al., 2014: 3).
23 As opposed to aspects that could affect corrosion indirectly.
24 STUK gave its statement concerning Posiva's construction licence application and safety case on 11 February 2015. It stated that 'The Olkiluoto encapsulation plant and disposal facility proposed by Posiva has been designed in such a way that the requirements on the nuclear and radiation safety during the operation of the facilities are fulfilled.' One of STUK's tasks was to evaluate whether Posiva has the competence and expertise for the construction of the facility. STUK concluded that Posiva has sufficient and extensive expertise available for constructing a nuclear waste facility, but was more concerned about society's ability to maintain enough societal infrastructures and services for the safe use of nuclear energy. The Finnish government granted a construction licence to Posiva for a used nuclear fuel encapsulation plant and final disposal facility at Olkiluoto on 12 November 2015.

References

Äikäs, T. 2013. *The Finnish Nuclear Waste Management Programme: Experience, Status and Views on the Future.*. Posiva Oy. Presentation given at *The Stockholm Talks 2013*, October 2nd, 2013, Stockholm, Sweden. Available online at: www.skb.se/e316672a-7dad-416a-99d6-c06281da0cde.fodoc (accessed 6 May 2014).

Äikäs, T. & Sundell, R. 2014. *ONKALO – From Concept to Reality. WM2014 Conference.* Paper No 14494, March 2–6, 2014, Phoenix, Arizona, USA.

Andersson, K. 2014. Copper corrosion in nuclear waste disposal: A Swedish case study on stakeholder insight. *Bulletin of Science, Technology & Society* 33(3–4): 85–95. Doi: 10.1177/0270467613520538

Beck, U. 1992. *Risk society: Towards a new modernity.* London and Newbury Park, CA: Sage.

Borup, M., Brown, N., Konrad, K. & van Lente, H. 2006. The sociology of expectations in science and technology. *Technology Analysis and Strategic Management* 18(3–4): 285–298.

Dewulf, A., Craps, M. & Dercon, G. 2004. How issues get framed and reframed when different communities meet: A multi-level analysis of a collaborative soil conservation initiative in the Ecuadorian Andes. *Journal of Community & Applied Social Psychology* 14(3): 177–192.

Dewulf, A., Gray, B., Putnam, L., Lewicki, R., Aarts, N., Bouwen, R. & van Woerkum, C. 2009. Disentangling approaches to framing in conflict and negotiation research: a meta-paradigmatic perspective. *Human Relations* 62(2): 155–193.

Elam, M. & Sundqvist, G. 2009. The Swedish KBS project: A last word in nuclear fuel safety prepares to conquer the world? *Journal of Risk Research* 12(7–8): 969–988. DOI: 10.1080/13669870903126077.

Etzioni, A. 1991. The socioeconomic view of redevelopment. *Review of Political Economy* 3(4): 373–392.

Fairman, D., Chigas, D., McClintock, E. & Drager, N. 2012. *Negotiating public health in a globalized world global health diplomacy in action*. London, New York: Springer.

FANC. 2013. *Issue: Posiva's Contruction Licence Application for building capsulation and final disposal facility for nuclear fuel at Olkiluoto*. Statement by the Finnish Association for Nature Conservation. Available online at: www.sll.fi/ajankohtaista/liitto/2013/posivaluola (accessed 7 April 2014).

Flyvbjerg, B. 2005. Machiavellian megaprojects. *Antipode* 37(1): 18–22. DOI: 10.1111/j.0066-4812.2005.00471.x

Flyvbjerg, B., Bruzelius, N. & Rothengatter, W. 2003. *Megaprojects and risk: An anatomy of ambition*. Cambridge: Cambridge University Press.

Geels, F.W. & Raven, R.P.J.M. 2006. Non-linearity and expectations in niche-development trajectories: Ups and downs in Dutch biogas development (1973–2003). *Technology Analysis and Strategic Management* 18(3/4): 375–392.

Heinonen, J., Paltemaa, R. & Hämäläinen, K. 2014. Regulatory review and assessment of the 2012 Construction Licence Application for an SNF disposal facility at Olkiluoto, Finland. Paper no. 14243, *WM2014 Conference*, March 2-6, 2014, Phoenix, Arizona, USA.

Hellmich, S.N. 2015. What is socioeconomics? An overview of theories, methods, and themes in the field. *Forum for Social Economics* 44 (1): 1–23.

Hokkanen, P. 2007. *Kansalaisosallistuminen ympäristövaikutusten arviointimenettelyssä*, Doctoral Thesis, Acta Universitatis Tamperensis 1285, Tampere: Tampere University Press.

Hultquist, G. 1986. Hydrogen evolution in corrosion of copper in pure water. *Corrosion Science*. 26: 173–176.

Isaksson, R. 2007. Lessons from the EPR construction supervision. In *Transparency of Nuclear Regulatory Activities, Workshop Proceedings Tokyo and Tokai-Mura, Japan 22–24 May 2007*, OECD, NEA No. 6256. Available online at: www.oecd-nea.org/nsd/pubs/2007/6256-transparency-nra.pdf, pp. 177–185 (accessed 10 April 2014).

Kasperson, R.E., Renn, O., Slovic, P., Brown, H.S., Emel, J., Goble, R., Kasperson, J.X. & Ratick, S. 1988. The social amplification of risk: A conceptual framework. *Risk Analysis* 8(2): 177–187.

Kasperson, R.E., Jhaveri, N. & Kasperson, J.X. 2001. Stigma and the social amplification of risk: Toward a framework of analysis. In J. Flynn, P. Slovic & H. Kunreuther (eds), *Risk, media and stigma: Understanding public challenges to modern science and technology*. London: Earthscan.

King, F. 2010. *Critical review of the literature on the corrosion of copper by water*. Technical Report TR-10-69, SKB, Stockholm. Available online at: http://skb.se/upload/publications/pdf/TR-10-69.pdf (accessed 7 April 2014).

King, F., Ahonen, L., Taxen, C., Vuorinen, U. & Werme, L. 2002. *copper corrosion under expected conditions in a deep geologic repository*. POSIVA 2002-01, Helsinki, Posiva Oy. Available online at: www.posiva.fi/files/2620/POSIVA-2002-01_web.pdf (accessed 24 April 2014).

Klötzer, U., Mattsoff, A.-L. & Launokari, L. 2013. *Open letter for the Ministry of Employment and Economy, Posiva and the members of the Finnish Government, joint statement of three NGOs: Women Against Nuclear Power, Finland; No More Nuclear Power Movement in Finland and Women for Peace in Finland*. Available online at: www.naisetrauhanpuolesta.org/Posiva_avoin_kirje_10012013.pdf (accessed 7 April 2014).

Kojo, M. 2014. *Ydinjätepolitiikan osallistava käänne*, Doctoral Thesis, Acta Universitatis Tamperensis 1987, Tampere: Tampere University Press.

Kojo, M. & Oksa, A. 2014. *Adaption of the Swedish KBS disposal concept to Finland: A technology transfer case study*. InSOTEC Working Paper. Available online at: http://urn. fi/URN:ISBN:978-951-44-9515-1 (accessed 17 May 2016).

Konrad, K. 2006. The social dynamics of expectations: The interaction of collective and actor-specific expectations on electronic commerce and interactive television. *Technology Analysis and Strategic Management*, 18(3): 429–444.

Laaksonen, J. 2006. Regulatory management system for licensing, inspection and enforcement. Regulatory approach, planning, quality manual, feedback, and measurement and improvement of effectiveness. In *Proceedings Series of IAEA: Effective Nuclear Regulatory Systems: Facing Safety And Security Challenges Proceedings Of An International Conference On Effective Nuclear Regulatory Systems: Facing Safety And Security Challenges*, Moscow, 27 February–3 March 2006, International Atomic Energy Agency Vienna, 2006.

Lehtonen, M. 2014a. Evaluation of "the social" in megaprojects: Tensions, dichotomies, and ambiguities. *International Journal of Architecture, Engineering and Construction* 3(2): 98–109.

Lehtonen, M. 2014b. Evaluating megaprojects: From the 'iron triangle' to network mapping. *Evaluation* 20(3): 278–295. DOI: 10.1177/1356389014539868

Lempinen, A. and Silvan-Lempinen, M. 2011. *Reverse logic. Safety of spent nuclear fuel disposal*, Greenpeace International. Available online at: www.greenpeace.org/finland/ Global/finland/Ydinvoima/Reports/Safety%20of%20spent%20nuclear%20disposal,%20 no%20layot.pdf (accessed 7 April 2014).

Litmanen, T., Kojo, M. & Nurmi, A. 2012. The socio-technical challenges of Finland's nuclear waste policy. The technoscientific community's discussion on the safety of the geological disposal of spent nuclear fuel. *Risk, Hazards, and Crisis in Public Policy* 3(3): 84–103.

Litmanen, T., Kari, M., Vesalainen, J. & Kojo, M. 2014. *Socio-technical risk governance through dyadic risk dialogue: Copper corrosion as a safety challenge in the geological disposal of spent nuclear fuel*. InSOTEC Working Paper, WP 2 – Topic: Demonstrating Safety. Available online at: https://jyx.jyu.fi/dspace/handle/123456789/43849 (accessed 15 May 2016).

Mackenzie Valley. 2007. *Socio-economic impact assessment guidelines*. 2nd edition. Yellowknife: Mackenzie Valley Environmental Impact Review Board.

Melber, B. and Durbin, N.E. 2005. *Experience with Regulatory Strategies in Nuclear Power Oversight. Part 1: An International Exploratory Study, Part 2: Workshop Discussions and Conclusions*. SKI Report 2005:37. Available online at: www.stralsakerhetsmyndigheten. se/Global/Publikationer/SKI_import/050808/9816ab95e7f70677d42b0fe5b24a2b8f/ SKI_Rapport_2005_37.pdf (accessed 27 May 2016).

Michigan Sea Grant. 2009. *Northeast Michigan Integrated Assessment Final Report* [MICHU-09-207]. Available online at: www.miseagrant.umich.edu (accessed 25 July 2016).

Ministry of Employment and the Economy (MEE). 2015. Posiva receives a construction licence for a spent nuclear fuel disposal facility. Press release on 12 November 2015. Available online at: www.tem.fi/en/current_issues/press_releases/press_release_archive/ year_2015?120313_m=119285 (accessed 16 May 2016).

NEA. 2003. *The regulator's evolving role and image in radioactive waste management: lessons learnt within the nea forum on stakeholder confidence*, Nuclear Energy Agency, Organisation for Economic Co-Operation And Development. Available online at: www.oecd-nea. org/rwm/reports/2003/nea4428-regulator-role.pdf (accessed 27 May 2016).

Nikula, A., Raumolin, H., Ryhänen, V., Seppälä, T., Vira, J. & Äikäs, T. 2012. *Kohti turvallista loppusijoitusta. Ydinjätehuollon neljä vuosikymmentä* [Towards safety disposal. Four decades of nuclear waste management]. Eurajoki: Posiva.

Nuclear Energy Act 990/1987. Ministry of Trade and Industry, Finland. Available online at: www.finlex.fi/en/laki/kaannokset/1987/en19870990.pdf (accessed 27 May 2016).

Nurmi, A., Kojo, M. & Litmanen, T. 2012. *Identifying remaining socio-technical challenges at the national level: Finland.* InSOTEC Working Paper (WP 1 – MS 5). Available online at: https://jyx.jyu.fi/dspace/bitstream/handle/123456789/38353/978-951-39-4752-1.pdf?sequence=1 (accessed 1 December 2012).

OECD (Organisation for Economic Co-operation and Development). 2002. *Guidance document on risk communication for chemical risk management*, Series on Risk Management, No. 16, OECD Environment, Health and Safety Publications. Paris: OECD Publications Service.

OECD. 2008. *Nuclear legislation in OECD countries, regulatory and institutional framework for nuclear activities, Finland.* Available online at: www.oecd-nea.org/law/legislation/finland.pdf (accessed 5 February 2014).

Posiva. 2003. TKS-2003, *Nuclear waste management of the Olkiluoto and Loviisa power plants: programme for research, development and technical design for 2004–2006.* Available online at: www.posiva.fi/files/344/TKS-2003.pdf (accessed 24 April 2012).

Posiva. 2006. TKS-2006, *Nuclear waste management of the Olkiluoto and Loviisa power plants: programme for research, development and technical design for 2007–2009.* Available online at: www.posiva.fi/files/345/TKS-2006web.pdf (accessed 24 April 2012).

Posiva. 2008. *Safety Case Plan.* Posiva Oy. Available online at: www.posiva.fi/files/490/POSIVA_2008-05_28.8web.pdf (accessed 24 August 2012).

Posiva. 2010a. *Annual Report.* Available online at: www.tvo.fi/uploads/File/2011/Posiva_Vuosikertomus2010_EN.pdf (accessed 24 April 2012).

Posiva. 2010b. TKS-2009, *Nuclear waste management at Olkiluoto and Loviisa power plants review of current status and future plans for 2010–2012.* Available online at: www.posiva.fi/files/1078/TKS2009_Eng_web_rev1_low.pdf (accessed 2 May 2012).

Posiva. 2010c. *Interim Summary Report of the Safety Case 2009*, Posiva Oy. Available online at: www.posiva.fi/files/1226/POSIVA_2010-02web.pdf (accessed 24 August 2014).

Posiva. 2012a. *Safety case for the disposal of spent nuclear fuel at Olkiluoto – Synthesis 2012.* Available online at: www.posiva.fi/files/2987/Posiva_2012-12web.pdf (accessed 17 February 2014).

Posiva. 2012b. *Safety case for the disposal of spent nuclear fuel at Olkiluoto. Description of the Disposal System 2012*, Posiva 2012-5. Available online at: www.posiva.fi/files/2996/Posiva_2012-05v1web.pdf (accessed 7 February 2014).

Posiva. 2012c. *YJH-2012 Nuclear waste management at Olkiluoto and Loviisa power plants: review of current status and future plans for 2013–2015.* Posiva Oy May 2013. Available online at: www.posiva.fi/files/3056/YJH-2012eng.pdf (accessed 23 April 2014).

Posiva. 2013. *Safety case for the disposal of spent nuclear fuel at Olkiluoto – models and data for the repository system 2012.* Posiva 2013-01. Available online at: www.posiva.fi/files/3441/Posiva_2013-01Part1.pdf (accessed 6 May 2014).

Posiva. 2015. *Annual Report 2014.* Available online at: www.posiva.fi/files/4004/Annual_Report_2014.pdf (accessed 17 May 2016).

Reiman, T. & Norros, L. 2002. Regulatory culture: Balancing the different demands of regulatory practice in the nuclear industry. In A.R. Hale, A. Hopkins & B. Kirwan (eds.), *Changing Regulation – Controlling Hazards in Society.* Oxford, Pergamon.

Renn, O. 2008. *Risk governance: Coping with uncertainty in a complex world.* London, Earthscan.

Risley, A. 2011. The power of persuasion: Issue framing and advocacy in Argentina. *Journal of Latin American Studies* 43(4): 663–691.

Ruokola, E. 2000. *Posiva's application for a Decision in Principle concerning a disposal facility for spent nuclear fuel – STUK's statement and preliminary safety appraisal.* Report STUK-B-YTO 198, Radiation and Nuclear Safety Authority, Helsinki.

Sanderson, J. 2012. Risk, uncertainty and governance in megaprojects: A critical discussion of alternative explanations. *International Journal of Project Management* 30(4): 432–443. DOI: 10.1016/j.ijproman.2011.11.002

SNCNW. 2013. *Nuclear waste state-of-the-art report 2013, Final repository application under review: Supplementary information and alternative futures.* Report from the Swedish National Council for Nuclear Waste, Swedish Government Official Reports, SOU 2013: 11, Stockholm.

Strauss, H. 2011. *For the good of society. Public participation in the siting of nuclear and hydro power projects in Finland.* Universitatis Ouluensis, University of Oulu, Oulu.

Swedberg, R. 1995. Schumpeter's vision of socioeconomics. *Journal of Socio-Economics* 24(4): 525–544.

Szakálos, P., Hultquist, G. & Wikmark, G. 2007. Corrosion of copper by water. *Electrochemical and Solid-State Letters* 10(11): C63–C67.

Wahlström, B. 1999. Finnish and Swedish practices in nuclear safety. In J. Misumi, B. Wilpert & R. Miller (eds.), *Nuclear safety: A human factors perspective,* London: Taylor & Francis.

Wahlström, B. 2007. Reflections on regulatory oversight of nuclear power plants. *International Journal of Nuclear Law* 1(4): 344–377.

Wallace, H. 2010. *Rock Solid? A scientific review of geological disposal of high-level radioactive waste.* Brussels: Greenpeace EU Unit.

Wärnbäck, A. 2012. *EIA practice. examples of cumulative effects and final disposal of spent nuclear fuel.* Doctoral Thesis, Faculty of Natural Resources and Agricultural Sciences Department of Urban and Rural Development, Swedish University of Agricultural Sciences, Uppsala.

Wärnbäck, A., Soneryd, L. & Hilding-Rydevik, T. 2013. Shared practice and converging views in nuclear waste management: long-term relations between implementer and regulator in Sweden. *Environment and Planning A* 45(9): 2212–2226.

Unpublished STUK documents

Apted, M.J. 2004. *Review of "TKS-2003"* [Statement by STUK's external RTD review expert].

Apted, M.J., Hänninen, H., Reacl, D., Robinson, P.C., Stephansson, O., Suksi, J., Tirn, S. and Tsang, C.F. 2004. STUK External RTD 2003 Review Group Report.

Bath, A., Niemi, A., Tirén, S. and Stephansson, O. 2007. *Review of Posiva's TKS-2006 Programme for STUK, Finland,* Appendix 3.

Heinonen, J. 2010. *Käytetyn ydinpolttoaineen loppusijoituksen valmistelu - Posiva Oy:n alustavat selvitykset. Esittelymuistio* [STUK's presentation memorandum on Posiva's "Preparation of Spent Nuclear Fuel Disposal – Posiva Oy's Preliminary Report"].

Hämäläinen, K. 2010. *Olkiluodon ja Loviisan voimalaitosten ydinjätehuollon tutkimus- ja kehitystyön sekä teknisen suunnittelun ohjelma 2010–2012. Esittelymuistio* [STUK's presentation memorandum on Posiva's "YJH-2012. Nuclear waste management at

158   Tapio Litmanen, Matti Kojo, Mika Kari and Jurgita Vesalainen

Olkiluoto and Loviisa power plants: review of current status and future plans for 2013-2015].

Hänninen, H. 2003. *Review of "TKS-2003: Nuclear Waste Management of the Olkiluoto and Loviisa Power Plants" by Posiva Oy (manufacturing, closure, non-destructive inspection and durability)* [Statement by STUK's external RTD review expert on Posiva's RTD-2003].

Hänninen, H., Arthur, R.C. and Apted, M.J. 2007. *Review of TKS-2006: Summary Report, Appendix 2* [Statement by STUK's external RTD review experts on Posiva's RTD-2007].

Read, D. 2004. *Review of the Posiva Programme for Research, Development and Technical Design – 2004–2006 Geochemistry, Radionuclide Release and Transport* [Statement by STUK's external RTD review experts on Posiva's RTD-2003].

Read, D., Robinson, P., Tsang, C. and Hellmuth, K. 2007. *Review Report of the Safety Case Team. Appendix 4* [Statement by STUK's external RTD review experts on Posiva's RTD-2007].

STUK. 2004. *Olkiluodon ja Loviisan voimalaitosten ydinjätehuollon tutkimus ja kehitystyön sekä teknisen suunnittelun ohjelma 2004–2006* [STUK's statement on Posiva's "Nuclear Waste Management of the Olkiluoto and Loviisa Power Plants: Programme for Research, Development and Technical Design for 2004–2006"].

STUK. 2007a. *Olkiluodon ja Loviisan voimalaitosten ydinjätehuollon tutkimus ja kehitystyön sekä teknisen suunnittelun ohjelma 2007–2009* [STUK's statement on Posiva's "Nuclear Waste Management of the Olkiluoto and Loviisa Power Plants: Programme for Research, Development and Technical Design for 2007–2009"].

STUK. 2007b. *Perustelumuistio TKS–2006-arvioinnille. Liite 1* [STUK's argumentation memorandum on Posiva's RTD-2006, Appendix 1].

STUK. 2010a. *Käytetyn ydinpolttoaineen loppusijoituksen valmistelu – Posiva Oy:n alustavat selvitykset* [STUK's statement "Preparation of Spent Nuclear Fuel Disposal – Posiva Oy's Preliminary Account" on Posiva's pre-CLA].

STUK. 2010b. *Olkiluodon ja Loviisan voimalaitosten ydinjätehuollon tutkimus ja kehitystyön sekä teknisen suunnittelun ohjelma 2010–2012* [STUK's statement on Posiva's RTD-2009: "Nuclear Waste Management at Olkiluoto and Loviisa Power Plants Review of Current Status and Future Plans for 2010–2012"].

STUK. 2013. *Säteilyturvakeskuksen lausunto Olkiluodon käytetyn ydinpolttoaineen kapselointi- ja loppusijoituslaitoksen rakentamisesta.* Available online at: www.stuk.fi/documents/12547/207522/stukin-lausunto-posivan-rl-hakemuksesta-temille.pdf/9b62b852-e80e-4a57-b01b-619f6d5c09c0 (accessed 26 July 2016).

Part II

Novel approaches to evaluating the socioeconomic in megaprojects

8 Ex ante evaluation of megaprojects in a time of uncertainty

What counts and what is countable in the Canadian context?

Moktar Lamari, Jean-René Prévost and Line Poulin-Larivière

Introduction

Despite intense media coverage and recurring political controversy surrounding megaprojects, citizens, politicians and managers remain insufficiently equipped to understand and to mitigate the risks, uncertainties and mistakes in judgement marring ex ante evaluations of megaprojects. These uncertainties are decried and feared due to the extent of their damaging effects and impacts on society (social, environmental, economic, political impacts, etc.) when they have not been sufficiently integrated during initial planning.

Bruzelius et al. (2002) define megaprojects from the standpoint of their high cost (more than a billion dollars), their long life cycle (fifty years or more) and the extent of their environmental (ecosystem, biodiversity, climate etc.), social, and political uncertainties. Frick (2008) views megaprojects from the standpoint of six complexities (6C): colossal size, captivating symbolism, cost overruns, controversial nature, lack of certainty, and lack of control in their governance. Megaprojects are real vectors of societal, territorial and regional change that induce latent and multi-dimensional impacts: economic, social, environmental and political (Flyvbjerg, 2007b; de Bruijn and Leitjen, 2008). The latter constitute "major events" that are also communicated through passionate rhetoric (national, regional, local pride etc.) and with ambiguous and changing objectives according to the political context (Bruzelius et al., 2002). Furthermore, megaprojects are often associated with challenging new technologies whose economic effectiveness and efficiency are difficult to demonstrate ex ante (Kardes et al., 2013; Priemus, 2010; Zidane et al., 2013).

For several observers, the term megaproject is synonymous with mega-uncertainty (Levinson, 2013; Eliasson and Anker Nielsen, 2013). Such uncertainty is induced by various errors in judgement, numerous cognitive biases (optimism, pessimism) and strategies (opportunism, optimism, partisanship etc.), and some quite bad surprises as well: cost overruns and delays, less revenue than expected, pollution, iniquity and even corruption and collusion between project planners and developers. Added up, these ingredients heighten citizens' cynicism and political analysts' scepticism towards megaprojects and their fiscal repercussions.

This chapter is about the uncertainty surrounding megaproject evaluation (cost, benefit, impact etc.) and how to assess these uncertainties ex ante (before decision and construction). We have investigated this topic in a Canadian context (data and published reports), using what we know from the scientific literature about ex ante evaluation of megaprojects (approaches, practices and theories).

The chapter is divided into three sections. The first one describes the status of large infrastructure projects presently being developed in Canada. The second section identifies a typology of the risks threatening megaprojects. The third section analyses different evaluation approaches that would help reduce the incidence of these risks for the validity of an ex ante evaluation.

Megaprojects in Canada

In its review of the Top 100 megaprojects, *ReNew Canada* lists the costliest infrastructure projects presently being developed in the country. For these megaprojects, the overall cost varies from CAD 500 million to CAD 10 billion. The published ranking is based on an approach that includes eight main submission criteria and six additional data; nine sectors are included and two are specifically excluded. In addition, seven filters facilitate the analysis of the data collected over each year. Table 8.1 offers the synthesis of the Top 100 megaprojects in Canada and the methodology used to identify their attributes.

In 2014 the total value of these 100 megaprojects was CAD 140.47 billion (with an average cost of CAD 1.4 billion per project), compared to CAD 121.72 billion in 2012 for 105 megaprojects (average cost of CAD 1.16 billion per project).

As Table 8.2 illustrates, investments in transportation, including public transportation, take up a major and increasing portion of this Top 100. They represent 43.6 per cent of the total value of the projects listed in 2014, compared to 34.1 per cent in 2012, whereas the number of projects under development was practically the same (36 in 2014 versus 35 in 2012). Highways and bridges made up the largest proportion of these transportation infrastructure investments (82.1 per cent of the total value in 2014), while light rail transit represented almost 60 per cent of public transportation investments in 2014.

Energy infrastructure accounted for 42.1 per cent of the total value of projects in 2014, slightly less than in 2012 (45.1 per cent). On the other hand, the number of these projects included in the Top 100 increased from 30 to 39. Hydroelectric dams alone represented 57.5 per cent of the total value of investments in this sector.

In order of importance, the next category was public buildings, which took up a decreasing portion between the years 2012 and 2014. In fact, the 36 public building projects listed represented 19.6 per cent of the total value in 2012, whereas the 23 projects in 2014 constituted 13 per cent of that year's total value.

Table 8.1 Data and criteria for selecting the Top 100 Canadian megaprojects

Main submission criteria	Additional data
Total project cost	Level of government contribution
Project name	Associated funding programme
Funding source (private/government/public–private partnership)	Name of collaborating company
Estimated start date of construction	Value of contract (CAD)
Estimated completion date of construction	Architectural image
Company's role	Short project description
Project location	
Company name	

Sectors included

Public transit	Subways, light rail vehicle lines, bus rapid transit, heavy rail. Also all infrastructure associated with the project in question, such as bridge/tunnel work, storage/maintenance facilities and station revitalisation
Transportation	Highways, roads and bridges
Healthcare	Hospitals
Water/wastewater	Wastewater treatment facilities, pipe systems, water treatment facilities
Energy	Nuclear, coal, natural gas, renewables, hydroelectric and transmission infrastructure
Environment	Brownfields and flood prevention projects
Education	College or university campus facilities
Ports/airports	Ports, airports and their associated infrastructures
Public buildings	Social infrastructure, government facilities, courthouses, gaols and police stations

Sectors excluded

Mining, oil, and gas development projects; commercial buildings

Source: Based on Top100 Projects, 2016a.

Table 8.2 Megaprojects (number) and investments (CAD billion) by industrial sector in Canada (2012–2014)

Sectors	2012			2013			2014		
	N	Value (CAD billion)	% $	N	Value (CAD billion)	% $	N	Value (CAD billion)	% $
Energy	30	54.85	45.1	38	58.26	41.5	39	59.1	42.1
Transportation Infrastructure	17	16.08	13.2	19	33.43	23.8	17	32.4	23.1
Public Transportation	18	25.47	20.9	16	25.67	18.3	19	28.83	20.5
Public Buildings	36	23.92	19.6	24	21.04	15.0	23	18.3	13.0
Environment	3	1.06	0.9	3	2.08	1.5	2	1.84	1.3
Other	1	0.34	0.3	–	–	–	–	–	–
Total	**105**	**121.72**	**100.0**	**100**	**140.48**	**100.0**	**100**	**140.47**	**100.0**

Source: Top100 Projects (2016b; 2016c; 2016d).

Table 8.3 Megaprojects and investments according to type of funding in Canada (2012–2014)

Type of Funding	2012				2013				2014			
	N	Value (CAD billion)	% $	N		Value (CAD billion)	% $	N		Value (CAD billion)	% $	
Public	50	70.67	58.1	46		75.55	53.8	46		76.71	54.6	
Private	19	16.21	13.3	24		25.37	18.1	24		27.17	19.3	
Public & Private	8	11.70	9.6	7		6.4	4.6	8		5.72	4.1	
Public-Private Partnership (PPP)	27	22.36	18.4	22		32.38	23.1	21		30.09	21.4	
Unknown	1	0.78	0.6	1		0.78	0.6	1		0.78	0.6	
Total	105	121.72	100.0	100		140.48	100.0	100		140.47	100.0	

Source: Top100 Projects (2016b; 2016c; 2016d).

Table 8.3 illustrates certain changes in the sources of megaproject funding between 2012 and 2014. For example, the number of projects with public funding decreased slightly (50 in 2012 versus 46 in 2014), but their proportion in the total value of the Top 100 remained above 50 per cent (58.1 per cent in 2012 and 54.6 per cent in 2014). On the contrary, private projects saw their share of the total value increase from 13.3 per cent to 19.3 per cent. Public–private partnerships (PPPs) also continued to occupy a significant position among Canadian megaprojects, with 21.4 per cent of the total value, although the number of this type of project in 2014 fell by six, compared to 2012 (from 27 to 21 PPP projects).

Among these 100 megaprojects, 15 were located in Quebec in 2014, making for a total projected investment of CAD 27.11 billion. This represented 19.3 per cent of the total value of the projects listed throughout Canada. This percentage remained fairly constant between 2012 and 2014, although the number of projects varied from one year to the next (12 in 2012 and 19 in 2013). The most important in terms of projected costs were, in descending order, the La Romaine Complex, the new Champlain Bridge, the Turcot Interchange and the re-building of the Université de Montréal Hospital Centre.

It is relevant to note that the data used by ReNew Canada were supplied by project promoters and do not necessarily reflect the budget evolution of the selected projects. Having said this, a recent study (SECOR/KPMG, 2012) demonstrates that the major recently developed projects in Quebec have incurred cost overruns of about 78 per cent, on average. This observation is particularly glaring in the case of transport infrastructure, which makes up the largest proportion of the portfolio of Canadian and Quebec megaprojects. This situation has led the Government of Quebec to modify its planning and approval process for large infrastructure projects. The phenomenon of megaproject cost overrun appears to be very widespread across Canada (Rolstadas et al., 2011). In Western countries, experts estimate that close to nine out of ten megaprojects incur cost overruns ranging from 50 per cent to 100 per cent of the original projected costs (Flyvbjerg, 2007a; Flyvbjerg et al., 2003).

Typology of the risks threatening megaprojects

Megaprojects are marred by uncertainties on several levels, namely: 1) their technological design (innovation, size, rare expertise, etc.); 2) their socio-political governance process (lobbying, political agendas, electoral cycles, inter-governmental negotiations, etc.); 3) their implementation (complexity, unpredictability, public–private partnership, etc.); and iv) the accuracy of expected impacts during their whole life cycle (Flyvbjerg, 2007a; Kardes et al., 2013). Two broad categories of uncertainties are often put forward in scientific literature: 1) random and irreducible uncertainties due to the natural variability of random phenomena (inputs, actor behaviour, etc.); and 2) the epistemic uncertainties that can be limited through data collection and rigorous empirical research (Townley, 1998). These sources of uncertainty and risk are even more troubling when they involve major investments and numerous partners with often diverging interests.

Flyvbjerg (2007a) identified three factors that could explain why risks and uncertainties are not always sufficiently well defined in ex ante evaluations. The first deals with methodological shortcomings in anticipating all the uncertainties associated with a megaproject during its entire life cycle. The second deals with psychological mechanisms, that is, managers' and evaluators' propensity for an excess of optimism that amplifies the expected spin-offs and underestimates the anticipated costs based on 'idealised' scenarios that stir the passions of the electorate (optimism bias). The third factor deals with the fact that project promoters tend to manipulate uncertainties surrounding megaprojects to their advantage (strategic misrepresentation), thus benefiting from two information asymmetries: 1) adverse selection (hidden attributes of the transactions); and/or 2) moral hazard (attributes hidden by actors) (Williamson, 1981). In the megaproject context, adverse selection is mainly related to situations where stakeholders have access to different information (asymmetric information) about the quality and the hidden cost of a product (bridge, metro/tube, airport, etc.). In the same vein, moral hazard also occurs under conditions of asymmetric information where the risk-taking party to a transaction (firms, entrepreneurs, lobbyists, etc.) knows more about its intentions than the party paying the consequences of the risk (government, agency, bank, etc.). These manipulations are often not taken very seriously by governments and institutional mechanisms that are capable of understanding and countering them.

From the literature on the risks and uncertainties threatening the success of megaprojects, we have developed a typology listing the categories of risks that must be integrated into the ex ante evaluation process of megaprojects in Canada. The proposed typology includes eight categories of risk.

Risks related to project design and management

These risks are linked to decisions on the nature and size of the project: the use of innovative technologies, the level of control exercised on the size of the project, contract management, etc. The nature of the project refers to choosing between implementing a light train transit system or a tramway, for example, or between a natural gas power station and a wind farm. These risks are linked to the degree of complexity associated with a project: the more a project's success rests on carrying out interdependent activities and on the collaboration of a large number of actors with diverging interests, the more significant these risks will be (Kardes et al., 2013). This category also includes risks concerning the management structure selected. The greater the number of groups involved in developing the project (contractors, sub-contractors, funders, workers, citizens, interest groups, etc.), the larger the risk of losing control.

Legal and political risks

These risks refer to the possible political, legal and regulatory changes that can influence a megaproject (Atkinson et al., 2006). Priemus (2010) advances the concept of political discontinuity, which refers to the risks of fluctuating political support along the electoral cycle (changeover of party in power), budget cycle and the crucial stages of the life cycle of a megaproject. In an electoral context, the scale, the objectives and the political backing for a megaproject can change and significantly alter its nature, viability and socio-political consequences. Changing the standards governing the development of a project can also have impacts that are difficult to foresee.

Risks related to the construction and exploitation of the infrastructure

Megaprojects are also vulnerable to different risks surrounding their construction and exploitation: cost overruns, prolonged delays, discovery of a design error, labour disputes, etc. It is this type of risk that has the most impact on the financial viability of a megaproject (Irimia-Diéguez et al., 2014), since these risks can quickly accumulate. In a megaproject with a high level of complexity, there are great risks that unforeseen events provoke major cost overruns. Mitigating these risks relies on the presence of a high level of expertise in the engineering aspects related to a specific project.

Economic and financial risks

Megaprojects are vulnerable to various market fluctuations possibly affecting their profitability: variable interest rates; access to liquid assets; recession or economic growth context; shortage of labour, expertise, materials, etc. In addition to the spontaneous evolution of markets, planners must take into consideration the endogenous effects that a megaproject can provoke on markets and anticipated costs (Priemus, 2010). These different risks must be integrated into the different budget projections related to the project.

Risks related to the anticipated demand for the project

The risks related to demand refer to the probabilities that the use of the megaproject will not be as great as originally expected (Kardes et al., 2013). Flyvbjerg et al. (2003) report that the demand demonstrated for large road projects is much lower than predicted at the initial planning stage. These are risks that the profits initially foreseen by the promoters do not materialise. Beyond the strategic considerations identified by Flyvbjerg, these differences can also be explained by an unexpected change in the population's preferences. For example, a highway may not have as much traffic as expected, or an energy megaproject may create energy surpluses generating financial losses for the company. The use of consultation mechanisms (involving citizens, stakeholders, government, experts, etc.) during the project's planning stage can help take these risks into account.

Environmental risks

Environmental risks are at the heart of uncertainties that characterise megaprojects (IAIA, 1999). Several environmental risks must be integrated into ex ante evaluations, including the possible effects on pollutant emissions, energy consumption, water quality and biodiversity. One of the major challenges with regard to environmental risks is their monetisation, especially when impacts span over several decades. Environmental risks are particularly complex to measure and their study leverages expertise targeted according to the project to be studied and its supporting environment. The integration of environmental risks must also distinguish between strictly local (air quality), regional (acidification of lakes and rivers) and global (greenhouse gases) risks (Fischer, 2006).

Risks related to host communities

The risks related to insertion in communities refer to the unexpected social impacts of the megaproject on individuals, communities and social structures. A megaproject can have various kinds of effects on a community: level and distribution of revenue, public health, social exclusion, crime, etc. (Vanclay, 2002). Social conflicts concerning the acceptability of a megaproject can be very costly, since citizens or groups that feel wronged can repeatedly take legal or court action to make their dissatisfaction known. Legal action can considerably delay a megaproject whose acceptability among the local residents is very weak, as is the case with the construction of a highway necessitating expropriation of citizens.

Risks caused by major disasters

The risks caused by an unanticipated act or other major disasters refer to risks of a very serious event, like a natural disaster or violent conflict, that can compromise the completion of the project. Although certain risks from natural disasters are quantifiable thanks to methods applying modern technology, they remain difficult to integrate into the megaproject decision-making process.

Evaluation approaches and how to 'count' uncertainties

In this section, we examine how certain evaluation approaches would enable evaluators to better integrate the different categories of risk identified in our typology. We have retained five evaluation approaches: cost–benefit assessment (CBA), strategic environmental assessment, social impact assessment, multi-criteria analysis (MCA) and the assessment of the socio-political context.

Cost–benefit analysis

Cost–benefit analysis is widely used in the selection of megaprojects (Levinson, 2013; Eliasson and Anker Nielsen, 2013). It seeks to assess economic efficiency, involving an ex ante comparison of the flows of expected costs and benefits through discounting (an operation consisting of converting future monetary flows into present value) throughout the life-cycle of the megaproject being evaluated (Ramsey, 1928; Stern, 2006). Cost–benefit analysis requires transforming costs and benefits (direct and indirect, tangible and intangible, visible and invisible, etc.) into a monetary value, even though not all that is important to the society can be calculated (Rossi et al., 2004). Cost-benefit analysis has been criticised for its incapacity to account for all social, environmental and political impacts associated with a project (Sen, 1999; Ostrom, 2007). The paradigm underpinning cost–benefit analysis proposes measurement methods, econometric modelling and projected calculation simulations supported by software dedicated to the cost–benefit analysis of megaprojects (TREDIS, GOBOT, EFFECT, etc.). When the cost–benefit analysis is rigorously designed and conducted, it enables decision-makers to put a price on a large majority of the risks described above, with the exception of political risks that are difficult to control. CBA, a fundamental tool for policy design and decision-making, is based on welfare theory, the rationality of gain and loss and the consideration of alternatives. Initially applied in infrastructure appraisal, the developed methods and conceptual tools allow analysts to measure the impacts of public policy on communities. When applied to megaprojects, CBA can determine the collective welfare in a spirit of optimisation (limiting costs and maximising benefits). These approaches are also based on discounting future cost and benefit, using a social discount rate generally fixed by government and adjusted periodically (from 7 per cent to 12 per cent).

Pearce et al. (2006) argue that the main reason for using CBA is to provide a model of rationality focused on beneficiaries and disadvantaged individuals. Regarding recent developments of CBA, the authors point out that the theory has significantly evolved over the last fifty years. They also demonstrate that CBA is based on the notion of human preference measured through willingness to pay or to accept compensation. Aggregated, it represents the social preference for a project, and to qualify, a project needs to total more social benefits than social costs. In spite of its popularity and advantages, CBA remains controversial.

A recent literature review indicates that current application of CBA in major transport project appraisal remains heterogeneous (Korytárová and Papežíková, 2015). For example, the UK Department of Transport's best practice guidelines set out the general principles of CBA, recall the pertinence of multi-criteria analysis (MCA) and admit the incapacity to determine monetary values for impacts on townscape, historic environment, biodiversity, water environment and security (Department of Transport, 2014). Beyond the differences between countries' implementation in this sector, four criteria appear as the most frequently monetised: travel timesaving, travel and operating costs, safety, and environmental costs (Korytárová and Papežíková, 2015).

However, a literature review focusing on CBA use in megaproject planning shows that, in the past, politicians have seldom used CBA outcomes to support their decisions, and that it was not always considered indispensable or required (Priemus and van Wee, 2013). It appears that five main barriers explain the limited use of CBA dealing with megaprojects: 1) information overload; 2) lack of understanding; 3) refusal of specific premises and mistrust; 4) political limits; and 5) a combination of factors (Priemus and van Wee, 2013). Table 8.4 summarises the main strengths and challenges for CBA, in the context of megaproject evaluation, and provides a general overview of the rationales behind the criticisms.

Efforts to standardise the practice include official publications from international organisations such as the World Bank and the European Union as well as national initiatives in many countries: the *New Approach to Appraisal* (NATA) in the United Kingdom, the *Guide to Cost–benefit Analysis* and the *Guide to Cost-benefit Analysis of Investment Projects* in the Netherlands, and *Developing Harmonised European Approaches for Transport Costing and Project Assessment* (HEATCO) at the European level (Priemus and van Wee, 2013). In an effort to provide practical assistance in the alignment of approaches and taking into consideration international best practices with regard to major project appraisals, the European Commission defines CBA as 'an analytical tool to be used to appraise an investment decision in order to assess the welfare change attributable to it and, in so doing, the contribution to EU cohesion policy objectives. The purpose of CBA is to facilitate a more efficient allocation of resources, demonstrating the convenience for society of a particular intervention rather than possible alternatives' (European Commission, 2015: 15).

Primeus and van Wee (2013) examine the current state of decision-making processes with regard to megaprojects, with a focus on transport infrastructure. The authors describe CBA as a 'market-oriented approach', which provides 'an overview of all the pros (benefits) and cons (costs) of a project [...] quantified and expressed in monetary terms' (Primeus and van Wee, 2013: 271). The research results of Korytárová and Hromádkaa (2014) emphasise the importance of going beyond investment and operational cost in the economic evaluation of megaprojects in order to include numerous aspects such as the assessment of social impacts in their specific contexts.

Table 8.4 Strengths, theoretical weaknesses and practical challenges of CBA

Strengths	Theoretical weaknesses	Practical challenges
The costs and benefits are known	Some effects are difficult to monetise	Wider economic benefits are ignored
Models are generally available	Distribution of effects is ignored	Cross-border issues related to differences between countries, provinces or states
Offers a relatively objective tool	Limits to long-term impacts measurement	Dynamic uncertainties over time
	Limits to social exclusion evaluation	Communication of results and impacts
	Difficulty of estimating benefits associated with innovation, image and prestige	Cost overruns Capacity to deal with uncertainty Quality of demand forecasts

Source: Based on Priemus and van Wee (2013: 276–286).

Table 8.5 synthetises the legal foundation and main role of CBA in five countries including Canada. Similar to the situation in Australia, France, Germany and the United Kingdom, CBA has legal foundation in Canada. The method is seen as a decision tool by which the government allocates funding to agencies, its role differs depending on actors, and it is considered as one tool among other decision-making tools.

As stated above, CBA methodology varies across countries; it remains impossible to present an exhaustive listing of formulas. Nevertheless, the following four simple formulas offer general guidelines to calculate the present value of the costs (PVC), the present value of benefits (PVB), the difference of PVC and PVB (net present value – NPV) and the ratio of benefits to costs (B/C) of a megaproject. NPV results lower than 0 or B/C results lower than 1 indicate a project with no net social benefit compared to NPV results higher than 0 or B/C higher than 1, which indicate that the project generates a net social benefit.

$$PVC = \Sigma_{t=1}^{T} \frac{C_t}{(1+r)^t}; \quad PVB = \Sigma_{t=1}^{T} \frac{B_t}{(1+r)^t}$$

$$NPV = \sum_{t=1}^{T} \frac{B_t}{(1+r)^t} - \sum_{t=1}^{T} \frac{C_t}{(1+r)^t}$$

$$B/C = \frac{PVB}{PVC}$$

Ct: social costs, Bt: social benefits, t: time (year), T: life time and r: social discount rate

Table 8.5 Legal foundation and main role of CBA

		Main Role of CBA				
	Legal foundation of CBA	Decision tool in allocating funding to agencies	Differs depending on actors	One among other decision making tools	Does not play a decisive role in decision making	Is increasing in role and importance
Australia	Y	X				
Canada	Y	X	X	X		
France	Y		X	X		X
Germany	Y		X			X
United Kingdom*	N	X				X

Note: Adapted from OECD (2015). Chapter 5, Table 5.5, page 105.

Y: CBA is mandatory nationwide by legislation for all capital investment projects above a certain financial threshold; X: indicates feasibility and relevance; N: No legal requirement, but CBA is recommended by government and used anyway.

* In the UK CBA is not prescribed under a specific law but in the Green Book, which is required guidance for all projects receiving central government funding; it is therefore a requirement even though not legally mandatory.

Pearce et al. (2006) differentiate risk from uncertainty and maintain that a risk context is one where 'benefits and/or costs are not known with certainty, but a probability distribution is known [...] [whereas] a context of uncertainty is different as there is no known probability distribution' (p. 60). Connected to internal and external factors, uncertainty may be evaluated through CBA risk assessment which may include the following activities: sensitivity analysis, qualitative risk analysis, probabilistic risk analysis, assessment of acceptable levels of risk, and eventually risk prevention/mitigation (European Commission, 2015).

Other evaluation approaches

Strategic environmental assessment

Strategic environmental assessment is a mechanism that allows analysts to identify, predict, assess and possibly mitigate the environmental impacts prior to the decision to implement a programme with potential consequences for the environment, territories or sustainable development (IAIA, 1999). This programmatic focus therefore distinguishes SEA from environmental impact assessment (EIA), which examines the impacts of a single project. The principles underlying strategic environmental assessment include the application of a systematic and pluralistic approach, considering the multi-dimensional analysis framework of megaprojects and taking into account the stakeholders' viewpoints (Sadler, 1996). Strategic environmental assessment relies on both a highly specialised scientific expertise and mechanisms for consulting the populations concerned. These consultations allow the anlaysts to obtain information on the environmental impacts not considered, and also to inform and potentially reassure the population about the real anticipated impacts. These consultations provide new insights, involvement and interaction with citizens and stakeholders. Conducting a strategic environmental assessment enables a reduction in the incidence of other non-environmental risks. By acting as a communication tool for insertion communities, it fosters a project's social acceptability and reinforces its credibility among interest groups and political actors.

Social impact assessment

Social impact assessment brings a very useful evaluation perspective. This approach permits an identification of the impacts on individuals, communities and social structures (Esteves et al., 2012; Becker, 2001). Vanclay (2002) proposes a seven-dimensional social impact assessment grid: 1) impacts on public health; 2) impacts on quality of life (liveability); 3) impacts on the material standard of living; 4) cultural impacts; 5) impacts on families and communities; 6) impacts on equity; and 7) gender-differentiated impacts. Social impact assessment is based on a process of wide, inclusive and structured consultation of the affected communities, enabling them to reveal their strongly felt needs, concerns and social issues. Like strategic environmental assessment, one of its primary objectives is to enable the identification of avenues to minimise the negative impacts and foster the emergence of positive impacts for the communities. Furthermore, this evaluation approach also fosters the attainment of prior, free and enlightened consent of the host community (Esteves et al., 2012). Besides the risks for the host communities, adopting this approach allows better identification of the environmental risks, risks linked to a lower than expected demand, and political risks possibly impeding the success of the megaproject.

Assessment of the socio-political uncertainties

Drawing on the work of Sabatier (2007), Kingdon (1995) and Lemieux (2009), it emerges that the adoption (or refusal) of a megaproject depends on a judicious assessment of the socio-political context through the identification of the various political uncertainties conveyed by three random and unpredictable fluxes. The first has to do with the flux of issues onto the political agenda (societal priorities) ensuring only certain issues can make it onto this very coveted agenda. The second concerns the flux of solutions, that is, techniques aiming to resolve problems (alternatives and options) within budget, as well as legal and institutional constraints, among others. The most profitable and viable alternatives risk being simply evacuated from public choices due to financial, technical or procedural reasons. The third concerns political flux, referring to the negotiations and compromises among the political actors involved. The assessment of the socio-political context is thus based on a threefold analysis: of the social issue that the megaproject is expected to address; of the degree to which the solutions are realistic, feasible and acceptable; and of the interests of the different political actors present. The convergence of these three fluxes (problem, solution and political context) creates a window of opportunity to permit the adoption of one megaproject rather than another, of one given alternative and not another, in a given region and not elsewhere. The political context (electoral cycle, legislature, alliances, lobbying, etc.) and the institutional rules governing the power play between the actors (private, public, community, federal–provincial–municipal, etc.) become megaproject adjustment and selection variables (Lamari and Landry, 2003). Besides the legal and political risks, this approach enables the control of certain risks linked to project design, economic and financial risks, and risks linked to the expected demand. Although the assessment of the socio-political context is seldom the subject of an official report and is not conducted openly and transparently, political decision-makers have to deal with different lobbyists and pressure groups before making decisions.

These different approaches cannot measure and incorporate simultaneously all types of identified uncertainties. Based on our data, we have codified the main associations between types of risks and evaluation approaches documented in the Canadian context. Table 8.6 highlights these associations and suggests that CBA has monetised the highest number of risks. Compared to the other examined approaches, CBA seems to be the most useful for incorporating risks and uncertainties in the decision-making process.

Table 8.6 Taking risks into account according to the evaluation approaches within the Canadian context

Categories of risks	Cost–benefit assessment	Strategic environmental assessment	Social impact assessment	Socio-political assessment
Risks linked to project design and management	X			X
Legal or political risks	X	X	X	X
Risks linked to construction and exploitation of the infrastructure	X			
Economic and financial risks	X			X
Risks linked to the expected demand for the project	X		X	X
Environmental risks		X	X	
Risks linked to host communities		X	X	X
Risks caused by major events (war, disaster, accident, severe recession, social disorder, etc.)	X	X		

Multi-criteria analysis (MCA)

Multi-criteria analysis (MCA) identifies the negative and positive effects of a project based on different scenarios, and compares their value in order to define the scenario that denotes optimal net benefit. The methodology facilitates the selection of alternatives based on a set of criteria and their attributed weight, and is mainly applied in development programmes (European Commission, 2015). The procedure incorporates qualitative and quantitative information and is structured in two phases: the analytical phase (problem definition) and the evaluation per se (Priemus and van Wee, 2013). Despite the variance between organisations' and countries' internal standards, MCA is usually composed of four key phases: 1) definition of objectives by decision-makers (generally civil servants); 2) selection of criteria in collaboration with experts (not limited to monetary criteria); 3) assignation of scores and weights; and 4) calculation of weighted average of scores and rankings (Pearce et al., 2006). It is possible to aggregate the score obtained by MCA with this generic formula:

$$S_i = \sum_j m_j \cdot S_j$$

Where: i = i[th] option, j = j[th] criterion, m = weight and S = score

In addition to the transparency in the definition of the objective and the criteria for evaluation, four main issues emerge during the implementation of MCA: 1) the method is limited to choosing between alternatives and does not include the measurement of economic efficiency; 2) it reveals experts' preferences; 3) the method entails certain ambiguities concerning the inclusion of time discounting and changing valuations; and 4) MCA must include distributional issues in its objectives (Pearce et al., 2006). The shortcomings of MCA in integrating multiple stakeholders motivated the development of the multi-actor multi-criteria analysis (MAMCA), which integrates different stakeholders' points of view (Priemus and van Wee, 2013). In fact, the methodology developed by Macharis has been applied in the transport sector and is structured in seven steps: 1) definition of the problem and identification of alternatives; 2) identification of relevant stakeholders; 3) identification of stakeholders' key objectives; 4) construction of indicators; 5) construction of an evaluation matrix; 6) ranking of alternatives; and 7) implementation.

As CBA focuses on maximising social welfare, MCA may include different objectives that may not be aggregated in regular CBA (European Commission, 2015). Table 8.7 offers a comparison of the CBA and MCA methodologies and clearly illustrates their similarities as frequently used evaluation tools. On the other hand, the table also highlights five characteristics that distinguish MCA from CBA: it does not assess viability, the political valuation of effects, the potential limitations due to the potential manipulation of the weights given to different criteria, the risk of double counting, and the integration of non-monetised attributes.

Table 8.7 CBA and MCA: similarities and differences

	CBA	MCA
Systematic comparison of alternatives	Yes	Yes
Assessment of the viability of a project	Yes	No
Explicit formulation of weights in trade-offs	Yes	Yes
Basis for weights of various effects	Valuation by consumer preferences	Political valuation
Opportunities for abuse by policymakers	By manipulation of inputs	By manipulation of inputs and weights
Degree of compensation between various attributes of alternatives	Every unfavourable attribute can in principle be compensated by a favourable outcome for another attribute	Various degrees of compensation are possible by using the minimum requirements
Risk of double counting	Limited*	Yes
Opportunities to take into account attributes that cannot be valued in monetary terms	No	Yes
Possibility to attach weights to the interests of specific actors	No	Yes

Note. Adapted from Priemus and van Wee (2013, Chapter 12, Table 12.1, p. 275) and Rietveld (2013).
* It is often stated that the risk of double counting is not present in the case of CBA. This holds true for the case of perfect markets. For imperfect markets where wider economic effects are incorporated, there is a certain risk of double counting.

Conclusion

Several actors denounce the fact that the decision process governing the adoption of public megaprojects too often underestimates the risks inherent in their development (Flyvbjerg, 2007b; Priemus, 2010; de Bruijn and Leitjen, 2008). Their great complexity and the interdependence of their components make megaprojects particularly vulnerable to costly management and invisible socio-political determinants. These risks are especially prominent in transportation megaprojects, which constitute the majority of megaproject investments in Canada.

To make the best decisions possible, politicians are faced with a twofold challenge: they must be able to familiarise themselves with all available options, and at the same time assess the large number of diffuse and intangible risks associated with each of these options. They are thus faced with a high level of ambiguity when attempting to determine which alternative would be the most beneficial for society. Megaproject decisions are so sensitive that they are always linked to holistic considerations concerning the type of society we want to live in (for example, supporting polluting energy projects rather than more innovative, but riskier, projects) (Stirling, 2013).

The matrix presented in the previous section is part of a reflection process that has not yet been completed. Our investigation suggests that risks and uncertainties require a holistic approach combining different evaluation paradigms and approaches. Although cost–benefit assessment is able to integrate several of the risks threatening megaprojects, not all social actors accord the same importance and credibility to monetising environmental and social impacts.

To further our understanding of the incidence of the types of risks identified on the validity of ex ante evaluations, new research needs to be conducted, including in particular case studies tracing the evolution of decision processes. This research should specifically deal with the content and rigour of ex ante evaluations that have led to the adoption of specific megaprojects, thus enabling the identification of both prioritised and neglected risks.

References

Atkinson, R., Crawford, L. and Ward, S. 2006. 'Fundamental uncertainties in projects and the scope of project management.' *International Journal of Project Management* 24(8): 687–698.

Becker, H.A. 2001. 'Social impact assessment.' *European Journal of Operational Research* 128(2): 311–321.

Bruzelius, N., Flyvbjerg, B. and Rothengatter, W. 2002. 'Big decisions, big risks. Improving accountability in mega projects.' *Transport Policy* 9(2): 143–154.

de Bruijn, H. and Leitjen, M. 2008. 'Management characteristics of megaprojects.' In H. Priemus, B. Flyvbjerg and B. van Wee (eds.), *Decision-making on megaprojects: Cost-benefit analysis, planning and innovation.* Cheltenham: Edward Elgar, pp. 23–39.

Department of Transport. 2014. *Transport Analysis Guidance Unit A1.1: Cost-Benefit Analysis.* Available online at: www.gov.uk/government/uploads/system/uploads/

attachment_data/file/427086/TAG_Unit_A1.1_-_Cost_Benefit_Analysis_November 2014.pdf (accessed 10 March 2016).

Eliasson, J. and Anker Nielsen, O. 2013. 'How Cost-Benefit Analysis influence decisions: Empirical evidence for Sweden, Norway and Denmark.' *International Conference on Uncertainties in Transport Project Evaluation* (Unite), Denmark University of Technologies, Copenhagen, September 17.

Esteves, A.M., Franks, D. and Vanclay, F. 2012. 'Social impact assessment: The state of the art.' *Impact Assessment and Project Appraisal* 30(1): 34–42.

European Commission. 2015. *Guide to Cost-Benefit Analysis of Investment Projects: Economic appraisal tool for Cohesion Policy 2014–2020.* Available online at: http://ec.europa.eu/ regional_policy/sources/docgener/studies/pdf/cba_guide.pdf (accessed 10 March 2016).

Fischer, T.B. 2006. 'Strategic environmental assessment and transport planning: Towards a generic framework for evaluating practice and developing guidance.' *Impact Assessment and Project Appraisal* 24(3):183–197.

Flyvbjerg, B. 2007a. 'Policy and planning for large-infrastructure projects: Problems, causes, cures.' *Environment and Planning B: Planning and Design* 34(4): 578–597.

Flyvbjerg, B. 2007b. 'How optimism bias and strategic misrepresentation undermine implementation.' Concept report 17, chapter 3, Norwegian University of Science and Technology. Available online at: http://citeseerx.ist.psu.edu/viewdoc/download?doi=1 0.1.1.307.5094&rep=rep1&type=pdf (accessed 1 March 2016).

Flyvbjerg, B., Bruzelius, N. and Rothengatter, W. 2003. *Megaprojects and risk: An anatomy of ambition*, 4th edition. Cambridge: Cambridge University Press.

Frick, K.T. 2008. 'The Cost of the technological sublime: daring ingenuity and the new San Francisco-Oakland Bay Bridge.' In H. Priemus, B. Flyvbjerg and B. van Wee (eds.), *Decision-making on megaprojects: cost-benefit analysis, planning and innovation.* Cheltenham: Edward Elgar, pp. 239–263.

Haidar, A. and Ellis, R.D. Jr. 2010. 'Analysis and improvement of megaprojects performance: Engineering project organizations conference.' Working Paper Proceedings. Available online at: http://academiceventplanner.com/EPOC2010/Papers/EPOC_2010_Haidar Ellis.pdf (accessed 1 March 2016).

IAIA (International Association for Impact Assessment). 1999. *Principles of environmental impact assessment best practice.* Dakota, US: IAIA.

Irimia-Diéguez, A.I., Sanchez-Cazorla, A. and Alfalla-Luque, R. 2014. 'Risk management in megaprojects.' *Procedia – Social and Behavioral Sciences* 119: 407–416.

Kardes, I., Ozturk, A., Cavusgil, S.T. and Cavusgil, E. 2013. 'Managing global megaprojects: Complexity and risk management.' *International Business Review* 22(6): 905–917.

Kingdon, J.W. 1995. *Agendas, alternatives and public policies.* New York: Harper Collins.

Korytárová, J. and Hromádkaa, V. 2014. 'The economic evaluation of megaprojects – Social and economic impacts.' *Procedia* 119: 495–502.

Korytárová, J. and Papežíková P. 2015. 'Assessment of large-scale projects based on CBA.' *Procedia Computer Science* 64: 736–743.

Lamari, M. and Landry, R. 2003. 'Contexte socio-politique de la prise de décision dans le domaine de la préservation de l'environnement.' In M. Guérin et al. (eds.), *Environnement et santé publique: fondements et pratiques.* Paris: Tec&Doc.

Lemieux, V. 2009. *L'étude des politiques publiques: les acteurs et leur pouvoir*, 3rd edition. Québec: Presses de l'Université Laval.

Levinson, D. 2013. 'Evaluation in time of uncertainty.' *International Conference on Uncertainties in Transport Project Evaluation* (Unite), Denmark University of Technologies, Copenhagen, September 16.

OECD. 2015. Government at a Glance 2015. Paris: OECD Publishing. doi: http://dx.doi.org/10.1787/gov_glance-2015-en

Ostrom, E. 2007. 'Institutional rational choice: An assessment of the institutional analysis.' In P.A. Sabatier (ed.), *Theories of the policy process*, 2nd edition. Boulder: Westview Press.

Pearce, D., Atkinson, G. and Mourato, S. 2006. *Cost-Benefit Analysis and the Environment: Recent developments*. Paris: OECD Publishing.

Priemus, H. 2010. 'Decision-making on megaprojects: Drifting on political discontinuity and market dynamics.' *European Journal of Transport and Infrastructure Research* 10(1): 19–29.

Priemus, H. and van Wee, B. 2013. *International Handbook and Megaprojects*. Cheltenham, UK and Northampton, US: Edward Elgar Publishing.

Ramsey, F.P. 1928. 'A mathematical theory of saving.' *Economic Journal* 38(152): 543–559.

Rietveld, P. 2013. 'Appraisal methods for transport policy.' In B. van Wee, J.A. Annema and D. Banister (eds), *The transport system and transport policy. An introduction*. Cheltenham, United Kingdom: Edward Elgar Publishing Limited and Northampton, United States: Massachusetts, pp. 329–352.

Rolstadas, A., Hetland, W., Jergeas, G.-F. and Westney, R. 2011. *Risk navigation strategies for major capital projects: Beyond the myth of predictability*. London: Springer.

Rossi, P.H., Lipsey, M.W. and Freeman, H.E. 2004. *Evaluation: A systematic approach*, 7th edition. Thousand Oaks: SAGE Publications.

Sabatier, P.A. (ed.) 2007. *Theories of the policy process*, 2nd edition. Boulder: Westview Press.

Sadler, B. 1996) *Étude internationale sur l'efficacité de l'évaluation environnementale: l'évaluation environnementale dans un monde en évolution – Évaluer la pratique pour améliorer le rendement*. Rapport final, Canadian Environmental Assessment Agency. Available online at: www.ceaa-acee.gc.ca/Content/2/B/7/2B7834CA-7D9A-410B-A4ED-FF78AB625BDB/iaia8_f.pdf (accessed 1 March 2016).

SECOR/KPMG. 2012. *Étude sur la gestion actuelle du Plan québécois des infrastructures et sur le processus de planification des projets*. Document principal, Infrastructure Québec. Available online at: www.tresor.gouv.qc.ca/fileadmin/PDF/publications/e/Etude/Etude_SECOR-KPMG.pdf (accessed 1 March 2016).

Sen, A. 1999. 'The possibility of social choice.' *American Economic Review* 89(3): 349–378.

Stern, N. 2006. *The Stern Review on the Economics of Climate Change*. London: HM Treasury.

Stirling, A. 2013. 'Evaluation and social appraisal: Risk, precaution and participation in infrastructure governance.' *Dealing with uncertainties in socioeconomic evaluation of megaprojects*, Agence nationale pour la gestion des déchets radioactifs. Paris: ANDRA, June 24.

Top100 Projects. 2016a. Available online at: http://top100projects.ca/submit-a-project/ (accessed 9 March 2016).

Top100 Projects. 2016b. 'Top 100 Projects for 2012.' Available online at: http://top100projects.ca/2012filters/ (accessed 9 March 2016).

Top100 Projects. 2016c. 'Top 100 Projects for 2013.' Available online at: http://top100projects.ca/2013filters/ (accessed 9 March 2016).

Top100 Projects. 2016d. 'Top 100 Projects for 2014.' Available online at: http://top100projects.ca/2014filters/ (accessed 9 March 2016).

Townley, P.G. 1998. *Principles of cost-benefit analysis in a Canadian context.* Scarborough: Prentice Hall Canada.

Vanclay, F. 2002. 'Conceptualising social impacts.' *Environmental Impact Assessment Review* 22(3): 183–211.

Williamson, O.E. 1981. 'The economics of organization: The transaction cost approach.' *The American Journal of Sociology* 87(3): 548–577.

Zidane, Y.J.T., Johansen, A. and Ekambaram, A. 2013. 'Megaprojects – Challenges and lessons learned.' *Procedia – Social and Behavioral Sciences* 74: 349–357.

9 The potential contribution of social impact assessment to megaproject developments

Frank Vanclay

Introduction

Megaprojects tend to be defined as multi-billion dollar/euro infrastructure projects characterised by complexity (van Marrewijk et al., 2008). Typically, they are multi-stakeholder projects, often public–private partnerships, comprise political sensitivities, and are highly contested (Flyvbjerg et al., 2003). Frick (2008) describes them in terms of the 'Six Cs': *colossal* in size and scope; *captivating* because of their size, engineering achievements or aesthetic design; *costly*, not only in the absolute cost of construction, but also in that costs are typically underestimated; *controversial*, attracting much public protest; *complex* in the sense of high levels of risk and uncertainty; and laden with *control* issues related to confusion over who makes the decisions, who manages, operates and/or regulates them, as well as potential interference by the project funders. Arguably, megaprojects are frequently anti-competitive, and are rife with, or at least highly prone to, corruption (Flyvbjerg, 2005; 2014).

The complexity megaprojects face is of both a technical and a social nature. The social complexity experienced by megaprojects often gives rise to wicked problems (Rittel and Webber, 1973) in that they are frequently novel or at least outside the normal experience of the impacted communities; the issues and people's perceptions of the issues change over time; and it is impossible to reach solutions that are acceptable to all stakeholders, partly because the issues are seen and framed in different ways by the various stakeholders.

Social impact assessment (SIA) is the process of managing the social issues of projects (Vanclay et al., 2015). Around the world, SIA has frequently been applied with respect to large projects, especially when there are locally impacted communities. Sometimes SIA is required by national legislation, either as a standalone response or as part of environmental impact assessment (EIA), although in some industries, notably the extractive industries, the use of SIA is an industry norm and SIA will be routinely undertaken whether or not it is legally required. Curiously, however, SIA and a discussion of social impacts have been strangely absent from the discourse on megaprojects (Lehtonen, 2014). This chapter therefore outlines what SIA is, and discusses how it can contribute to improving decision-making around and outcomes from megaprojects.

Social impact assessment as a changing discourse, field of practice and paradigm

Superficially, SIA is like EIA except that it considers the social rather than the biophysical issues associated with project development. However, this view is inadequate because social issues play out in very different ways than biophysical issues, and thus a different approach is needed to properly address them. Therefore, compared to EIA, there is a much greater focus in SIA on *managing* the issues (not just predicting, assessing, mitigating and monitoring them) (Vanclay, 2006; Esteves et al., 2012; Vanclay et al., 2015). A further major difference is that in SIA there is a much greater focus on enhancing the benefits of the project to local communities (Esteves and Vanclay, 2009; João et al., 2011). Nevertheless, the history of SIA is very much interlinked with the development of EIA, starting in North America in the early 1970s (Vanclay, 2014). In certain countries around the world, the legal definition of 'the environment' includes the social aspects by the use of expressions such as '*the qualities and characteristics of locations, places and areas*' or '*the social, economic and cultural aspects*'. In those countries, SIA tends to be part of EIA. In other countries, EIA only addresses the soil, the water and the air (and sometimes physical cultural heritage or historical artefacts), and SIA tends not to be undertaken, or must be separately commissioned (Vanclay, 2004). Nevertheless, whether SIA is standalone or integrated into EIA, it has an important role to play, and potentially will be of much use in the development of megaprojects (Lehtonen, 2014).

In the same way that other professional groupings or discourses – e.g. science, technology and society; public health; environmental engineering; or life-cycle analysis – are fields of research and practice, so too is SIA. There is a group of scholars and practitioners interested in SIA; there is a professional association, the International Association for Impact Assessment (IAIA, web address www.iaia. org); there is an extensive literature on SIA; there are theories and methods applicable to SIA; and there is a set of historical cases that would normally be expected to comprise the background understanding of any SIA practitioner. SIA thus has its own paradigm. This paradigm has been codified by the International Association for Impact Assessment at various points in time, including in the International Principles for Social Impact Assessment (Vanclay, 2003) and in a guidance document (Vanclay et al., 2015).

Over its forty-five or so years of practice, the SIA paradigm has changed considerably. SIA has transformed from being only a step undertaken in EIA to becoming a discourse, paradigm and field of practice in its own right (Vanclay, 2003). Within that discourse, SIA has moved beyond being only a regulatory tool like EIA; instead, SIA is now regarded as being the process of managing the social issues of projects at all phases of project development (Esteves et al., 2012; Franks and Vanclay, 2013; Vanclay et al., 2015). Although SIA remains a process of ensuring that community concerns will be considered in decision-making, SIA has positioned itself much more as a management process within the development of the project, from conception, through inception, construction, operation and even closure.

Demands for Social Impact Assessment

Given the absence of mandatory or regulatory requirements specifically for SIA, selling the business case to project proponents, i.e. justifying why SIA should be conducted, has become a major part of the SIA discourse (Esteves and Vanclay, 2009; Vanclay et al., 2015). Many companies will do SIA because it is best practice and/or because they are convinced of the value it contributes to their business operations. Furthermore, SIA is now often required not because of national regulatory agencies, but because of the expectations of the financial backers of projects. The World Bank, the International Finance Corporation (IFC – the private sector lending arm of the World Bank) and the Equator Principles group of banks (www.equator-principles.com/), which includes most of the world's major banks, all require due consideration of social issues as a condition of project financing. The United Nations Principles for Responsible Investment (www.unpri. org/) also encourage assessment of social issues by the investment industry, and ultimately ensure that social issues are properly considered in the governance and implementation of large projects.

The unanimous endorsement of the United Nations Guiding Principles on Business and Human Rights (United Nations, 2011) has led to a greater awareness about how many of the social issues created by projects of all sizes, especially megaprojects, can be interpreted in human rights terms (Kemp and Vanclay, 2013; Timo, 2013). One aspect of this shift to a human-rights-based approach is that impacted people are no longer stakeholders to be considered or ignored according to stakeholder management theory, they are now rights-holders whose rights must be properly considered. Thus, to comply with international standards and expectations, all companies (including state-owned companies) must consider the actual and potential adverse impacts they cause or contribute to, and any impacts that are linked to their operations, products and services through their business relationships, i.e. their supply chain (Götzmann et al., 2016). SIA can play a considerable role in understanding and managing social issues so that they do not become human rights issues.

Societal trends and the response of the SIA paradigm

There are some societal trends that are especially relevant to consider when thinking about SIA as more than a regulatory tool. One of these is the process of neoliberalism – a market-based ideology of reform in economics and governance that over time has resulted in governments changing their views about their responsibilities for regulation, and to a lowering of concern about social issues (Swyngedouw, 2005). Arguably, SIA was invented because governments were concerned about protecting communities from project-related harm. Now, governments tend not to fill the same roles of provider and protector that they did several decades ago. Furthermore, typically communities want much more than the minimal protection governments tended to provide. Communities want a greater say in the projects and policies that affect their lives. They also expect to be beneficiaries of the projects in their neighbourhoods, not just to have some regulatory agency speak on their behalf about what impact may or may not occur. 'Do no harm' is no longer sufficient, 'do good' is needed – local communities want positive outcomes. Communities want opportunities for social development: jobs, local content, local procurement and other benefits.

Another trend that has been under way over the last half century is the rise of the concept of 'corporate social responsibility' (CSR). Arguably, the concept of CSR has existed since the early 1950s (Bowen, 1953; van der Ploeg and Vanclay, 2013) but, by and large, the CSR and social performance practices of most corporations were poor. In contrast, at the present time, under the rubrics of sustainable development and corporate social responsibility, many companies willingly do more than just meet the minimum regulatory requirements. They want to be the 'developers of choice', and they are willing to negotiate with local communities and a wider set of stakeholders to address considerations beyond those required by law. In subscribing to the notion of 'shared value' (Porter and Kramer, 2011), they undertake SIA not because the government requires them to do it, but because they believe that being committed to SIA and doing it properly enables them to manage their social issues and social risks better, and that this adds value to their business (Esteves and Vanclay, 2009; Vanclay et al., 2015).

Yet another trend is increasing local community activism, international NGO support of local communities, and the rise of watchdog NGOs. Alongside growing perceptions that communities should have a bigger say and a bigger slice of the cake, local communities are becoming more adept at advancing their concerns across a wide range of settings – in the political arena, in the mass media and social media, and by protest actions in an ever-increasing number of forms (Hanna et al., 2016a; 2016b). All projects need to have a social licence to operate – in other words, the acceptance, if not approval, of local people and other stakeholders – otherwise they will be targeted by protest action (Dare et al., 2014).

In fact, it could be argued that to some extent, the regulators of today and into the future are not governments; rather, they are local and international NGOs and environmental watchdog organisations. These are the organisations that monitor corporate activities, that bring legal action when there is a transgression or infringement, and that create pressure and advocate for standards. Even where companies may have regulatory approval for their projects in particular jurisdictions, this does not mean that they have international NGO acceptability or a social licence to operate. Corporations need to ensure that they have established their case for project legitimacy in a bigger forum than just the local regulatory context – they must be acceptable to stakeholders all around the world, or else the global social and environmental NGOs will take action against them.

All these issues lead the advocates of SIA to claim, not that SIA is the perfect tool for governance – although there remains an important regulatory role for SIA – but that there is a strong business case for why companies should do SIA in order to achieve improved outcomes for businesses as well as for communities (Vanclay and Esteves, 2015).

SIA at each stage in the project life cycle

As previously indicated, the social impacts of projects occur even before the project starts, and continue to arise at all stages in project development. If a project is to be effectively modified to address the potential social issues (i.e. mitigation), thinking about and addressing (i.e. SIA) needs to happen long before the step of getting regulatory approval for the project – it has to happen up-front, or, in engineering or project management-speak, by 'front-loading'. Thus, rather than having SIA as a regulatory process that happens at some midpoint in project development, we need to front-load the consideration of social issues and build it into project design much earlier on in the project cycle. The paradigm of SIA has in effect become equivalent to what is in industry circles called 'social performance' – the process of managing the social issues at all stages of a project. SIA is applicable at closure, operations and construction phases, and for all pre-construction activities – it is useful at every stage of project development (see Figure 9.1).

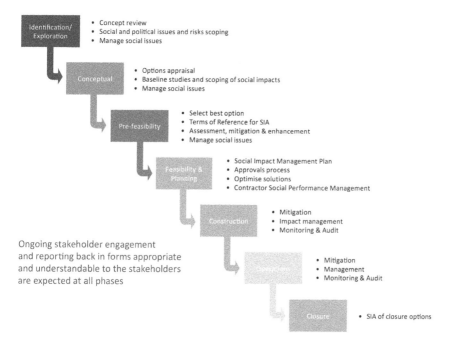

Figure 9.1 SIA is useful at each phase of project development.
Source: Vanclay et al., 2015.

The activities comprising social impact assessment

Since SIA is applicable at all stages of the project, it necessarily must cover a wide range of activities. The activities will vary across the project life cycle. While the guidance document of the International Association for Impact Assessment (Vanclay et al., 2015) identified twenty-six separate steps (see Figure 9.2 and Box 9.1), essentially falling under four headings: gaining an understanding of the community; predicting, analysing and assessing the likely impacts; developing and implementing strategies to address the impacts; and designing and implementing monitoring and adaptive management programmes. Having ongoing participatory processes for information input and reporting back are essential and should occur across the whole process.

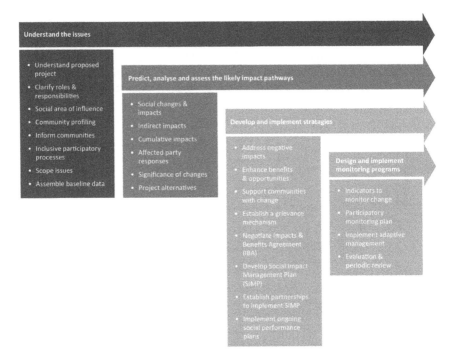

Figure 9.2 The overlapping activities in undertaking an SIA.
Source: Vanclay et al., 2015.

Box 9.1 The twenty-six tasks that comprise social impact assessment (Source: Vanclay et al., 2015)

Phase 1: Understand the issues

1   Gain a good understanding of the proposed project, including all ancillary activities necessary to support the project's development and operation.

2   Clarify the responsibilities and roles of all involved in or associated with the SIA, including relationships to the other specialist studies being undertaken, and establish what national laws and/or international guidelines and standards are to be observed.

3   Identify the preliminary 'social area of influence' of the project, likely impacted and beneficiary communities (nearby and distant), and stakeholders.

4   Gain a good understanding of the communities likely to be affected by the project by preparing a Community Profile which includes: (a) a thorough stakeholder analysis; (b) a discussion of the socio-political setting; (c) an assessment of the differing needs, interests, values and aspirations of the various subgroups of the affected communities including a gender analysis; (d) an assessment of their impact history, i.e. their experience of past projects and other historical events; (e) a discussion of trends happening in those communities; (f) a discussion of the assets, strengths and weaknesses of the communities; and (g) optionally the results of an opinion survey. This task is typically called profiling.

5   Fully inform community members about: (a) the project; (b) similar projects elsewhere to give them a sense of how they are likely to be affected; (c) how they can be involved in the SIA; (d) their procedural rights in the regulatory and social performance framework for the project; and (e) their access to grievance and feedback mechanisms.

6   Devise inclusive participatory processes and deliberative spaces to help community members: (a) understand how they will be impacted; (b) determine the acceptability of likely impacts and proposed benefits; (c) make informed decisions about the project; (d) facilitate community visioning about desired futures; (e) contribute to mitigation and monitoring plans; and (f) prepare for change.

7   Identify the social and human rights issues that have potential to be of concern (i.e. scoping).

8   Collate relevant baseline data for key social issues.

Phase 2: Predict, analyse and assess the likely impact pathways

9   Through analysis, determine the social changes and impacts that will likely result from the project and its various alternatives.

10 Carefully consider the indirect (or second and higher order) impacts.

11 Consider how the project will contribute to the cumulative impacts being experienced by the host communities.

12 Determine how the various affected groups and communities will likely respond.

13 Establish the significance of the predicted changes (i.e. prioritise them).

14 Actively contribute to the design and evaluation of project alternatives, including no-go and other options.

Phase 3: Develop and implement strategies

15 Identify ways of addressing potential negative impacts (by using the mitigation hierarchy).

16 Develop and implement ways of enhancing benefits and project-related opportunities.

17 Develop strategies to support communities in coping with change.

18 Develop and implement appropriate feedback and grievance mechanisms.

19 Facilitate an agreement-making process between the communities and the developer leading to the drafting of an Impacts and Benefits Agreement (IBA).

20 Assist the proponent in facilitating stakeholder input and drafting a Social Impact Management Plan (SIMP) which puts into operation the benefits, mitigation measures, monitoring arrangements and governance arrangements that were agreed to in the IBA, as well as plans for dealing with any ongoing unanticipated issues as they may arise.

21 Put processes in place to enable proponents, government authorities and civil society stakeholders to implement the arrangements implied in the SIMP and IBA, and develop and embed their own respective management action plans in their own organisations, establish respective roles and responsibilities throughout the implementation of those action plans, and maintain an ongoing role in monitoring.

22 Assist the proponent in developing and implementing ongoing social performance plans that address contractor obligations implied in the SIMP.

Phase 4: Design and implement monitoring programmes

23 Develop indicators to monitor change over time.

24 Develop a participatory monitoring plan.

25 Consider how adaptive management will be implemented and consider implementing a social management system.

26 Undertake evaluation and periodic review (audit).

Typical social impacts caused by large projects

An important difference between EIA and SIA is that environmental impacts tend only to occur when the project starts – when the first sod of soil is turned (Vanclay, 2012). Conversely, social impacts begin to happen immediately following even a rumour about a possible project. In some contexts, when there is a rumour that a project is going to happen nearby (and sometimes even a long way away), there may be some very real, immediate and direct impacts. Local people may become very concerned or anxious about their future – including the future of their place and their community. They may create and/or harbour many fears and anxieties, which may have no technical basis. They may become very angry and resentful, and they will likely mobilise against the project. This period of uncertainty about the project will typically be very stressful for them. Megaprojects, especially relating to risky industries, will most certainly create controversy and provoke local opposition. It is essential that all projects consider their engagements with local communities and how they will obtain a social licence to operate.

If the project is regarded as socially undesirable, property prices in the neighbourhood may go down as the region becomes stigmatised. Alternatively, if the project is socially desirable, it may lead to gentrification, displacing poor people (Slater, 2006; Watt, 2013). People may speculate in property, which can also distort the local real estate market. In low- to middle-income countries a different phenomenon tends to occur. People may flock to the likely project site – to pretend that they are locals so they might receive compensation from the project, in search of jobs, or as entrepreneurs (small and medium-sized enterprises) to ply their services. The industry term for this phenomenon is the 'honey pot effect'. A more technical expression might be 'project-induced in-migration' (IFC, 2009).

What is important, whether in high or low- to middle-income country contexts, is that the process of managing the social issues needs to start very early on, well before any regulatory procedure is required. Therefore, thinking about how projects create impacts and how these impacts can be mitigated and managed from the very beginning of the project is important.

Many large projects lead to the displacement of many people. Arguably, when done properly, the effective resettlement of people could potentially lead to them becoming better off, at least in the longer term (Perera, 2014; Reddy et al., 2015). However, the experience of most projects is that resettled people are made worse off (Scudder, 2013). The International Finance Corporation (2012) Performance Standard 5 on Land Acquisition and Involuntary Resettlement is generally regarded as the 'gold standard' for best practice in resettlement. The first principle of best practice is to avoid resettlement if at all possible. The second principle is to always attempt to come to a negotiated agreement rather than to rely on legal powers of expropriation or eminent domain. A third principle is that the livelihoods of those being resettled should be improved, or at the very least these people must not be made worse off. A handy summary of the principles of resettlement is provided in the International Association for Impact Assessment's guidance document on social impact assessment (Vanclay et al., 2015). A good outline of how to do resettlement can be found in Reddy et al. (2015).

Large projects are often a 'boom' for a local economy, and will typically create local inflation, especially when the project is located in a rural community. The increased demand for all goods and services from the project, subcontractors and their combined workforce and associated families (which often number in their thousands, if not tens of thousands) will always cause pressure on local resources, especially housing. People who work for the project most likely have incomes that can accommodate the high local inflation rates. However, other local people may have fixed salaries that can become very inadequate if inflation is severe. This disparity in wages related to living costs creates further social impacts because of the shortage of teachers, police officers, nurses and all other types of professional and service staff that it generates. It also becomes extremely difficult for local shopkeepers and other businesses to attract staff. Demands for social services increase, and many of these demands remain unmet. Appointments with doctors, dentists, accountants etc. must be made months in advance. Queues at the shopping centre checkouts become longer. There may be traffic jams at major intersections, and bottlenecks of all forms may develop. The level of frustration with everyday life increases.

The in-migration, local inflation, increasing inequality and frustration together lead to other social issues. People's sense of place is disrupted, and their sense of security is affected. They will start to feel unsafe. Their perception of their community changes. Whether or not actual crime rates increase, people will often perceive that there is more crime. This reduces their sense of well being, and reduces the sense of community cohesion. People may experience psychological and physiological symptoms of stress. The presence of strangers and the fear of difference (xenophobia) promoted by this sense of decreased well being will likely lead to anti-social behaviour.

Government agencies also experience difficulties. Their workload increases considerably. They cannot adequately respond to cost-of-living issues, and their staff therefore become very prone to being poached by the project. Their highly competent staff are especially attractive to the project because they may have special skills, knowledge or connections that can make things work for the project. However, the consequence is a diminished capacity in the government agencies, and a loss of organisational memory. Lack of oversight may develop. With delays and incompetence because of diminished capacity, the potential for corruption increases. With many opportunities for rent-seeking, facilitation payments will often be offered and accepted. All of this in turn leads to a loss of trust in these agencies and to government in general.

Megaprojects are particularly complex

Megaprojects will likely create the same social impacts as other large projects, but they are also likely to present some particular issues relating to their complexity and extended time frames. Projects go through distinct phases (see Figure 9.1), with different benefits and impacts in each phase. Typically, with large projects the construction phase has the greatest impacts, but this phase is usually short-lived and the longer-term benefits compensate for any short-term inconveniences to local communities. In megaprojects, however, construction time frames can be very long (into decades), making the trade-off of impacts against benefits very difficult to determine. Even if an economist might be brave or foolish enough to attempt such a calculus, there is an equity issue. For some megaprojects the benefits might not even accrue to the current generation; they may only be realised many years later, after the people who experience the negative impacts have long passed. This was particularly the case with the Stuttgart 21 railway development (Novy and Peters, 2012).

Another problem is that there are often major delays between decision-making and implementation. With megaprojects, it is not uncommon for there to be decades between when decisions on projects are decided and when construction actually commences. This has many social consequences, primarily that the baseline data are no longer adequate and conditions and people's preferences may have changed considerably. Even if community consultation pertaining to the original decision indeed took place, such decision-making no longer has legitimacy with current generations.

A final problem is that the extended life and complexity of many megaprojects may mean that unforeseen consequences arise. These issues may not necessarily change the overall assessment of the project as a whole, but may mean that at certain times, the people experiencing these impacts feel they are unduly affected. One example here is gas extraction from the Groningen gas field. For fifty years or so gas was extracted from the Groningen gas field with little environmental consequence and with much benefit to the national economy. However, the depletion of gas reserves in the field has led to sudden subsidence events which have created minor earthquakes, causing damage to houses and much consternation generally (van der Voort and Vanclay, 2015).

Some personal observations about how SIA can make an effective difference

Whereas EIA tends to be about producing an environmental impact statement that, once signed off by the regulatory authority, has no role anymore, SIA is a process that directly interacts with the project itself in order to ensure there is a real commitment within the company and project to addressing all the issues and implementing appropriate measures. The SIA field has moved away from statements of social impact towards producing Social Impact Management Plans. The best practice in the governance of impact assessment is about assessing the management plan rather than the statement of impacts (Franks and Vanclay, 2013).

Another good governance practice is the use of an Impacts and Benefits Agreement (IBA), sometimes called a Community Development Agreement. These are legal documents outlining the agreement made between the proponent and the local community. Arguably, it should be a three-way agreement also including government at multiple levels. An IBA makes transparent what the project is about, what the likely impacts will be, how the proponent will manage those impacts, how the project will benefit the local community, and what the responsibilities of each partner or stakeholder are (Gibson & O'Faircheallaigh, 2010).

A common question is: "what is 'social'?" The answer is that 'social' is everything. Any impact is a social impact because it affects people and their lives. All environmental impacts ultimately translate into social impacts, because they unavoidably influence people (Vanclay, 2002). Although there are a plethora of new types of impact assessments being developed (Vanclay, 2004; 2015), SIA is an umbrella that covers all the issues. This also means that doing an SIA for a large project is a major undertaking that cannot be done by small teams of people.

People often ask what the measurable indicators of social impact should be. It is important to realise that determining what the indicators might be is quite difficult, because the impacts experienced by people depend on several factors: the characteristics of the project; the characteristics of the mitigation; and the characteristics of the community. Some communities are adaptable, flexible and resilient, while others are not. It also depends on the characteristics of particular individuals. It is also important to realise that the way in which people relate to the impacts changes over time, and also that impacts affect people differentially: there are always winners and losers. Part of the discussion in impact assessment is thinking about how each person is negatively affected and what it would take to change those people from being negatively affected to being positively affected by the project. A critical question is: **How can the losers be turned into winners?**

The concept of 'impact history' is particularly important. Impact history refers to the previous experience a community has had with projects. In situations where that experience is bad, people are sceptical about new projects. Hence, even when the new project is arguably very good, it might still be hard for the project to win the trust of the local people, who have in mind their previous experiences. One of the ways social impacts differ from environmental impacts is that environmental impacts are to a certain extent deterministic (when they occur there is little doubt about them), whereas social impacts are very different in nature – they are individually experienced by people. Social impacts also very much depend on the legitimacy of the project and the ways in which this legitimacy came about.

From analysis of the case history in SIA, we know that **second and higher-order impacts tend to cause more harm than first-order impacts**. Far too much impact assessment has been merely about identifying the first-order direct impacts. This feeds what is called 'checklist thinking', in which the consultant merely goes down the list to consider whether each impact is likely to be a consequence of the project. However, this usually leads to inadequate assessments. We know that impacts interact with each other in complex ways, one impact leading to another impact which in turn engenders a third impact, and so on. Furthermore, people respond to the impacts that they experience, and their responses themselves create more impacts. Thus it is necessary to think about the impact pathways, or the chains or the web of impacts. Drawing mental maps of these links is a useful way of conceptualising and presenting them. Indeed, one of my favourite sayings is:

'almost all projects almost always cause almost all impacts'. While that is very evident for megaprojects, it is also arguably true for small projects.

Due to these complexities, it is often extremely difficult to predict what the social impacts will actually be. It would be ludicrous to believe that impact assessment could be all-knowing and all-powerful – that the impacts could be accurately predicted, that interventions could be designed to mitigate the impacts, and that everything would proceed as planned. Therefore, not only must there be impact prediction early on; it is also important to have an open process of continuous monitoring and adaptive management.

In most countries, because really dangerous projects tend not to be approved or even proposed, typically *a key impact of any project is the fear and anxiety generated by the project*. Fear and anxiety are real social impacts that we need to take seriously and manage effectively. We need to be mindful of how projects might generate fear and anxiety and what needs to be done to reduce them.

Another issue is that many projects have promised lots of benefits that they then fail to deliver. This annoys communities, and contributes to the impact history of the community and that community's reluctance to agree to new projects. Another impact is that many projects could have been enhanced to improve the way they provide benefits to communities. So an impact is the difference between what actually eventuates and what benefits could have been obtained if those projects had been more carefully designed from a social perspective.

Free, Prior and Informed Consent is part of getting a Social Licence to Operate

The notion of 'free, prior and informed consent' (FPIC) is an important international legal concept that comes out of the International Labour Organization Convention 169 and the United Nations Declaration on the Rights of Indigenous Peoples (Hanna and Vanclay, 2013). Originally it was a concept that was only applicable to indigenous peoples, deriving from their special connection to the land, and therefore projects needed a special process for dealing with indigenous peoples. In human rights terms, FPIC was a mechanism to ensure indigenous peoples could exercise their rights (Götzmann et al., 2016). However, many in the SIA field argue that FPIC should apply to all communities (Vanclay and Esteves, 2011; Buxton and Wilson, 2013), since it constitutes an important overarching philosophical concept about the rights of communities. Although its origin lies with indigenous communities, FPIC is an appropriate way of demonstrating respect to all communities. No project should proceed without the free, prior and informed consent of the local people.

- 'Free' means no coercion, intimidation, manipulation or harassment.
- 'Prior' means that all the issues need to be considered and consultations undertaken in adequate time before any decisions about the project are made.

- 'Informed' means that the proponent has to disclose fully, but also that the affected communities have enough ability to be able to consider what the impacts of those activities will be for them.
- 'Consent' means that communities themselves have a choice about whether they say yes or no, depending on whether the project is of value to them.

The business case for doing social impact assessment

Introductory courses in business management generally teach that the key drivers of business are: revenue growth and access to markets; cost savings and productivity; access to capital (and the rate of interest charged); effective management of risks; access to skilled human capital; and the reputation of the company and its products. It is easy to make a case for SIA as a positive contributor to all these business drivers (Vanclay et al., 2015). While there are some differences between public sector enterprises and the private sector, the differences are not that great. Even projects initiated by the public sector and by NGOs need to have a social licence to operate, and have to operate efficiently (Jijelava and Vanclay, 2014).

There is a strong business case for social impact assessment (Esteves et al., 2012; Vanclay et al., 2015). Even though the goal of SIA is to improve the well being of communities, SIA also assists projects by:

- effective identification and management of social risks
- identifying issues early on so that they can be addressed before they become problems
- cost reductions in a wide variety of areas by, for instance, preventing problems from escalating; reducing the risk of strikes, sabotage and stakeholder-induced stoppages or blockades; and reducing the risk of future litigation
- full-cost consideration, which means that by knowing all the likely 'full costs', decision-making can be improved and the risk of cost overruns can be reduced
- providing greater certainty and reassurance about the project to key stakeholders including government, investors, and the affected communities
- improving stakeholder relations
- improving access to a skilled local workforce and suppliers
- improving company and product reputation
- creating an ongoing social licence to operate and grow
- enabling better access to land and resources
- as a combined result of all of the above, contributing to the long-term success of the project and the company.

In many sectors, but particularly in the extractive industries, many costs to industry have arisen from community protests, community retaliation against companies, sabotage of plant and equipment, legal action and court cases, and so on. Whether the companies win or lose the court cases, they always incur costs, not only in terms of legal costs but also in terms of the considerable reputational harm that accompanies such action. Therefore, there is a clear business case for companies to build better relationships with local communities and establish a social licence to operate (Davis and Franks, 2014; Franks et al., 2014; Hidalgo et al., 2014).

One reason why companies and projects should consider their social risks carefully is because the cost of finance, or even their access to finance, may be affected. Around the world, many banks are signing up to the Equator Principles (see www.equator-principles.com). As of 2015, over eighty banks, representing over 70 per cent of project financing in emerging markets, had done so. The Equator Principles constitute a credit risk management framework for determining, assessing and managing environmental and social risk in project finance transactions. In effect, banks signing up to the Equator Principles make a public pledge that they will not lend money for bad purposes – in other words to projects that violate human rights or cause environmental or social harm. To receive project financing, companies need to demonstrate to the financial institutions that they are meeting or exceeding a set of sustainability and social guidelines – in practice, the equivalent of the IFC's performance standards (see www.ifc.org/performancestandards). Thus, the need to ensure that the project is compatible with high social standards is also now vested in financial institutions – which otherwise run the risk of being rejected from the Equator Principles organisation and/or harassed by international watchdog NGOs.

Conclusion

Megaprojects have the potential to create a great deal of harm for nearby communities and to attract the attention and wrath of civic stakeholders across the world. Social impact assessment, understood as the process of managing the social issues of projects at all phases of project development, can contribute to reducing this harm, and, ideally, to ensuring that projects contribute positively to communities. The activities that comprise SIA contribute to managing the social issues from conception of the project, through design stages, construction, implementation and closure. SIA should not be seen as a cost, but as an essential investment that assists in getting better outcomes for the project and the community.

References

Bowen, A.B. 1953. *Social Responsibilities of the Business Man*. New York: Harper & Row.

Buxton, A. & Wilson, E. 2013. *FPIC and the Extractive Industries: A Guide to applying the Spirit of Free, Prior and Informed Consent in Industrial Projects*. London: International Institute for Environment and Development. Available online at: http://pubs.iied.org/pdfs/16530IIED.pdf (accessed 25 July 2016).

Dare, M., Schirmer, J. & Vanclay, F. 2014 Community engagement and social licence to operate. *Impact Assessment and Project Appraisal* 32(3): 188–197.

Davis, R. & Franks, D.M. 2014. *Costs of Company-Community Conflict in the Extractive Sector*. Corporate Social Responsibility Initiative Report, John F. Kennedy School of Government, Harvard University, Cambridge, MA. Available online at: www.hks.

harvard.edu/m-rcbg/CSRI/research/Costs%20of%20Conflict_Davis%20%20Franks.pdf (accessed 25 July 2016).

Esteves, A.M., Franks, D. & Vanclay, F. 2012. Social impact assessment: The state of the art. *Impact Assessment and Project Appraisal* 30(1): 35–44.

Esteves, A.M. & Vanclay, F. 2009. Social development needs analysis as a tool for SIA to guide corporate-community investment: Applications in the minerals industry.' *Environmental Impact Assessment Review* 29(2): 137–145.

Flyvbjerg, B. 2005. Design by deception: The politics of megaproject approval. *Harvard Design Magazine* 22: 50–59.

Flyvbjerg, B. 2014. What you should know about megaprojects and why. *Project Management Journal* 45(2): 6–19.

Flyvbjerg, B., Bruzelius, N. & Rothengatter, W. 2003. *Megaprojects and Risk: An Anatomy of Ambition*. Cambridge: Cambridge University Press.

Franks, D. & Vanclay, F. 2013. Social Impact Management Plans: Innovation in corporate and public policy. *Environmental Impact Assessment Review* 43: 40–48.

Franks, D.M., Davis, R., Bebbington, A.J., Ali, S.H., Kemp, D. & Scurrah, M. 2014. Conflict translates environmental and social risk into business costs. *Proceedings of the National Academy of Sciences* 111(21), 7576–7581.

Frick, K. 2008. The cost of the technological sublime: Daring ingenuity and the new San Francisco-Oakland Bay Bridge. In: H. Priemus, B. Flyvbjerg & B. van Wee (eds.), *Decision-Making on Mega-Projects*. Cheltenham: Edward Elgar, pp. 239–262.

Gellert, P. & Lynch, P. 2003. Mega-projects as displacements. *International Social Science Journal* 55: 15–25.

Gibson, G. & O'Faircheallaigh, C. 2010. *IBA Community Toolkit: Negotiation and Implementation of Impact and Benefit Agreements*. Toronto: Walter & Duncan Gordon Foundation. Available online at: www.ibacommunitytoolkit.ca (accessed 25 July 2016).

Götzmann, N., Vanclay, F. & Seier, F. 2016. Social and human rights impact assessments: What can they learn from each other? *Impact Assessment & Project Appraisal* 34(1): 14–23.

Hanna, P., Langdon, J. & Vanclay, F. 2016a. Indigenous rights, performativity and protest. *Land Use Policy* 50: 490–506.

Hanna, P. & Vanclay, F. 2013. Human rights, Indigenous peoples and the concept of Free, Prior and Informed Consent. *Impact Assessment & Project Appraisal* 31(2): 146–157.

Hanna, P., Vanclay, F., Langdon, J. & Arts, J. 2016b. Conceptualizing social protest and the significance of protest action to large projects. *Extractive Industries and Society* 3(1): 217–239.

Hidalgo, C., Peterson, K., Smith, D. & Foley, H. 2014. *Extracting with Purpose: Creating Shared Value in the Oil and Gas and Mining Sectors' Companies and Communities*. FSG. Available online at: www.fsg.org/publications/extracting-purpose (accessed 25 July 2016).

IFC. 2009. *Projects and People: A Handbook for Addressing Project-Induced In-migration*. Washington, DC: International Finance Corporation. Available online at: http://commdev.org/wp-content/uploads/2015/06/In-Migration-Handbook.pdf (accessed 25 July 2016).

IFC. 2012. *Performance Standard 5 Land Acquisition and Involuntary Resettlement*. Washington, DC: International Finance Corporation. Available online at: www.ifc.org/wps/wcm/connect/3d82c70049a79073b82cfaa8c6a8312a/PS5_English_2012.pdf?MOD=AJPERES (accessed 25 July 2016).

Jijelava, D. & Vanclay, F. 2014. Assessing the social licence to operate of the work of humanitarian and development cooperation organizations: A case study of Mercy Corps in Samtskhe-Javakheti, Georgia. *Social Epistemology* 28(3–4): 297–317.

João, E., Vanclay, F. & den Broeder, L. 2011. Emphasising enhancement in all forms of impact assessment: Introduction to a special issue. *Impact Assessment and Project Appraisal* 29(3): 170–180.

Kemp, D. & Vanclay, F. 2013. Human rights and impact assessment: Clarifying the connections in practice. *Impact Assessment & Project Appraisal* 31(2): 86–96.

Lehtonen, M. 2014. Evaluation of 'the social' in megaprojects: Tensions, dichotomies, and ambiguities. *International Journal of Architecture, Engineering and Construction* 3(2): 98–109.

Novy, J. & Peters, D. 2012. Railway station mega-projects as public controversies: The case of Stuttgart 21. *Built Environment* 37(3): 128–145.

Perera, J. (ed.) 2014. *Lose to Gain: Is Involuntary Resettlement a Development Opportunity?* Manilla: Asian Development Bank. Available online at: www.adb.org/sites/default/files/ publication/41780/lose-gain-involuntary-resettlement.pdf (accessed 25 July 2015).

Porter, M. & Kramer, M. 2011. Creating shared value. *Harvard Business Review* 89(1–2): 62–77.

Reddy, G., Smyth, E. & Steyn, M. 2015. *Land Access and Resettlement: A Guide to Best Practice*. Sheffield: Greenleaf.

Rittel, H. & Webber, M. 1973. Dilemmas in a general theory of planning. *Policy Sciences* 4: 155–169.

Scudder, T. 2013. Development-induced community resettlement. In F. Vanclay & A.M. Esteves (eds.), *New Directions in Social Impact Assessment: Conceptual and Methodological Advances*. Cheltenham: Edward Elgar, pp. 186–201.

Slater, T. 2006. The eviction of critical perspectives from gentrification research. *International Journal of Urban and Regional Research* 30(4): 737–757.

Swyngedouw, E. 2005. Governance innovation and the citizen: The Janus face of Governance-beyond-the-State. *Urban Studies* 42(11): 1991–2006.

Timo, P.B. 2013. Development at the cost of violations: The impact of mega-projects on human rights in Brazil. *SUR – International Journal on Human Rights* 10(18): 137–157.

United Nations. 2011. *Guiding Principles on Business and Human Rights*. Available online at: www.ohchr.org/Documents/Publications/GuidingPrinciplesBusinessHR_EN.pdf (accessed 25 July 2016).

van der Ploeg, L. & Vanclay, F. 2013. Credible claim or corporate spin: A checklist to evaluate corporate sustainability reports. *Journal of Environmental Assessment Policy and Management* 15(3): 1350012 (21 pages).

van der Voort, N. & Vanclay, F. 2015. Social impacts of earthquakes caused by gas extraction in the Province of Groningen, The Netherlands. *Environmental Impact Assessment Review* 50: 1–15.

van Marrewijk, A., Clegg, S.R., Pitsis, T.S. and Veenswijk, M. 2008. Managing public–private megaprojects: Paradoxes, complexity, and project design. *International Journal of Project Management* 26(6): 591–600.

Vanclay, F. 2002. Conceptualising social impacts. *Environmental Impact Assessment Review* 22(3): 183–211.

Vanclay, F. 2003. International principles for Social Impact Assessment. *Impact Assessment and Project Appraisal* 21(1): 5–11.

Vanclay, F. 2004. The triple bottom line and impact assessment: How do TBL, EIA, SIA, SEA and EMS relate to each other? *Journal of Environmental Assessment Policy and Management* 6(3): 265–288.

Vanclay, F. 2006. Principles for Social Impact Assessment: A critical comparison between the International and US documents. *Environmental Impact Assessment Review* 26(1): 3–14.

Vanclay, F. 2012. The potential application of Social Impact Assessment in integrated coastal zone management. *Ocean and Coastal Management* 68: 149–156.

Vanclay, F. 2014. Developments in Social Impact Assessment: An introduction to a collection of seminal research papers. In F. Vanclay (ed.), *Developments in Social Impact Assessment*. Cheltenham: Edward Elgar, pp. xv–xxxix.

Vanclay, F. 2015. Changes in the impact assessment family 2003–2014: Implications for considering achievements, gaps and future directions. *Journal of Environmental Assessment Policy and Management* 17(1): 1550003 (20 pages).

Vanclay, F. & Esteves, A.M. 2011. Current issues and trends in social impact assessment. In F. Vanclay & A.M. Esteves (eds.), *New Directions in Social Impact Assessment: Conceptual and Methodological Advances*, Cheltenham: Edward Elgar, pp. 3–19.

Vanclay, F. & Esteves, A.M. 2015. Current trends in social impact assessment: Implications for infrastructure developments. In J. Woltjer, E. Alexander, A. Hull, & M. Ruth (eds.), *Place-Based Evaluation for Integrated Land-use Management*. Aldershot: Ashgate, pp. 99–112.

Vanclay, F., Esteves, A.M., Aucamp, I. & Franks, D. 2015. *Social Impact Assessment: Guidance for assessing and managing the social impacts of projects*. Fargo ND: International Association for Impact Assessment. Available online at: http://bit.ly/SIAguidance (accessed 25 July 2016).

Watt, P. 2013. It's not for us. *City* 17(1): 99–118.

10 Collective construction of social indicators of wellbeing

Analytical insights from an experiment

Michel Renault

The collective construction of social indicators of wellbeing has been my main area of research for the past five or six years. The relevance of my work for megaproject evaluation stems from the significant impacts that such projects may have on people's daily lives and wellbeing. The controversies surrounding megaprojects entail scientific, social, ethical and many other dimensions. In such controversies, the representations and perceptions of people play an important but often neglected role, since even agreeing upon a common definition of the situation is often impossible. Social indicators could help to overcome such difficulties or at least reveal the representations underlying individual or collective positions.

The pragmatic/transactional approach that I advocate in this chapter calls for attention to time and uncertainty. Such attention is particularly relevant in the governance of megaprojects that engage communities over long time periods. This is typically the case, for instance, in the Cigéo project, for the deep geological disposal of high-level radioactive waste in France. The pragmatic/transactional perspective does not entail a 'quest for certainty', whereby decision-making would be transformed into a techno-scientific process or reduced to a merely theoretical matter. Decision-making is instead perceived as a practical and operational issue open to debate and deliberation. In the words of John Dewey: *'Man finds himself living in an aleatory world; his existence involves, to put it boldly, a gamble. The world is a scene of risk; it is uncertain, unstable, uncannily unstable. Its dangers are irregular, inconstant, not to be counted upon as to their times and seasons'* (quoted in Thompson, 2005: 187). The quest for certainty, for example through the transformation of uncertainty into risk by using actuarial and probabilistic calculus as mentioned by Knight (1921), tends to neglect this practical and operational character of decision-making. One of the causes that Dewey identified for this quest for certainty is the refusal to consider ordinary life and its contingencies as objects of legitimate knowledge (Thompson, 2005: 197). But according to Dewey, since we cannot escape the everyday contingencies related to 'events', it is necessary to find ways to 'make do with'. Hence, in a world characterised by uncertainty, *'a "more ordered and intelligent happiness" is the most "certainty" we can hope for'* (Thompson, 2005: 204). It is then necessary to find ways to develop a 'collective intelligence'. Organising participatory procedures that engage citizens and communities into a process of inquiry appears as one way of mobilising this collective intelligence in order to solve problematic situations. Dialogue and deliberation appear as means of making the '*stability of meaning prevail over the instability of events*', and it '[…] *is the main task of intelligent human effort*' (Thompson, 2005: 204). The SPIRAL methodology appears as a possible instrument for putting into practice this quest for meaning.

Uncertainty appears from this perspective not only as a technical issue but also as a matter of meaning. It also challenges the false idea that the 'problematic situations' we are facing and which entail decision-making are clear and perfectly defined. Plurality of meanings is the rule rather than the exception in the situations we face, each situation raising its own challenges. We must therefore confront this plurality of meanings by integrating into the process of inquiry as many perspectives as possible. The SPIRAL methodology provides an opportunity to juxtapose multiple perspectives, while the elaboration of 'indicators of situation' (which describe situations from the worst to the best) allows one to define and redefine situations. From a pragmatic/transactional point of view, in particular within the framework developed by Mead (1934), defining a situation implies adopting the point of view of the other (or putting oneself in the place of the other) or of a group or a community. This 'perspective-taking' process may also open the way for the consideration of what the economist John Roger Commons (1950) called 'futurity'. The SPIRAL methodology indeed enables the individuals involved to adopt the perspective of the others, including the perspective of a future community. This was the approach adopted, for instance, in an exercise involving the analysis of quality of life by the Mid-America Regional Council in its 'Metro outlook' model. One can also imagine giving a status to the concerns of future generations in debates that seek to systematically explore the imagined and hypothetical views of those future generations. In this way, deliberative methodologies that engage citizens and communities in an inquiry allow the future to be truly taken into account in a collective endeavour of exploring the possible futures and the consequences of our actions.

Economists often use indicators such as GDP as the sole measure of progress, although this situation may be changing. For example, the Stiglitz–Sen–Fitoussi commission report on the measurement of performance and social progress (Stiglitz et al., 2009: 12) states: '*the time is ripe for our measurement system to shift emphasis from measuring economic production to measuring people's well-being. And measures of well-being should be put in a context of sustainability.*' This was a key message and a unifying theme of the report.

This work is in line with other research, for example on economic, social and environmental concerns, such as the OECD Better Life Initiative.[1] Two main themes can be identified: the limitations of traditional indicators in addressing issues of wellbeing – for example, GDP can no longer be considered as an indicator of wellbeing and social progress – and the need to involve citizens in the process of quantifying wellbeing and social progress. For instance, the 'community indicators movement', which emerged in the United States in the 1960s[2] but has since spread across the world, highlights the importance of democratic processes. '*The idea of community indicators of well-being reflects a change in focus from the "top down" imposition of what well-being, sustainability, quality of life, etc. should look like to a "bottom up" approach that emphasises democratic participation and empowerment in the development of locally significant understanding of well-being and its measurements'* (Jēkabsone et al., 2013). This movement also reflects other trends: the need to move beyond controversies over projects affecting the 'public'; the devolution of control over many programmes to the local level (local authorities); the need to measure progress towards the objectives of Agenda 21 and sustainable development strategies; and the need for better performance and accountability indicators (for example, measuring the outcome of public spending).

This chapter starts by describing an experiment that aimed, through a participatory process, to develop 'situation indicators'. The experiment adapted a method initiated by the Social Cohesion Division of the Council of Europe (CoE). The method seeks not only to define indicators, but also to use them as guidance in public policy, following the logic of co-responsibility. Compared to conventional approaches, its main original feature is the involvement of citizens or communities at all stages of the process. It thus provides original data to complement the data conventionally used for describing and understanding the various dimensions of quality of life, wellbeing and happiness. In the following, I shall first present the efforts aimed at developing social indicators of wellbeing through a participatory process, and will then draw some methodological insights from this experiment of collaborative indicator development.

An experimentation: developing social indicators of wellbeing together

Generally speaking, social indicators can perform three functions. First, they can provide information that serves as a basis for decision-making. Second, they may assist in evaluating projects from an internal or external point of view. Third, they *'may also constitute elements of a collective definition of a common world ... or even a common good (objectives to reach, norms to be respected), and means of achieving it (measure of well-being)'*[3] (Boulanger, 2004: 14).

A collective definition of the common world

It was from this third point of view – the ambition of collectively defining a common world – that our experiment took off. This experiment was aimed at constructing social indicators of wellbeing jointly with citizens and communities in rural areas of France. The starting point was what can be called 'a problematic situation'. Of course, the focus could be on any other issue – which would obviously first have to be defined through a process of social inquiry. A social inquiry, with the engagement of the 'public' – those directly or indirectly affected by the human activity in question – is necessary in order to at least partly reduce the uncertainty relating to the definition of the 'situation'. This collective process of defining the situation would entail, in particular, identifying the relevant cause–effect relationships concerning the wellbeing of the people involved. In the words of

Desrosières (2008), the process of quantification therefore implies qualifying before measuring or counting.

Our project, ISBET (Societal Indicators of Territorial Wellbeing), was composed of three phases. The first phase was devoted to elaborating human development indicators and other alternative synthetic indicators at the regional and sub-regional levels. The aim was to take a step towards more adequate local policies orientated towards human development and not only towards increasing the national or local-level GDP. However, such indicators are still defined by experts; they are not easily understood and handled by citizens.

The second phase of the project aimed at constructing indicators with citizens and for citizens. We drew inspiration from the SPIRAL (Societal Progress Indicators and Responsibilities for ALL) methodology developed by the Council of Europe (CoE 2005; 2010) and applied it in two local communities in Brittany. The third part was devoted to analytical reflection concerning the indicators and the process of their social construction.

One original feature of the SPIRAL methodology is that it considers wellbeing for all, and not just individual wellbeing. For example, in economics we are used to measuring the wellbeing of a community as an aggregation of all individual opinions in order to obtain the average opinion of a community or a group as a whole. This is, for example, how European Values Studies[4] and World Values Surveys[5] construct their wellbeing estimates. The wellbeing of us all would hence be the average opinion constructed by aggregating all individual opinions. This is not the approach adopted by the SPIRAL methodology.

The most widespread indicators, those promoted by international organisations and bodies which seek to direct public policies, such as the indicators following the recommendations of the Stiglitz–Sen–Fitoussi report (Stiglitz et al., 2009), are based on a rather clear theoretical vision and epistemological position (Cassiers and Delain, 2006; Méda and Jany-Catrice, 2013; Thiry and Roman, 2014). They align themselves with the framework of orthodox, neo-classical economics, adopting its subjectivist, individualistic and utilitarian postulates. For example, the new 'economics of happiness' (Davoine, 2012; Layard, 2005) broadly adheres to the thinking of Jeremy Bentham and the associated subjectivist and utilitarian conception of value. These perspectives share several defining characteristics:

- They consider only individuals.
- These individuals are taken as passive objects of investigation.
- The questions asked and the methods used do not take into account the institutional framework.
- Wellbeing is handled only via predetermined cognitive filters, such as closed questions, 'ladders' used in subjective inquiries such as World Values Surveys, or methods designed to reveal individual preferences (e.g. contingent valuation or even magnetic resonance imaging equipment) (Layard, 2005).

These approaches do not take into account processes of 'formation of values' and the 'social worlds' in which individuals and communities are embedded. Likewise, they fail to consider language as one of the main vectors of sociality. These perspectives rely instead on the classic conception of language as a transparent medium that allows a person to communicate her thoughts to another person. Language is seen simply as the vehicle through which arguments can be conveyed and truth be discovered (Brown, 1994). The dualistic epistemology that underpins such a conception is clear: truth (or reality) exists independently of the process of its discovery or expression, just like economic preferences are supposed to pre-exist and only need to be 'revealed'.

The SPIRAL methodology

In contrast with these conventional approaches, the SPIRAL methodology that we adopted in our experiment focuses on wellbeing for all. As Farrell (2008: 16) has argued, '*The concept of well-being for all has to be a properly thought out construct, subject to constraint, consultation and mutual concessions. It embodies elements of equity and empathy and must be viewed over the long term.*'

The main point of this approach, according to the Council of Europe (2010: 72), is that '*The well-being of all can be defined and measured only by means of deliberative and interactive methodological approaches that identify disparities between situations of well-being and ill-being within a society.*'

Not each and every phase of the SPIRAL methodology will be discussed in detail here, but some insights into the different steps will be provided (see Figure 10.1). The first phase consists of mobilising and getting organised. The second phase involves co-designing progress goals, whereas the third entails co-evaluation, planning, comparing, co-deciding, engaging, acting together, *ex post* co-evaluating, reviewing, and improving.

The aim of this approach was to identify shared key dimensions of wellbeing on a territory and to establish 'situation' indicators related to these dimensions. This approach can be applied in the context of joint public policy – for example, Agenda 21, local projects and so on. Citizens and stakeholders are involved at each stage of the process.

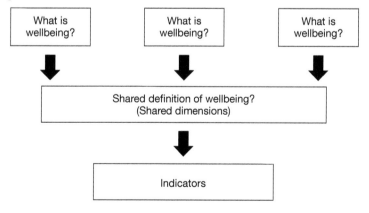

Figure 10.1 A simplified view of the SPIRAL process.

In simple terms, the key task of the endeavour is to ask people: 'What is wellbeing?' We then define the shared dimensions of this general idea of wellbeing. Of course, this set of dimensions is specific to each community, and is therefore not necessarily comparable with other communities. Indicators for measuring wellbeing along these different shared dimensions can then be defined.

The methodology postulates that the definition of wellbeing for all must be based on the way in which citizens themselves see the phenomenon. The process begins by setting up small homogenous groups of a maximum of eight to ten people. We might have groups composed of the young, the elderly, housewives, people with disabilities, and so on. One can have as many groups as one can identify criteria of homogeneity. The main objective of this phase is to invite people that are not used to participating; such often overlooked categories of people who are seldom involved in participatory processes include, for instance, children and the elderly.

These groups are invited to consider the matter individually (by writing Post-it© notes) and then collectively, by taking stock of their thoughts in the light of three simple and completely open questions:

1   What do you understand by wellbeing?
2   What do you understand by illbeing?
3   What do you do to ensure your individual or collective wellbeing?

This generates a long list of diverse criteria for wellbeing, put forward by the various groups. These criteria are then pooled and organised, in order to generate a list of dimensions of wellbeing.

Next, a heterogeneous group of citizens – a mix of individuals selected from each of the homogeneous groups – is invited to conduct a process of consolidation. The next stage is to devise indicators for progress and wellbeing on the basis of the criteria allocated to each of the indicators identified. A progress indicator must be able to measure progress along the entire continuum of situations ranging from 'very bad' to an 'ideal situation' or the 'ultimate goal'.

Progress indicators are elaborated in relation to five situations that are categorised as very unsatisfactory (or 'very bad'), unsatisfactory (or 'bad'), medium, good, or ideal. The five situations describe the path to progress upon which local actors and local players embark in their efforts to ensure wellbeing in all its dimensions.

Figure 10.2 is a simplified representation of the process that starts from the criteria of illbeing and wellbeing. This leads on to an indicator of wellbeing elaborated jointly by citizens and stakeholders.

For example, the list below presents the shared dimensions and sub-dimensions we obtained for a local community during our experiment. In the communities that we worked with, seven dimensions were identified, but other communities might just as well identify a different number of dimensions. The title given to each dimension could also vary widely from one community to another.

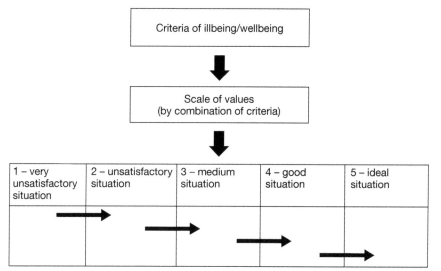

Figure 10.2 Elaboration of value for each situation.
Adapted from Jēkabsone et al., 2013.

1   Health
    1-1 Individual health (behaviour)
    1-2 Access to health (proximity, cost…)
    1-3 Dependence/disability
2   Environment
    2-1 Pollution
    2-2 Nature protection/conservation
    2-3 Individual and collective behaviour
3   Solidarity and mutual help
    3-1 Interpersonal level
    3-2 Collective level
4   Social relations
    4-1 Interpersonal relations (friends, family…)
    4-2 Mutual respect
    4-3 Community involvement, citizenship
5   Modes/conditions of living
    5-1 Job/work
    5-2 Material conditions of living (income, housing…)
    5-3 Education, culture and entertainment
    5-4 Consumption and proximity (sustainability of lifestyles)
    5-5 Transportation
6   Public institutions and policies
    6-1 Infrastructure and policy services
    6-2 Economic and social development policies
    6-3 Social cohesion

7   Personal wellbeing
    7-1 Recognition
    7-2 Living well.

This naming process is very significant, as it typically engenders lively debate among the involved people on which label to give to each dimension. For example, the meaning of 'the environment' is not self-evidently the same for all. In some communities this dimension was named 'pollution', while others might name it differently. These are concrete examples of processes of 'defining a situation'.

Each dimension includes sub-dimensions. These can be broken down according to the five categories of situations ranging from 'very unsatisfactory' to 'ideal' (Figure 10.2). For each sub-dimension we obtain 'situation indicators'.

Participants constructed these indicators from the criteria that they wrote on Post-it© notes during the first step of the process. Working on from this, together with the citizens, we produced a questionnaire designed to enable the measurement of wellbeing in the local community in question. The resulting indicators were too complicated to constitute a basis for the elaboration of a questionnaire by themselves. We therefore worked with these citizens to streamline the indicators and to come up with questions that could be understood by everyone.

We then used the questionnaire to take a snapshot of wellbeing in the local community at that moment in time (see Figure 10.3). Of course, this only represents a picture of community wellbeing at a specific moment in time and for this specific group. As the figure shows, for the dimensions concerned, most people surveyed considered the situation of their local community to be relatively good, good, or very good.

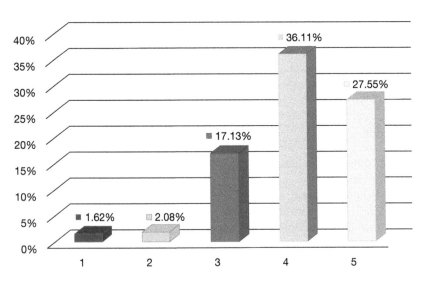

Figure 10.3 An example of the appreciation of wellbeing for a local community (one dimension).

This work raises a number of analytical questions, associated primarily with the initial task: that of providing the necessary conceptual and methodological foundations for the construction of indicators with the citizens and the communities. In the following, I shall explore these questions in more detail.

Elaborating indicators with citizens and communities: an analytical framework

It seems that the profusion of 'alternative' indicators suffers from a *'notorious absence of theoretical foundations'* (Perret, 2003: 261).[6] This insight is based upon the belief that the participatory processes of developing wellbeing indicators should be based on a clear analytical framework, for which pragmatism provides an ideal intellectual foundation (Hayden, 1983; Boulanger, 2014). I think this framework would also help to answer challenges such as those highlighted by Perret (2002), who advocates a *'communicative approach to indicators'*. In this sense, the objective of developing wellbeing indicators in collaboration with citizens is to challenge the aggregative conception of value and the currently dominant 'valuation' processes that model and structure the market. It instead adopts a 'social' conception of value (and of all valuation activities).

Our framework builds upon a transactional approach based upon the work of Dewey and Bentley (1973) and pragmatism. A transaction may be defined as *an exchange in which actors continuously construct and reconstruct their relationships and identities, share and create value, agree on compromises and become integrated into a network of mutual obligations.* This implies that, unlike in the aggregative model, agents' preferences are not fixed but are contextual and subject to change through communication processes. This perspective therefore considers wellbeing in a different way than traditional approaches. Our conception goes beyond individualistic and aggregative mainstream approaches, which employ methods such as subjective surveys, drawing upon experimental economics and neuroeconomics.

In Dewey's view, it was necessary to go beyond the *"subjectivist moment of European philosophy"* which is embodied, for example, in economic approaches. To highlight the language, communication, deliberation and so on in the formation of values (valuation process) means paying attention to what is 'common' and to the definition of a 'common good'. In *The Public and Its Problems* (1927: 48) Dewey wrote that *'the public'* is born of an awareness of 'externalities': *'The public consists of all those who are affected by the indirect consequences of transactions to such an extent that it is deemed necessary to have those consequences systematically cared for'*. This awareness leads people to engage in a social inquiry process mediated by dialogue.

The political models of valuation

In *The Theory of Valuation* (2011), Dewey argues that the determination of the desirable, which according to him lies in the domain of evaluation, is a reflexive activity, which implies convening the other individuals, protagonists or entities into the problematic situation to be solved by collective action. This links the development of wellbeing indicators to the theories and practices of participatory and deliberative democracy. Indeed, the process of elaborating indicators entails the determination of ends (a common good), that is, a process of collectively defining what is valuable and dear to us. However, we have to collectively take into account also the available and envisageable means, if we are to 'pay attention to' and to 'take care of' what is valuable (Renault, 2012). This entails a confrontation with other points of view and other legitimacies, because the problematic situations that we face in the shared course of events invite us to 'negotiate reality', to define the situation, and to *'make compromises'* (Hache, 2011). It is a question of giving a chance to the mobilisation of what Dewey called *'collective intelligence'* (*ibid.*). However, this political model, which we can qualify as 'communicative' – and which Dewey called 'transactional' (Woodward, 2000), because it emphasises debate and deliberation – is not the only possible model. We can distinguish three models of organising the processes of indicator production (Boulanger, 2007):

1   The autocratic model. Ends are determined with reference to the 'public interest', supposedly embodied by the sovereign or the government (the Hobbesian Leviathan). Policies are designed in line with this public interest. In such a frame, the individual appears as passive and her actions are essentially determined by the constraints imposed upon her by those in power. Measurement takes the form of a discretionary process by the 'sovereign'; legitimacy is viewed in essentialist terms, as arising from the source of the power that is exercised (the 'divine right', the tradition, or the constitution, for example). The GDP and the system of national accounts appear, at least initially, as symbolic embodiments of such logic.

2   The rational model. Ends are considered as exogenous and given (the maximisation of wellbeing or efficiency, for example). The problem is then to determine the means for achieving the ends in an efficient way. This model rests upon a calculative, objectivist and instrumental logic, with policy being guided by a continuous effort at 'rationalisation'. In this frame, indicators arise from a technical and scientific process aimed at determining targets to be achieved and measures for monitoring progress towards these objectives. The conventions underpinning these measurement processes correspond to the scientific ideals entailed in the logic of social engineering. Legitimacy rests on the reference to 'Science', objectivity, and expertise.

3   The communicative, transactional model. The preferred mode of *'regulation of the activities'* (Dewey, 2011) consists of deliberation, discussion, debate and negotiation designed to create a 'common world' and a 'common good'. In this frame, both means and ends are subject to discussion. Measuring implies defining what is valuable, what 'counts', and thus agreeing upon shared definitions and ends, before producing, via a social process of inquiry, adapted, reasonable 'measures' in order to attain these ends. It also implies a permanent process: as Dewey underlines, an agreement never closes the question and is still subject to subsequent revision.

These models of organising indicator production correspond, in turn, to three models of political organisation:

- The autocratic model corresponds to an authoritarian, hierarchical, centralised power.
- The rational model corresponds to the aggregative or representative democracy often associated with rational bureaucracy.
- The communicative/transactional model corresponds to participatory, deliberative or collaborative democracy.

Table 10.1 summarises these '*political models*' of quantification.[7]

The CoE methodology relies on an epistemology in line with American pragmatism insofar as it emphasises democratic processes of collective deliberation designed to establish a shared conception of what really matters. It also contributes to a process of redefining the modalities of evaluation of the quality of life, wellbeing and societal progress in terms of societal value (Béraud and Cormerais, 2011).

Table 10.1 The political models of quantification (adapted from Boulanger, 2007)

	Communicative/ transactional model	*Rational/instrumental model*	*Autocratic model*
Decision-making logic	Debate, deliberation, discussion	Calculation, engineering	Discretion, hierarchy
Type of reasoning	Communicative rationality (Habermas, 1984), transactive rationality (Kuruvilla and Dorstewitz, 2010)	Instrumental rationality	Essentialist rationality (connected to the nature of the authority)
Object of the decision-making process	Ends, means, values	Means (and means–ends relationship)	The realisation of the public interest
Foundation of the decision	Agreement, convention, compromise	Logic, coherence	Power
Political model	Participatory democracy, association	Aggregative democracy, representative democracy, rational bureaucracy	Hierarchy, centralised power
Quantification process	Situation indicators, participatory methodologies	Scientific, 'statistical engineering': parameters, data, barometers, dashboards	'Political engineering': statistics in the etymological sense (State)
Difficulties, worrisome trends	Lack of realism, subjectivism, uneven distribution of the argumentative capacity, participative biases	Scientism, bureaucratic and/or technocratic biases	Dictatorship, authoritarianism, manipulation, Machiavellism

The pragmatic framework: some insights

This pragmatic tradition, drawing on works of C.S. Peirce, J. Dewey and G.H. Mead, has widely influenced the social sciences and has given rise to new approaches of understanding and conceptualising processes in the public sphere. The recent revival of interest in participatory procedures, especially in the area of indicators (see e.g. Bell and Morse, 2008) owes much to the rediscovery and reinterpretation of this tradition, relatively underutilised in France. One of the fundamental characteristics of pragmatism is its refusal of the dualisms associated with the Cartesian epistemology that tend to separate, for example, thought and action, theory and practice, and the positive and the normative. These dualisms lie at the heart of numerous approaches, including notably the social sciences and the humanities. As Bidet (2008) argues, '*The tendency to establish a clear-cut distinction between means and ends, between the order of the calculation and that of the values [...] leads one to consider the genesis of values as extrinsic to acting and to rationality, presumed to determine only the most effective means for given ends – in a dichotomy between thought and action, between ethics and technics.*' Bidet also evokes Dewey's concern of not reducing value only to the emotional dimension (that of the affects and sensations), a common tendency in economics of happiness. She continues: '*The notion of valuation – a process by which an element of the experience takes value, importance, for the human body – rejects the separation between affect and cognition, emotion and intelligence, valuation (pricing) and appreciation (appraisal)*' (Bidet, 2008).[8] The valuation process does not simply refer to the revelation of pre-existent preferences through technical procedures or to the steering of behaviour by pre-existing values (prices for example), but to the – at least ideally – deliberative processes whereby these values are constructed (Béraud and Cormerais, 2011).

The process of valuation is embedded in a relational and situational perspective, which sees the attribution of value as part of a process of reconfiguration of situations considered as problematic. One of the striking observations from our experiment concerns the inquiry process in which the participants were engaged. From the three simple questions evoked at the start of the process, the individuals were led to ponder issues relating to wellbeing/illbeing and to consider questions from an angle that many admitted having never envisaged before. This way of reconfiguring a situation invites one to judge what is good, adequate, useful, desirable, etc. Valuations are the products of this process of inquiry. The structure of the questionnaire also encouraged this logic of inquiry, given that the respondents were free to add comments. Indeed, the participants did make numerous comments, some of which were critical. Many of the comments demonstrated that the questionnaire had spurred reflection and introduced new ideas and perspectives. The process of inquiry therefore did not leave the individuals unchanged (cf. Dewey, 1916).

This inquiry is not individual but social in nature, and it unfolds as part of the transactions in which the actors are engaged. This concept entails the idea that individual preferences are not fixed and pre-given, but change in the course of the transaction (Bouvier, 2007). Also the goods and values have no meaning 'in and of themselves', but their meaning is constructed only through the process of transaction (Dewey and Bentley, 1973). In this way, the actors are still trying to define themselves through a process of individuation (Bidet, 2008: 214). Engaging in an 'inquiry' entails, in the pragmatic sense, defining the 'common', which in turn requires that the participants adopt, to varying degrees, the perspective of the other (Mead, 1934). The logic of inquiry illustrates this well. Indeed, for Dewey (1938), language forces the individual to adopt the point of view of other people, to see the world and to investigate events from a viewpoint that is not strictly individual, but is common to the participants in a shared experience. In this sense, the process involving citizens in developing indicators constitutes what Bohman (2008), following Mead, calls multiperspectival forms. As Young (1997: 398) noted: '*However experienced, the availability of multiple perspectives provides everyone with the resources to take a distance on any one of them, and to communicate in one way with people with whom one does not share perspectives.*'

The CoE method thus relies on epistemological foundations different from the methodologies usually applied to address issues of welfare or happiness in mainstream economics. Individuals (and their affects and emotions) are not considered as passive objects of study but as active subjects within the framework of a social inquiry process, whose ultimate aim is not so much to define indicators as to (re)define the conditions for a 'regulation of the activities', in the words of Dewey (Woodward, 2000). The pragmatic approach therefore postulates that individuals are 'intelligent' actors (Dewey, 1922) who constantly face problematic situations and – in order to render these situations manageable – need to engage in a deliberative process in which actors will gradually institute themselves (that is, define their roles, rights and duties) (Zask, 2008). This does not necessarily presuppose that we reach an agreement, but that the process for defining what really matters, what 'living well together' means, offers an opportunity to define a 'public' in the Deweyan sense and provides this public with the conditions enabling it to define the means of resolving situations perceived as problematic.

Language, narratives and indicators

Communicative processes are at the heart of the initiatives to develop indicators in a participatory way. In these processes, words and language appear as fundamental data that deserve attention. A number of studies, including those conducted by IWEPS[9] (Ruyters et al., 2013), seem to go in the direction of an approach stressing what could be called 'relational' data. Frequency of specific words, semantic registers, clusters, and the like are in this approach seen as products of communicative processes that take place during the construction of a situation indicator. In our case study experiment, a few keywords around the notion of wellbeing had a high occurrence. Words such as the other(s), family, child/children, health, and life denote essential elements of individual wellbeing. Many of these words are associated with sociality, conviviality, relationships, etc. We should be careful not to understand these words in a static way. Developing a transactional understanding requires that we further explore the very process of 'qualifying' the situations, as defined by the CoE. Indeed, the process proposed by the CoE brings into the discussion the 'words of all' to arrive at a 'common world'. These words are thus the product, at the same time, of an individual opinion and of a collective discussion – a communicative process. Behind these words there are thus processes of negotiation, explicitation, clarification and agreement, which constitute a set of 'data' that allows one to understand the social background of indicators. These 'data' are likely to help better understand a sociality that is constituted through mediators and meaningful artefacts, such as words, texts, conversations, narrations and qualifications.

Such insights are not new and have been evoked in different contexts – for instance by pragmatists, by Norbert Elias and Margaret Archer (Türk, 2009). We could postulate the hypothesis that words, narratives and qualifications reflect the 'inner conversations' – the reflexions of an individual (Archer, 2003), as mediators between the agency on one hand, and the subjectively perceived objective structures – as realisations of the perspectives of action – on the other. Therefore, not only the words but also the conversations and their traces as manifested in the words and in the stories need to be considered as 'data'. The methodology that we have outlined here probably does not fully reveal the 'inner conversations' of individuals, but it nevertheless opens new avenues for inquiry. First of all, it makes available for further analysis the material from our experiment as well as from other similar experiences – a reservoir of thousands of words, qualifications and narratives is out there for the research community to examine. The following remarks serve to illustrate the ideas developed above.

- In the CoE method, we ask questions (e.g. *'what is ill/wellbeing for you?'*). On the basis of the answers that the participants write on Post-it© notes, we define the criteria for a collective definition of wellbeing. For example, a participant can answer that wellbeing is to possess *'a car'* (a word) but also *'to have a car, in order to be able to go for a walk in the countryside'*, which already reveals a projection, a perspective, a mediation between an objective situation as perceived by the individual and the perspectives of action. We thus have a 'trace' of an 'inner' conversation, in the sense described above.
- The conversations are not only 'inner' ones. The method opens these words, narratives, and qualifications to discussion, and subjects them to a process of reconstruction. For example, during our experiment, a child had written on a Post-it© note *'to have a Logan'* as a criterion of wellbeing. Initially, the group decided to classify this criterion as one related to material wellbeing (together with criteria such as 'owning a house'). However, the child that had written the Post-it© note firmly opposed this choice, and wanted us to place his criterion in the category of 'the environment'. This of course aroused questions from the other participants, and the ensuing conversation revealed what the child had wanted to say. For him, a Logan symbolised a simpler lifestyle, as a car that contains no useless gadgets and serves simply as a means of transportation from point A to point B. In other words, 'to have a Logan'

referred to the register of 'voluntary simplicity', or 'frugality' – a form of more environmentally friendly lifestyle. Unlike most of us thought at first, the child here reasoned in terms of 'being' instead of 'having'. What appears significant in this example is the double interactive process at work: first, an inner conversation as described above, then a collective conversation that rendered explicit what had thus far remained implicit, in a discussion that converged towards a 'common world'. The CoE method therefore calls for methodological innovations that would allow the conversations to remain traceable, through words, stories, and processes of discussion (Ruyters, 2013).

It is not enough to focus on words, however, because by doing so we risk losing some of the sociality, as well as the universe of meanings and perspectives that they contain. We must also keep in mind that the inner conversations are not soliloquies – instead, they are relational and 'perspectival' (Mead, 1934). They reflect the inscription of the individual in a meaningful social world. Furthermore, an inner conversation is never perfectly clear and can be rendered intelligible through discussion, by making the inner conversation available to the other participants. In other words, contrary to 'economicist' assumptions, not only information but also the individuals themselves are incomplete. This incompleteness can be overcome through relationships and the insertion of the individual into processes of transaction. Words or narratives are likewise incomplete and acquire a meaning in interpretative frameworks and communication processes. There is not enough space here to further elaborate on these issues, which are nevertheless important if social and economic theories are to regain 'traction in the world' that they lost by seeking to imitate science designed to explore worlds without friction (Türk, 2009). According to Türk (2009: 85), '*For economics to have any traction in the real world, we need to develop ways of using interview material to allow our theories to come into contact not just with data, but with real-world phenomena made tangible through data; thus, to have any practical use, they must do more than merely explain data – they must explain some real phenomenon in the world. We must also expect that since the social world is qualitatively different than the physical world, the methods we invent to study it are also likely to be different.*'

Summing up, central to this methodology and the associated analytical framework are language, communication, words and narratives. In pragmatic methodology, language and dialogue allow an individual to adopt the point of view of the other, to investigate phenomena from a perspective that is not strictly personal but that brings together participants in a process of common inquiry. Such a social inquiry process encourages people to consider what wellbeing means for all, and not only for themselves. The social construction of wellbeing indicators entails a process whereby the character of a problematic situation is defined. At the start this definition is often not quite clear, but a social inquiry helps to elaborate solutions, goals and ideals, to construct indicators capable of highlighting the problem and implementing solutions.

Such a process results in what has been called a '*transactive rationality*' (Kuruvilla and Dorstewitz, 2010). This is based upon four postulates. First, the starting point is not a predefined problem or goal, but an indeterminate situation. Second, rationality is a product of inquiry in democratic communities. Third, rationality integrates scientific, moral and ecological reasoning. Fourth, rationality is only successful if it serves as a guide towards satisfactory consequences in both theory and practice.

A central assumption underpinning our approach is that the social world is shaped by language and that sociality operates through mediators and meaningful artefacts: words, texts, conversations, stories, qualifications and so on. Our material – as well as that collected in many other similar exercises – consists to a large extent of these types of artefacts. On the basis of this 'raw' material, participants collectively construct qualifications, which hence emerge as products of these transactions. These qualifications then provide the basis for the final step in the process – the elaboration of indicators.

Transactions and structuring phenomena

The selection of citizens entitled to participate in these processes raises tricky questions. For example, in the context of the method of the Council of Europe, the goal is the wellbeing of all, but who are to be included in this group called 'all'? Who actually participates in this qualification process that leads to the shared definition of wellbeing in a community? When we look at the actual participatory processes it is easy to see that the 'all' in reality very often means 'some'. While numbers are not everything, and the lack of full representation by no means delegitimises such processes, the impossibility of actually including 'all' introduces limitations that one must be aware of. Moreover, even if methodologies such as that of the Council of Europe try to overcome these limitations, 'participatory biases', as a result of the impossibility of reaching full representation, are well documented and must be accounted for. These biases raise a number of concrete questions that I shall explore in the following.

First, if the reorganisation of spaces and institutions of valuation is seen as important, then the considerations underpinning and justifying the procedures and the instruments of participation must be carefully documented. The procedural dimensions appear indeed central if we want to move from participatory experiments that are often limited in time and space to a truly participatory society. This implies rethinking essential dimensions of social organisation. Matters of time, notably the 'social temporalities', are of fundamental importance. Participatory processes indeed take time, and time is always scarce. Another difficulty concerns the tension between the contingent character of participatory approaches on the one hand, and the need for indicators with a minimum of longevity to allow guidance and evaluation of policies on the other. In megaprojects, such considerations take an even greater prominence as they engage societies for a long period (such as in the case of high-level long-lived nuclear waste, for example).

The procedural choices are obviously not neutral. The processes of engaging citizens occur in '*negotiation spaces*' (Dillenbourg and Baker, 1996), through transactions that can produce shared definitions of wellbeing, for example. The structuring of these processes raises very concrete and practical questions. For example, do and should elected representatives be present during the debates? Is anybody 'leading' the debates? In the case of the Post-it© method used by the CoE, is the task of displaying Post-it© notes on a blackboard given to a 'facilitator', or is everyone entitled to display notes? These types of processes that define the structures within which negotiations and transactions take place significantly shape the outcomes of citizen engagement. An example from our experiment serves as an illustration: in one of our case study communities, so many situational indicators were identified that we could not realistically have enough time to develop and administer a questionnaire. It was therefore necessary to eliminate items, to simplify, and to elaborate criteria for selection. Since the objective of the project in question was to improve public policies, the project steering committee decided to eliminate a suggested indicator relating to 'love relations'. While legitimate as such, this criterion does not have an apparent and direct connection to public policy. Yet eliminating this indicator from the list unavoidably contributed to structuring the negotiation and transaction.

The processes of constructing societal indicators therefore define particular negotiation spaces, in which the definition of a problematic situation is negotiated, agreement on its dimensions is reached, variables to be taken into account as well as their relative weights are agreed and so on. These negotiation spaces can be defined and structured according to different dimensions that affect discursive processes (adapted from Dillenbourg and Baker, 1996):

- **The object of negotiation.** For example, are we talking about wellbeing, about indicators, or perhaps about megaprojects?
- **The mode of negotiation** refers in particular to the negotiation process, and to the concrete procedural rules adopted.
- **The degree of symmetry** defines the degree of power held by each agent or stakeholder in the final decision. The agents may or may not be in a situation of symmetry if the voice of some agents prevails for some reason (for example, for institutional or rhetorical reasons).
- **The degree of complexity** of what is under negotiation. For instance, it is not the same thing to negotiate about the dimensions of wellbeing as about statistical tools.
- **The degree of flexibility**, or the degree of freedom allowed for the agents in the negotiation process. The degree of flexibility is often determined by procedural constraints and limitations.
- **The degree of systematicity** denotes the extent to which agents provide relevant information. An agent or a stakeholder is 'systematic' if she provides all the information and opinions whenever these are relevant. For example, some agents may choose, for various reasons, not to speak at all or not to express exactly what they want.
- **The degree of directness** relates to the salience of procedural rules and power in the process. For example, are strict deadlines for achieving the results

imposed? It also refers to issues such as the potential difference between what has been planned (from the designer's point of view) and what actually happens (from the user's point of view).

All these elements structure the transactions. Lefevbre's (2013) analysis of the consensus conference organised in the Nord-Pas-de-Calais region to develop new indicators of wealth highlights crucial structuring issues that need to be taken into account in participatory initiatives.

Another phenomenon of structuring relates to the so-called 'rhetorical spaces' (Code, 1995). Indeed, communicative transactions, beyond aspects relative to negotiation spaces, are also subject to structuring effects. Some find it easier than others to speak in public and/or have better linguistic and rhetoric skills – hence, the choice of words and terms, for instance, is not a neutral undertaking, but influences the qualification process. Thus, while the limitations of 'traditional' indicators and associated political models are evident, as argued in this chapter, one should not underestimate the problems that come with the new indicators and the procedures through which they are elaborated.

Conclusion

Understanding the issue of wellbeing from a transactional approach invites us to be explicit about and care about what we, as a collective, hold precious. The Council of Europe method provides citizens with opportunities for discussion and dialogue, allowing them to place themselves in the perspectives of others (Mead, 1934). Societal indicators can help to open up a new public space, to redefine the valuation/evaluation institutions, and to reconfigure the modes of governance by taking into account the diverse interests emanating from plural and sometimes conflicting voices.

What emerges from our experiment is that it is not only the indicators as such that matter. Crucially, the procedures of their elaboration, the debates that take place, the learning that is generated, and, perhaps most crucially, the conviviality that these processes generate, produce social cohesion. This is a call to build a society of participation within which: '[…] *policies and proposals for social action [should] be treated as working hypotheses, not as programs to be rigidly adhered to and executed. They will be experimental in the sense that they will be entertained subject to constant and well-equipped observation of the consequences they entail when acted upon, and subject to ready and flexible revision in the light of observed consequences*' (Dewey, quoted in Tracy and Tracy, 2000: 8).

Acknowledgement

The ISBET project mentioned in the chapter was funded by the Regional Council of Brittany (France).

Notes

1 www.oecd.org/statistics/better-life-initiative.htm
2 www.communityindicators.net/
3 'Ils peuvent aussi constituer des éléments de la définition collective d'un monde commun (...), voire d'un bien commun (buts à atteindre, normes à respecter) et des moyens de l'atteindre (mesure du bien-être).' Author's translation.
4 www.europeanvaluesstudy.eu/
5 www.worldvaluessurvey.org/wvs.jsp
6 Author's translation.
7 Quantification is here understood broadly, including also classifications and rankings that do not necessarily apply absolute, cardinal measures, but rely instead on ordinal valuation, for instance. Essentially, to quantify implies to first qualify – establish the relevant conventions – and then to measure – regardless of whether measuring takes a cardinal or an ordinal form (Desrosières, 2008).
8 Author's translation.
9 Institut wallon de l'Evaluation, de la Prospective et de la Statistique.

References

Archer, M.S. 2003. *Structure, Agency and the Internal Conversation.* Cambridge: Cambridge University Press.

Bell, S. & Morse, S. 2008. *Sustainability Indicators: Measuring the Immeasurable?* London: Earthscan.

Béraud, P. & Cormerais, F. 2011. Économie de la contribution et innovation sociétale. *Innovations* 2011/1(34): 163–183.

Bidet, A. 2008. La genèse des valeurs: une affaire d'enquête. *Tracés. Revue de Sciences Humaines* 15: 211–216.

Bohman, J. 2008. Realizing deliberative democracy as a mode of inquiry: Pragmatism, social facts, and normative theory. *The Journal of Speculative Philosophy*, New Series. 18,(1 – *Pragmatism and Deliberative Politics*): 23–43.

Boulanger, P.M. 2004. Les indicateurs de développement durable: un défi scientifique, un enjeu démocratique. *Les séminaires de l'Iddri,* 12, Institut pour un développement durable. Available online at: www.iddri.org/Publications/Collections/Idees-pour-le-debat/id_0421_boulanger.pdf (accessed 25 July 2016).

Boulanger, P.M. 2007. Political uses of social indicators: Overview and application to sustainable development indicators. *International Journal of Sustainable Development* 10(1/2): 14–32.

Boulanger, P.M. 2014. *Elements for a comprehensive assessment of public indicators.* Report procured by the European Commission-Joint Research Centre, Econometrics and Applied Statistics (DDG.01).

Bouvier, A. 2007. Démocratie délibérative, démocratie débattante, démocratie participative. *Revue Européenne des Sciences Sociales* Tome XLV(136): 5–34. Available online at: http://ress.revues.org/82 (accessed 25 July 2016).

Brown, V. 1994. Higgling: The language of markets. In N. de Marchi, N & M.S. Morgan (eds.), *Higgling – Transactors and their markets in the history of economics.* London, Durham: Duke University Press, pp. 66–93.

Cassiers, I., & Delain, C. 2006. La croissance ne fait pas le Bonheur, les économistes le savent-ils? *Regards économiques* 38 (March). Available online at: www.regards-economiques.be/images/reco-pdf/reco_47.pdf (accessed 25 July 2016).

Code, L. 1995. *Rhetorical spaces: Essays on gendered isolation*. London: Routledge.

Commons, J.R. 1950. *The economics of collective action*. New York: McMillan.

Council of Europe. 2005. *Concerted development of social cohesion indicators – Methodological guide*. Strasbourg: CoE Publishing.

Council of Europe. 2010. *Involving citizens and communities in securing societal progress for the well-being of all. Methodological guide*. Strasbourg: CoE Publishing.

Davoine, L. 2012. *Economie du Bonheur*. Paris: La Découverte, Coll.

Desrosières, A. 2008. *L'argument statistique 1: Pour une sociologie historique de la quantification*. Paris: Presses des Mines.

Dewey, J. 1916. *Democracy and education*. New York: Macmillan.

Dewey, J. 1922. *Human nature and conduct*. New York: Henry Holt & Co.

Dewey, J. 1927. *The Public and its Problems*. New York: Henry Holt & Co.

Dewey, J. 1938. *Logic, the theory of inquiry*. New York: Henry Holt & Co.

Dewey, J. 2011. *La formation des valeurs*. Paris: La Découverte.

Dewey, J. & Bentley, A.F. 1973. Knowing and the known (1949). In R. Handy & E.C. Harwood, *Useful procedures of inquiry*. Great Barrington, MA: B.R.C.

Dillenbourg, P. and Baker, M.J. 1996. Negotiation spaces in human-computer collaboration. In COOP '96, *Second International Conference on Design of Cooperative Systems*, INRIA, Juan-les-Pins, pp. 187–206.

Farrell, G. 2008. Well-being for all as the objective of social cohesion. *Trends in Social Cohesion* 20: 15–34.

Gadrey, J.and Jany-Catrice, F. 2012. *Les nouveaux indicateurs de richesse*, 3rd edition. Repères, Paris: La Découverte.

Habermas, J. 1984. *Theory of Communicative Action* (2 Vol.) (1981). Boston: Beacon Press.

Hache, E. 2011. *Ce à quoi nous tenons. Pour une écologie pragmatique*, Paris: La découverte.

Hayden, F.G. 1983. Integration of social indicators into holistic geobased models. *Journal of Economic Issues* XVII(2 – June): 325–334.

Jany-Catrice, F. 2012. *La performance totale nouvel esprit du capitalisme?* Villeneuve d'Asq: Presses Universitaires du Septentrion.

Jēkabsone, I., Thirion, S., Grantiņš, A. and Sloka, B. 2013. Challenges of the SPIRAL methodology for wellbeing studies. Paper presented to *New Challenges of Economic and Business Development* conference, Riga, University of Latvia, 9–11 May.

Knight, F. 1921. *Risk, uncertainty and profit*. Boston, MA: Hart, Schaffner & Marx; Houghton Mifflin Company.

Kuruvilla, S., & Dorstewitz, P. 2010. There is no "point" in decision-making: A model of transactive rationality for public policy and administration. *Policy Sciences* 43(3): 263–287.

Layard, R. 2005. *Happiness: Lessons from a new science*. New York: Penguin Books/Penguin Group.

Lefebvre, R. 2013. "L'introuvable délibération": Ethnographie d'une conférence citoyenne sur les nouveaux indicateurs de richesse. *Participations*, 2013/2(6): 191–214.

Mead, G.H. 1934, *Mind, self and society*. Ed. Charles W. Morris. Chicago: University of Chicago Press.

Méda, D. & Jany-Catrice, F. 2013. Nouvelles mesures des performances économiques et du progrès social. Le risque de l'économicisme. *Revue du Mauss* 41 (1er semestre): 271–398.

Ogien, A. 2010. La valeur sociale du chiffre. La quantification de l'action publique entre performance et démocratie. *Revue Française de Socio-Economie* 5: 19–40.

Perret, B. 2002. *Indicateurs sociétaux, état des lieux et perspectives*, Rapport au Conseil de l'Emploi, des Revenus et de la Cohésion Sociale (CERC), January.

Perret, B. 2003. Indicateurs sociaux et théorie sociale. *Revue du MAUSS* 2003/1(21): 261–275.

Renault, M. 2009. Perspectivisme, moralité et communication. Une approche transactionnelle de la responsabilité sociale des entreprises. *Revue Française de Socio-Economie* 4: 15–37.

Renault, M. 2012. Dire ce à quoi nous tenons et en prendre soin-John Dewey, La formation des valeurs, Note critique. *Revue Française de Socio-Économie* 9: 247–253.

Ruyters, C. 2013. Mesure du bien-être et du progrès en Wallonie: Pratiques et méthodes de construction d'une connaissance partagée au service de nouveaux modes de gouvernance territoriale. Paper presented to the Séminaire pluridisciplinaire *Constructions et Représentations du Bien-Etre. Pratiques et méthodes*, MSH Grenoble, 3–4 décembre.

Ruyters, C., Laffut, M., Defays, D. and Colicis, O. 2011. *Élaboration concertée d'indicateurs de bien-être dans les communes wallonnes. Partie 1 : la genèse du projet et les premiers résultats de l'expérience en cours.* Working papers de l'IWEPS, 3, September.

Stiglitz, J.E., Sen, A. & Fitoussi, J.-P. 2009. *Report by the Commission on the Measurement of Economic Performance and Social Progress.* Available online at: www.stiglitz-sen-fitoussi. fr/documents/rapport_anglais.pdf (accessed 25 July 2016).

Thiry, G. & Roman, P. 2014. The Inclusive Wealth Index. A Sustainability Indicator, Really? *FSMH Working Paper*, no 71, June. Available online at: https://halshs.archives-ouvertes.fr/halshs-01011250/ (accessed 25 July 2016).

Thompson, J.K. 2005. *John Dewey and Pragmatic Economics.* Doctoral thesis. Faculty of the Graduate School of Vanderbilt University. Nashville, Tennessee. May, 2005. Available online at: http://etd.library.vanderbilt.edu/available/etd-04012005-080229/ unrestricted/Dissertation.pdf (accessed 21 July 2016).

Tracy, P.D. and Tracy, M.B. 2000. A conceptual framework of social capital and civil society: The re-emergence of John Dewey. Paper presented to *The Year 2000 International Research Conference on Social Security*, Helsinki, September 25–27.

Türk, J.D. 2009. Traction in the world: economics and narrative interviews. *International Journal of Green Economics.* 3(1): 77–92.

Woodward, M. 2000. Transactional philosophy as a basis for dialogue in public relations. *Journal of Public Relations Research* 12(3): 255–275.

Young, I.M. 1997. Difference as a resource for democratic communication. In J. Bohman & W. Rehg (eds), *Deliberative Democracy: Essays on Reason and Politics*. Cambridge, MA and London: MIT Press, pp. 383–406.

Zask, J. 2008. Le public chez Dewey: une union sociale plurielle. *Tracés, revue de sciences humaines* 15: 169–189.

11 Addressing the evaluation–implementation gap in infrastructure megaproject research with qualitative comparative analysis

Stefan Verweij

Introduction

Methods such as environmental impact assessment, multi-criteria analysis, and especially cost–benefit analysis are now commonly applied in the planning of megaprojects (e.g. Priemus et al., 2008). Still, megaprojects – i.e. 'large-scale, complex projects delivered through (…) partnerships between public and private organisations' (Van Marrewijk et al., 2008: 591) – regularly overrun their budgets and planned construction time, and they are confronted with socio-political dissatisfaction. A topical example from the Netherlands is the A15 Maasvlakte-Vaanplein project. The construction of this €2,031 million public–private partnership project started in 2011. It concerns the reconstruction of a 37 km highway corridor between the Maasvlakte port area and the city of Rotterdam (Ministerie van Infrastructuur en Milieu et al., 2013). Newspapers recently reported an estimated cost overrun of about €250 million and tense relationships between the project principal, project contractor, and project stakeholders (Verbraeken and Weissink, 2014; Houtekamer, 2015). This example shows that in implementation – which concerns the execution of a contract after project planning, i.e. infrastructure construction and/or service delivery (Jones and Noble, 2008) – sound plans and good intentions developed in megaproject planning can easily fail (cf. Pressman and Wildavsky, 1984). Therefore, it is important to evaluate project implementation, in order to learn how to improve the planning and implementation of similar projects in the future (Short and Kopp, 2005). Pressman and Wildavsky aptly said: 'learning is the key to both implementation and evaluation. We evaluate to learn, and we learn to implement (1984: xviii).

However, there is a gap between the evaluation and the implementation of megaprojects. As explained by Lehtonen (2014), although the evaluation of megaprojects receives increasing attention, it remains preoccupied with comparing 'before-and-after' situations. Although important, the drawback of this focus is that less insight is gained on how the 'after' was produced in-between, that is, on the implementation processes of projects (cf. Love et al., 2015). One possible explanation for this gap is that the evaluation of infrastructure projects post-planning receives little attention (Verweij, 2015a), for example because data or resources are insufficient (Short and Kopp, 2005). It could also be that once a project has been implemented, managers rush to the next project, which makes evaluation of the previous project less of a priority. Another and more fundamental reason for the gap is the mismatch between the nature of megaproject implementation and the methods used to evaluate them (cf. Pattyn and Verweij, 2014). Megaproject implementation processes are inherently and systemically complex (Verweij, 2015a). This means that the causes and outcomes in/of projects cannot be predicted and identified unambiguously (Rittel and Webber, 1973). However, this is often not recognised or acknowledged in evaluation. Megaprojects face uncertainty and ambiguity but their evaluation is often informed by a linear-rationalist, objectivist worldview and corresponding methods (cf. Salling and Nielsen, 2015), as explained by the editors in the introduction to this volume.

The problems with linear-rationalist methods for evaluating megaproject implementation are twofold. First, the evaluation methods assume that project outcomes can be clearly identified, calculated and predicted in project planning. By extension, it is argued that actors can choose to miscalculate, and that outcomes are due to, for instance, the optimistic and/or strategic identification and calculation of project risks (e.g. Flyvbjerg et al., 2002; Flyvbjerg, 2009). Although these explanations are not necessarily untrue, they focus on questions of accountability and identifying culprits, and therefore are not conducive to learning (cf. Van der Meer and Edelenbos, 2006; Lehtonen, 2014). Furthermore, linear-rationalist methods do not tell us what works, when, in which contexts, for whom, and why (Rogers, 2011; Verweij and Gerrits, 2013). They disregard, inter alia, the fact that actors in megaprojects can have different and changing goals and interests, and that explanations for project outcomes may not hold across all projects because of different and changing project contexts. Evaluation methods that ignore this complex nature of megaproject implementation do not create a realistic understanding of project implementation, and thereby sustain the evaluation–implementation gap. This also hampers learning from megaproject evaluations (Verweij, 2015a).

Learning from megaproject evaluation requires evaluation approaches that recognise and acknowledge the ambiguities and complexities of project implementation. In other words, they need to be complexity-informed (Verweij, 2015a; 2015b).[1] In this contribution,[2] qualitative comparative analysis, commonly abbreviated as QCA (Ragin, 1987; 2000; 2008), is put forth and demonstrated as an approach that allows evaluating complex megaprojects. First, the fundamental building blocks of the complexity of megaproject implementation are explained, followed by a description of the implications of this complexity for evaluation. The subsequent section then applies QCA to the A15 Maasvlakte-Vaanplein megaproject, leading to the argument that QCA indeed is a suitable evaluation method. The chapter ends with a reflection on the method for addressing the evaluation–implementation gap, including a discussion of the scope of applicability of QCA for megaproject research and an agenda for future applications.

The complexity of megaprojects

To say that implementing infrastructure megaprojects is complex does not just mean that implementation processes are very difficult. Complexity is a property of social reality (Bhaskar, 1975; Byrne, 1998; Sayer, 2000; Byrne and Callaghan, 2014). The world of megaproject implementation is not a closed system controlled by a single project actor or organisation (Teisman et al., 2009). Rather, it is composed of open systems (Engwall, 2003) that are nested and interrelated (Teisman et al., 2009). This implies that reality is non-decomposable, contingent, non-compressible and time-asymmetric (see Verweij 2015a; cf. Gerrits and Verweij, 2013).

Non-decomposability means that infrastructure megaproject implementation cannot be understood by decomposing the project into its individual parts and then only studying these individual parts. Instead, the implementation and its outcomes emerge from interactions between parts. These include both project-internal (i.e. within the project's organisation) and project-external parts (i.e. the socio-physical environment or context). In terms of internal parts, inter alia, public and private organisations are bound by a construction contract and based on this contract they interact in various formal and informal ways to construct, manage and deliver the project. As for external parts, when a megaproject is being implemented, it interacts with an existing socio-physical system. This socio-physical system can be understood as a 'syntax' or a specific mix of physical and social elements (Marshall, 2009; Verweij and Gerrits, 2013). That is, the system consists of roads, tunnels, bridges, rivers, dykes, residential areas with dwellings, etc. – which are distributed (spatially) in a certain way – and public organisations (e.g. municipalities and provinces) bear responsibilities for these physical elements, which are also used by citizens and businesses. When the megaproject is being implemented, the socio-physical system reacts – events occur (see, e.g. Verweij 2015c; Verweij and Gerrits 2015). For instance, citizens may protest and hamper implementation, *force majeure* may impact on the project planning, and stakeholders may demand design changes and/or refuse to grant permits for construction activities (cf. Love et al., 2002). These events are managed by public and private actors for the purpose of the project's construction and delivery. The megaproject and its outcomes emerge from this myriad of dynamic interactions within the project and between the project and the context. This emergent nature means that the whole outcome can be less or more than the assessments of its individual internal or external parts indicate. For instance, public and private partners can be satisfied with a particular construction contract (an internal element) but, in implementation, unforeseen social events – that is, events that originate from stakeholders (Verweij, 2015c) – in the project's context may affect the functioning of the contract, making it a less effective model for achieving intended project outcomes (see, e.g. Reynaers and Verweij, 2014).

The *contingency* of reality implies that because infrastructure megaprojects interact with their socio-physical contexts, and because projects' contexts are unique, the process of implementation is unique for each project. This assumption helps to understand why certain management strategies that are effective in one project may not be so in another one. Context is crucial (Buijs et al., 2009). The contexts of megaprojects, though, also share common features. For instance, certain laws and regulations enforced by governmental actors apply nationwide. Summing up, the socio-physical system with which a megaproject interacts has both unique and similar aspects compared to other projects (Verweij and Gerrits, 2013). Whereas similarities may be managed by applying standardised project management strategies, unique situations may need to be managed with tailor-made strategies (Edelenbos et al., 2009). Contingency further means that explanations for megaprojects and outcomes in/of projects are time-sensitive: a management strategy in a project at t_n may not work at t_{n+1}. It signals that the causal relationships between the interacting internal and external parts of project implementation are inherently emerging and can only be known for a specific time and place. The contingent understanding of megaproject reality boils down to the notion that explanations for project implementation processes and outcomes are case-specific, but patterns may be explored and recognised across cases.

The third property of reality is *non-compressibility*: 'while reduction or compressibility [of reality] may be inevitable given the limits of human cognition and for practical research purposes, such a reduction or compression implies the loss of some of reality's properties such that any explanation is reductionist' (Gerrits and Verweij, 2013: 170). People in infrastructure megaprojects cannot perceive and understand the full complexity of the project. This means that public and private actors draw boundaries (cf. Cilliers, 2001), i.e. that their perceptions of projects are simplifications of the projects' reality. Moreover, because actors have different backgrounds, tasks, roles, responsibilities etc., they draw the boundaries differently. They have a specific understanding of the project and their action is guided by their own way of simplifying the project reality. The perceptions underpinning these actions are unavoidably subjective and partial, comprising only a part of the relevant project reality. This also gives rise to ambiguities and conflicts between various rationalities and cultures represented in megaprojects (Van Marrewijk et al., 2008; Sanderson, 2012).

Time-asymmetry means that the trajectory of an infrastructure megaproject is unidirectional or irreversible (cf. Prigogine, 1997). Causality is emergent (see Goldstein, 1999). This signals that, although the outcomes in/of implementation may in hindsight appear to follow from a logical sequence of events, this sequence of events is not there at the start of the project's implementation. The sequence unfolds in the future. If time were reversible, causality in social reality would be linear, and a particular sequence of events that occurred in the past could be used to perfectly predict future (sequences of) events. Reality, however, is 'developmentally open' (Rescher, 1995). Thus, public and private actors can have (quite accurate) expectations about events, and they can plan the implementation of a project (which is based on compressions of reality) to manage prospective events, but these plans cannot foresee all possible future eventualities (Söderholm, 2008). It means that projects and outcomes emerge in time and that infrastructure megaproject implementation faces uncertainty.

Requirements for evaluating complex megaprojects

What are the implications of these four building blocks of the complexity of megaproject implementation for evaluation? In order for evaluations to create a realistic understanding of implementation, the evaluation method used needs to be complexity-informed, which implies that it has to meet the following requirements (see Verweij, 2015a).

Non-decomposability

Because megaproject implementation and outcomes emerge from the interactions between internal and external project parts, the method has to be able to evaluate how combinations of parts produce outcomes. Evaluation methods that inquire into the effect of singular variables on outcomes do not create a realistic understanding of megaproject implementation and are therefore inadequate.

Contingency

Because context is explanatory for how implementation and outcomes emerge, the method has to be able to evaluate the role of context in explaining megaproject outcomes. More specifically, it needs to be capable of identifying project-specific aspects that explain outcomes and simultaneously identifying patterns across cases of megaproject implementation (cf. Marsden and Stead, 2011). Also, it should accept that the possibilities of generalisation will be limited because causal relationships do not apply to all cases at all times. Evaluation methods that 'control for context' or aim to establish 'universal laws of implementation' are unrealistic and inadequate.

Non-compressibility

Because actors in megaproject implementation hold different perceptions of project reality on which they base their behaviour and actions, the method has to be able to include the different project realities in explaining outcomes. Evaluation methods that ignore the diversity of project goals, rationalities, and cultures have an unrealistic understanding of megaproject implementation, and are therefore inadequate.

Time-asymmetry

Because causality is emergent, the evaluation method needs to be able to capture the dynamics of megaproject implementation through time. Additionally, it needs to recognise the uncertain nature of implementation, disregarding the idea that outcomes could be linearly predicted. If it does not, the focus easily shifts to questions of accountability and identifying culprits instead of learning, and to the absurd idea that what worked in one project works by necessity in other projects as well.

A QCA evaluation of the A15 megaproject

Qualitative comparative analysis (Ragin, 1987; 2000; 2008) is an approach that meets the requirements to a very large extent (Verweij, 2015a). In this section, this is demonstrated by presenting the evaluation of the implementation of the A15 Maasvlakte-Vaanplein megaproject (see also Verweij, 2015c) that was introduced in the beginning of this chapter. The purpose of this demonstration is not to provide a set of guidelines for evaluating infrastructure projects with QCA. Guides are available elsewhere (e.g. Jordan et al., 2011; Schneider and Wagemann, 2012). Note also that the example discussed here concerns the evaluation of a single megaproject, but QCA may be used to evaluate multiple projects as well (e.g. Verweij, 2015d; see also the concluding section of this chapter). After the empirical demonstration, section 5 explicates how exactly QCA meets the requirements.

In order to facilitate the increased transport from the Maasvlakte port area, via Rotterdam into the European hinterland (see Figure 11.1), Rijkswaterstaat (RWS) signed a Design–Build–Finance–Maintain (DBFM) contract with the private consortium A-Lanes A15 in December 2010 (Ministerie van Infrastructuur en Milieu et al., 2013). RWS is the executive branch of the Dutch Ministry of Infrastructure and the Environment, which is responsible for the national highway network (Rijkswaterstaat, 2012). The megaproject includes the design and construction of approximately 85 km of additional traffic lanes, a dynamic traffic management system on the 37 km route, the renovation of thirty-six civil structures, the construction of twelve new structures, the renovation of two large tunnels, the replacement of the old Botlekbridge with a new and larger one, and the maintenance of the whole system up to 2035.

Leading up to the contract closure, RWS concluded various implementation agreements with fourteen local stakeholders in the project's environment. The idea of these agreements was to reach a consensus with the stakeholders about the megaproject's implementation beforehand, so as to ensure a smooth construction and delivery of the project. The agreements were made part of the DBFM contract between RWS and A-Lanes A15. Nevertheless, when the implementation started, unforeseen events occurred. The evaluation inquired into the events that occurred, how implementation managers responded to the events, and which management responses produced satisfactory outcomes (Verweij, 2015c).

Data were collected mainly via twenty open qualitative interviews with public and private managers between May 2012 and January 2013. The open and grounded nature of the interviews (e.g. Weiss, 1994) helped to account for the various project realities of the actors. Because of their different roles and backgrounds, different (sets of) managers were involved in dealing with different events. Moreover, they had different goals in mind when managing the events. For instance, controlling costs and schedule was pivotal for private managers: if these were not controlled, this would translate into loss of profit for the construction companies. For the public managers, costs and time were less of a concern, because these risks were transferred to A-Lanes A15. Instead, the RWS managers were more concerned with goals such as stakeholder satisfaction and quality. In

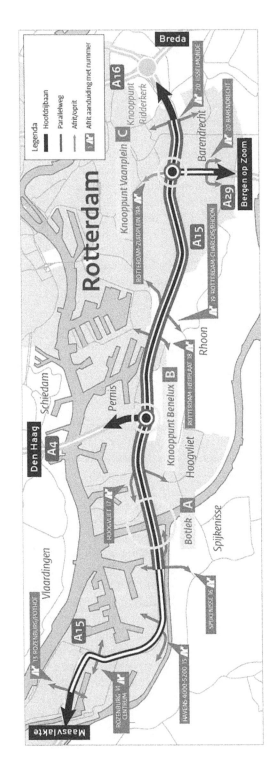

Figure 11.1 Overview A15 Maasvlakte-Vaanplein project.
Source: Rijkswaterstaat.

addition, having a good public–private relationship was important to both public and private managers, especially because they were going to be partners in the project for a long time, at least up to 2035. The importance of taking into account the diversity of outcomes, beyond the 'iron triangle' criteria of cost, time, and predefined performance criteria, is increasingly acknowledged in the literature (e.g. Atkinson, 1999; Jeffares et al., 2013). The outcome measure of 'satisfaction' was used in the evaluation, as it was better able to address the complex, heterogeneous, and subjective nature of outcomes in infrastructure project implementation processes (Lehtiranta et al., 2012; Kärnä et al., 2013). The interviews were transcribed and then coded using ATLAS.ti software.

A total of twenty events were identified in the implementation. An example of an event was a case where ProRail, the national railway network manager in the Netherlands, changed the design it had chosen in the implementation agreement on the railway system for the Botlekbridge. Another example was the discovery of an explosives risk zone containing World War II bombs. A third example concerned citizens who complained about noise produced by the construction works, which was due to an uncommon, hence unexpected, northeast wind. For each event, based on the coded data, the first task was to determine whether the event was social or physical, i.e. whether it originated from local stakeholders or from the physical (natural) system. A second distinction concerned the managers' choice of strategy: whether they opted for an internally-oriented or an externally-oriented strategy when responding to the event. The former has a closed and project-inward orientation, emphasising 'structure, administrative systems and the execution of plans' (Söderholm, 2008: 81), insisting on achieving predetermined goals. The latter strategy is characterised by an open and project-outward orientation, where solutions to emerging problems are sought together with stakeholders (see e.g. De Bruijn et al., 2010). The third task entailed identifying who was involved in managing the event: did the public and private partners work together, or were private managers from A-Lanes 15 left to deal with the events by themselves? The fourth step consisted of determining whether or not the managers involved in dealing with the event were satisfied with the outcome of the applied management strategy. The coding scheme for these four aspects and the resulting 'data matrix' are provided as Tables 11.1 and 11.2 (adapted from Verweij, 2015c).

Table 11.1 Four conditions

Condition	Abbreviation	Explanation
Nature of the event	EVENT	0 = Physical 1 = Social
Management	MAN	0 = Internally-oriented 1 = Externally-oriented
Cooperation	COOP	0 = Contractor A-Lanes A15 acts autonomously 1 = A-Lanes A15 and RWS cooperate
Satisfaction (outcome)	SATIS	0 = Dissatisfaction 1 = Satisfaction

Table 11.2 Data matrix

Case-ID	EVENT	MAN	COOP	SATIS
CAB1	0	0	1	1
CIT1	1	1	1	1
CIT2	1	1	0	1
CIT3	1	0	0	0
CIT4A	1	0	0	0
CIT4B	1	0	1	0
DOW	0	0	0	0
EXP	0	0	0	0
GRO	0	0	0	0
HBR1	1	0	1	0
HBR2	1	1	0	1
HBR3	1	0	1	0
LEI	1	1	1	1
MUN1	1	0	1	0
MUN2	1	0	0	0
PRO	1	1	1	1
PRV1	1	1	0	1
PRV2	1	1	0	1
RWS1	1	0	0	0
RWS2	1	0	1	0

Table 11.2 summarises in a very succinct way the twenty events, their management, and the outcomes that were produced. The table signals that combinations of conditions – the conditions being EVENT, MAN, and COOP – produce the outcome satisfaction (SATIS). The objective is to understand how the combinations of conditions produce outcomes, and what patterns can be identified across the cases. To answer these questions, QCA uses set-theoretic and Boolean logic (Schneider and Wagemann, 2012). Set-theory allows the articulation of necessary and/or sufficient conditions for producing a certain outcome of interest. When an outcome cannot be produced without a certain condition, this condition is necessary. A condition is sufficient if it can produce the outcome by itself. Causality, however, is often more complex than this. First, conditions combine to form configurations that produce outcomes. Second, different configurations may be capable of producing the same outcome (i.e. equifinality). Third, a condition may contribute to producing the outcome or the non-outcome, depending on how it combines with other conditions. Application of Boolean logic allows us to trace back these complex relations. To do this, first, a so-called 'truth table' needs to be constructed. The truth table groups similar cases from the data matrix together, thereby simultaneously separating dissimilar cases. The truth table is shown as Table 11.3 (adapted from Verweij, 2015c).

Each row in the truth table represents a statement of sufficiency. For instance, the second row states that in the context of social events (EVENT{1}), an externally-oriented management strategy (MAN{1}) combined with a cooperative approach (COOP{1}) is sufficient for producing satisfactory outcomes in megaproject implementation. By pairwise comparing truth table rows that have the same outcome but which differ in but one of the three conditions, more generalised patterns can be identified. This pairwise comparative process is called truth table minimisation, which results in so-called minimised configurations. For instance, comparing the second truth table row – i.e. EVENT{1}*MAN{1}*COOP{1} – with the third one – i.e. EVENT{1}*MAN{1}*COOP{0} – leads to the conclusion that irrespective of the nature of the cooperation, that is, whether it is {0} or {1}, an externally-oriented management strategy in response to social events is sufficient for achieving satisfactory outcomes: EVENT{1}*MAN{1} → SATIS{1}. The complete comparative process, conducted with QCA software (Cronqvist, 2011) yielded the results as shown in Table 11.4 (adapted from Verweij, 2015c).[3] The table shows that there are two sufficient minimised configurations that produce satisfaction and two that produce dissatisfaction.

The first minimised configuration is covered by one case: CAB1. In this physical event, A-Lanes A15 and RWS cooperatively responded in order to find a solution. The partners had different responsibilities for dealing with different types of underground pipelines and cables, but because some pipelines and cables were physically intertwined, working together in this issue was chosen as the solution. The second configuration is covered by more cases, and can therefore be considered as empirically more relevant. This configuration states that in the case of social events, an externally-oriented management strategy produces satisfactory

Table 11.3 Truth table

EVENT	MAN	COOP	SATIS	Cases
0	0	1	1	CAB1
1	1	1	1	CIT1, LEI, PRO
1	1	0	1	CIT2, PRV2, HBR2, PRV1
0	0	0	0	DOW, GRO, EXP
1	0	0	0	CIT3, CIT4A, MUN2, RWS1
1	0	1	0	CIT4B, RWS2, HBR1, HBR3, MUN1

Table 11.4 Results of the truth table minimisation

SATIS	Configuration	Cases	N
{1}	EVENT{0}*MAN{0}*COOP{1}	CAB1	1
	EVENT{1}*MAN{1}	CIT1, LEI, PRO + CIT2, PRV2, HBR2, PRV1	7
{0}	EVENT{1}*MAN{0}	CIT3, CIT4A, MUN2, RWS1 + CIT4B, RWS2, HBR1, HBR3, MUN1	9
	MAN{0}*COOP{0}	DOW, GRO, EXP + CIT3, CIT4A, MUN2, RWS1	7

outcomes. For instance, in the HBR2 event, the Rotterdam Port Authority objected to a particular rerouting designed by A-Lanes, and through a deliberation process with the Port Authority and other stakeholders, a solution was found to the rerouting problem that satisfied all stakeholders. The condition COOP is absent in this minimised configuration, which signals that in some cases contractor A-Lanes A15 acted autonomously and in other cases A-Lanes and RWS cooperated.

Two minimised configurations are associated with dissatisfaction (Table 11.4). In nine events, managers responded to social events with an internally-oriented strategy, i.e. by not interactively engaging with the local stakeholders who were at the basis of the occurrence of the events. As a consequence, the stakeholders' interests were not catered for, which resulted in stressful relationships with the stakeholders, delays, extra costs, and an unhappy RWS. This happened, for instance, in the HBR3 event, where A-Lanes failed to check the design of a temporary road for transporting hazardous substances with the Port Authority, and as a result, the design was rejected and a tense relationship developed between A-Lanes and the Port Authority. The other configuration is covered by seven cases. It indicates that irrespective of the nature of the event, internally-oriented management responses by A-Lanes result in dissatisfactory outcomes. An example is case MUN2, where the municipality of Rotterdam did not give its approval for the construction of the Botlekbridge pillars as it remained unconvinced about the safety and quality of the design. A-Lanes focused on finding technical solutions and on continuing the purchase of steel for the bridge, which entailed great financial risks and high costs.

The evaluation shows that stakeholder complexity dominated the implementation of the A15 Maasvlakte-Vaanplein megaproject, as sixteen out of twenty events were of a social nature (see Tables 11.2 and 11.3). In the majority of the cases (i.e. thirteen out of twenty), internally-oriented strategies were applied, resulting in dissatisfactory outcomes, while in contrast, externally-oriented management is a strategy that results in better outcomes in responding to stakeholder complexity in megaproject implementation (see Table 11.4). The evaluation corroborates findings from previous studies (e.g. Edelenbos and Klijn, 2006; 2009) that show that flexibility, openness, and interaction with the societal environment result in more satisfactory outcomes in the implementation of complex megaprojects than management strategies that stress the execution of projects according to plans, specified goals, and contractual relations.

QCA for complexity-informed evaluation

The brief QCA demonstration helps to understand the complexity-informed nature of the QCA approach for infrastructure megaproject evaluation (see Verweij, 2015a; cf. Gerrits and Verweij, 2013; Verweij and Gerrits, 2013). As the analysis of the A15 Maasvlakte-Vaanplein projects clarifies, QCA is able to evaluate how combinations of parts, for example events, management, and public–private cooperation, produce outcomes. This means that the first requirement of *non-decomposability* is met. QCA is a decidedly configurational approach: it assumes a priori that causes operate in configurations. In QCA, cases are conceptualised as combinations of conditions, and these configurations explain outcomes. Although a QCA evaluation could, in principle, point to singular conditions being necessary or sufficient for the outcome of interest, it is *a priori* assumed that configurations, not singular variables, produce outcomes.

QCA is also a *contingent* evaluation approach. A qualitative comparative analysis starts from the premise that megaprojects are unique and implemented in unique contexts. It is a decidedly case-based evaluation method (Verweij and Gerrits, 2013), assuming that the unique properties of cases can hold explanations for the outcome of interest. A project is first studied in depth on various context- and project-specific properties (see Verweij, 2015c). The coding process (e.g. with ATLAS.ti) then results in a data matrix (Table 11.2), and via the grouping of cases in the truth table (Table 11.3), patterns (i.e. minimised configurations) in or across project implementations are explicated, as shown in Figure 11.2 (Verweij, 2015a). Importantly, because the studied cases group together in different configurations, the method implicitly accepts that generalisation is limited. The patterns, as shown in Table 11.4, only apply to the subset of cases covered by the minimised configuration.

Although QCA in itself does not necessarily imply that the diversity of project goals, rationalities, and cultures is included in explaining outcomes in/of megaproject implementation processes, this option is certainly not ruled out. QCA is often considered as a theory-driven evaluation approach, for instance when it is suggested as a method to formalise pattern finding in the context of a so-called realistic evaluation approach (Befani et al., 2007; Befani 2013), but it can also be applied in a grounded fashion so as to include the different project realities in the evaluation (e.g. Verweij, 2015c; Verweij and Gerrits, 2015). By

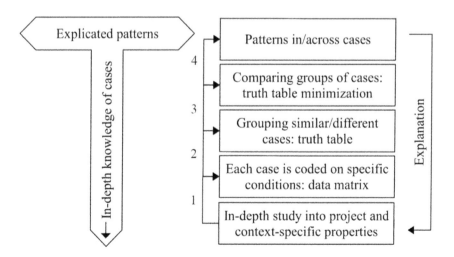

Figure 11.2 The T-structure of QCA.
Source: Adapted from Verweij (2015a).

constructing cases via an inductive process, as little as possible of the complexity of the megaproject is reduced at the start of the evaluation. This means that the third requirement, *non-compressibility*, is also met. It is important here that the outcome measure is derived from the empirical data, for example through the concept of 'satisfaction', as in the empirical example in the previous section, instead of focusing a priori only on time, costs, and predefined performance criteria.

The fourth requisite, *time-asymmetry*, is only partly met in QCA. In essence, the time dimension is not captured with the method (Verweij and Gerrits, 2013). Cases as configurations are compared at a certain point in time, not through time. Although proposals to include time in QCA are available (e.g. Caren and Panofsky, 2005; Hak et al., 2013), the approach is unable to capture the dynamics of megaproject implementation through time. QCA does address the question of uncertainty in the evaluation of megaprojects. Conventionally, the method is deployed to identify necessary and/or sufficient conditions for outcomes – this nomenclature might suggest that QCA is deterministic, and therefore would not allow for uncertainty. However, the logical deterministic nature of QCA should not be confused with causally deterministic relations. In QCA, similar configurations may have contradictory outcomes, the relationships are not linear but configurational (i.e. conditions combine in configurations) and equifinal (i.e. multiple configurations may lead to an outcome), as mentioned in the previous section, and generalisation is modest. QCA does not allow planners and managers of megaprojects to predict the outcomes produced by certain strategies; for one thing, changes in the selection and/or coding of conditions can result in the alteration of patterns. However, patterns found in a QCA evaluation do provide a basis for suggestions on how to improve megaproject development, for example by employing externally-oriented management strategies. In this sense, QCA is better suited for *ex post* evaluation, which does not seek to produce estimations or predictions but focuses instead on identifying successful and failed cases and on systematically distinguishing between relevant and irrelevant conditions, so as to contribute to the successful development of future megaprojects.

An agenda for learning from evaluation with QCA

This chapter has described the way in which QCA was applied to the evaluation of a single megaproject: the A15 Maasvlakte-Vaanplein project in the Netherlands (Verweij, 2015c). The evaluation of this project implementation was shaped by the specific Dutch institutional setting and the specific contractual features of the project, which both had an influence on the organisation and management of the implementation process. For instance, an important criterion for RWS was that stakeholders, with which it concluded various agreements prior to the implementation, were kept satisfied during the implementation process. Another example was the policy of RWS to develop projects through a specific type of public–private partnership contract, which defines the roles and responsibilities of the partners in the project. When QCA is applied to other cases in other countries, sectors, or settings, different conditions and outcomes may need to be selected for the analysis.

As shown in Figure 11.3, QCA may also be applied to foster consensus-building and collaboration in megaproject development, and to comparatively and systematically evaluate development strategies of multiple projects. There are three dimensions along which QCA can foster learning (see Verweij, 2015a for the extended argument).

The first involves learning across projects (see Figure 11.3) using, for example, data from existing megaproject research programmes. QCA is especially suitable for research settings that fall between case studies ('small-N') and broad surveys ('large-N'). In such 'medium-N' research settings, QCA can strike a balance between rich and in-depth case knowledge on the one hand and cross-case pattern recognition on the other hand (Verweij and Gerrits, 2013). Research programmes containing medium-N of cases could usefully be analysed with QCA. Relevant examples of such programmes include the OMEGA Centre for Mega Projects in Transport and Development at the Bartlett School of Planning (see Chapter 3 in this volume; Dimitriou et al., 2013, Dimitriou, 2014), the NETLIPSE network on the management and organisation of large infrastructure projects in Europe (see Hertogh et al., 2008), and the MEGAPROJECT Action under the European Cooperation in Science and Technology (COST) framework (Brookes and Locatelli, 2015). These research programmes generate a lot of knowledge about megaproject development and cases, resulting in many lessons and best practices.

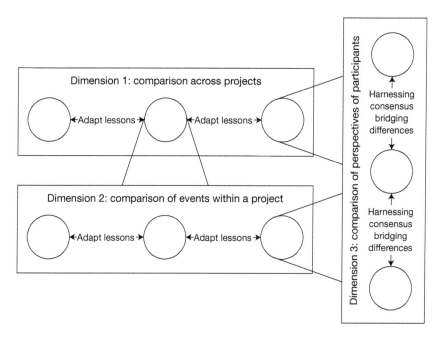

Figure 11.3 The dimensions of learning with QCA.
Source: Adapted from Verweij (2015a).

However, their danger may be that because of the richness and in-depth nature of the studied cases, the cross-case patterns, and by extension the lessons learned, may lack in systematic and transparent comparative analysis that would help to identify exactly those strategies that would be necessary and/or sufficient in developing megaprojects under any given conditions. In fact, the MEGAPROJECT Action observes (Brookes et al., 2015: 5; emphases added):

> The successful transfer of learning across projects has been a long-held desire by project professionals. The difficulties in achieving this activity are created by the very nature of projects themselves: their separation from a 'permanent' organization and *their uniqueness*. (…) In the context of megaprojects, the ability to learn across megaprojects becomes even more difficult. *The size and complexity of megaprojects make it very difficult to discern which actors and elements of its myriad configurations have actually influenced performance*. (…) The situation is further complicated by much of the learning that is transferred between megaprojects being anecdotal in nature. Many 'lessons learnt systems' rely solely on unreflective recollections of individuals. *No rigorous attempt is made to discover if characteristics ascribed to the project's performance were actually associated with the ensuing project performance*.

QCA can be a valuable method to address these hiatuses. For instance, a systematic QCA evaluation may point to configuration A*B*C*D being associated with high performance (Y), and configuration A*B*C*~D with low performance (~Y). The insight here could be that megaprojects characterised by the latter configuration, in which condition D is absent (i.e. ~D), might improve their performance by ensuring the presence of D (see Verweij, 2015a). In addition to analysing megaprojects as configurations of binary conditions, i.e. {0} or {1}, other types of QCA are available that allow multi-value or continuous conditions (e.g. Verweij, 2015a; see Rihoux and Ragin, 2009; Schneider and Wagemann, 2012).

The second dimension is learning within projects (see Figure 11.3), by comparing events or situations within project implementation. The evaluation of the A15 Maasvlakte-Vaanplein project presented above is an example of this. Such an evaluation tells project managers what kinds of situations require what kind of management, and how adapting their management strategy may generate better outcomes. For instance, as can be inferred from Table 11.4, managers that responded to social events with internally-oriented management (i.e. EVENT{1}*MAN{0}) are advised to adapt: responding with an externally-oriented strategy to social events (i.e. EVENT{1}*MAN{1} produces better outcomes. Other QCA evaluations conducted in the same way as the A15 Maasvlakte-Vaanplein study substantiate this finding, and furthermore provide additional options for generating better outcomes (see Verweij and Gerrits, 2015).

The third dimension concerns learning about project participants' perspectives (see Figure 11.3) – with regard to the project or events/situations within a project – by comparing these perspectives on certain aspects (e.g. Kort et al., 2015). In this situation, the evaluator would consider each participant as a case, with his or her perspectives on certain issues as the conditions that constitute the case. For example, instead of comparing events in a project, one could examine each manager's perspective on the way that an event was managed. Comparison of perspectives then tells the participants where there is common ground or mutual understanding between them (i.e. when managers are positioned in the same or similar truth table rows), and in which respects perspectives diverge. The assessment of similar and dissimilar perspectives could show where consensus between participants can be harnessed, and where there is potential for bridging the existing differences. This evaluation of perspectives is important in developing megaprojects: the projects are large-scale and complex, and involve interests that easily and often clash because of, among other things, the different cultures and value systems of the project participants involved (cf. Van Marrewijk et al., 2008).

In order to move away from the tendency to use evaluations purely for questions of accountability and identifying culprits, and to foster instead the use of evaluation for learning purposes, planners and evaluators have to accept the uncertain and complex nature of megaproject development. Moreover, instead of seeing the diverging cultures and interests involved in public–private megaprojects as a threat to a smooth project implementation, the heterogeneous nature of project participants and stakeholders can also be regarded as an opportunity for evaluation. Project stakeholders and participants draw different boundaries to simplify their project realities. By implication, including a multitude of actors and perspectives in the evaluation, the different partial perspectives can be combined to broaden and strengthen the data, knowledge, and experience base in evaluation. It may also provide opportunities for consensus-building and mutual learning across the evaluation participants (cf. Greene, 2001) and for enhanced evaluation utilisation and learning (Patton, 2011). This chapter has sought to demonstrate the potential of QCA for complexity-informed evaluation of megaprojects and other infrastructure projects. Although QCA is gradually becoming recognised in infrastructure research, more applications are welcomed.

Acknowledgements

I thank Geert Teisman for his comments on previous versions of this chapter. This chapter derives from a research project that was funded by Next Generation Infrastructures under grant 03.24EUR.

Notes

1 For an overview of differences between the linear-rationalist worldview and a complexity worldview, consult e.g. Morçöl (2001).
2 This chapter is based on the research *Once the shovel hits the ground: Evaluating the management of complex implementation processes of public–private partnership infrastructure projects with qualitative comparative analysis* (Verweij, 2015a).
3 A complete overview of available software packages for conducting QCA can be found at www.compasss.org.

References

Atkinson, R. 1999. Project management: Cost, time and quality, two best guesses and a phenomenon, it's time to accept other success criteria. *International Journal of Project Management* 17(6): 337–342.

Befani, B. 2013. Between complexity and generalization: Addressing evaluation challenges with QCA. *Evaluation* 19(3): 269–283.

Befani, B., Ledermann, S. & Sager, F. 2007. Realistic evaluation and QCA: Conceptual parallels and an empirical application. *Evaluation* 13(2): 171–192.

Bhaskar, R. 1975. *A realist theory of science*. London: Routledge.

Brookes, N. and Locatelli, G. 2015. *A megaproject research framework: A guide for megaproject researchers*. Leeds: University of Leeds.

Brookes, N., Locatelli, G. and Mikic, M. 2015. *Learning across megaprojects: The INNOMET working group report*. Leeds: University of Leeds.

Buijs, J.M., Eshuis, J. & Byrne, D.S. 2009. Approaches to researching complexity in public management. In G.R. Teisman, A. Van Buuren & L.M. Gerrits (eds.), *Managing complex governance systems: Dynamics, self-organization and coevolution in public investments*. New York: Routledge, 37–55.

Byrne, D.S. 1998. *Complexity theory and the social sciences: An introduction*. Abingdon: Routledge.

Byrne, D.S. & Callaghan, G. 2014. *Complexity theory and the social sciences: The state of the art*. London: Routledge.

Caren, N. & Panofsky, A. 2005. TQCA: A technique for adding temporality to qualitative comparative analysis. *Sociological Methods & Research*, 34(2): 147–172.

Cilliers, P. 2001. Boundaries, hierarchies and networks in complex systems. *International Journal of Innovation Management* 5(2): 135–147.

Cronqvist, L. 2011. *Tosmana: Tool for small-n analysis*. Trier: University of Trier.

De Bruijn, H., ten Heuvelhof, E. & In't Veld, R. 2010. *Process management: Why project management fails in complex decision making processes*. Berlin: Springer.

Dimitriou, H.T. 2014. What constitutes a 'successful' mega transport project? *Planning Theory & Practice* 15(3): 389–392.

Dimitriou, H.T., Ward, E.J. & Wright, P.G. 2013. Mega transport projects – Beyond the 'iron triangle': Findings from the OMEGA research programme. *Progress in Planning* 86: 1–43.

Edelenbos, J. & Klijn, E.-H. 2006. Managing stakeholder involvement in decision making: A comparative analysis of six interactive processes in the Netherlands. *Journal of Public Administration Research and Theory* 16(3): 417–446.

Edelenbos, J. & Klijn, E.H. 2009. Project versus process management in public–private partnership: Relation between management style and outcomes. *International Public Management Journal* 12(3): 310–331.

Edelenbos, J., Klijn, E.H. & Kort, M.B. 2009. Managing complex process systems: Surviving at the edge of chaos. In G.R. Teisman, A. Van Buuren & L.M. Gerrits (eds.), *Managing complex governance systems: Dynamics, self-organization and coevolution in public investments*. New York: Routledge, 172–192.

Engwall, M. 2003. No project is an island: Linking projects to history and context. *Research Policy* 32(5): 789–808.

Flyvbjerg, B. 2009. Optimism and misrepresentation in early project development. In T. Williams, K. Samset & K. Sunnevag (eds.), *Making essential choices with scant information: Front-end decision making in major projects*. New York: Palgrave Macmillan, 147–168.

Flyvbjerg, B., Holm, M.S. & Buhl, S. 2002. Underestimating costs in public works projects: Error or lie? *Journal of the American Planning Association* 68(3): 279–295.

Gerrits, L.M. & Verweij, S. 2013. Critical realism as a meta-framework for understanding the relationships between complexity and qualitative comparative analysis. *Journal of Critical Realism* 12(2): 166–182.

Goldstein, J. 1999. Emergence as a construct: History and issues. *Emergence* 1(1): 49–72.

Greene, J.C. 2001. Dialogue in evaluation: A relational perspective. *Evaluation* 7(2): 181–187.

Hak, T., Jaspers, F. and Dul, J. 2013. The analysis of temporally ordered configurations: Challenges and solutions. In P.C. Fiss, B. Cambré & A. Marx (eds.), *Configurational theory and methods in organizational research*. Bingley: Emerald Group Publishing Limited, 107–127.

Hertogh, M.J.C.M., Baker, S., Staal-Ong, P.L. & Westerveld, E. 2008. *Managing large infrastructure projects: Research on best practices and lessons learnt in large infrastructure projects in Europe*. Baarn: AT Osborne.

Houtekamer, C. 2015. Bluffen en pokeren om de A15. NRC, 23 Apr.

Jeffares, S., Sullivan, H. & Bovaird, T. 2013. Beyond the contract: The challenge of evaluating the performance(s) of public–private partnerships. In C. Greve & G.A. Hodge (eds.), *Rethinking public–private partnerships: strategies for turbulent times*. New York: Routledge, 166–187.

Jones, R. & Noble, G. 2008. Managing the implementation of public–private partnerships. *Public Money & Management* 28(2): 109–114.

Jordan, E., Gross, M.E., Javernick-Will, A.N. & Garvin, M.J. 2011. Use and misuse of qualitative comparative analysis. *Construction Management and Economics* 29(11): 1159–1173.

Kärnä, S., Junnonen, J.M., Manninen, A.P. & Julin, P. 2013. Exploring project participants' satisfaction in the infrastructure projects. *Engineering Project Organization Journal* 3(4): 186–197.

Kort, M., Verweij, S. & Klijn, E.H. 2015. In search for effective public–private partnerships: An assessment of the impact of organizational form and managerial strategies in urban regeneration partnerships using fsQCA. *Environment and Planning C: Government and Policy*, doi: 10.1177/0263774X15614674.

Lehtiranta, L., Kärnä, S., Junnonen, J.M. & Julin, P. 2012. The role of multi-firm satisfaction in construction project success. *Construction Management and Economics*: 30(6): 463–475.

Lehtonen, M. 2014. Evaluating megaprojects: From the 'iron triangle' to network mapping. *Evaluation* 20(3): 278–295.

Love, P.E.D., Holt, G.D., Shen, L.Y., Li, H. & Irani, Z. 2002. Using systems dynamics to better understand change and rework in construction project management systems. *International Journal of Project Management* 20(6): 425–436.

Love, P.E.D., Smith, J., Simpson, I., Regan, M. & Olatunji, O. 2015. Understanding the landscape of overruns in transport infrastructure projects. *Environment and Planning B: Planning and Design* 42(3): 490–509.

Marsden, G. & Stead, D. 2011. Policy transfer and learning in the field of transport: A review of concepts and evidence. *Transport Policy* 18(3): 492–500.

Marshall, S. 2009. *Cities, design and evolution*. Abingdon: Routledge.

Ministerie van Infrastructuur en Milieu, Ministerie van Economische Zaken & Ministerie van Binnenlandse Zaken en Koninkrijksrelaties. 2013. *MIRT projectenboek 2014*. Den Haag: Ministerie van Infrastructuur en Milieu.

Morçöl, G. 2001. What is complexity science? Postmodernist or postpositivist? *Emergence* 3(1): 104–119.

Patton, M.Q. 2011. *Developmental evaluation: Applying complexity concepts to enhance innovation and use.* New York: The Guilford Press.

Pattyn, V. & Verweij, S. 2014. Beleidsevaluaties tussen methode en praktijk: Naar een meer realistische evaluatiebenadering. *Burger, Bestuur & Beleid* 8(4): 260–267.

Pressman, J.L. & Wildavsky, A. 1984. *Implementation: How great expectations in Washington are dashed in Oakland; Or, why it's amazing that federal programs work at all, this being a saga of the economic development administration as told by two sympathetic observers who seek to build morals on a foundation of ruined hopes.* Berkeley: University of California Press.

Priemus, H., Flyvbjerg, B. & Wee, B.V. (eds.). 2008. *Decision-making on mega-projects: Cost-benefit analysis, planning and innovation.* Cheltenham: Edward Elgar.

Prigogine, I. 1997. *The end of certainty: Time, chaos, and the new laws of nature.* New York: The Free Press.

Ragin, C.C. 1987. *The comparative method: Moving beyond qualitative and quantitative strategies.* Berkeley: University of California Press.

Ragin, C.C. 2000. *Fuzzy-set social science.* Chicago: University of Chicago Press.

Ragin, C.C. 2008. *Redesigning social inquiry: Fuzzy sets and beyond.* Chicago: University of Chicago Press.

Rescher, N. 1995. *Luck: The brilliant randomness of everyday life.* Pittsburgh: University of Pittsburgh Press.

Reynaers, A. & Verweij, S. 2014. Kritisch kijken naar kansen: De schaduwzijden van DBFMO. *ROmagazine* 32(4): 32–34.

Rihoux, B. and Ragin, C.C. (eds.). 2009. *Configurational comparative methods: Qualitative comparative analysis (QCA) and related techniques.* Thousand Oaks: Sage.

Rijkswaterstaat. 2012. *Rijkswaterstaat: About us.* The Hague: Ministry of Infrastructure and the Environment.

Rittel, H.W.J. & Webber, M.M. 1973. Dilemmas in a general theory of planning. *Policy Sciences* 4(2): 155–169.

Rogers, P.J. 2011. Implications of complicated and complex characteristics for key tasks in evaluation. In K. Forss, M. Marra & R. Schwartz (eds.), *Evaluating the complex: Attribution, contribution, and beyond.* New Brunswick: Transaction Publishers, 33–52.

Salling, K.B. & Nielsen, O.A. 2015. Uncertainties in transport project evaluation: Editorial. *European Journal of Transport and Infrastructure Research* 15(3): 282–285.

Sanderson, J. 2012. Risk, uncertainty and governance in megaprojects: A critical discussion of alternative explanations. *International Journal of Project Management* 30(4): 432–443.

Sayer, A. 2000. *Realism and social science.* London: Sage.

Schneider, C.Q. & Wagemann, C. 2012. *Set-theoretic methods for the social sciences: A guide to qualitative comparative analysis.* Cambridge: Cambridge University Press.

Short, J. & Kopp, A. 2005. Transport infrastructure: Investment and planning. Policy and research aspects. *Transport Policy* 12(4): 360–367.

Söderholm, A. 2008. Project management of unexpected events. *International Journal of Project Management* 26(1): 80–86.

Teisman, G.R., van Buuren, A. & Gerrits, L.M. (eds.). 2009. *Managing complex governance systems: dynamics, self-organization and coevolution in public investments.* New York: Routledge.

Van der Meer, F.B. & Edelenbos, J. 2006. Evaluation in multi-actor policy processes: Accountability, learning and co-operation. *Evaluation* 12(2): 201–218.

Van Marrewijk, A., Clegg, S.R., Pitsis, T.S. & Veenswijk, M. 2008. Managing public–private megaprojects: Paradoxes, complexity, and project design. *International Journal of Project Management* 26(6): 591–600.

Verbraeken, H. & Weissink, A. 2014. Nieuwe Botlek-brug zorgt voor grootste kostenoverschrijding A15-project. *Het Financieele Dagblad*, 10 Jul.

Verweij, S. 2015a. *Once the shovel hits the ground: Evaluating the management of complex implementation processes of public–private partnership projects with qualitative comparative analysis*. Rotterdam: Erasmus University Rotterdam.

Verweij, S. 2015b. Voorsorteren op de belofte van DBFM: Het juist managen en evalueren van de complexiteit in DBFM-transportinfrastructuurprojecten. *Verkeerskunde* 66(2): 16–17.

Verweij, S. 2015c. Achieving satisfaction when implementing PPP transportation infrastructure projects: A qualitative comparative analysis of the A15 highway DBFM project. *International Journal of Project Management* 33(1): 189–200.

Verweij, S. 2015d. Producing satisfactory outcomes in the implementation phase of PPP infrastructure projects: A fuzzy set qualitative comparative analysis of 27 road constructions in the Netherlands. *International Journal of Project Management* 33(8): 1877–1887.

Verweij, S. & Gerrits, L.M. 2013. Understanding and researching complexity with qualitative comparative analysis: Evaluating transportation infrastructure projects. *Evaluation* 19(1): 40–55.

Verweij, S. & Gerrits, L.M. 2015. How satisfaction is achieved in the implementation phase of large transportation infrastructure projects: A qualitative comparative analysis into the A2 tunnel project. *Public Works Management & Policy* 20(1): 5–28.

Weiss, R.S. 1994. *Learning from strangers: The art and method of qualitative interview studies*. New York: The Free Press.

12 Conclusions

Markku Lehtonen, Luis Aparicio
and Pierre-Benoît Joly

This book has been about opening up megaproject evaluation to 'the socioeconomic' in the two senses of the term described in the introductory chapter: evaluation of the various dimensions of socioeconomic impacts, and a broader, more reflexive approach to evaluation that would be better able to accommodate the complexity and irreducible uncertainty inherent in megaprojects. The central question addressed in this book can be summarised as follows: how can socioeconomic evaluation contribute to better governance and governing of megaprojects, including through dialogue among the various actors involved, when the governance context is characterised by strong political and economic interests, radical uncertainty, potential irreversibilities, and exceptionally long timescales?

The chapters in this volume address this fundamental question from two distinct angles. The first part consists of critical empirical analyses of current megaproject evaluation practices, while the chapters in the second part of the book explore possibilities for improved methodologies for the socioeconomic evaluation of megaprojects. Instead of seeking to capture the full richness of the insights provided by the different chapters, we shall here highlight some recurring themes of this volume, as well as a number of relatively neglected issues.

Opening up as a means of dealing with uncertainties in megaproject evaluation

A constant theme running through the chapters in this book concerns the role of evaluation in situations involving strong economic and political interests and passions. The choices of evaluation methods and approaches are important, but at the same time inseparable from the surrounding political and institutional context – including notably the framing of the issues at hand. Many of the chapters in this book draw attention to the chronic tendencies in megaproject evaluation towards a premature closure, 'irreversibilisation', and attempts to hide essential political choices behind presumably neutral and technical methods. All chapters manifest the call for greater 'opening up' (Stirling, 2008) of megaproject evaluation, as a means of counteracting these tendencies. Dimitriou et al. (Chapter 3) highlight the tension between project managers who focus on 'getting things done', and the policymakers and planners more concerned with sustainability – and presumably more amenable to greater openness. The risk dialogue between the Finnish safety regulator and the radioactive waste management company (Chapter 7) illustrates the 'getting things done' mentality shared by a restricted group of key technical experts – a convergence of mentalities as a result of continuous dialogue and a search for consensus amongst this 'inner circle'. Saraç-Lesavre (Chapter 2) observes similar pressures towards closing down, as key political and ethical choices concerning responsibilities for nuclear waste management are reduced to supposedly neutral technical discussions on the 'correct' discount rate. The progressive closing down in the case of the Lyon–Turin high-speed railway (Chapter 4) concerned not so much evaluations, but instead the successive financing and implementation decisions that rendered the project increasingly irreversible. The chapters in the second part of the book present various alternative ways of 'opening up', either through participatory elaboration of community well-being indicators (Chapter 10), evaluation methods that seek to foster reflexivity and learning by bridging between quantitative and qualitative approaches (Chapter 11), or through a systematic analysis of various, potentially complementary, evaluation methodologies that would be better capable of addressing risk, complexity and uncertainty (Chapter 8).

Beyond the iron triangle – learning and accountability

A form of 'opening up' specific to megaprojects entails moving beyond the 'iron triangle' criteria of cost, timetables and predefined project specifications. As argued throughout the chapters, this triangle of objectives – and the associated rational actor model and a linear-rational view of policymaking – is clearly insufficient if evaluation is to foster learning and reflexivity that are necessary in the face of the multiple challenges of megaproject governance.

While most of the chapters underline learning as the often forgotten function of evaluation, many of the chapters remind us of the continuing relevance of the accountability objective. Accountability appears particularly relevant in the evaluation of the economic and financial viability of megaprojects (e.g. Chapters 2, 5, 6 and 8). The chapters in this book provide many reasons to believe that the balance in megaproject evaluation is currently skewed in favour of accountability, and that greater attention to learning is needed. A central challenge still remains, however: how to combine the often mutually conflicting objectives of learning and accountability (e.g. Blalock, 1999; Lehtonen, 2005)? We argue that a vital task in such efforts of combining the two functions entails redefining accountability, drawing on the ideas of network governance (Hertting and Vedung, 2012; Lehtonen, 2014).

Opening up or managing the socioeconomic? The politics of socioeconomic evaluation

Vanclay's (Chapter 9) discussion on social impact assessment (SIA) illustrates another form of the tension between opening up and 'getting things done', mentioned above. As a method designed to 'manage social issues', SIA fully embraces the objective of making sure that the project in question gets done, albeit in the socially least obtrusive – or indeed most favourable – manner. It also implicitly postulates that there is an actor sufficiently motivated to strive for good management of the social issues, and capable of implementing such management. In a similar vein, Chapter 8 focuses on the importance of control and management, in particular, managing costs and timetables. Dimitriou et al. (Chapter 3), together with Bergmans and Verhaegen (Chapter 6) and Verweij (Chapter 11), put forward perhaps most explicitly the argument in favour of opening up. For them, the objective is not so much managing the social, but more of embracing uncertainty and complexity: one could perhaps evoke the notion of management through flexibility, vagueness and indeterminacy.

Tensions between the desire to control and the need to foster learning are crucial, and directly related to different approaches to uncertainty. An approach emphasising control would postulate that the main *raison d'être* of evaluation is to smooth out conflicts, reduce uncertainties, and thereby improve the efficiency and effectiveness of the governance processes – in the spirit of 'getting things done'. An alternative, learning-oriented perspective would instead see evaluations as an instrument that helps us to explore new problem framings and question the convenient and consensual assumptions underpinning our governance and evaluation approaches. These two approaches can be labelled, respectively, as 'internal' and 'external'. The former assumes that the overarching political decisions have already been made, and that evaluation would be left merely with the task of examining the alternatives and impacts within that predetermined framework. From an external perspective, by contrast, evaluating would imply stepping 'outside of the system', and evaluation would explore not only the impacts of a project, but also the overall framing of the problem and the *raison d'être* of the project. The external view therefore contests the assumption that the prevailing framing is automatically legitimate.

The key questions raised by this distinction are therefore familiar to evaluation research and practice: what types of evaluation will be needed, at which point in time, conducted by whom, and for which purpose? The chapters in this book provide varying answers to these questions, with those of Vanclay (Chapter 9) and Lamari et al. (Chapter 8) perhaps falling most clearly within the internal category. As a process for managing a project at the local level, SIA would take place once a national-level deliberation has taken place, and the project would already be shaped at least to some extent. Public involvement would then contribute to shaping the details of the project and to negotiations of community benefit packages, for instance. The apparently neat distinction between 'internal' and 'external' is obviously blurred to the extent that any given method or approach can usually adopt an internal and external perspective. The Lyon–Turin railway project (Chapter 4) is a case in point: relatively conventional 'internal' evaluation methods (e.g. CBA) are applied in an 'external' manner, precisely as a tool that allows the original framing of the project to be problematised.

The chapters in this book also address the political and symbolic functions of evaluation (e.g. Pawson and Tilley, 1997; Vedung, 1997; Weiss, 1999). These could take the form of 'greenwashing', as Chapter 3 suggests in relation to sustainability evaluations, or 'social greenwashing' – such as when social impact assessment is used merely as a means of obtaining local acceptance to predefined project plans. Such instrumental functions (Fiorino, 1990) are, of course, well known from participatory planning and decision-making in general (e.g. Wüstenhagen et al., 2007; Chateauraynaud and Debaz, 2011; Cowell et al., 2011). Some chapters in this book provide such examples of evaluation being used to legitimise predetermined agendas and justify project decisions made in advance. In Finnish nuclear waste policy development, socioeconomic evaluation seems to have served primarily a legitimising function – while at the same time helping the waste management company to better deal with public opinion (Chapter 5). Socioeconomic evaluations are particularly prone to such legitimising use in highly technical megaprojects such as nuclear waste management, when safety and technical evaluations constitute the primary concerns and there is overwhelming political pressure to 'get things done' and obtain local acceptance.

Participation – gaining acceptance or constructing legitimacy?

Social acceptance and social acceptability have indeed become watchwords in modern-day project planning and management (e.g. Wüstenhagen et al., 2007; OECD-NEA, 2010; Chateauraynaud and Debaz, 2011; Cowell et al., 2011). The chapters in this book illustrate some of the problems associated with the use of such terms. In particular, these terms clearly entail an 'internal' approach, in accepting that the overall framing has been chosen, and that the role of the citizens would be merely to give their passive acceptance, a 'licence to operate', to a project whose interest to the nation/society/mankind has been determined in advance. However participatory any evaluation might then be, its function would be to strengthen the acceptance by (especially local) citizens of a project whose contours have been defined by others. Greater public participation may in such situations fail to achieve significant 'opening up'. If indeed key decisions have already been made, citizen participation is likely to do more harm than good, producing deep frustration among citizens that have been called upon to contribute, only to realise that their opinions have no impact whatsoever. Megaproject literature has been rather ambivalent about the role of public participation – as exemplified, for example, by Flyvbjerg et al. (2003: 7), who expressed scepticism concerning the virtues of public participation in the face of overwhelmingly powerful vested interests.

Nevertheless, many of the chapters in this volume make a strong case for early citizen and stakeholder engagement as a means of improving megaproject evaluation. Dimitriou et al. (Chapter 3) argue that upstream public participation is a precondition for successful megaprojects and for their evaluation. However, they concede that sometimes the need to get the project up and running on time (e.g. the Olympic Games) may prevent genuine participation. In the light of the downsides of participation when crucial decisions have already been made, the 'Finnish wonder' of seemingly smooth and consensual implementation of the spent fuel disposal project gives food for thought. Maybe the exclusion of civil society from the 'risk dialogue' between the regulator and the waste management company (Chapter 7) has been a pragmatic and reasonable solution when the institutional actors have no intention whatsoever of halting or even fundamentally modifying the project. Comparisons between the lessons from the Finnish and Belgian nuclear waste management experiences (Chapters 6 and 7) illustrate the importance of context – as amply highlighted by the OMEGA centre research on transport megaprojects (Chapter 3). Is the 'Finnish wonder' a truly culture-bound phenomenon, and would the 'extended project management' strategy advocated by Bergmans and Verhaegen (Chapter 6) fail to obtain sufficient societal support in Finland? More broadly, this raises questions about the attribution of blame, and the respective roles of demand for participation from civil society and the 'supply' of participation by authorities and industry. In the Finnish nuclear waste policy there seems to be little demand for social impact monitoring – for instance, using indicators developed through a process such as the one described by Renault in Chapter 10. Socioeconomic evaluation had its time in Finland, during the EIA preceding site selection, but once this key choice was made, social issues again faded to the background.

The usually significant asymmetries of power among policy actors in megaproject governance and evaluation have direct implications for participation. In such situations, the oft-cited objective of participation – building consensus among the participants – appears as potentially problematic. Many megaprojects are characterised by a long and conflict-laden history and mutual mistrust among participants. Nuclear waste disposal megaprojects are a typical, but by no means the only, example of such entrenched mistrust (e.g. Blowers, 2016). A lack of genuinely inclusive governance processes is certainly one of the most common sources of mistrust: when people feel that their concerns are not heard, they lose trust in the actors responsible for project governance. If opening up socioeconomic evaluation entails making a virtue out of a vice – exploiting uncertainty rather than seeking to minimise it – would the same apply to conflict and controversy? From the 'internal' perspective described above, conflict should be minimised, whereas 'opening up', in the sense advocated in this book, also requires explicit recognition and even elicitation of controversy. Both efforts are certainly needed yet, arguably, the balance is in favour of seeking consensus, while key sources of conflict and controversy are toned down. The 'case for controversy' also brings a frequently skewed angle to the claim that the lack of shared understanding of the meaning of sustainable development represents a major obstacle to megaproject evaluation (Chapter 3). If exploring conflicts and controversies is a major virtue of socioeconomic evaluation, would not the lack of shared values and definitions constitute an opportunity rather than an obstacle?

It is of course crucial what methods are used to organise participation, consensus-building and controversy-stirring. Approaches such as those suggested by Bergmans and Verhaegen (Chapter 6) and Renault (Chapter 10) are designed to allow the most to be made of both consensus and controversy in politically charged megaproject evaluation contexts. However, even the most participatory processes of indicator development do not mean a permanent 'opening up'. For instance, an agreement on a jointly accepted set of well-being indicators can be seen as a temporary closure, whereby the multiple dimensions and perceptions of well-being – including the underlying normative assumptions and values – are aggregated and reduced into a given set of indicators.

Insights from radioactive waste management

One of the distinct contributions of this volume consists of its treatment of radioactive waste management as a specific domain of megaprojects. Two challenges that such megaprojects pose for socioeconomic evaluation deserve particular attention: 1) the extremely long temporal scales involved – and the associated challenges related to ethics and justice; and 2) the nature of radioactive waste management as a 'societal problem in need of a solution', rather than as a project primarily justified by its promise of generating added social value and socioeconomic well-being in a particular community or region. The first question entails intergenerational justice considerations: the need to agree upon the sharing of the burden of the costs of the disposal project (or any other radioactive waste management solution, for that matter) between the current and future generations. Decisions on burden-sharing should be informed by calculations of the total costs of the project, yet ultimately the decision is political, and should therefore be subject to a broad societal discussion. Ensuring that this debate is truly political and inclusive, and that crucial normative choices are not hidden behind a façade of presumably technical calculations, is a central challenge for socioeconomic evaluation (Chapter 2).

Radioactive waste management projects constitute a rather extreme example of the challenges involved in socioeconomic evaluation over very long timescales. Two main arguments are usually put forward to justify the use of cost–benefit analysis (CBA) in the evaluation of such megaprojects, with discounting as the key instrument designed to address the questions of long-term intergenerational justice. CBA would, first, allow a comparison of the net benefits of alternative waste management options for the entire society, and second, provide certainty for the waste producing companies concerning the amount of money they must set aside to finance the project. However, one could argue that in the case of radioactive waste management the society actually has no true choice – the waste problem needs a solution, hence the 'benefit' side in the cost–benefit equation entails in fact a legal obligation. To conduct a CBA, we therefore would not have to calculate the value of this benefit, but could instead take it as a given. Calculating the cost, in turn, would require a stepwise learning process, in order to accommodate the multiple uncertainties that prevail over many of the input parameters. Uncertainties over the technical management solutions are well known: it is not self-evident which alternative best serves public interest. For instance, deep geological disposal and interim near-surface storage both have their strong advocates and adversaries. However, uncertainties concern more general political choices as well: waste management solutions are significantly shaped by decisions such as whether or not to continue the use of nuclear power or the reprocessing of spent nuclear fuel. Any estimate of the total cost is therefore a convention, an agreement, concerning what the total cost seems like, in the light of the current state of knowledge. As aptly demonstrated by Saraç-Lesavre (Chapter 2), the discount rate used for calculating the total cost of the project is a key element of such a convention.

Radical uncertainties – can they be 'positive'?

Evaluation of the costs of radioactive waste disposal projects can be seen as a typical example of decision-making under radical uncertainty: there are huge unknowns concerning even the relatively near – let alone the distant – future, and yet decisions have to be made on the financing arrangements. In turn, these decisions have direct consequences for the balance sheets of private companies, here and now. In addition to the intergenerational justice issues evoked above, cost evaluations of long-term megaprojects therefore also entail considerations of intragenerational justice – the distribution of burden among actors in the present. Even a small downward correction in the discount rate could significantly increase the financial burden on the waste producing companies – and lower their share value. The mutual dependence between the cost estimates and the applied interest rate complicates matters further: the discount rate itself is affected by (uncertain) estimates of how much it would cost to construct a safe and secure disposal repository.

Two distinct ways of dealing with the 'radical' uncertainties can be imagined. Methods such as cost–benefit analysis do this by seeking to determine the most appropriate discount rate for cost calculations, whereas an alternative approach would seek 'opening up'. Uncertainty would, from the perspective of opening up, appear both as a reason and a means for exploring what is unknown and has been neglected. The framing of the issue would again be crucial: the problem would appear radically different, depending on whether it is conceived as one of choosing among a range of possibilities – which would entail genuine uncertainty, ambiguity, and ignorance – or whether it is framed in terms of managing calculable risk, measured by attributing probability distributions to given parameters. The latter, the risk-management based approach, is typically defended as the 'realistic' option when one needs to provide practical policy advice. The 'realism' of such an approach can be called into question, however. Is it realistic to simply 'sweep under the carpet' issues for which economic theory does not offer satisfactory answers and operational rules? Realism would then translate to 'the need to be operational'. An alternative way of proceeding would be to critically scrutinise the realism of what Andy Stirling in the workshop called 'our convenient assumptions' – the basis upon which we define 'being operational'. From this starting point it would hardly appear 'realistic' to simply discard issues that do not fit smoothly into our theoretical frameworks.

These alternative approaches to uncertainty also entail different conceptions of transparency. Defenders of methods such as the CBA often describe the method as transparent, since it does not conceal anything – the assumptions underpinning the calculations are laid open for scrutiny by anyone. Critics contend that 'radical' uncertainties should be taken seriously, and economic evaluation should help to explore a broader opportunity space instead of attributing values to variables whose very relevance is uncertain. From this perspective, the transparency of methods such as CBA is limited, since the underlying hypotheses tend in practice to be forgotten and pushed under the carpet. What remains is a false image of accuracy and certainty conveyed by the quantitative estimates.

The chapters in this volume illustrate distinct ways of dealing with radical uncertainties, yet the majority seem to converge around the approach of 'opening up'. Dimitriou et al. (Chapter 3) emphasise uncertainties that stem from the evolving nature of project objectives – evaluating megaprojects merely in the light of the 'iron triangle' criteria therefore appears inadequate in the face of such dynamism. Bergmans and Verhaegen (Chapter 6) echo these ideas, calling for an alternative way of dealing with uncertainties, based on 'organised flexibility', inclusive management culture, and the use of mainly qualitative performance criteria. This would certainly introduce a degree of vagueness into project management and evaluation, but in doing so it would also constitute a reasonable strategy in the face of multiple irreducible uncertainties. Verweij (Chapter 11) follows a similar line of reasoning: reflexivity and opening up of the process are needed in order to take into account the characteristics of megaprojects and promote learning. Conflict and uncertainty appear, again, as assets rather than problems to be minimised.

As counterpoints to the majority of the chapters that emphasise 'opening up' as the preferred strategy, Chapters 4 (Reverdy and Lehtonen) and 8 (Lamari et al.) remind us of the enduring importance of control and accountability. The Canadian examples of megaprojects (Chapter 8) clearly demonstrate the need to continuously improve the techniques of prediction, as well as cost and time management, while the Lyon–Turin rail project (Chapter 4) shows that rigorous economic assessment employing standard methods can, ideally, help safeguard public interest against the multiple vested interests.

Integrating the socioeconomic impacts into megaproject evaluation criteria: paradigms, approaches and methods

The contributions to this volume also highlight the importance of national characteristics that shape the governance and the evaluation of megaprojects. The importance of culture appears, for instance, when it comes to defining 'the community' considered relevant in a given situation of megaproject evaluation. Some differences are primarily semantic, but nevertheless important: the term 'community' generally carries a positive connotation in countries such as the UK and the US, while in France it is associated with ideas such as exclusion, oppression and the control of individuals by a group, and as such poses a threat to the nation. Another dimension is geographic: the relevant community in a given megaproject evaluation situation can be geographically bound, but it can just as well include, for instance, international NGOs, as crucial actors when companies seek to obtain a 'social licence to operate' (Chapter 9).

The question of how to define the relevant 'community' brings yet another angle to the issues of framing and to the distinction between an 'internal' and an 'external' approach. It brings to the fore the processes and procedures through which the general interest – or the overall 'good of the society', as the Finnish nuclear legislation puts it – are to be determined. The chapters by Dimitriou et al. (Chapter 3), Bergmans and Verhaegen (Chapter 6), Renault (Chapter 10), and Vanclay (Chapter 9) stress the importance of engaging with local citizens in attempts to determine 'what counts'. By contrast, especially the Lyon–Turin example (Chapter 4) but to a certain extent also the chapters by Lamari et al. (Chapter 8) and Verweij (Chapter 11) remind us of the opposite perspective, amply highlighted by Flyvbjerg (2009: 352–353): powerful local-level alliances of actors sharing a common interest tend to capture the control over evaluation processes, against the poorly organised national-level actors supposed to represent the general interest. Also, the processes of defining the general interest vary widely, between the idea of the state as the only legitimate source of general interest, and the Anglo-Saxon, especially American, perception of the state as the arbiter between competing private interests (e.g. L'intérêt general..., 2006; Saurugger, 2007). These contrasting perspectives highlight the ambiguity of community empowerment as a key objective of megaproject evaluation. Who should in fact be empowered and how? Clearly, the local-level actors are not always the underprivileged. Empowerment evaluation (e.g. Fetterman, 2000), along the lines suggested by Renault (Chapter 10) in his plea for participatory processes of indicator development, certainly has its role to play, as do participatory processes in general (e.g. Chapters 6 and 9). This kind of process can also help to reconcile the functions of learning and accountability in evaluation: for instance, participatory development of indicators would constitute venues for learning, while the indicators themselves could help to hold policymakers accountable. For indicators to truly foster learning and reflexivity, their development and use should obviously take place through continuous and iterative processes, if the pitfalls of 'checklist' approaches are to be avoided (see Chapters 1 and 9).

How do we know when to open up and when to close down?

The idea of 'opening up' as the crosscutting theme in this book raises the question of the balance between closure and openness. Keeping things open cannot carry on forever, since decisions have to be made, sooner or later. On a general level, the question is: how does one know when a situation is 'ripe' for closing down? To be more specific, by whom and through which processes should the decision of closure be made? How long do we have to 'reflect', explore alternative pathways, and avoid closure around a single consensual solution? Can we have objective criteria upon which to base the decision to close down the debate and make a decision? For megaprojects in general, and for radioactive waste disposal projects in particular, these questions are crucial.

Three distinct types of answers to the question of 'when to close down' can be considered. From an 'internal' project management perspective characteristic to SIA, for instance, participation is crucial. A decision to close down must result from a proper process of stakeholder involvement; it must be clear that all relevant stakeholders have been involved; and the vast majority of stakeholders must feel that the process has been legitimate. Another perspective focuses on the institutional setting of megaproject governance, which provokes constant pressure towards closure. Dedicated agencies are set up to ensure quick and efficient delivery of these projects, while the public sector alone has to deal with the broader consequences of megaprojects. Continuous monitoring throughout the project could then constitute the basis for decisions on closure. Monitoring would serve both learning and accountability: checking whether the project has achieved its predefined objectives would allow project managers to be held accountable, but monitoring would also provide information on whether modifications to the project might be needed. The constant tendency towards privatisation of knowledge in megaproject management poses a true challenge for such monitoring, by compromising access to key knowledge that is increasingly in the hands of private actors. Considerations about the sharing of responsibilities between private and public actors also raise the question of the extent to which the project developer should be held responsible for evaluating and managing the broader impacts, including in particular the socioeconomic impacts.

Finally, at our workshop that provided the initial impetus for publishing this book, Andy Stirling gave a two-pronged answer to the question of when to close down. First, he argued that closing down 'takes care of itself', insofar as our current governance and policymaking structures constantly push towards closure. Hence, the argument for 'opening up' is not about removing closure, but a plea for greater attention to the conditions of that closure. Second, he called for a distinction to be made between closing down technology choices and closing down knowledge. Keeping the knowledge open does not by any means prevent closing down technology choices; it is perfectly feasible to decide on the construction of a specific radioactive waste management facility, for instance, while at the same time acknowledging that it is not the knowledge concerning such a facility that compels such a closure. Decisions need to be made when the institutional setting obliges us to converge along a given pathway or technology, but this does not imply closing the doors to new knowledge and problem framings that might again justify an opening up of the technological choice as well.

References

Blalock, A.B. 1999. Evaluation research and the performance management movement: from estrangement to useful integration? *Evaluation* 5(2): 117–149.

Blowers, A. 2016 (forthcoming). *The Legacy of nuclear power*. London: Routledge.

Chateauraynaud, F. & Debaz, J. 2011. *Observer la sécurité sanitaire dans la durée. Leçons cognitives et pratiques d'un observatoire socio-informatique. Socio-informatique et argumentation: sociologie argumentative des controverses, concepts et methods socioinformatiques*. Available online at: http://socioargu.hypotheses.org/2786 (accessed 30 May 2016).

Cowell, R., Bristow, G. & Munday, M. 2011. Acceptance, acceptability and environmental justice: The role of community benefits in wind energy development. *Journal of Environmental Planning and Management* 54(4): 539–557.

Fetterman, D.M. 2001. *Foundations of empowerment evaluation*. Thousand Oaks, CA: Sage.

Fiorino, D. 1990. Citizen participation and environmental risk: A survey of institutional mechanisms. *Science, Technology & Human Values* 15(2): 226–243.

Flyvbjerg, B. 2009. Survival of the unfittest: Why the worst infrastructure gets built – and what we can do about it. *Oxford Review of Economic Policy* 25(3): 344–367.

Flyvbjerg, B., Bruzelius, N. & Rothengatter, W. 2003. *Megaprojects and risk: An anatomy of ambition*. Cambridge: Cambridge University Press.

Hertting, N. & Vedung, E. 2012. Purposes and criteria in network governance evaluation: How far does standard evaluation take us? *Evaluation* 18(1): 27–46.

Lehtonen, M. 2005. OECD Environmental performance review programme: Accountability (f)or learning? *Evaluation* 11(2): 169–188.

Lehtonen, M. 2014. Evaluating megaprojects: From the "iron triangle" to network mapping. *Evaluation* 20(3): 278–295.

L'intérêt général et les intérêts particuliers. 2006. Vie publique; La Documentation Française. 30/05/2006. Available online at: www.vie-publique.fr/decouverte-institutions/citoyen/approfondissements/interet-general-interets-particuliers.html (accessed 30 May 2016).

OECD-NEA. 2010. *Partnering for long-term management of radioactive waste: Evolution and current practice in thirteen countries*. Paris: OECD Nuclear Energy Agency.

Pawson, R. & Tilley, N. 1997. *Realistic Evaluation*. London, Thousand Oaks and New Delhi: Sage.

Saurugger, S. 2007. Democratic 'misfit'? conceptions of civil society participation in France and the European Union. *Political Studies* 55(2): 384–404.

Stirling, A. 2008. 'Opening up' and 'closing down': Power, participation, and pluralism in the social appraisal of technology. *Science, Technology & Human Values* 33(2): 262–294.

Vedung, E. 1997. *Public policy and program evaluation*. New Brunswick: Transaction Publishers.

Weiss, C.H. 1999. The interface between evaluation and public policy. *Evaluation* 5(4): 468–486.

Wüstenhagen, R., Wolsink, M. & Bürer, J. 2007. Social acceptance of renewable energy innovation – an introduction to the concept. *Energy Policy* 35(5): 2683–2691.

Index

For Product Safety Concerns and Information please contact our EU
representative GPSR@taylorandfrancis.com
Taylor & Francis Verlag GmbH, Kaufingerstraße 24, 80331 München, Germany

www.ingramcontent.com/pod-product-compliance
Ingram Content Group UK Ltd.
Pitfield, Milton Keynes, MK11 3LW, UK
UKHW021618240425
457818UK00018B/634